Political Activists

The N D P in Convention

From
the Library
of

Political Activists

The NDP in Convention

Keith Archer
and
Alan Whitehorn

Toronto   Oxford   New York
OXFORD UNIVERSITY PRESS
1997

Oxford University Press
70 Wynford Drive, Don Mills, Ontario M3C 1J9

Oxford   New York
Athens   Auckland   Bangkok   Bombay
Calcutta   Cape Town   Dar es Salaam   Delhi
Florence   Hong Kong   Istanbul   Karachi
Kuala Lumpur   Madras   Madrid   Melbourne
Mexico City   Nairobi   Paris   Singapore
Taipei   Tokyo   Toronto

and associated companies in
Berlin   Ibadan

Oxford is a trademark of Oxford University Press

Canadian Cataloguing in Publication Data

Archer, Keith, 1955–
    Political activists: the NDP in convention

Includes bibliographical references and index.
ISBN 0-19-541145-5

1. New Democratic Party.   I. Whitehorn, Alan.   II. Title.

JL197.N4A72 1997   324.27107   C97-930693-0

Cover art: Juan M. Sanchez, 1997
Design: Max Gabriel Izod
Formatting: Janette Thompson (Jansom)

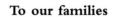

To our families

Table of Contents

ACKNOWLEDGEMENTS

This book has benefited from the contributions of many individuals and agencies. Numerous research assistants have provided support over the years, including Janet Harvie, Merrill Cooper, Roseanne Reimer, Mebs Kanji, Janice Stokes, Jennifer Stewart, Maurie Barron, Janet Alford, and Faron Ellis at the University of Calgary, Linda Trimble and Kali Deonandan while they were graduate students at Queen's University, and Simi Desor and Wendy Miko at Simon Fraser University. Students of the Woodsworth seminar on the CCF-NDP at Simon Fraser University provided welcome feedback. Translation services have been provided by Josette Arassus and Marie-Thérèse Ferguson in Kingston and by Syntax Language Services Ltd. in Calgary. We have enjoyed extremely helpful secretarial support from Judi Powell in the Department of Political Science and Joey Dyrholm in the Dean's office in the Faculty of Social Sciences at the University of Calgary, and Ursula Butz at the Royal Military College of Canada.

Research is a shared endeavour, and we have benefited from the comments of many fellow academics, including Thérèse Arsenau, Herman Bakvis, Sylvia Bashevkin, Sandra Burt, Ken Carty, John Courtney, Jean Crête, Jane Jenson, Larry LeDuc, Joe Levitt, Ian McClymont, Simon McInnes, Terry Morley, George Perlin, Leonard Preyra, Jack Vowles, and many anonymous reviewers. We are also grateful to the following editors whose books included material from this project: Hugh Thorburn; François-Pierre Gingras; Maureen Mancuso, Richard Price and Ron Wagenberg; Alan Frizzell, Jon Pammett, and Anthony Westell; Carol Williams, and Herman Bakvis. Among the colleagues who have provided intellectual discussions and advice, we thank Tom Flanagan, Roger Gibbins, and Rainer Knopff at the University of Calgary; Neil Nevitte at the University of Toronto; Les Pal at Carleton University; H. Binhammer, Jim Cairns, Mahinder Chaudhry, Joel Sokolsky, and Jack Treddenick at the Royal Military College of Canada; Trish Graham and Jery Zaslove at the Institute for the Humanities at Simon Fraser University; and Len Evenden, Steve McBride, Allan Seager, and Mary Ann Stouck at Simon Fraser University. In the area of public opinion research, Canada's pollsters have a unique vantage point; we thank Donna Dasko, the late Dave Gotthilf, Jim Matsui and Lorne Bozinoff for their comments over the years.

This project has received financial support from a variety of sources, including the Douglas-Coldwell Foundation, the Social Sciences and Humanities Research Council of Canada (SSHRC) (grant numbers 410-90-1726 and 410-93-0440), the SSHRC President's Fund (grant number 421-90-0002), the University of Calgary Research Grants Committee, the Summer Temporary Employment Program (STEP) Grants (Province of Alberta), the Summer Employment/Experience Development (SEED), and the Summer Career Placement Program (SCPP) of the federal government, the Department of Political Science, and Faculty of Social Sciences at the University of Calgary, the Department of Politics and Economics, the Arts Research Programme (ARP) and the Principal's Discretionary Fund (PDF) at the Royal Military College of Canada, the Work Study Program sponsored by the Province of British Columbia, and the Boag Foundation. We are particularly grateful to Kalmen Kaplansky at the Douglas-Coldwell Foundation and Jim McKenzie of the Boag Foundation for their encouragement.

Over the years the executive officers and staff at the federal office of the NDP have provided responses to many of our queries. We thank the following federal secretaries: Robin Sears, Dennis Young, Bill Knight, Dick Proctor, Fraser Green, and David Woodbury. Others at the federal office who provided assistance include Carmel Belanger, Marion Dewar, Raymond Guardia, Shirley Johnson, Peter Julian, Audrey Kari, Leslie Kerr, Brian McKee, Ian McLeod, Abby Pollenetsky, and Judy Randall. At the Canadian Labour Congress, advice and assistance was provided by Bob White, Nancy Riche, Pat Kerwin, Carole Phillips and Murray Randall.

Among the individuals at provincial NDP offices who offered assistance were Jill Marzetti and Ed Dale (Ontario), Dick Proctor and Rod Dickinson (Saskatchewan), and Brian Gardiner and Sherry Hyde (British Columbia). We are also grateful to many NDP activists and MPs, including Dawn Black, Kerri Brinkert, Gerry Caplan, Wendy Hughes, Lynn Hunter, Joy Langan, Mario Lee, Michael Lewis, Tommy McLeod, Lynn McDonald, Donald MacDonald, Dave Mackenzie, Margaret Mitchell, George Nakitsas, Patrice Pratt, Olga Oleinikow, Keith Reynolds, Maya Russell, Janet Solberg, Ish Theilheimer, and Gary Wilson. Despite their busy schedules, NDP leaders Ed Broadbent, Audrey McLaughlin, and Alexa McDonough found time to talk with us, as did the other candidates in the 1995 leadership contest, Svend Robinson, Lorne Nystrom, and Herschel Hardin. A mass party such as the NDP has tens of thousands of members and we particularly are grateful to the scores of activists who granted interviews and completed our many survey questionnaires over the years.

At Oxford University Press we benefited from the kind patience and expertise of Ric Kitowski, Phyllis Wilson, and Jo MacKinnon. We wish to acknowledge a special debt to Sally Livingston, our editor, whose sound advice on both content and style and generous tolerance of delays in our schedule are much appreciated. We are also grateful to the distinguished artist Juan Sanchez for his evocative cover painting.

Among the numerous CCF–NDP activists who have died in recent years, we particularly note the loss of two remarkable individuals. Cliff Scotton was a key party and labour official whose keen sense of the party's history was of great assistance to us. Dave Gotthilf was a brilliant party pollster who engineered the NDP provincial victories in Ontario in 1990 and British Columbia in 1991; his commitment to politics and public opinion research will be greatly missed.

Our greatest debts of gratitude are owed to our families. On more occasions than we wish to recall, Keith found the time for this project before the sun rose, or Alan long after it had set, and both of us on too many weekends. To Lisa Hurst-Archer and Suzanne Whitehorn, and to Justin, Caitlin, Ben, Will, and Isaiah Archer and Kate Whitehorn, or deepest thanks for their patience and love. We hope that our children will inherit a world made better by the political activists we have sought to study.

Part I

The Organizational and Ideological Structure of the NDP

CHAPTER
1

Party Structure and Character

INTRODUCTION

This book examines the federal New Democratic Party as it seeks to define a role for itself in the new millennium. In the dynamic process of Canadian politics, parties are not static entities. If they are to remain relevant, they must change in response to changes in the context in which they operate. As it is for other parties, so it is for the NDP: if it is to have a continuing life in Canadian politics, it must succeed in its quest for relevance.

The social and economic context of Canadian politics has undergone, and continues to undergo, profound change. The past generation has seen major shifts in family and gender relations; many young people who in the past would have been establishing careers and starting families feel shut out of the job market by the aging but demographically powerful baby-boomers; and a general increase in life-span has important implications for everyone in Canadian society. In the economic sphere, dramatic changes have occurred in the labour market, with unprecedented numbers of women in the work force, the movement towards a 'post-industrial' economy, liberalization of global trade, and decreasing job security in many sectors. Meanwhile, environmental consciousness has been growing among many segments of the population.

These changes have been accompanied by changes in the context of party competition. The partisan landscape experienced fundamental shifts in the 1993 federal election. The rise of the Reform Party and the Bloc Québécois reinforced regional and linguistic divisions, while the collapse of the Conservatives, and to a lesser extent the NDP, challenged conventional understandings of the Canadian party system. At the same time there has been a significant increase in both the number and the importance of interest groups in Canadian society—for example, the Business Council on National Issues and the National Citizens Coalition on the right, and the Council of Canadians and the National Action Committee on the Status of

Women on the left—that provide outlets for political activism. If political parties hope to remain relevant in federal politics, they must be prepared to respond to these and other changes in the context of electoral competition.

One argument of this book is that parties not only respond to the external environment (social, economic, and political) but endeavour to shape the environment of party competition. As Brodie and Jenson (1980, 1988) put it, every party attempts to 'define the political' in its own way. Targeting certain groups within the electorate, it selectively emphasizes some political issues or cleavages and downplays others; that is, it tries to highlight those issues on which it stands to gain a political advantage and to avoid discussing those on which it risks losing support. A second argument is that a party's internal structure—the range of groups (representing various segments of the electorate) it consists of, and the formal and informal arrangements it makes to give them a voice in decision-making—affects both its policy positions and its leadership selection process. The interplay of groups within a party can have an important effect on the way it 'defines the political'. In the case of the NDP, organizational structure has been particularly important to its functioning both in its earlier incarnation as the Co-operative Commonwealth Federation and in the contemporary period.

The major parties in Canadian federal politics differ significantly in their organizational structure and bases of support. The Liberal and Conservative parties have adopted a broadly pan-Canadian organizational focus, although their bases of support have often had a regional and/or linguistic slant (Johnston et al., 1992: 102–10). In recent years, attitudes towards Canada's relationship to the United States have been especially important in distinguishing between Liberals and Conservatives. The most salient feature of the organizational structure of both the Liberals and Conservatives is their relative 'diffuseness'.[1] Many have argued that this diffuseness has given rise to a politics of personality in federal elections (Clarke et al., 1996).[2] The Reform Party is more firmly rooted in the principle of individualism than are the other parties. There are very few layers of organization that come between the party members and leaders, a characteristic feature of populist organizations (Laycock, 1990). Reform's targeted base of support initially was centred in the West, and after 1991 was extended to 'English Canada' (Ellis and Archer, 1994; Flanagan, 1995).

The New Democratic Party has a much more fully developed organizational structure than the other parties. One reason is the formal participation of organized labour through unions affiliated with the party. In addition, however, provincial sections and a variety of caucuses (women's, youth, environmental, left, and gay and lesbian) all play important roles. The following section outlines the development of this rich organizational structure.

THE CCF–NDP AS A MASS PARTY

In the 1950s the French political scientist Maurice Duverger (1951/1963) identified two basic types of political party: the older 'cadre' party controlled by the wealthy and powerful few, and the newer 'mass' party representing the interests of the many with little money or power. Although the distinctions between the two have lessened in the course of the twentieth century, in its original form the cadre party was typically a loose alliance of like-minded individuals focusing their activities on the parliamentary forum and sustained by the virtually unlimited resources of their wealthy patrons. By contrast, according to Duverger, a mass party typically has its origins in extraparliamentary organizations, depends for financial support on large numbers of individuals paying modest membership dues, and, because of its size, requires a somewhat more formal organizational structure.

In Canada, the cadre party was exemplified by the Conservative and Liberal parties as they operated in the late nineteenth century, a time when the franchise was limited to property-owning males of European descent aged 21 or older,[3] and their monopoly of the political system was unchallenged by any third party. Representing the country's economic élite—a small group with strong interpersonal ties—these parties constituted an informal caucus of notables who pursued their own interests in Parliament and had little need to reach out to the less affluent strata of Canadian society (Carty, 1991; Reid, 1996; Thorburn, 1996).[4]

By the early twentieth century, however, the franchise was being extended, and with increasing industrialization, the development of a manufacturing sector, and the opening of the West, local organizations—trade unions, labour clubs, farmers' co-operatives—were forming to defend and promote the interests of workers and farmers (Archer, 1990; Brodie and Jenson, 1988; Forsey, 1982; King, 1918/1973; MacPherson, 1979; Mooney, 1938).[5] One of the key questions that these groups had to decide was whether to tie their activities to a political party or confine them to the workplace or other specific area of concern. Differences over this question delayed the establishment of formal links, but finally, in 1932, delegates to the annual Western Labour Conference[6] in Calgary, believing that their interests were not represented by the two cadre-style parties, voted to form the Co-operative Commonwealth Federation, a mass party representing three groups: labour, farmers, and progressive left intellectuals (Horowitz, 1968; McHenry, 1950; Young, 1969; Zakuta, 1964).

With its roots in extraparliamentary organizations, its mass-based membership, and its written constitution requiring the payment of membership dues, the CCF was consistent with Duverger's description of a mass party. Yet it differed in one important respect, for while the Duverger model emphasizes the role of individual members,[7] the CCF from the beginning was characterized by a significant group element. In fact, collective representation was woven into the mass fabric of the CCF, not only through its founding groups—trade unions, workers' and farmers' co-ops, and the left intellectual League for Social Reconstruction (see Horn, 1980)—but through the formation of provincial sections and regional and youth caucuses.[8] However, the roles of all these groups remained largely unspecified at the time of the party's first full convention, in 1933. The roles that the various groups were to play emerged over time. For example, although labour had been a founding partner of the CCF, it was not certain in 1933 how its voice would be heard. In 1938, District 26 of the United Mineworkers of America on Cape Breton Island decided to affiliate formally with the party, thereby necessitating the development of formal procedures for affiliation (Archer, 1990: 15; Lewis, 1981: 153–4, 158). Five years later, the Canadian Labour Congress (CLC) declared the CCF to be the 'political arm of labour' and encouraged its locals to affiliate with the party (Horowitz, 1968: 78; McHenry, 1950: 104–6; Young, 1969: 82).

In 1961, when the CCF was dissolved and reconstituted, by its former members together with the CLC, as the New Democratic Party, the group character of the party was firmly entrenched in its constitution. Over the three decades of the CCF's existence, Canadian society had changed significantly. With increasing industrialization and urbanization, the electoral importance of farmers, particularly in the West, had been steadily decreasing; the beginning of the Quiet Revolution was raising hopes that with modernization Quebec would become more receptive to secular trade unions and a social-democratic party (Baum, 1980); and growing numbers of liberal-minded people closer to the political centre were becoming dissatisfied with the older cadre-style parties. The designers of the NDP sought to reflect these social changes—and improve on the federal CCF's disappointing, and worsening, electoral record—by broadening the party's ideological base to appeal to a wider spectrum of voters[9] while strengthening the organizational base provided by the CLC and its affiliated unions. Thus the constitution of the NDP included a collective membership category for members of affiliated trade unions, alongside the original mass base of individual members of constituency associations. In addition to this formal recognition, other formal and informal arrangements ensured labour representation in various positions within the party hierarchy. For example, central labour bodies and affiliated unions may send delegates to party conventions, and labour is guaranteed representation on the party's federal council. In addition, labour has representation on the party executive, and labour representatives can be found on such important bodies as the

Strategy and Election Planning Committee (SEPC) (Archer, 1990, 1991b; Whitehorn, 1994). Many of the provisions for labour representation in the NDP developed over time, and exist by virtue of custom rather than formal constitutional provisions.[10]

Similarly, the provisions for other types of group representation developed over time and are a combination of formal rules and informal understandings. The representation of provincial and regional groups provides a good example. Within the NDP, even individual memberships have a group component, since individuals may join the federal party only by joining a provincial section. Indeed, the provincial sections, along with the affiliated unions, are the primary building blocks of the party. Entitlements to send delegates to the party's conventions are based on the number of party members in each constituency, and the delegates often have strong provincial ties and loyalties, which are reinforced through attendance at provincial caucuses at the convention. In addition, the provincial sections are guaranteed representation on the federal council, and more informally on the party executive and the SEPC.

However, social realities are not frozen in time, nor are party structures and constitutions.[11] In the period since the founding of the NDP, the number of women in the work force has risen dramatically, as has the importance of women's issues. Gays and lesbians have become more willing to participate openly in the political process, and the ranks of people identifying environmental issues as their primary concern have increased significantly. Aboriginal people have become increasingly active in seeking political change both through conventional forms of participation in the party system and by a variety of other means, from formal constitutional negotiations to armed confrontation. Similarly, over the past two generations the ethnic composition of the country has become increasingly diverse, and with this diversity have come demands for greater and more effective representation of the interests of multicultural communities. Many in these groups see a social-democratic party as their natural political home, and as they have become more involved in the NDP, the party has come under increasing pressure to broaden its provisions for group representation.[12]

GROUP REPRESENTATION AND NDP CONVENTIONS

Thus the federal NDP is a much more complex entity than the Duverger model of a social-democratic mass party implies. In addition to its individual membership base, it has a very significant group component. Today there are four group categories with a formally recognized place in the party's constitution and governing structure: organized labour; the various provincial sections and regional caucuses; the youth wing; and women,[13] who since 1991 have endeavoured to achieve gender parity in the nomination of candidates for Parliament (Bashevkin, 1993: 100) but who remain under-represented at federal conventions (see Chapter 6). Other groups, such as gays and lesbians, environmentalists, Aboriginal people, and ethnic groups, which are formally recognized in some provincial sections (e.g., Ontario), at present exist only informally within the federal party, but may well take on more prominent roles in the future.

The varied points of view that all these groups bring to the party are likely to be reflected in differences in ideology and policy priorities, as well as attitudes towards party leadership, democracy, and decision-making. These differences can also give rise to tensions, especially between older male trade-union delegates who want to maintain the status quo and younger female activists who want to widen the decision-making circle.[14] Is the presence of these groups changing the character of the party? We will attempt to provide at least a provisional answer to this question through analysis of an abundance of survey data collected at federal NDP conventions.

Our focus on conventions is appropriate for two reasons. First, conventions play an extremely important role in the NDP. In fact, as Article V.2 of the NDP constitution states, the convention is 'the supreme governing body of the Party and [has] final authority in all matters of federal policy, program, and constitution'. All of the party's key manifestos and most of its official policy resolutions have been drafted at conventions, and conventions have selected all of its leaders.

The second reason for focusing on conventions is that they provide a unique opportunity to study a country-wide sample of party activists at regular intervals.[15] A large portion of the data for the present study is drawn from surveys administered at the 1983, 1987, and 1989 NDP federal conventions, which provide a detailed portrait of the party over nearly a decade. For the most part, we draw on the latter two surveys, which represent the greatest source of survey data collected on the federal NDP to date, and are among the richest sources of data on the political attitudes and behaviour of any Canadian political party. The 1987 federal convention was the first the NDP had ever held in Montreal, and coincided with the height of the party's popularity. The 1989 convention was held in Winnipeg following a disappointing third-place finish in the 1988 federal election, and resulted in the election of Audrey McLaughlin. Since the time of these surveys, the federal NDP has held a policy convention in 1991 in Halifax and a leadership convention in 1995 in Ottawa, at which Alexa McDonough was elected to head the party. We supplement the survey findings from the earlier conventions with participant observations from the later ones and from meetings of the federal council throughout this period and of the Strategy and Election Planning Committee during the 1993 federal election, as well as many personal interviews with leading party officials.

Although our analysis draws on a wide range of data sources, the 1987 and 1989 surveys of convention delegates form the core evidence. There are a number of advantages to using these data. In designing the surveys, we were mindful of similar surveys that had been administered previously to delegates at Liberal and Conservative conventions are well as at earlier NDP conventions. The 1987 and 1989 NDP surveys were thus designed to facilitate comparison both with the other major federal parties of the era and with the NDP over time. The 1987 NDP survey was, to our knowledge, the largest survey ever undertaken of party activists in Canada, and contains a wealth of information on their ideology, attitudes, policy orientations, and behaviour.[16] We believe it provides a highly revealing portrait of the federal party. The 1989 NDP survey used a shorter questionnaire, focusing specifically on leadership selection within the party.

OVERVIEW

Part I of this book provides an overview of the NDP as a whole. Following a demographic profile of convention delegates in Chapter 2, Chapter 3 explores ideology and opinion structure within the NDP through comparison with the two older parties. Especially in a mass party, ideology is central both to members' self-identification and to the alternative vision that the party offers to the public at large. It is the framework within which first general attitudes and then specific policy positions are developed.

Part II narrows the focus to examine the four principal groupings within the party today: organized labour (Chapter 4), the regions (Chapter 5), women (Chapter 6), and young people (Chapter 7). In each case, a brief historical outline of the group's role in the party lays the groundwork for analysis of its positions on various policy issues and its differences with other groups.

Part III shifts the analytical perspective to explore three broad policy areas and the attitudes towards them expressed by various groups within the party. Chapter 8 focuses on the role of the state, particularly with respect to public ownership and social welfare; Chapter 9 on defence and foreign policy, including relations with the US; and Chapter 10 on 'postmaterialist' issues—a broad category of concerns relating to the environment, political equality, and quality of life.

Part IV examines intra-party democracy in the NDP and the party's changing approach to leadership.[17] Following a brief historical review and explanation of delegate selection procedures in Chapter 11, Chapter 12 provides a detailed analysis of the 1989 contest, in which Audrey McLaughlin was elected as the first woman in Canada's history to head a federal party, and Chapter 13 examines the revised selection process followed in 1995, a hybrid of a direct ballot of all party members and a traditional convention, which resulted in the election of the party's current leader, Alexa McDonough. Chapter 14 offers some concluding comments.

It is sometimes said that a week is a long time in politics, and some would argue that surveys of party activists conducted in the late 1980s cannot provide sufficient insight into politics in the late 1990s and beyond. There is some truth to that observation. Much has changed in both Canadian and global politics over the past decade. The Berlin wall has come down and communism has collapsed in the Eastern bloc; global trade has undergone considerable liberalization; and everywhere, it seems, governments have moved to reduce the size and scope of their debt, in some instances calling into question the very core of the welfare state. On some matters, our delegate surveys do not fully capture the new circumstances.

However, the 1987 and 1989 surveys are highly relevant to understanding the NDP in the late 1990s for three reasons. First, despite the appearance of continual change in politics, many of the issues that Canadians wrestle with today have their origins in the past. Although the Canada–US Free Trade Agreement and NAFTA were new issues in the 1988 and 1993 federal elections respectively, debates over Canada's economic relationship with the United States extend back to the founding of this country. Likewise, although the 1995 Quebec referendum seems to have defined a new era in Quebec–Canada relations, the role of Quebec in confederation has been a perennial issue. Thus surveys from the late 1980s continue to have a direct relevance to the political debates of today, and where events have overtaken the surveys, we have supplemented these data with other observations. Second, there is a high level of stability among delegates to federal NDP conventions. Whereas the more traditional cadre parties typically undertake intensive recruitment efforts at convention time, NDP delegates tend to be party members and activists of long standing, and in fact many of the delegates surveyed in 1987 and 1989 are still active in the party today. Third, it is only through retrospective examination of developments over time—a purpose to which our delegate surveys are ideally suited—that the dynamics underlying a party's decision-making process become visible. Understanding these dynamics is essential if we are to make realistic predictions about the future.

NOTES

1 The *Shorter Oxford English Dictionary* defines 'diffuse' as meaning 'confused', 'vague', or 'spread out in space'. All these descriptions fit the relatively non-programmatic character of the Liberal and Conservative parties.

2 A poetic expression of this theme can be seen in Frank Scott's ode to Prime Minister Mackenzie King, entitled 'W.L.M.K.', which reads in part:

> He blunted us.
> We had no shape
> Because he never took sides,
> And no sides
> Because he never allowed them to take shape . . .
> He seemed to be in the centre
> Because we had no centre,
> No vision
> To pierce the smoke-screen of his politics.

3 For a discussion of changes to the franchise in Canada, see Archer et al. (1995).

4 In this period, party organization and structures were still somewhat fluid and tended to centre on Parliament instead of society. Personal ambition and political patronage were the glue that held cadre parties together (Carty, 1991).

5 Geographical isolation should not be overlooked as a factor contributing to the development of the Canadian party system. The late nineteenth and early twentieth centuries saw the rise of a number of municipal labour parties and regional farmers' parties. However, the vastness of the country inhibited the weaving of a strong pan-Canadian organization among these local groups.

6 The economic depression of the 1930s was particularly harsh in Western Canada. In the midst of economic hardship, labour representatives from the West began meeting annually in search of common solutions to their economic problems.

7 Although Duverger discusses the distinction between direct and indirect parties (the latter being typified by the British Labour Party and its affiliated trade unions), the bulk of his analysis centres on the linkage between individual members and the political party. The present analysis also extends beyond Duverger in arguing that key groups of party members may form within a party to gain more effective representation. Thus actual relations within a party are more complex than Duverger suggests and involve both individual and group members.

8 The CCF began as a confederation of relatively independent regional and/or provincial parties, which were transformed into relatively autonomous provincial sections of the federal party (see Young, 1969; Whitehorn, 1992).

9 Including increasingly disgruntled Liberal voters.

10 The roles and relative strength of different groups within political parties may change, sometimes with explicit change in the party's constitutional and representational structure and sometimes without such formal change. For example, when the CCF was created in 1932–33, the official name of the party was 'Co-

operative Commonwealth Federation: (Farmer, Labour, Socialist)'. While the input from the three charter groups was significant, the party's constitution in the early days was relatively simple. To the extent that these groups did have representation, it was often informal and subject to change; for example, the United Farmers of Ontario left the party in 1934. In addition, it is worth noting that only a minority of trade-union locals chose to affiliate formally with the party, while the 'socialist' element in the CCF's full name did not really represent an organized group; rather, it was a concession to Marxist members of the party and certain radicals in British Columbia.

11 This argument is in contrast to the position of Lipset and Rokkan (1967).

12 This may be so for all parties. Even the Conservatives and Liberals are making concessions to represent key groups. It is particularly true, however, for social-democratic parties like the NDP which purport to represent those whose interests have not been adequately represented in the past. Relationships have always existed between interest groups and political parties, whether between businessmen and capitalist parties or labour and workers' parties. However, a society is not so dichotomous, particularly one that is continental in size. As a society becomes more populous, heterogeneous, and complex, more interest groups arise (Pross, 1986). The increasing complexity of Canadian society is finding reflection in changes in the structure of interest-group representation (Pal, 1993; Cairns, 1986). Interest groups have grown significantly over the past generation in their size, number, economic and political resources, and power. Changes in the relative power of interest groups and political parties may raise important strategic questions for individuals attempting to decide which is the most effective vehicle for social action (Brodie and Jenson, 1988). Interest groups themselves, as organizations, must ask whether it is better to work independently—outside any established political party—to influence public policy, or to operate within the decision-making structures of a formal political party. These groups—feminist organizations, gay rights groups, environmental associations, abortion lobbies, Aboriginal people, multicultural groups—have made the system of interest representation, and the task of political parties, increasingly complex.

13 These categories are not necessarily mutually exclusive.

14 These tensions were often evident at renewal conferences that followed the 1993 election, where the major differences within the party were the result of this cleavage.

15 See Chapter 14. The party's constitution states (in Article V.1) that convention will meet 'at least once every other calendar year'. Since 1961 the convention has been held at different sites across the country every second year. The exception to this trend, and to the party's constitutional stipulation of biennial conventions, occurred following the 1991 convention, which was the last to be held until 1995. The delay was due to several factors, most notably the scheduling of a federal election in 1993, at the very end of the Mulroney government's mandate; this led the NDP to delay a convention that year so that it could concentrate its energies and efforts on the election campaign. Following the election, the convention was further delayed because of the party's very poor electoral showing

(it fell below twelve seats and lost official party status in the House of Commons), the subsequent announcement by Audrey McLaughlin that she intended to step down as leader, and the decision to undertake a 'renewal' process to examine party principles, policies, and structure.

The leadership question in turn created a thorny administrative problem for the party on when to hold a convention. One of the key responsibilities of conventions is to elect party officers (president and associate president, eleven vice-presidents, and a treasurer). The federal council's decision to delay the convention call meant that no new election of officers took place.

16   An ideology provides the context through which general attitudes and specific policy positions are developed; as in a system of concentric circles, the ideology forms the largest circle, general attitudes operate within that ideology, and specific policy positions are embedded within those attitudes. General attitudes are more narrow than ideological beliefs, but more overarching than orientations toward specific policy issues. Attitudes may cluster on a variety of dimensions (see Chapter 3). For a social-democratic mass party, one of the key dimensions of attitude clustering is left versus right, which may also incorporate elements of equality versus inequality, pluralism versus hegemony, decentralization versus centralization, and democracy versus authoritarianism (Lipson, 1960).

17   As Robert Michels (1915/1962) suggested in his classic study of the German social-democratic party, mass parties are not immune to tensions between leaders and rank-and-file members; in fact, according to Michels, an 'iron law of oligarchy' exists whereby the powerful few prevail over the mass membership even in parties with a democratic ethos and a formal democratic structure.

CHAPTER
2

Party Insiders: A Demographic Profile

As we have seen, the NDP is a mass party, depending for its financing on a large dues-paying membership base. In contrast to the Liberal, Progressive Conservative, and Reform parties, which rely solely on individual members, the NDP has two types of members. The first type have joined as individuals (including members of riding associations, campus clubs, or organized study groups) and pay dues directly to the party. The second belong to trade unions affiliated to the party; each of these people pays dues to the union, which collectively has decided to affiliate with the NDP, and in turn the union forwards a certain monthly sum to the party. In 1995 there were 78,815 individual party members (see Table 13.1) and 217,102 affiliated members (NDP, April 1995; for earlier data see Whitehorn, 1992: 6).

To explore the nature of the NDP and its activists, we have analyzed five surveys of NDP convention delegates carried out between 1971 and 1989. Survey research on party activists was first conducted at Queen's University by George Perlin in his study of the federal Conservative and Liberal leadership conventions in 1967 and 1968, respectively. In 1971 Perlin joined forces with his colleagues Hugh Thorburn and Jayant Lele to survey delegates to the NDP's federal leadership convention. A second survey of NDP delegates was conducted by Perlin following the 1979 convention. In 1983 Whitehorn administered a survey questionnaire to delegates attending the Regina convention and in 1987 he joined with Archer to survey activists at the convention in Montreal. Finally, in 1989, Archer surveyed delegates attending the leadership convention.[1] The analyses in this book focus on the two most recent surveys, although on occasion reference is made to the earlier studies.[2]

DEMOGRAPHIC PROFILE

In the early years of the CCF, conventions were annual assemblies, but today they are normally held every other year.[3] Those early conventions were small, intimate affairs; the founding convention of 1932 attracted only 131 people. In 1987, by contrast, 1,391 delegates gathered to debate policy and elect various party officers. Leadership conventions are usually even larger, attracting over 1,600 voting delegates in 1971 and 1975, and 2,510 in 1989.

Federal convention delegates are from six categories: the federal council, the parliamentary caucus, youth, central labour (i.e., co-ordinating bodies such as the CLC), affiliated union locals, and constituencies. The two largest contingents of delegates represent constituency associations (one delegate per 50–100 individual members) and union locals (one delegate per 1,000–1,500 affiliated union members); while the first group is by far the largest (67% of all delegates in 1987),[4] a significant minority of delegates (17.2% in 1987 and ranging from a low of 16.1% in 1983 to a high of 31.2% in 1971) come from affiliated organizations (both union locals and central labour bodies).[5] A smaller group are *ex-officio* delegates: members of caucus and the federal council (the latter consisting of the party executive and table officers). The youth wing sends very few delegates to federal conventions (1 to 3%).

Most of the delegates in 1987 indicated that they had previously attended either a federal (64.2%) or provincial (82.0%) NDP convention; almost half (43.1%) had attended the previous federal convention, two years earlier. Among those who had been delegates before, in 1983 the average number of provincial or federal conventions previously attended was six. In addition, true to the NDP's tradition of involvement in extra-parliamentary political activity, a high proportion of 1987 delegates were members of unions (45.6%) or co-operatives (44.9%); almost all (98.1%) had signed a petition; and 90.4% had participated in a protest march. Just over half (57.7%) had been involved in a strike,[6] and more than one-third (34.7%) had engaged in a sit-in demonstration.

Membership data also suggest substantial continuity and background experience, with most of the delegates (54.2% in 1987, 55.2% in 1989) having been party members for 6 to 20 years. A great many (76.6% in 1987) have had experience as election canvassers. In addition, many delegates have held executive posts in constituency associations (see Table 2.1): about two-fifths (39.7% in 1987, 41.7% in 1989) were on federal riding executives, and roughly half (51.2% in 1987, 47.9% in 1989) were members of provincial riding executives. What is perhaps most interesting about the data on convention attendance and service on riding association executives is that the numbers are higher for the provincial level in both cases; as we shall see in Chapter 5, when federal delegates in 1987 were asked which level of the party they felt closest to, a convincing majority (63.2%) indicated the provincial level.

Table 2.1

Selected Party Activity Characteristics, 1983, 1987, and 1989

	1983 %	1987 %	1989 %
Delegate type			
Constituency	74.1	64.7	68.6
Affiliated unions	12.4	17.3	18.4
Federal council	7.1	8.5	4.7
Central labour	3.7	5.2	4.6
Youth	1.0	2.7	2.3
Caucus	1.7	1.7	1.4
Years of NDP membership			
1–5	23.3	26.9	20.4
6–10	26.7	24.0	21.8
11–20	26.5	30.2	33.4
21–30	14.6	12.2	17.7
31–40	6.9	3.3	3.4
more than 40	2.9	2.0	3.4
Federal conventions previously attended			
0/no response	23.8	37.1	52.1
1	13.0	19.9	13.6
2	10.8	11.2	9.3
3	10.1	10.6	9.5
4	7.6	6.4	4.8
5	5.7	4.3	3.7
6–10	18.3	8.8	5.8
11–20	8.1	1.6	1.1
More than 20	3.3	0.0	0.0
Party positions			
Provincial/territorial riding executive	50.4	51.2	47.9
Federal riding executive	38.3	39.7	41.7
Provincial/territorial council	19.9	22.6	20.0
Provincial/territorial executive	10.3	10.3	9.1
Federal council	5.7	8.6	7.0
Federal executive	1.7	2.2	1.6
Election activity			
Canvasser	28.0	76.6	N.A.
Canvass organizer	37.8	31.5	
Campaign manager	25.6	23.8	
Paid party worker	N.A.	21.9	
Caucus attendance			
Provincial	N.A.	58.0	48.8
Labour		24.0	17.6
Women		21.6	14.6
Environment		N.A.	13.6
Regional		8.4	8.3
Left		8.2	7.7
Youth		10.9	6.6
Gay/Lesbian		N.A.	3.3
Municipal		1.4	2.0

SOURCES: Data on delegate type are based on actual convention attendance and are taken from NDP, *Report of the Credentials Committee*, 1983, 1987, and 1989 conventions.
N.A.: Data not available in similar question format.

Table 2.2

Selected Social Background Characteristics, 1983, 1987 and 1989

	1983 (Regina) %	1987 (Montreal) %	1989 (Winnipeg) %
Region			
Prairies	44.0	25.0	36.9
Ontario	30.3	44.7	33.8
British Columbia (and territories)	22.6	14.5	21.0
Atlantic	2.1	7.0	6.2
Quebec	0.7	7.7	2.1
Gender			
Male	69.1	67.0	63.4
Female	30.9	33.0	36.6
Education			
Less than grade 12	17.1	10.8	10.2
Grade 12/13	14.4	11.1	10.0
Some or complete college/university	68.3	78.1	79.9
Age			
21 and under	4.9	3.7	3.5
22–29	12.5	14.1	9.9
30–39	31.7	31.7	31.4
40–49	14.7	23.9	23.6
50–59	16.7	14.5	12.9
60 and over	19.4	12.2	18.6
Language spoken at home			
English	96.8	91.4	93.6
French	1.7	6.8	1.7
Both	0.9	1.5	4.7
Other	0.5	0.3	0.0
Community size			
Metropolis (500,000 or more)	32.7	36.7	29.5
Medium city (100,000–499,999)	20.9	26.7	25.5
Small city (10,000–99,999)	20.4	17.6	19.4
Town (1,000–9,999)	12.8	6.1	11.4
Rural (less than 1,000)	4.9	6.4	6.8
Farm	8.4	5.7	7.4
Family income[a]			
Less than $40,000	68.7[b]	44.1	37.3
$40,001–$60,000	31.3	34.3	29.0
More than $60,000	0	21.5	33.7
Occupation[c]			
Skilled white-collar	14.6	22.6	N.A.
Skilled blue-collar	10.1	10.8	
Union administrator/official	7.9	9.6	
Professional	10.6	9.5	
Educator	10.6	8.0	
Student	7.2	7.4	
Retired	11.4	6.1	
Small proprietor	3.0	4.3	
Unskilled labour	4.0	4.3	
Homemaker	5.4	3.6	
Sales/clerical	3.5	3.2	
Farmer	5.9	3.2	
Manager	3.5	2.8	
Unemployed	1.7	2.7	
Owner/senior executive	0.5	1.8	

[a] Does not account for inflation; percentages may not add to 100 because of rounding.

[b] Includes $40,000.

[c] Open-ended question. For comparable data from earlier periods see Whitehorn (1992).

In the past, party politics, both within the NDP and elsewhere, was an overwhelmingly male preserve (see Chapter 6; see also Whitehorn and Archer, 1995). While the most recent survey samples suggest that increasing proportions of delegates are women, in 1989 men still predominated by almost two to one (for a detailed breakdown, see Table 2.2; for further evidence and commentary, see Archer, 1991a; Bashevkin, 1993; Whitehorn, 1992).

NDP conventions tend to attract a disproportionate number of delegates in their thirties. Even though the party prides itself on being 'new', 'progressive', and in tune with youth's problems, very few people attending its conventions have been under 21 years of age—only 3.7% in 1987 and 3.5% in 1989 (see Chapter 7); recent Liberal and Conservative leadership conventions have attracted far larger percentages of young delegates.[7] Among the factors that may help to explain the NDP's poor record in this area is the party's reluctance to encourage and subsidize youth involvement.[8]

In terms of convention location, the party has a decided bias, with the West hosting 11 of 16 CCF federal conventions and to date 8 of 17 in the NDP era (1961–95). Reflecting the growth in Ontario's importance as a party base, 3 of the CCF and 7 of the NDP conventions have been held there. By contrast, until Halifax was selected for the 1991 convention, no federal CCF–NDP convention had been held in Atlantic Canada; this may help to account for the party's continuing poor electoral record in the region. Similarly, although Quebec accounts for almost one-quarter of Canada's population, it has been chosen only three times (twice in the CCF era and, surprisingly, only once in the NDP period). Given the organizational weakness, and at times disarray, of the party's Quebec wing, the tendency to hold meetings elsewhere is perhaps understandable, but it does little to encourage Quebeckers to become involved in the party.

In substantial contrast to the Liberal and Conservative parties, which allocate the same number of delegates to every constituency across the country, the NDP allocates delegates according to the constituency's party membership, with the result that delegate representation is always regionally skewed (see Chapter 5).[9] In 1987 the largest percentage of NDP delegates came from Ontario (44.7%), followed by British Columbia (13.0%) and Saskatchewan (12.7%). Clearly the NDP, like the CCF before it, retains a distinctive Western emphasis (38.8% in all).[10] Even though the convention was held in Montreal, attendance from Quebec (7.7%) and the Atlantic region (7.0%) was very low, and the great majority of delegates were anglophones. At the 1989 leadership convention, held in Winnipeg, the largest percentage of delegates came from the Prairies (36.9%), followed by Ontario (33.8%) and British Columbia (21.0%). Representation from Quebec (2.1%) and the Atlantic region (6.2%) was very limited. As was noted above, most of the delegates at both conventions came from constituency associations, and large proportions (58.8% in 1987, 48.8% in 1989) attended a provincial caucus during the convention (Table 2.1).

In 1987 and 1989 the largest proportions of delegates identified themselves as middle-class (40.7%, 47.3%). The second largest segment, those who described their background as working-class, declined from 24.7% to 18.2%, while those choosing the upper or upper-middle category increased from 14.9% to 21.2%. While these changes may in part reflect demographic shifts in Canadian society at large (and increases in convention fees, from $175 in 1983 to $300 in 1989 and $340 in 1995) they fuel allegations by left-wing critics (Brodie and Jenson, 1988) that the party has forsaken its primary audience, the working class, and shifted its allegiance to the middle class. Such charges are not easily answered by one measure, particularly a subjective one. However, comparable indications of the class profile of delegates to Liberal and Conservative conventions suggest that these are skewed to the upper strata. For example, the proportions of delegates with family incomes over $60,000 were 34% for the NDP in 1989, 52% for the Liberals in 1990, and 53% for the Conservatives in 1993 (Courtney, 1995: 336–7). Perlin (1988) found comparable differences in earlier surveys. Thus important socio-economic differences remain between activists in these three parties.

The most common occupational categories listed by NDP delegates in 1987 were skilled-white collar (22.6%), skilled blue-collar (10.8%), union administrator/official (9.6%), professional (9.5%), educator (8.0%), student (7.4%), retired (6.1%), unskilled labour (4.3%), small proprietor (4.3%), and homemaker (3.6%). The high cumulative percentage of the skilled white-collar, educator, professional, and union administrator/official categories (49.7%) lends further support to the middle-class profile of NDP convention delegates,[11] as do the very high percentages (78.1% in 1987, 79.9% in 1989) of delegates with at least some university or college education. This too suggests that delegates are more likely to be recruited from the more articulate 'haves' in society than from the least skilled and educated strata.

Assessing the significance of the size of the community in which delegates live is complicated by the fact that NDP conventions have been held in different regions of the country. In general, the rural/urban profile seems reasonably consistent over time, with the majority of delegates coming from medium-sized cities or metropoli. The relatively low percentages of delegates from farms or rural locations is yet another indicator that the NDP, in sharp contrast to the early CCF, is to a significant degree no longer a rural-based populist party.

IDEOLOGICAL COMPOSITION OF NDP CONVENTIONS

Ideologically, New Democratic activists tend to be more distinctive and more consistent than delegates to Liberal and Conservative party conventions (see Chapter 3).[12] Nevertheless, any large party is an aggregation of many diverse interests, and the policy differences within a party are often as significant as those between parties.[13] Like the CCF before it, the NDP today is a blend of several colours of the political rainbow. Whereas in 1971 a plurality (45.7%) of party members saw themselves as 'socialists', since then decreasing numbers have opted for this label (38.9% in 1979, 29.6% in 1983, and 27.6% in 1987; see Table 2.3). Instead, pluralities have selected 'social democrat' as their preferred self-description (40.6% in 1971, 52.9%

Table 2.3
Selected Ideological Characteristics, 1983, 1987, and 1989

	1983 %	1987 %	1989 %
Subjective class			
Upper	0.5	0.3	0.7
Upper middle	11.1	14.6	20.5
Middle	45.1	40.7	47.3
Lower middle	14.2	14.5	12.1
Working	27.7	24.7	18.2
Lower	1.3	1.6	1.3
Ideological self-description			
Social democrat	44.6	48.4	N.A.
Socialist	29.6	27.6	
Reformer[a]	4.3	3.9	
Social gospel	3.5	2.6	
Progressive	0.0	2.6	
Ecologist	1.3	2.2	
Marxist	3.0	2.0	
Liberal[a]	1.5	0.9	
Populist	1.0	0.7	
Other	2.3	6.0	
Multiple entry	8.9	3.8	
Placement on left–right scale			
(left = 1, right = 7; mean scores)			
Self	2.8	2.7	2.5
Federal NDP	3.4	3.4	3.6
Provincial/territorial NDP	N.A.	3.5	3.6
Federal Liberals		5.3	5.6
Federal Progressive Conservatives		6.2	6.6
Communist Party of Canada		1.9	N.A.
Most Canadians		4.5	4.8
People in your province/territory		4.6	N.A.
Most Americans		5.9	6.2

NOTE: For comparable data from earlier periods see Whitehorn (1992).
[a] These labels do not refer to political parties.

in 1979, 44.6% in 1983, and 48.4% in 1987).[14] To some scholars, these data indicate a growing de-radicalization of the party and a significant shift away from commitment to socialist programs such as nationalization (Brodie, 1985a; Hackett, 1979; 1980). While a case can be made for this position, there is also evidence to the contrary. In 1983 and 1987, for example, the overwhelming majority (76.0%, 77.7%) of delegates reported that they saw the NDP as a socialist party. These findings, coupled with the fact that a third of the respondents described themselves as socialists or Marxists, suggest that it would be premature to dismiss the party, as some have done, as merely 'liberals in a hurry',[15] or 'populists' (Richards, 1983; 1988).

Many socialist parties have experienced ideological schisms, purges, and defections. From 1932 to the present, there has always been a 'ginger group' endeavouring to guide the CCF–NDP into a more radical or even revolutionary path. Policy debates, votes on resolutions, and leadership contests are often interpreted in left–right terms by participants and scholars alike. In the 1980s, convention delegates continued to believe that there was a 'significant'/'big' difference (68.3% in 1983, 63.3% in 1987) between left and right factions within the NDP. To what degree ideological disagreements have hampered the party's growth in the past is not easily determined, but many party members have asserted that the rhetoric of the radical minority at conventions has weakened efforts to attract new supporters into the party. Nevertheless, in the 1980s there seemed to be little support (only 11.8% in 1983 and 13.2% in 1987) within the party rank and file for expelling 'ultra-left elements'.

It is conventional wisdom within the NDP that most members feel they are politically to the left of the party. While delegates placed the party left of centre on the political spectrum on a 7-point left–right scale (mean = 3.4 in 1987 and 3.6 in 1989), they placed themselves even further to the left (2.7 in 1987 and 2.5 in 1989). Does this suggest a widespread desire among delegates to see the party shift to the more left-wing position for which many radicals have called? Although survey data from the 1980s indicate that significant numbers of delegates wished to see the party 'move more clearly to the left' (55.6% in 1983, 39.9% in 1987), and strong majorities opposed the idea that the NDP should 'present a more moderate image to the general public' (76.8% in 1983, 64.2% in 1987), in both cases the proportions supporting the more left-wing position had declined by 1987.

INTRA-PARTY DEMOCRACY

Most NDP members believe that their party is more open and democratic than the Conservative and the Liberal parties. In both 1983 and 1987, a

majority of delegates (55.7% and 57.7%) agreed with the statement that
NDP conventions are extremely democratic. In addition, majorities, albeit
declining ones (83.0% in 1979 and 61.7% in 1987), indicated that they felt
they were effective in influencing party policy (see Whitehorn, 1992: 119;
Table 2.4). Yet significant numbers (29.7% in 1983, 29.0% in 1987) did not
believe that NDP conventions were 'extremely democratic'. Even in 1979,
nearly half (46.7%) of the delegates felt there was not enough 'rank and file
participation in party decisions'.

In the context of intra-party decision-making and influence levels, it is
particularly important to look at the role of organized labour (see also

Table 2.4
Delegates' Views on Intra-Party Democracy, 1987

Statement	Agree[a] %	Uncertain %	Disagree %
The NDP should become more of a social movement and less of a political party	15.9	12.2	71.8
Trade unions have too much influence in the NDP	14.8	11.1	74.1
The NDP should move more clearly to the left	39.9	22.2	37.9
There are significant differences between the left and right within the party	63.3	17.4	19.3
NDP conventions are extremely democratic	57.7	13.4	29.0
The NDP should ensure that a significant percentage of its candidates and party officers are women	82.8	6.7	10.5
Women are discriminated against within the NDP	14.0	10.2	75.8
Fifty per cent of the federal council should be composed of women	63.4	12.8	23.8
Resolutions passed at federal NDP conventions should be binding on the federal leader	65.4	14.3	20.3
I feel effective in influencing NDP policy	61.7	21.8	16.6
The party leader should have the right to reject a candidate nominated by a constituency association if that candidate does not accept party policies	64.1	12.3	23.5
Provincial sections of the NDP should have the right to develop policies on issues of fundamental importance independent of the federal party	54.3	15.9	29.8

[a] 5-point Likert scale collapsed into 3 categories.

Chapter 4). Although, as we have seen, in the 1980s fewer than 20% of the delegates were selected as representatives of affiliated unions, labour caucuses attracted relatively high proportions of delegates (24.0% in 1987, 17.6% in 1989); only the provincial caucuses attracted more. The question of labour's actual influence within the party will be discussed in later chapters. Judging by delegates' perceptions, however, it is not excessive. Although, at the sharply polarized Lewis–Laxer leadership convention of 1971, almost two-thirds (63.3%) of the delegates responded that trade unions have too much influence within the party,[16] at more recent conventions the overwhelming majority (67.0% in 1983, 74.1% in 1987) indicated that they did not believe unions have wielded too much power within the party; in fact, by a ratio of almost two to one, delegates called for closer ties with unions.

Delegates to the 1987 policy convention were also asked their views on the effectiveness of women's representation in the party (see also Chapter 6). As we noted earlier, women's participation in the NDP has increased, and at the 1989 leadership convention the third highest percentage of respondents (14.6%) reported attending the women's caucus, no doubt in part because of the presence of a woman as a high-profile leadership candidate. Although a substantial majority of delegates in 1987 (75.8%) believed that women were not discriminated against in the NDP, a significant minority either were uncertain (10.2%) or agreed (14.0%) that women did face discrimination. Most delegates thought the party should take concrete steps to redress the historic imbalance in gender representation within the party. However, it also appeared that support for gender-based affirmative action within the party weakened when the proposal entailed specific quotas for gender equity as opposed to a more abstract commitment to equity. For example, while an overwhelming 82.8% of delegates in 1987 agreed that the party should ensure that a significant number of its candidates and party officers are women, the meaning of 'a significant number' appears to have been ambiguous. Whereas some delegates may have interpreted this as a commitment to gender parity, others may have seen it as simply a move in that direction. When a clear target for gender parity was suggested—i.e., '50% of the federal council'—support dropped to 63.4%, and almost one-quarter (23.8%) of respondents disagreed. Thus any move towards complete gender parity in all aspects of party governance may meet some resistance.

With respect to party leadership, two-thirds (65.4%) of delegates in 1987 endorsed the rule that policy resolutions passed at convention are binding on a leader and presumably any future premier/prime minister. Perceptions of the leadership's responsiveness to 'ordinary members' have varied over the years. In 1979, only a small percentage (17%) felt that the leader (Ed Broadbent) was 'cut off too much from the opinions of ordinary party members'. Four years later, however, with the party at only 16% in the Gallup polls and still strained by intra-party differences over both the Canadian constitutional amendments in 1981 (see Gruending, 1990) and the proposed new Regina manifesto, almost half the delegates (48.7%) believed 'the NDP leadership does not pay sufficient attention to ordinary party members'. By 1987 the majority (61.7%) again seemed satisfied with their influence on party policy. Nevertheless, an increasingly common criticism has been that party leaders too often rely on pollsters and technical advisers; in 1979 almost three-quarters of respondents did not agree with this suggestion, but in 1989 two-thirds (67.8%) agreed that 'the NDP paid too much attention to pollsters and not enough to principles in the 1988 election campaign'.

Delegates to the 1987 convention also believed that one of the responsibilities of the leader is to ensure that other party representatives and spokespersons 'toe the party line'. Almost two-thirds (64.1%) agreed that the leader has the right to reject a nominated candidate who does not accept party policies. Delegates were somewhat more evenly divided over whether the provincial sections of the party should be able to develop policies independent of, and possibly in direct opposition to, those adopted by the federal party; whereas slightly more than half (54.3%) the delegates thought that provincial sections should have such a right, almost three in ten (29.8%) disagreed.

CONCLUSION

This chapter has provided a profile of the people, most of them volunteers, who as convention delegates play an important role in developing NDP policy. According to our survey data, the typical convention delegate would be an English-speaking male, middle-aged or older, from Western Canada, representing a constituency association. With respect to the ideological self-image of NDP activists, respondents situated themselves further to the left than the party itself, which they saw as nearer to the centre of the political spectrum (though still left of the Liberal and Conservative parties), and tended to describe themselves as social democrats or socialists. However, these left-wing self-images do not necessarily translate into consistent class self-images. The data show that the most common class image is middle-class. Thus there is a tension between activists' ideological self-image and their class self-image. This latter finding may have implications for the group identity of NDP activists. An important part of class identity is identification with a collectivity, or group consciousness. In contrast, locating oneself as left-wing on an ideological spectrum, or choosing a label such as social democrat, is a more individualistic kind of identification.

This chapter has examined the general ideological orientations of NDP activists, focusing on the labels they used to describe themselves and their placements on a left–right scale. The following chapter will extend this analysis in three ways. First, it examines the ideological positions of NDP activists in comparison with those of their counterparts in the Liberal and Progressive Conservative parties. Second, instead of examining summary ideological orientations and labels, it focuses on attitudes towards specific public-policy issues. Third, it examines both the extent to which NDP activists differ from their Liberal and Conservative counterparts across a range of issues and the extent to which they agree among themselves.

NOTES

The first part of this chapter is based on Whitehorn (1992).

1 NDP convention surveys have differed in sample size and method of data collection. The 1971 survey used a mailed questionnaire and had a sample size of 776 respondents. A mailed questionnaire was also used in 1979, with a sample of 520. In 1983, questionnaires were distributed in the delegates' convention kits and returned to special boxes at the convention hall; of 1,433 delegates, 407 filled out questionnaires (see Whitehorn, 1992: 137). The 1987 survey was based on a sample of 731 of the 1,391 delegates attending the convention. The 1989 survey, using a mailed questionnaire following the convention, was answered by 1,060 of the 2,510 delegates.

2 Each sample of convention delegates, like a cross-sectional sample of the Canadian population, presents a 'snapshot' of a given moment. However, unlike a sample of the national electorate, whose base tends to be very stable over time, a sample of convention delegates is drawn from a base that is much more mobile and open to significant fluctuations over relatively brief periods of time. The mobility is caused by two factors: first, the higher rates of turnover in party membership than in the electorate, and, second, and potentially most important, the physical shifting of convention sites across the country (see also note 9 below).

3 For details on the timing of conventions, see Chapter 11.

4 Although the proportions of people in each delegate category attending the convention differ somewhat from the proportions in each category that responded to the various surveys (see Table 2.1), these differences are modest.

5 Data provided through correspondence with the federal office of the NDP. These data do not include labour representatives already on the federal council (see Chapter 4). It should also be noted that all convention delegates from affiliated unions must be individual members of the party as well, even though most of the people they represent need not be. Thus the differences between riding delegates and union delegates at convention should not be overstated; all are individual members of the party, despite the differences in their roles, the people they represent, and their methods of selection. See also Lele et al. (1979: 84).

6   While this rate is certain to be significantly higher than for delegates at either Conservative or Liberal conventions, it is perhaps lower than might be expected for a labour-based party. The reason will become evident below, when the educational, income, and job profiles of NDP convention delegates are analyzed.

7   Data from Liberal and Conservative convention reports, Perlin's (1988) surveys of the 1984 Liberal and 1983 Conservative conventions indicate that delegates 20 and under represented 6.6% and 19.2% of the delegates respectively.

8   The NDP leadership has been cautious about fostering youth groups since the Waffle episode (see Chapter 7). In the history of the CCF–NDP, it has not been uncommon for the youth section, when it existed, to embrace a more hard-line Marxist ideology. See Lewis (1981: 385–7; Laxer, 1996).

9   In addition, convention location affects transportation and accommodation costs for delegates, who in many cases must pay at least part of their own way. Thus regional representation also depends on individual activists' ability to attend.

10 As Courtney (1973) points out, a delegate-selection mechanism based on rewarding larger riding memberships with more convention delegates is hardly likely to alleviate this problem.

11 This is actually a conservative estimate, since undoubtedly the 'student', 'retired', and 'homemaker' categories would also include people from middle-class homes; also, managers and executives account for 4.5% of delegates. See Lele et al. (1979) for more detail on the income, education, and occupational background of NDP delegates.

12 For comparable data on the Reform Party see Archer and Ellis (1994).

13 The issues of bilingualism and abortion in particular have divided most Canadian parties (Blake, 1988). The British Labour Party exhibits similar intra-party differences of opinion on policy issues (Whiteley, 1983).

14 Some care should be taken in the interpretation of the data. For a number of delegates several terms seemed equally apt, and for many the terms 'socialist' and 'social democrat' are interchangeable (Lewis, 1981: 301).

15 Louis St. Laurent originally made this remark in 1949, but it has been reiterated by scholars such as Teeple (1972). Laycock (1990) suggests that the terms 'populism' and 'socialism' are not necessarily incompatible.

16 Union attendance varies; in fact, many locals do not send all the delegates they are entitled to. However, union participation does generally rise at leadership conventions, particularly if one of the candidates is seen as significantly pro-union. Certainly the candidacy of David Lewis—the prime architect of the party–union relationship—in 1971 attracted a larger union contingent than usual.

Ideology and Opinion Structure:
A Comparison with Liberals and Conservatives

The preceding chapter has outlined the ideological self-image of NDP activists. To gain a more complete and objective picture of the party's ideological orientation, this chapter will compare the attitudes of NDP delegates with those of their Liberal and Conservative counterparts. It is a paradox that much of the existing analysis of the degree to which Canadians are guided by some ideology (liberal, conservative, socialist, nationalist, etc.)[1] has been conducted without the benefit of direct research on the values, attitudes, and beliefs of Canadians.[2] Nor has the prevailing methodology in this area, comparative historical analysis, produced consensus on either the colouration of the ideological lens or the extent to which it is shared by Canadians (Gibbins and Nevitte, 1985: 581).

Recently this area of inquiry has attracted considerable attention from scholars wishing to test the empirical foundation of research on political culture and attitudes[3] (e.g., Elkins and Simeon's [1980] finding that Canada has a set of regional political cultures and regional party systems) through individual-level survey research (e.g., to see whether the regional breakdown of attitudes supports those earlier findings). What individual-level analysis loses in historical reach it gains in a common framework of measurement.

Empirical survey-based research in Canada has only begun to unravel the complex issue of ideological space. One central challenge is to specify the linkages that may (or may not) exist between ideologies, political issues, and political parties.[4] If those linkages are not present—if, for example, Canadians use a left–right or liberal–conservative ideological lens to view politics, and organize their positions on issues accordingly, but the parties do not occupy distinct positions on that continuum—then ideology will have very little bearing on voting behaviour. Identifying the parties' ideological positions, therefore, is important in evaluating the currency of ideology in Canadian politics.

One way of assessing a party's underlying ideological foundations is through surveys of the delegates to national party conventions. Such surveys are particularly useful because they can gather data on a host of policy items at a similar point in time, and because attendance at such conventions is typically high enough to provide reasonably large samples for analysis. If we do not find significant ideological clarity and distinctiveness among the delegates to national party conventions, who, as activists, constitute a political élite, at least within the party,[5] then there is reason to conclude that the party is not organized along ideological lines.[6]

Empirical studies on the degree to which Canadian partisan politics reflects distinctive ideological choices and perspectives have generally found low levels of attitude consistency (or 'constraint'; see Converse, 1964) in the mass public; in other words, individuals' opinions on various issues do not show the kind of consistency that a firm ideological stance would require. Political élites, on the other hand, do tend to show some degree of consistency (Gibbins and Nevitte, 1985). In a recent contribution to this debate, Donald Blake (drawing on surveys conducted by George Perlin) examined ideological differences between delegates to Liberal and Progressive Conservative leadership conventions. Blake (1988: 47–8) found that Liberal and Conservative activists held significantly different opinions on most matters of policy. However, the variations within each party produced a substantial overlap in the positions held on various issues. Richard Johnston (1988: 65) took the argument a step further, demonstrating that ideological consistency explained only a small part (25–30%) of the differences in attitudes of Liberal and Conservative activists. Johnston concluded that in both cases the lack of agreement on ideology among party activists leaves considerable latitude for the leadership to act as political brokers, negotiating compromises between competing interests.

This chapter extends Blake's analysis by adding data on NDP convention delegates to his comparison of attitude structures among activists in the Liberal and Conservative parties.[7] This comparison indicates that the attitudes of New Democrats differed from those of Liberals and Conservatives in two ways: their positions on various issues were further from those of both Liberals and Conservatives than the latter two were from one another, and they displayed a much higher degree of attitude consistency than did activists in either of the other major parties. In other words, ideology appears to play a significantly greater role in the NDP than in the two older parties. In light of the formal policy-making role assigned to conventions by the NDP's constitution, this emphasis on ideology may mean that NDP leaders have less latitude than Liberal and Conservative leaders in shaping party policy and brokering competing political interests.

ANALYSIS OF SPECIFIC ISSUE ITEMS

Effective comparison is best achieved by using clusters of survey instruments in the same time period. Accordingly, the current analysis is based on three surveys conducted over a span of four years. Although the 1987 NDP survey did not always pose the same questions as those presented to the delegates at the 1984 Liberal and 1983 Progressive Conservative leadership conventions,[8] we have included as many comparisons of policy items and indexes as possible and have indicated where the items in question differ.

Using Blake's Table 1, we located 30 variables[9] from the Liberal and Conservative convention surveys that were either identical or comparable to the 1987 NDP data; items from Blake's table that could not be matched with the NDP survey are not included. Our version of Blake's table also includes equivalent statistics for the NDP with respect to the percentage agreeing with the specific statements and the index of difference[10] between the NDP and each of the two other parties (see Table 3.1). The 31 comparable attitude statements that we found are clustered into 11 policy areas: continentalism, hawkishness on defence and foreign affairs, social security, privatization, government spending, corporate power, moral conservatism, civil liberties, minority equality, constitutional powers, and, finally, bilingualism and Quebec.[11]

The first hypothesis that this comparison explores is the idea that the NDP, as a mass party, differs significantly from the Liberal and Conservative parties. Posited not only by political scientists but by political activists on both the left and the right, this hypothesis is especially current among NDP activists, who often tend to dismiss the differences between Liberals and Conservatives. We conjectured that this hypothesis would be invalidated if the policy differences between Liberals and Conservatives proved to be on the whole greater than the differences either between New Democrats and Liberals or between New Democrats and Conservatives.

First we compared Liberal–Conservative differences with Liberal–NDP differences on the 31 items. Calculating the difference to consist in the percentage agreeing with a statement in one party minus that agreeing in a second party, we found the differences between NDP and Liberal activists to be greater than those between Liberal and Conservative activists on 18 items, smaller on 11 items, and identical on 2. Thus our hypothesis was, in general, confirmed, although the number of items on which Liberal–NDP differences exceeded Liberal–Conservative differences was slightly smaller than we had initially expected. For most or all of the items in the areas of continentalism, hawkishness, government spending, corporate power, moral conservatism, and civil liberties, the differences between Liberals and New Democrats were greater than the differences that Blake found between Liberals and

Table 3.1
Liberal, Conservative, and NDP Attitudes on Selected Policy Items

Variable	Agree (%) Lib. (1984)	PC (1983)	NDP (1987)	Difference (rounded %) Lib.–PC	Lib.–NDP	PC–NDP
Continentalism						
favour freer trade with US	63.9	53.7	14.1	10	50	40
foreign ownership threatens independence	51.5	27.3	95.8	24	44	69
independent Canada even if income declines	58.1	33.3	76.8	25	19	44
Hawkishness						
refuse Cruise testing	28.7	18.3	94.0	10	65	76
more aid to underdeveloped countries	35.1	15.4	79.7	20	45	64
increase defence spending	44.7	75.3	21.9	31	23	53
Social security						
too much abuse of social programs	21.9	37.7	11.4	16	11	26
means test for some social programs[a]	54.4	74.1	28.6	20	26	46
Moral conservatism						
abortion private matter[a]	47.3	44.0	85.9	3	39	42
reintroduce capital punishment	48.9	79.9	5.6	31	43	74
legalize marijuana possession	47.3	43.2	51.5	4	4	8
society too permissive	54.7	64.1	17.1	9	38	47
Corporate power						
big business has too much political influence	57.4	46.6	98.2	11	41	52
Bilingualism and Quebec						
bilingual federal government[a]	79.7	38.3	88.4	41	9	50
special status for Quebec	33.7	36.9	66.6	3	33	30
Civil liberties						
restrict rights to reduce crime	48.8	53.7	18.5	5	30	35
restrict right to strike[a]	32.7	30.8	36.6	2	4	6
Privatization						
less public ownership: rail	13.6	36.5	2.3	23	11	34
less public ownership: airlines	22.5	54.2	3.4	32	19	51
less public ownership: radio/TV	13.4	38.3	3.8	25	10	35
less public ownership: oil/gas	13.8	61.8	2.0	48	12	60
Government spending (increase)						
foreign aid	35.1	15.3	76.7	20	42	61
education[a]	71.4	55.1	90.0	16	19	35
arts	31.2	23.9	65.5	7	34	42
develop new technology	90.2	89.6	75.8	0	14	14
welfare payments to poor[a]	48.5	32.3	87.0	16	39	55
defence	44.7	75.3	21.9	31	23	54
Minority equality						
take immigrants from all groups	79.1	67.3	90.8	12	12	24

Table 3.1 continued

Liberal, Conservative, and NDP Attitudes on Selected Policy Items

Variable	Agree (%)			Difference (rounded %)		
	Lib. (1984)	PC (1983)	NDP (1987)	Lib.–PC	Lib.–NDP	PC–NDP
Constitutional powers						
more power to federal government	38.8	9.1	26.6	30	12	18
more power to provincial government	7.9	47.1	18.6	39	11	29
monarchy essential	54.0	69.0	22.4	15	32	47
Items with differences greater than Lib./PC differences					18	29
Items with differences smaller than Lib./PC differences					11	2
Items with differences equal to Lib./PC differences					2	0
Mean					26.3	42.6

NOTE: Some items are scored positively, others negatively. One item (defence spending) appears twice both here and in Blake's analysis. Index of differences is calculated by subtracting the percentage agreeing with a particular statement in one party from the percentage agreeing in the other party. Because this method is slightly different from the one used by Blake, we have recalculated and, where necessary, adjusted his figures for Liberals and Conservatives (see note 17, p. 41).
aSurvey items are comparable but differences in questionnaire wording may affect results.

Conservatives. In two areas (privatization and constitutional powers), however, the NDP–Liberal differences were on the whole less than those between Liberals and Conservatives. In three other areas the differences in the pairings balanced out: on minority equality the differences were equal, while on social security and bilingualism and Quebec, both of which included two items, the difference was larger in one case and smaller in the other.

The differences between NDP and Conservative delegates on the same questions were greater than those between Liberals and Conservatives on 29 items and smaller on 2. For all items in each policy area except one (constitutional powers), the differences in position between the Conservatives and New Democrats were greater than the differences between Liberals and Conservatives in Blake's data. The gulf between the NDP and Conservatives seems substantial and the consistency of these findings significant. Hence these data seem to confirm the ideological placement of the NDP to one side of the political spectrum (presumably the left) and the Conservatives on the other side (presumably the right), with the Liberals somewhere in the middle. They also appear to belie the arguments of the 'end of ideology' school of thought (Bell, 1962) in any comparisons between the NDP and Conservatives. On almost every policy item, the NDP–Conservative differences are significant.[12]

In addition, Table 3.1 sheds light on the levels of internal agreement among NDP respondents on the issues in question. If we assume that ideology will act as an important constraint on the opinions of NDP activists, we would expect the NDP to occupy one of the polar positions: that is, to have the highest numbers agreeing or disagreeing with a particular policy statement. (Note that a random distribution of the three parties would have any one party appearing in the middle range, between the other two parties, on one in three occasions, on average.) In fact, NDP responses appeared in the middle (between the Liberals and Conservatives) on only two occasions (6.5%)—far less than the three in ten (33%) one would expect with a random distribution. Thus again the evidence suggests that NDP activists clearly position themselves on one side of the political spectrum.

More specifically, on the issue of continentalism NDP delegates were the least likely of the three groups to favour freer trade with the United States and the most likely to feel that foreign ownership threatens Canadian independence. In the area of foreign affairs they were the least committed to increases in defence spending and the most strongly opposed to Cruise missile testing. Reflecting their internationalism, they were also far more tolerant than their Liberal and Conservative counterparts of accepting immigrants from all groups. In the area of social security, they were the least inclined to perceive abuses in social programs and the most opposed to the imposition of means tests on such programs. Not surprisingly, New Democrats were the least sympathetic to efforts at privatization. In the area of government spending, they were the most in favour of education, payments to the poor, and foreign aid, and least in favour of defence. Reflecting traditional socialist beliefs, they were almost universal in their perception that corporations have too much political influence.

New Democrats were the least likely to endorse opinions associated with moral conservatism. They were not inclined to see society as too permissive or to favour a reintroduction of capital punishment, and they were the most likely to regard abortion as largely a private matter. While New Democrats were the least willing of activists in the three parties to accept restrictions on human rights, they were, surprisingly, the most sympathetic to some restrictions on the right to strike.[13] Finally, New Democrats were the least inclined to see the monarchy as essential and the most inclined to favour both a bilingual federal government and special status for Quebec. Only on the two questions relating to federal and provincial constitutional powers did New Democrats place themselves midway between the Liberals (more power to the federal government) and the Conservatives (more power to provincial governments).

ISSUE INDEXES

Having compared the positions of NDP delegates on a number of policies with those of Liberal and Conservative delegates, we can extend that analysis by grouping positions on related policy matters into issue indexes. Our indexes are based on Blake's, and we have attempted to replicate his analysis as closely as possible. For the questions used in the NDP survey see the Appendix on pp. 38–40; for the Liberal and Conservative indexes, see Blake (1988: 49–50, note 3).[14]

Examining the attitudinal differences within and between the convention delegates in Canada's three major parties reveals the spatial dimensions of those issue positions. Are the parties' positions, as reflected by the attitudes of convention delegates, arrayed along a consistent left–right dimension, with New Democrats furthest left, Conservatives furthest right, and Liberals occupying the middle ground? Or is there a multidimensional element to party positions, with attitudes on some issues arrayed along a left–right axis and others along some different dimension, independent of the left–right cleavage?[15] To the extent that spatial distances between parties can be mapped along a given ideological dimension, does that distance remain constant across issue domains, or does it vary, with party activists situating themselves further from one pole in some issue domains than in others?

In addition to the relationship between parties, we examine the degree of issue consensus within the parties. To what degree do party workers agree among themselves on a given issue area? Is one party consistently either more or less consensual than the others? Do the parties' levels of consensus remain constant for all issue domains, or are they stronger on some issues than on others? The answers to these questions should help to refine our understanding of the nature of attitudinal divisions among activists in the three parties.

The first portion of Table 3.2 lists the indexes, their ranges, and the direction in which each was scored (i.e., pro- or anti-).[16] For example, in the first index each item relates to the respondents' view of the relationship between Canada and the United States on economic matters. The index was constructed using four questions and was scored in a pro-continentalist direction. One point was added to a respondent's score for a response of 'agree' or 'strongly agree' to the statement 'Canada should have freer trade with the United States'. Three other questions similarly tapping continentalist attitudes were included. (See the Appendix, pp. 38–40), for a complete list of the items used in each index.) The pro-continentalist responses to the four items were summed, producing an index ranging from 0 to 4. The table shows the mean scores and standard deviations for Liberal, Progressive Conservative, and New Democratic convention delegates (the data for the

Table 3.2

Attitudinal Differences Within and Between Parties

Index (range) (direction)	Liberal		Party Progressive Conservative		New Democrat		Difference Lib.–PC	Lib.–NDP	PC–NDP
	mean	s.d.	mean	s.d.	mean	s.d.			
Continentalism (0–4) (pro–)	1.80	1.22	2.90	1.16	0.32	0.59	–1.10	1.48	2.58
Hawkishness (0–6) (pro–)	2.65	1.41	4.17	1.42	0.87	1.14	–1.52	1.78	3.30
Social security (0–5) (pro–)	2.63	1.34	1.67	1.25	4.06	1.09	0.96	–1.43	–2.39
Moral conservatism (0–3) (pro–)	1.65	1.14	2.16	1.04	0.58	0.76	–0.51	1.07	1.58
Corporate power (0–3) (anti–)	1.98	1.01	1.58	1.11	2.64	0.69	0.40	–0.66	–1.06
Bilingualism (0–2) (pro–)	1.71	0.58	1.01	0.85	1.76	0.65	0.70	–0.05	–0.75
Civil liberties (0–3) (pro–)	1.22	1.01	1.51	1.06	1.92	0.85	–0.29	–0.70	–0.41
Privatization (0–6) (pro–)	2.21	1.79	4.00	1.72	0.17	0.75	–1.79	2.04	3.83

NOTE: For the questions on which indexes are based, see Appendix, p. 38.

Liberals and Conservatives are taken directly from Blake, although we use standard deviations instead of the coefficient of variation[17]) and, finally, the differences in means for each of the three pairings of parties.

Several patterns emerge from the data in Table 3.2. First, comparison of the means[18] indicates that on almost all items, party delegates aligned themselves in similar ways. This suggests a single overarching, presumably left–right, dimension, with the New Democrats and Conservatives occupying the polar positions of left and right. Second, NDP delegates tended to be closer to the left pole than the Conservatives to the right pole;[19] for example, on the four-point continentalist index, New Democrats (0.3) were one-third of a unit away from the left pole, whereas Conservatives (2.9) were a full point from the right pole and the Liberals (1.8) were close to the centre. Likewise on the six-point hawkishness measure, New Democrats were on average less than one unit from the left pole, and Conservatives were almost two units from the right, and Liberals near the centre. This general finding holds for the indexes measuring attitudes towards social security, moral conservatism, privatization, and, to a lesser extent, corporate power.

On bilingualism, however, the parties arrayed themselves differently on the left–right axis, and on civil liberties party alignment was not so obviously based on a left–right cleavage. With respect to bilingualism, the attitudes of Liberals and New Democrats were almost indistinguishable, falling towards the 'pro-' end of the spectrum, whereas Conservatives were near the mid-point.[20] On the question of civil liberties, New Democrats were the most strongly opposed to restrictions on such liberties, Liberals the least, and Conservatives at the mid-point of the range.[21]

The dispersion of data as measured by standard deviation also illuminates aspects of the ideological nature of respondents in the three parties. In general, attitudinal consistency and consensus were greater in the NDP than in the other parties.[22] On every index except bilingualism, New Democrats had the greatest consistency (i.e., the lowest standard deviation score). The Liberals and Progressive Conservatives were barely distinguishable in the degree of consensus they showed in all instances but one (bilingualism). Typically, the Liberals and Conservatives had very similar standard deviation scores, with the latter showing marginally greater consistency except in the case of bilingualism, where the greatest consensus was shown by the Liberals and the least by the Conservatives.

Thus comparison of means and standard deviations indicates that NDP delegates tended to be ideologically more distinctive and internally more consistent than Liberal and Conservative delegates. In addition, on most issues the Conservatives occupied a position near the right pole, although not quite so near as the New Democrats were to the left pole. Internally, however, Conservative delegates were less unanimous in their views than were New Democrats, displaying as wide a range of views as Liberals.

In order to make comparisons between as well as within indexes, we adjusted for the range of the index by dividing the absolute difference in means between each pair of parties (from Table 3.2) by the range for that index. The resulting 'standard difference in means', which ranges from 0 to 1, appears in Table 3.3.[23] However, the standard deviations from Table 3.2 are not directly comparable across indexes because they are based on different ranges. Thus we adjusted the standard deviations by dividing by the range of the index. The 'adjusted standard deviations', therefore, are also based on indexes ranging from 0 to 1. Thus we are able to compare levels of division and cohesion among the parties across each of the issue areas.

Table 3.3 illustrates the ideological divides in Canadian politics in the 1980s, at least at the level of political activists. The greatest differences were between Conservatives and New Democrats,[24] and the two areas in which they were most pronounced concerned economic relations between Canada and the United States (continentalism) and the role of the government in managing a mixed economy (privatization). (Since the data on the

Table 3.3
Standardized Attitudinal Differences Between and Within Parties

Index (direction)	Standardized absolute differences between parties			Adjusted standard deviation		
	Lib.-PC	Lib.-NDP	PC–NDP	Lib.	PC	NDP
Continentalism (pro-)	0.28	0.37	0.65	0.31	0.29	0.15
Hawkishness (pro-)	0.25	0.30	0.55	0.24	0.24	0.19
Social security (pro-)	0.19	0.29	0.48	0.27	0.25	0.22
Moral conservatism (pro-)	0.17	0.36	0.53	0.38	0.35	0.25
Corporate power (anti-)	0.13	0.22	0.35	0.34	0.37	0.23
Bilingualism (pro-)	0.35	0.03	0.38	0.29	0.43	0.33
Civil liberties (pro-)	0.09	0.23	0.14	0.34	0.35	0.28
Privatization (pro-)	0.30	0.34	0.64	0.30	0.29	0.13

Conservatives and Liberals were gathered before the Conservative government took office in 1984—before the free-trade initiative and policy of privatization were introduced—the differences would likely have been even greater in the late 1980s or early 1990s.) Conservatives and New Democrats were also sharply divided over Canada's foreign policy (hawkishness), issues such as the right of homosexuals to teach in schools (moral conservatism), the legitimacy of the welfare state (social security), bilingualism, and corporate power.

The divisions between Liberals and Conservatives were in general smaller and were most pronounced in quite a different area: French–English relations (bilingualism). The data also suggest that the New Democrats were very close to the Liberals in this area (a difference of only 0.03). However, whereas the bilingualism index revealed the greatest distinction between Liberals and Conservatives, it was of comparatively modest importance in separating New Democrats from Conservatives. Although the Liberal–Conservative differences on issues such as privatization, continentalism, and hawkishness were important, they were markedly smaller than the NDP–Conservative differences on the same issues. In fact, in most instances the differences between Liberals and Conservatives were smaller than those between Liberals and New Democrats.

Examining the adjusted standard deviations, we find the highest levels of internal consensus among the NDP delegates. Strong opposition to privatization, to closer economic ties with the United States, and to militarization in foreign policy were among the key issues uniting New Democrats. Indeed, the agreement among NDP delegates on each of these issues was greater than that among the delegates of the other parties on *any* issue area. The Liberals found their greatest levels of agreement on the issues of hawkishness, social security, and bilingualism; the Conservatives, on hawkishness, social security, privatization, and continentalism.

As we have already noted, there is reason to suspect that some of these findings reflect the fact that the three surveys were conducted at different times over four years. Conservative delegates were interviewed in 1983, before the Conservative government elected in 1984 undertook important initiatives in areas such as free trade (i.e., continentalism) and privatization. It is likely that by the late 1980s the distance between the Conservatives and the other parties on these issues was greater, and that the consistency in the attitudes of Conservatives was greater as well. Whether Conservative attitudes on these issues would have been as consensual as NDP attitudes is impossible to tell. It is clear, however, that over the range of indexes examined, the levels of consensus and ideological clarity among NDP respondents were considerably higher than among their Liberal and Conservative counterparts.

CONCLUSION

The data presented in this chapter reveal considerable differences in the attitudes of party activists in the 1980s, and indicate that these divisions were stable across issue areas. In most cases the New Democrats were clearly on the ideological left and the Progressive Conservatives on the ideological right. Furthermore, the Liberals were strikingly consistent in their tendency to locate themselves at the ideological centre, a tendency that was reaffirmed after the 1993 federal election. In general, the Liberals were closer to the Conservatives than to the New Democrats, although clearly the two older parties were not as indistinguishable as some have suggested (see Brodie and Jenson, 1988; Underhill, 1960). However, our data also cast doubt on analyses that group Liberals and New Democrats together on the ideological left and contrast them with Conservatives (see Alford, 1963).

The content of delegates' attitudinal differences provides an interesting perspective on the nature of the ideological divisions between the parties. Differences on bilingualism, for example, were most pronounced between Liberals and Conservatives. As long as partisan conflict was generally centred on a choice between Liberals and Conservatives, political debate focused on non-economic issues.[25] This finding helps to explain the relative unimportance of economic performance in conditioning levels of support for the parties in the 1970s and 1980s (see Archer and Johnson, 1988: 569–84; Monroe and Erickson, 1986).[26] This is not to suggest that Liberals and Conservatives did not differ on other issues as well: significant differences were evident in attitudes towards continentalism, privatization, and so on. However, while we suspect that some of these differences increased following the 1984 federal election, they have probably diminished somewhat since the Liberals' return to power in 1993.

Attitudes towards bilingualism also distinguished New Democrats from Conservatives, but these differences paled in comparison with those evident in attitudes towards continentalism and privatization. Although traditionally there has been a regional component in Canadians' attitudes towards the United States, with Westerners much more amenable to forging closer economic links than many of those in the rest of the country, for all parties these issues cut across provincial and regional boundaries in a way that the bilingualism issue does not.

Finally, on almost every index our study has revealed much higher levels of ideological consistency among NDP delegates than among their Liberal and Conservative counterparts. This relatively high degree of ideological clarity[27] suggests that NDP policies are less liable to shift with changes in leadership than are Liberal and Conservative policies, and that new NDP leaders have less latitude than their counterparts in those 'brokerage' parties to move the NDP in new directions.

However, the NDP's general ideological consistency does not mean that there are no systematic divisions or cleavages within it. To explore these, the following chapters will examine key caucuses and policy issues.

APPENDIX: NDP ATTITUDE INDEXES

Each index was produced by counting the number of statements on which the individual's response corresponded to the direction (pro- or anti-) of the scale. Most variables were measured with a 5-point scale ranging from (1) strongly disagree to (5) strongly agree, with (3) signifying uncertainty. Items identical or very similar to Blake's are marked with an asterisk. For the operationalization of the Liberal and Conservative respondents' scores, see Blake (1988: 49–50, note 3).

Continentalism (pro-)

*1. Canada's independence is threatened by the large percentage of foreign ownership in key sectors of the economy (DISAGREE OR STRONGLY DISAGREE).

*2. We must ensure an independent Canada even if it means a lower standard of living for Canadians (DISAGREE OR STRONGLY DISAGREE).

*3. Canada should have freer trade with the United States (AGREE OR STRONGLY AGREE).

4. We ought to seek greater American investment in Canada (AGREE OR STRONGLY AGREE).

Hawkishness (pro-)

1. Canada should seek closer relations with communist countries (DISAGREE OR STRONGLY DISAGREE).

2. Canada ought to devote much more effort and money to aiding the underdeveloped countries (DISAGREE OR STRONGLY DISAGREE).

*3. Canada should refuse to permit the testing of the Cruise missile on Canadian soil (DISAGREE OR STRONGLY DISAGREE).

4. Soviet communism is no longer a threat to Canada (DISAGREE OR STRONGLY DISAGREE).

*5. The spending on foreign aid should be (SLIGHTLY DECREASED OR GREATLY DECREASED).

*6. The spending on defence should be (SLIGHTLY INCREASED OR GREATLY INCREASED).

Social security (pro-)

*1. There is a great deal of abuse of social security and welfare programs in Canada (DISAGREE OR STRONGLY DISAGREE).

2. Social security programs, such as old-age pensions and family allowances, should be based on family income needs, and people who don't need this type of assistance should not receive it (DISAGREE OR STRONGLY DISAGREE).

⋆3. Government-sponsored child-care services should be greatly expanded (AGREE OR STRONGLY AGREE).

4. More money should be spent on social services (AGREE OR STRONGLY AGREE).

⋆5. The spending on welfare payments to the poor should be (SLIGHTLY INCREASED OR GREATLY INCREASED).

Moral conservatism (pro-)
⋆1. Abortion is a private matter which should be decided between the pregnant woman and her doctor (DISAGREE OR STRONGLY DISAGREE).

⋆2. The possession of marijuana should be legalized (DISAGREE OR STRONGLY DISAGREE).

⋆3. Our society has become too permissive (AGREE OR STRONGLY AGREE).

Corporate power (anti-)
⋆1. Big business has too much influence in Canadian politics (AGREE OR STRONGLY AGREE).

2. The government ought to take stronger measures to break up monopolies and create competition in the economy (AGREE OR STRONGLY AGREE).

(This index was multiplied by 3/2.)

Bilingualism (pro)
⋆1. A bilingual federal government is necessary (AGREE OR STRONGLY AGREE).

(This index was multiplied by 2.)

Civil liberties (pro-)
⋆1. Certain restrictions on civil rights would be acceptable if it would help police reduce crime (DISAGREE OR STRONGLY DISAGREE).

2. People who are homosexuals should be permitted to teach in schools (AGREE OR STRONGLY AGREE).

3. Racists should not be allowed to hold public meetings and rallies (DISAGREE OR STRONGLY DISAGREE).

Privatization (pro-)
With regard to public ownership in different sectors, how much do you think there should be?

★1. Oil and gas (LESS)
★2. railroads (LESS)
★3. airlines (LESS)
★4. radio-television (LESS)
(This index was multiplied by 3/2.)

NOTES

This is a revised and expanded version of Archer and Whitehorn, 'Opinion Structure among Party Activists: A Comparison of New Democrats, Liberals and Conservatives', in Thorburn (1991). A shorter, earlier version was published in the *Canadian Journal of Political Science* (March 1990).

1 These categories are from Christian and Campbell (1995).

2 Some use the comparative historical method *à la* Louis Hartz (see Horowitz, 1968; Wiseman, 1983). Some use aggregated electoral returns (Brodie and Jenson, 1988). Some use a combination of party platforms, leaders' statements, and government initiatives (Christian and Campbell, 1996).

3 This research is often cast as examining the extent to which attitudes are 'constrained'. 'Attitude constraint' refers to the degree of consistency in an individual's positions across a series of issues (see Elkins, 1974; Gibbins and Nevitte, 1985; Kornberg et al., 1975; Lambert et al., 1986; Laponce, 1981; Ogmundson, 1975).

4 The importance of an unambiguous link between issue and party was initially proposed by Campbell et al. (1960) and further developed by Butler and Stokes (1974). For an application to Canada, see Clarke et al. (1979).

5 The term 'political élite' can refer to political participation as well as political power. Thus the fact that the New Democrats have never formed a national government does not mean that NDP activists cannot be considered members of the political élite. The term 'political élite' is used in this way in Kornberg et al. (1979) and Presthus (1978).

6 For discussions of the very different ways in which political élites and mass publics understand politics, see Converse (1964); Gibbins and Nevitte (1985); Kornberg et al. (1975); Lambert et al. (1986).

7 For a similar analysis of the Reform Party see Archer and Ellis (1994).

8 Surveys of the 1983 Progressive Conservative and 1984 Liberal conventions were undertaken by George Perlin. For analyses based on these earlier surveys, see Perlin (1988).

9 Although Table 3.1 shows 31 items, one of these, defence, is included under two separate categories (hawkishness and government spending).

10 For an explanation of this term see Blake (1988: 34). It should be noted that we use the index somewhat differently from Blake, who computes the 'difference index' as follows: the absolute differences between parties in the percentages in

each response category are summed, then divided by 200 (Blake, 1988: 51, note 2). Our index of difference is less complex: a straight difference between the percentage in one party who agree on one item subtracted from the percentage who agree on the same item in another party. We have applied the same method to all three parties, recalculating Blake's indexes for the Liberals and Conservatives; in the overwhelming majority of cases, there is little or no difference in the results obtained by our less complex method of calculation.

11 Three of our headings differ slightly from Blake's: our 'moral conservatism' is his 'moralism (restrictive)' our 'corporate power' is his 'anti-corporate power'; and our 'government spending' is his 'spending increases'.

12 Although the Reform Party did not exist when these data were collected, its ideological placement and issue positioning in the early 1990s suggest that the differences between it and the NDP would be even greater than those between the Conservatives and the NDP.

13 Differences in questionnaire wording may account for some of this result. Compare the questions in Blake (1988: 49–50) with those in the Appendix (pp. 38–40).

14 To ensure that our indexes have the same range as Blake's, in most instances we have included the same number of items as Blake's indexes. Where sufficient comparable items were not available (i.e., on the corporate-power, bilingualism, and privatization indexes), the values on the indexes were adjusted to produce an equivalent range. For example, Blake included six items in his privatization index, producing a range of 0–6. Since we had only four comparable items, the resulting index was multiplied by 1.5 to produce a range of 0–6. This procedure enables us to compare directly the means within, but not across, indexes. The standard deviation, if affected, is likely increased under this procedure.

15 The argument has recently been made that the Canadian party system is characterized by multidimensional issue positioning: on some issues, positions are based on an economic cleavage, and on others they are based on a linguistic cleavage (see Johnston, et al., 1992).

16 We follow Blake in omitting three categories—'spending', 'minority equality', and 'constitutional powers'—from these indexes.

17 We have used standard deviation rather than the coefficient of variation (CV) because we find it is a more accurate measure of dispersion in this instance. CV is obtained by dividing the standard deviation of each distribution by its mean. With these measures, however, the size of the mean is heavily dependent on the direction of the index, which in itself is arbitrary. (It doesn't matter whether continentalism is measured in a pro-continentalist or an anti-continentalist direction, as long as it measures feelings toward continentalism.) However, since CV divides the standard deviation by the mean, the direction in which the index is measured has a large bearing on the perceived dispersion.

The use of CV led Blake to infer (1988: 41) that 'continentalism and hawkishness came closest to reflecting a consensus within Conservative ranks, but were a source of considerable disagreement with the Liberal party'. When standard deviation is used as a measure of dispersion, however, we find identical consensus within the two parties on each issue. Had the index been measured in the opposite direction (i.e., anti-continentalist), resulting in a reversal of means (Liberal=2.20, Conservative=1.10), CV would change dramatically and standard deviation would remain the same. To compare dispersion across indexes, the standard deviation must be adjusted according to the range rather than the mean, a procedure we use in Table 3.3.

18   Whereas Blake took into account the percentage of respondents in each category of the dependent variable, we used the less complex method of subtracting the mean for one party from the mean for another.

19   This finding may reflect the way we operationalized our measures of left and right, which as noted were based on answers to a series of policy questions. Our respondents were asked to place Canada's parties on a seven-point left–right scale, with 1 indicating farthest left and 7 farthest right. The mean score in left–right placement for the NDP was 3.4. Respondents placed the Liberal Party at 5.3 and the Progressive Conservative Party at 6.2. For complete data on left–right placement, see Chapter 2.

20   When delegates to the 1992 Reform Party Assembly (the party's term for its convention) were asked their views on bilingualism and the place of Quebec in the confederation, their distinctive position became apparent. For example, 30.9% of Reform delegates thought 'a bilingual federal government is necessary', whereas fully 60.3% disagreed and 8.8% were uncertain. On the role of Quebec, 97.5% thought the province should not have a veto in the Canadian constitution, and 89.3% thought it should not be granted 'distinct society' status (Archer and Ellis, 1994). These positions place Reformers to the right of the Conservatives.

21   Conservative positioning on this item likely reflects the inclusion of a question concerning the 1970 imposition of the War Measures Act by the Liberal government, a question that may have provoked a partisan response.

22   In its high levels of attitudinal consistency and consensus, Reform parallels the NDP, although it is located at the opposite end of the left–right ideological continuum, and also at the opposite end of the linguistic ideological divide (i.e., rejecting bilingualism).

23   This is an attempt to standardize the 'standard deviations', which are based upon indexes of different ranges. Note that standard deviation is in part range-dependent (see note 17 above).

24   Today the greatest differences on left–right issues are between New Democrats and Reformers.

25   See Brodie and Jensen (1988) for an explanation of this finding, which centres on explicit strategic decisions within the Liberal and Progressive Conservative parties.

26   In the 1990s, of course, economic cleavages have become more apparent, largely as a consequence of the economic crisis and the coming to power of neo-conservative governments in several provinces and the rise of the fiscally conservative Reform Party.

27 The substantial degree of ideological clarity that we have observed among the
    convention delegates, especially from the New Democratic and Conservative
    parties, does not necessarily lead us to conclude that political choice in Canada
    is based on a model of minimizing the perceived distance between one's own
    ideological positions and those of the various parties, as postulated by Downs
    (1957). One of the prerequisites of the Downs model is that the parties organize
    their positions on issues in an unambiguous way. Examining the attitudes of con-
    vention delegates, as we have done, leads to the conclusion that there are con-
    siderable differences between Canada's major political parties as well as relative
    cohesion within each party. In examining the broader question of the role of ide-
    ology in structuring choices at Canadian elections, our observations suggest that,
    for party activists, the ideological divisions are clear and straightforward, even if
    those perceptions do not necessarily extend to the mass public.

Part II

Intra-Party Caucuses and Major Policy Issues

CHAPTER
4

Organized Labour

Since the transformation of the Co-operative Commonwealth Federation into the New Democratic Party in 1961, a change intended to integrate labour more fully within the party, differing views over the role that organized labour should play have engendered some of the most intense debates and divisions that the party has experienced. To some degree the role of organized labour in the NDP remains controversial. On the one hand, some commentators, particularly on the left, have seen organized labour as a conservative force both in its approach to labour–management relations and in its political positions and preferences (Brodie, 1985a; Brodie and Jenson, 1988; Hackett, 1979; Waffle Manifesto, 1969). According to these critics, the prominence of a conservatively oriented labour element within the NDP has prevented the party from articulating a clear socialist response to capitalism (Brodie and Jenson, 1988). They also suggest that this failure in turn has been directly responsible for the NDP's electoral marginalization (Bradford, 1989; Brodie and Jenson, 1989).

On the other hand, some of the earliest and most severe public criticism of the NDP's strategy in the 1988 federal election came from leaders of the two unions that historically have been the party's strongest supporters, the Canadian Auto Workers (CAW) and the United Steelworkers of America. On the advice of an American public-opinion pollster, the party had chosen to downplay the issue of the free-trade agreement, an important decision in light of its continentalist implications, and instead centred its campaign on the preservation of social-welfare programs. Intended to woo voters from the non-socialist ideological centre, the large Canadian middle class, and the key province of Quebec, this strategy failed to achieve the desired breakthrough even though the party did better than ever before in seats, votes, and percentage of the vote. Almost immediately after the election, the leader of the CAW at the time, Bob White, accused the NDP of having ignored labour by not focusing its campaign on the free-trade agreement, while the Steelworkers' Gerard Docquier condemned the party's betrayal of its principles for electoral expediency. Both White and Docquier were harshly critical of the lack of labour input into the 1988 election campaign strategy and tactics, particularly on the crucial free-trade issue (Whitehorn, 1989: 51–2). Similarly, from mid-1993 until its defeat in June 1995, some affiliated unions criticized the Ontario NDP government for insufficient adherence to party policies.

We seem to be faced with a paradox. Some critics see labour as responsible for the party's poor electoral fortunes and argue that it is a conservative force that prevents the party from taking a more left-wing ideological stance. Others claim that labour has too little voice in the party, is too often ignored, and, if given the opportunity, would lead the party in a progressive direction. To understand this apparent paradox, this chapter will focus on two fundamental questions: (1) Is organized labour a defender of conservatism and the status quo within the NDP, or is it a progressive force offering renewal and innovation? (2) Is labour a unified and powerful intra-party interest group capable of setting and altering party preferences, or is it internally divided and often ignored or over-ridden by the party's institutional hierarchy and/or rank-and-file party members?

LABOUR AND THE CCF–NDP

For much of the history of the CCF, the labour movement in Canada remained divided along a number of important lines. The major union central during the first half of the twentieth century, the Trades and Labour Congress (TLC), organized mainly craft-based international unions, the majority of which had their headquarters in the United States. The organizing preferences of the TLC were most clearly shown in its 1903 decision to exclude from its membership those unions attempting to organize workers whose jurisdiction was claimed by existing TLC affiliates. Thus many all-Canadian unions were excluded from the major union central in Canada.[1]

A denominational and linguistic cleavage was superimposed on the national cleavage when the Roman Catholic Church began to support the creation of denominational unions (see Baum, 1980: 71–92), the vast majority of which were created in the province of Quebec under the Canadian Catholic Confederation of Labour (CCCL; founded 1921). In 1961 the CCCL, which had become more secular over time, dropped the religious dimension of its identity while preserving its linguistic distinctiveness, becoming the French-speaking Confederation of National Trade Unions (CNTU). However, it remained separate from the English-speaking union centrals.

A further division was created with the emergence of industrial union organizations in the 1930s. In the United States, the new industrial organizations were first accommodated through a committee of the American Federation of Labour (AFL), but following their expulsion from the AFL, in 1937, they created a new central labour body, the Congress for Industrial Organizations (CIO). What followed was a generation of internecine jurisdictional disputes that continued into the mid-1950s.

Developments in Canada paralleled those in the United States. Following the expulsion of the CIO from the AFL, the Trades and Labour Congress in Canada expelled its industrial-based affiliates of CIO unions. Canada's industrial unions then united with the All-Canadian Congress of Labour (ACCL) unions in opposition to the TLC to form the Canadian Congress of Labour (CCL). Although the CCL was much friendlier towards the CCF than was the TLC, the jurisdictional divisions within the union movement effectively prevented harmony on political action. However, a major barrier was removed with the AFL–CIO merger in 1955, and the following year their Canadian counterparts, the TLC and CCL, merged to form the Canadian Labour Congress (CLC). The creation of the CLC dramatically reduced the political significance of the national–international and craft–industrial cleavages within the trade-union movement. Meanwhile, although the denominational cleavage was soon to dissolve of its own accord, it would be replaced by a linguistic division that has reinforced the distinctiveness of Quebec labour.[2] By the late 1960s, a public–private sector divide would be added to the linguistic cleavage, further complicating the challenge of achieving labour unity in Canada.

Nonetheless, the creation of the Canadian Labour Congress in 1956 represented an important new opportunity for the CCF to forge stronger ties with the labour movement. Although the CCF was ostensibly based on a tripartite alliance of farmers, labour, and socialists, in fact divisions internal to the labour movement had always prevented the development of strong labour bonds with the party. By the late 1950s and early 1960s, the internal divisions in the labour movement were weaker than they had been at any time in this century, and about as weak as they would become. At the same time, the ascendancy of CLC leaders who favoured strengthening labour's commitment to partisan political action provided the necessary impetus for a re-evaluation of labour's political strategy.

These positive developments in the labour movement combined with negative trends in the electoral performance of the CCF to increase the numbers of voices calling for a new and stronger relationship between the social-democratic left and labour. By the mid-1950s the CCF had effectively stalled as a national political party, averaging only 11% of the popular vote, and in the 1958 Diefenbaker landslide it was reduced to a mere 9.5% of the popular vote and its lowest total of seats (8) in the House of

Commons since the 1930s; among the vanquished were the party's leader, M.J. Coldwell, and one of its leading figures, Stanley Knowles. The defeat of prominent CCFers in 1958 was not an isolated setback, but one in a long series of disappointments. Party strategists and members alike were frustrated by the federal party's inability to make significant and sustained inroads into the industrial heartlands of Ontario and Quebec. If the prospects for long-term growth were to improve, it was imperative that the party gain support among the urban, industrial electorate of Central Canada. Yet the vast majority of the party's seats continued to come from the Prairie provinces of Manitoba and Saskatchewan, and to a lesser extent from British Columbia (Whitehorn, 1992). Faced with the CCF's decline, many in the party began to focus their efforts on appealing to an increasingly urbanized and industrialized electorate by integrating the party more closely with organized labour.[3]

However, it was clear from the outset that the CCF was not to become simply a labour party along the lines of the British model; rather it had to become a social-democratic party based on an alliance of different classes. In practice, this meant establishing formal ties with organized labour while preventing trade unions from taking control of any of the crucial organs of the party—the executive, the federal council, and their specialized committees. Even party conventions would be beyond labour's domination. Instead, constituency organizations would remain the basic units of the party.

The representation of organized labour at party conventions is one of the key differences between the NDP in Canada and the British Labour Party (Archer, 1987, 1990), and illustrates clearly the ways in which constituency delegates have retained overall control of the NDP. In the British Labour Party, unions are awarded a party conference vote for each member who maintains (i.e., has not 'opted out' of) political affiliation. Typically, the votes of individual union members are pooled together and a key official from the trade union casts all these votes in a unified bloc. Thus there are many British union leaders who by themselves are able to cast more votes than all constituency delegates combined.

By contrast, NDP conventions, rejecting bloc voting, operate on the principle of 'one delegate, one vote'. No union official is able to cast all the votes on behalf of his or her union members. Another curb on the potential power of union officials is the fact that the rates of delegate entitlements differ for constituency associations and affiliated labour unions. In general, constituency associations are entitled to one delegate for every 50 to 100 members or major fraction thereof, whereas affiliated unions are entitled to one delegate for every 1,000 to 1,500 members or major fraction thereof.[4] The representational ratio of 10 to 1 in favour of constituency associations over affiliated unions has strengthened substantially the constituency presence at party conventions. The express intention of these two provisions—no bloc voting, and a different representational formula for constituencies and unions—was to prevent union domination of the convention and hence of the party (Lewis, 1981). The data on convention attendance by type of delegate indicate that these rules have achieved their goal.

The intent of the NDP constitution was to make labour an important but not dominant force within the party.[5] Nevertheless, labour remains a key presence on the party's policy-making bodies, especially at conventions. The rest of this chapter will explore the magnitude and the implications of that presence with a case study of the 1987 NDP federal convention.

PROFILES OF UNION AND NON-UNION DELEGATES

To assess labour's influence in NDP policy-making, it is necessary to understand its representation at the all-important biennial policy conventions. On average, about two-thirds of all delegates to NDP conventions come from constituency associations; another 6 to 10% come from federal council and caucus; and 1 to 3% represent the party's official youth wing (under 26 years of age; see Chapter 7).[6] The remaining delegates fall into two categories of labour representation: those accredited as representatives from central labour bodies and those belonging to affiliated union locals; the latter are always more numerous. (This finding belies the common perception of centralized bureaucratic control of trade unionists by CLC headquarters.) Whatever the means of selection, unions, especially affiliated locals, rarely send their full allotment of delegates to conventions, and accredited labour representatives generally make up between 15 and 25% of delegates (see also Chapters 12 and 13). The exception was the highly politicized 1971 leadership convention, at which the proportion of delegates from affiliated union locals reached almost 30%. Clearly the 1971 leadership convention, for all its importance, was not necessarily a representative one from which to generalize, as some have done, about the typical composition of NDP conventions (see also comments by Courtney, 1995).

Both the general pattern and the 1971 exception are of interest. The data suggest that labour has been a distinct minority, albeit a substantial one, at all NDP conventions, and has never come close to constituting a majority of delegates. At the 1975, 1989, and 1995 conventions (each of which chose a new party leader), only 1 in 4 delegates was a union delegate. The strongest challenge to labour's position in the party occurred in 1971, when the more militant socialist and nationalist grouping known as the Waffle contested the party leadership through the candidacy of James Laxer (see Laxer, 1996).

Despite this student-inspired new-left challenge within the party, organized labour was still able to muster less than one-third of all delegates.

Affiliation with the NDP has not been the typical practice among Canadian unions. Never have more than 15% of union members belonged to NDP-affiliated unions. In fact, the proportions of union members in Canada affiliated with the NDP have consistently declined since the early 1960s;[7] in 1997, fewer than 1 in 10 union members belonged to an NDP-affiliated union. Rates of affiliation are strongly related to region of residence (Whitehorn, 1992). For example, approximately three-quarters of all the unions affiliated with the NDP are located in Ontario (see Chapter 5), a province with slightly more than 35% of Canada's population. The four Western provinces, with almost 30% of the population, are home to approximately 20% of all affiliated unions. By far the greatest under-representation is found among Quebec unions: with approximately one-quarter of the national population, its unions account for less than 2% of NDP affiliates. The union–party link remains weak as one moves further east; Atlantic Canada, which makes up approximately 9% of Canada's population, accounts for only 2% of NDP affiliates.

The system by which the NDP allocates convention delegates also has an important effect on the regional imbalance at conventions, an imbalance that is brought into bold relief when one compares union and non-union delegates.[8] Because the number of delegates that each constituency or labour organization is permitted to select depends on the size of the organization, more delegates come from areas and organizations where the party is strong than from those where it is weak. Historically, both the CCF and NDP have received their greatest levels of support in Ontario and the four Western provinces, where they have formed either the government or the official opposition. Hence the West provided the largest number of non-union delegates at the 1987 convention, followed closely by Ontario. These data are made more striking by the fact that this was the first federal convention the NDP had ever held in the province of Quebec, and the size of the Quebec delegation had reached an unprecedented level.

However, in keeping with the regional skew of union affiliates in the country, union delegates to the convention came overwhelmingly from Ontario (72.0%). Only modest proportions of union delegates came from the West (15.2%), Quebec (6.4%), and the Atlantic region (6.4%). With large numbers of both affiliated union and riding members, Ontario always has a particularly strong presence at the conventions. It is also the only province or region for which the numbers are high in both cases: Western delegates are much more likely to represent constituencies, and the representation of both union and non-union members from Quebec and the Atlantic region is relatively poor.

The NDP has sometimes been described as a bifurcated party, with two quite distinctive bases of support: on one side, blue-collar workers with relatively low levels of education (sometimes called the proletariat) and on the other, highly educated, well-paid professionals (the intellectuals). The profiles of union and non-union delegates lend weight to this perception. As Table 4.1 indicates, non-union delegates tend to be professional and white-collar, while union delegates are much more likely to be skilled blue-collar workers. Comparative research on political parties has shown repeatedly that political élites and party activists are not usually representative of the overall socio-demographic characteristics of the electorate and the party members they purport to represent (Kornberg et al., 1979). Within the NDP, that pattern is much weaker among union than non-union delegates. For example, whereas non-union delegates tend to report levels of education far above those of a cross-section of the Canadian public (in 1987 almost 3 in 4 non-union delegates had attended university or completed at least one university degree), barely 1 in 4 union delegates had any university training, and more than half had at most a high-school diploma, compared with only 14.8% of non-union delegates.

Interestingly, however, higher levels of education among non-union delegates did not translate directly into higher levels of family income.[9] Union delegates were more likely than others to live in families earning $20,000 to $60,000 annually. Non-union delegates, on the other hand, were more likely than union delegates to be located in either the lowest income grouping (less than $20,000) or the highest (more than $60,000).

Profound differences were evident in the ways in which union and non-union delegates earned their income. In 1987, about 6 in 10 non-

Table 4.1
Occupational Characteristics by Delegate Type, 1987

	Delegate Type	
Occupation	Non-union %	Union %
Professional/skilled white-collar	58.4	8.5
Sales/clerical	2.8	4.6
Skilled blue-collar	6.0	32.3
Unskilled labour	2.0	15.4
Union representative	4.3	32.3
Farmer/fisher	3.7	0.8
Student	9.2	0.0
Homemaker	4.1	0.8
Not employed (retired, unemployed)	9.4	5.4
N	(563)	(130)

union delegates were employed in the professions or in skilled white-collar occupations, compared with just over 1 in 10 union delegates. In contrast, about half the union delegates were either skilled blue-collar or unskilled labour employees, compared with fewer than 1 in 10 non-union delegates. In addition, and not surprisingly, almost 1 in 3 union delegates was employed as a union representative, compared with only 1 in 20 non-union delegates. Non-union delegates are also more likely than union delegates to be students (9.2% vs 0.0%), homemakers (4.1% vs 0.8%), or not employed (unemployed or retired; 9.4% vs 5.4%).

One last important socio-demographic difference between union and non-union delegates is the gender breakdown. Delegates to NDP conventions are still predominantly male, although the gap is narrowing (Whitehorn, 1992; see also Chapter 6). In the total 1987 NDP convention sample, two-thirds (67.0%) of delegates were male and one-third (33.0%) female. Representation of women was somewhat higher among non-union delegates, of whom 37.0% were female. Among union delegates, however, more than 5 in 6 (83.5%) were men. Given the male skew in trade-union membership, it is not surprising that labour unions have been relatively slow to accept the principle of gender parity,[10] for which support appears to be growing elsewhere.

On the whole, the data in Table 4.1 suggest that the NDP is composed of several groups with a wide range of socio-demographic characteristics. This is perhaps not surprising, since from the CCF's founding, the party's goal has been to form an alliance of different classes and not to be simply a labour party reflecting trade-union priorities. The following section will explore whether the socio-demographic differences between union and non-union delegates provide these two groups with differing ideological lenses through which to view the world of partisan politics, and whether these different lenses lead to substantially different policy preferences.[11]

IDEOLOGICAL AND POLICY POSITIONS
OF UNION AND NON-UNION DELEGATES

As a first step in our survey, respondents were given a list of ideological labels (socialist, social democrat, reformer, marxist, social gospel, ecologist, liberal, populist, or some other designation) and were asked which one best described their self-image. The results for union and non-union delegates are comparable to earlier findings (Whitehorn, 1988, 1992; see also Table 2.3). More than 3 in every 4 respondents identified themselves as either socialists or social democrats.[12] For both delegate types, the most common response was social democrat (almost half the non-union delegates and more than 60% of union delegates). Nonetheless, the relative popularity of these descriptive labels differed between the two groups. Just under one-third of the non-union delegates chose the more leftist 'socialist' designation, compared with about one-fifth of the union delegates. In addition, whereas union delegates were almost three times as likely to consider themselves social democrats as socialists, non-union delegates were only one-and-a-half times as likely to do so. Similarly, when respondents were asked to place themselves on a 7-point left–right scale, with 1 designated as left and 7 as right, non-union delegates placed themselves further to the left (mean=2.6) than did union delegates (mean=3.1).[13]

Differences in ideological self-image also appeared in the subjective class orientations of union and non-union delegates. Approximately two-thirds of both delegate types reported that they thought of themselves as belonging to a social class,[14] with union delegates slightly more likely to hold this view. However, the nature of that self-image was quite different for the two groups. More than 40% of union delegates viewed themselves as working-class, while only half as many non-union delegates did so (21.4%). Conversely, 6 in 10 non-union delegates held a middle- or upper-middle-class self-image, compared with only 4 in 10 union delegates. The subject of family background also revealed differences: 4 in 10 non-union delegates but only 2 in 10 union delegates reported that they were raised in middle- or upper-middle-class families. Nevertheless, a generational trend towards perceived upward mobility was evident among both types of delegates.

Most NDP delegates disagreed (84.9%) with the assertion that there is no ruling class in Canada (see Table 8.10). The concept of class has frequently been linked to that of class struggle. Indeed, attitude towards class struggle is often a litmus test to differentiate between evolutionary and revolutionary variants of socialism. Like the labour and socialist movements in general, NDP delegates were somewhat divided on whether 'the central question of Canadian politics is the class struggle between labour and capital'. In 1987, a majority (53.9%) agreed, while a third (33.5%) disagreed (see Table 8.10). Not surprisingly, union delegates, some of whom were veterans of past labour–management conflicts, were even more likely to portray Canadian politics in terms of a class struggle (60.8% vs 52.5% for non-union delegates). In the more polarized political atmosphere of the 1990s, particularly in Ontario, where Mike Harris's neo-conservative revolution has provoked massive protest demonstrations by unionists and others generating crowds of up to 100,000 people, it seems probable that an even higher percentage of NDP activists would embrace the concept of class struggle.

Differences between union and non-union delegates in attitudes towards unions and business and towards Canadian political parties were explored using thermometer scales (see Table 4.2). Few meaningful differences emerged according to delegate type except in attitudes towards unions, which were rated more positively by the union delegates. However, non-union delegates also held far more positive attitudes towards unions than towards business.

If union/non-union delegate status has little bearing on thermometer scores for parties and institutions, does it affect attitudes towards political issues? Do union and non-union delegates differ substantially in their positions on specific issues? It has already been noted that the non-union delegates placed themselves further to the left than union delegates. Accordingly, we might ask whether the positions of union delegates are more similar to those of Liberal and Conservative party delegates than to those of their non-union counterparts in the NDP. To put it bluntly, is labour aligned with the wrong party? Would unions find a more fitting ideological home elsewhere—for example, in the Liberal Party?

To explore this question we can draw on the comparison, introduced in Chapter 3, of attitudes of delegates to the 1983 Conservative and 1984 Liberal leadership conventions with the 1987 NDP delegates on a series of eight issue indexes. As we have seen, these indexes measured delegates' attitudes towards continentalism, a 'hawkish' approach in foreign policy, social security, bilingualism, moral conservatism, privatization, civil liberties, and corporate power. These data, along with a breakdown by NDP delegate type, are presented in Table 4.3.

On a four-point scale measuring attitudes towards continentalism (scored in a positive direction from zero to 4), non-union delegates (made up mostly of constituency members) had a mean score of 0.27, indicating strong opposition to continentalist policies. Union delegates also strongly

Table 4.2

Attitudes Towards Political Parties and Social Groups by Delegate Type, 1987 (mean thermometer scores)

Party/Group	Delegate Type		
	Non-union	Union	N
Canadian business	42.1	42.1	(693)
Canadian labour unions	69.0	79.8	(695)
Federal NDP	84.4	86.7	(704)
Provincial NDP	77.8	79.0	(702)
Federal Liberal Party	28.1	30.8	(702)
Federal Progressive Conservative Party	12.4	12.0	(700)

NOTE: Thermometer scores could range from 0 to 100, with 100 representing 'like the most', 0 'like the least', and 50 a mid-point.

opposed such policies (0.51), although their feelings were somewhat less intense than those of their non-union counterparts. By contrast, Liberal delegates in 1984 (four years before the 1988 election) were quite neutral on continentalist policies (1.80), whereas the Conservatives in 1983 strongly supported them (2.90). Likewise, on the 6-point 'hawkishness' scale, non-union delegates in the NDP registered the strongest opposition, followed closely by NDP union delegates. Once again Liberal delegates registered an aggregate neutrality and Conservatives were more supportive of a hawkish defence posture. The same general pattern held for attitudes towards social-security spending, moral conservatism, privatization, and civil liberties. In general, union delegates were closer to the mid-point of the various indexes than were non-union delegates.

On attitudes towards corporate power, however, union delegates, not surprisingly, expressed stronger feelings than did non-union delegates. And on the bilingualism issue union delegates were actually closer to the Liberal delegates in 1984 than to non-union NDP delegates, although the difference

Table 4.3

Attitudinal Differences Between Parties and Between Union Categories in the NDP (mean scores)

Index (range) (direction)	Delegate Type			
	NDP Non-union	NDP Union	Liberal	Conservative
Continentalism (0–4) (pro-)	0.27	0.51	1.80	2.90
Hawkishness (0–6) (pro-)	0.73	1.50	2.65	4.17
Social security (0–5) (pro-)	4.11	3.86	2.63	1.67
Moral conservatism (0–3) (pro-)	0.51	0.77	1.65	2.16
Corporate power (0–3) (anti-)	2.62	2.68	1.98	1.58
Bilingualism (0–2) (pro-)	1.82	1.54	1.71	1.01
Civil liberties (0–3) (pro-)	1.95	1.84	1.22	1.51
Privatization (0–6) (pro-)	0.17	0.37	2.21	4.00

SOURCE: Data for Liberals and Conservatives are taken from Blake (1988: 40).

was not great. Overall, on 6 of the 8 indexes, unionists positioned themselves between NDP non-unionists and the Liberal Party, and except on the bilingualism issue they were always significantly closer to the NDP non-unionists. While unions may appear to lean towards less radical policies, in general union delegates in 1987 did not favour a dramatic shift to the right for the party.

Nevertheless, in a few specific policy areas the differences between union and non-union delegates do seem significant. Respondents were asked several questions about women. On the topic of gender representation on party councils, 7 in 10 (69.5%) non-union delegates agreed that women should comprise 50% of the federal council,[15] whereas only 41.4% of union delegates were so inclined. Support for the suggestion that a significant proportion of the party's candidates and officers should be women was overwhelming among non-union delegates (86.4%), but more muted among union delegates (66.7%). When asked whether women were discriminated against in the NDP, union delegates almost unanimously disagreed (91.0%), whereas non-union delegates were less sweeping in their disagreement (72.3%). Thus a gap did exist between union and non-union delegates on the topic of the status of women, and this gap may have contributed to the gender gap within the NDP as a whole (see also Chapter 6).

There were also important differences in the attitudes of union and non-union delegates towards the NATO and NORAD military alliances—although we must point out that our survey dates from 1987, two years before the dramatic changes that brought an end to the Soviet Union. For many delegates, particularly those on the party's ideological left, opposition to Canada's participation in NATO and NORAD was among the most fundamental planks in the NDP's platform. Only about 1 in 5 non-union delegates in 1987 supported Canada's participation in either alliance. In contrast, half the union delegates felt that Canada should remain in NORAD, and even more (58.3%) endorsed participation in NATO. However, the changes that have taken place in Eastern Europe since the questionnaire was administered have led to a more general questioning of the utility and roles of the NATO and NORAD alliances. For this reason caution is required in extrapolating these data to the present.

Differences in attitudes towards other aspects of Canada's defence and foreign policy were evident in union and non-union delegates' responses when asked whether they believed government spending should be increased or decreased in specific policy areas. While, on the whole, neither group wished to see greater spending on defence, the percentage of non-union delegates supporting greater spending on defence was only 18.9%; among union delegates it was almost twice as high (34.6%). Both groups also wished to see more spending on foreign aid. However, whereas the proportion of non-union delegates supporting such spending was 4 in 5, only 3 in 5 union delegates favoured this position. Similarly, union delegates tended to be less supportive than non-union delegates of spending on education and the arts, although they were equally or more supportive of increased spending on housing and social-welfare programs—two policy areas with a more concrete, material foundation. Thus it would be inaccurate to say that either union or non-union delegates were more supportive of increased government spending across the board. Rather, the data suggest that each of these delegate groupings supported increased government spending in the areas that it valued and saw as important.

One area of potentially important disagreement between union and non-union NDP delegates, or more generally between labour unions and parties of the left, is labour relations. Conflict of this kind may be particularly likely to arise when the NDP forms the government, as has recently been the case in British Columbia, Saskatchewan, and Ontario. The data in Table 4.4 suggest that, on the one hand, union and non-union delegates agree that trade unions do not have too much power in Canada; 9 in 10 respondents expressed this view. However, on other labour-relations issues the two delegate types are marked more by division than by cohesion. While over half the union delegates agreed that an NDP government should never interfere with free collective bargaining (55.6%), fewer than 4 in 10 non-union delegates agreed. Some socialists might consider both percentages low for a party championing the working class. Union delegates were also substantially more supportive than non-union delegates of providing unemployment insurance for strikers (51.9% vs 40.5%) and of allowing no restrictions to be placed on strikes (74.4% vs 43.6%). But they were substantially less supportive of job-sharing.

On matters of labour relations, then, NDP union delegates are more likely than non-union delegates to take pro-labour positions. A clear example of this tendency in action was the union opposition to the Rae government's 'social contract' in the early 1990s, which rolled back the wages of Ontario's public-sector workers (Jenson and Mahon, 1995; Laxer, 1996; McBride, 1996; Monahan, 1995; Rae, 1996, Tanguay, 1995; Walkom, 1994). Some would point to such opposition as evidence of labour's progressivism, while others would suggest that it is more a matter of collective self-interest; perhaps it is a combination of the two. In any event, this is one area in which union delegates' views differ from those of their non-union counterparts.

We concluded our survey of labour and the NDP by asking delegates a series of questions aimed at evaluating the link between unions and the party. Some very interesting differences emerged. When asked whether unions have too much influence in the NDP, both groups disagreed. However, while the rate among union delegates reached 90%, with over 50% disagreeing strongly, the rate was only 70.2% for non-union delegates, of whom only one-fifth strongly disagreed (see Table 4.5). Conversely, whereas only 1 in 20 union delegates agreed that unions have too much power in the party, 1 in 6 non-union delegates subscribed to this critical view. However, these differences should not detract from the more general finding that, by a very wide margin, union and non-union delegates alike believed that unions do not have too much influence in the party. At the same time it seems fair to say that this view was held less strongly among non-union than union delegates.

A similar pattern was evident in attitudes towards the benefits derived from the party's link with labour. The union delegates were almost unanimous (over 98%) in their perception that this link was beneficial. Although nowhere near as unanimous, an impressive 82% of non-union delegates also agreed that the trade-union link had been of benefit to the party.

Table 4.4

Attitudes Towards Labour Relations Issues by Delegate Type, 1987

| | Delegate Type | | | |
| | Non-Union | | Union | |
Statement/Attitude	%	N	%	N
Trade unions have too much power in Canada (disagree/strongly disagree)	90.1	(578)	95.5	(134)
An NDP government should never interfere with free collective bargaining (agree/strongly agree)	39.2	(570)	55.6	(133)
Strikers should be able to collect unemployment insurance (agree/strongly agree)	40.5	(570)	51.9	(133)
During difficult economic times, workers should be willing to share jobs (disagree/strongly disagree)	30.1	(569)	47.0	(134)
The right to strike should never be restricted (agree/strongly agree)	43.6	(569)	74.4	(133)
The central question of Canadian politics is the class struggle between labour and capital (agree/strongly agree)	52.5	(575)	60.8	(125)

Nevertheless, a significant minority—almost 20%—of non-union delegates were either skeptical or undecided.

Furthermore, when asked about the party's relationship with labour, a clear majority of almost 7 in 10 union delegates thought the relationship should be strengthened, compared with only 4 in 10 non-union delegates. The largest response among the non-union delegates (almost half) was supportive of the status quo. However, less than a third of union delegates chose this option. How these two positons can be reconciled remains to be seen. Yet very few delegates in 1987, union or otherwise, wished to weaken the labour–party nexus. Events such as the decisions of the Canadian Auto Workers and the Ontario Federation of Labour not to support the Ontario NDP government in the 1995 provincial election obviously reflected a tension between NDP government policies and the preferences of union members and leaders. Nevertheless, while the concerns expressed by some unionists about the Ontario NDP government suggest that labour's support for its links with the NDP has weakened, the 1987 data indicate such overwhelming approval for maintaining or strengthening labour ties to the party that the relationship can probably withstand some decline in support.

Table 4.5
Attitudes Towards Unions' Role in the NDP by Delegate Type, 1987

	Delegate Type	
Statement/Attitude	Non-union %	Union %
Unions have too much influence in the NDP.		
Strongly agree/agree	16.9	4.6
Uncertain	12.9	2.4
Disagree/strongly disagree	70.2	93.2
N	(574)	(132)
The union link with the party is beneficial.		
Very beneficial/beneficial	82.0	98.5
Uncertain	12.7	0.7
Harmful/very harmful	5.4	0.7
N	(577)	(134)
Strengthen or weaken relationship between unions and NDP.		
Strengthen	43.3	69.7
Keep about the same	47.0	29.5
Weaken	9.8	0.8
N	(564)	(132)
Was the CLC's parallel political campaign beneficial?		
Very beneficial/beneficial	71.8	88.0
Uncertain	25.9	10.5
Harmful/very harmful	2.3	1.5
N	(560)	(133)

Finally we turn to the question of the CLC's parallel political campaigns during elections, in which labour has supplied phone banks and workers to the party and actively encouraged members to vote for the NDP. Here again the results were consistent with the pattern noted above. Union delegates, some of whom were no doubt involved in the campaign, gave a high rating to this effort, whereas non-union delegates, though generally supportive, were less markedly so and more uncertain. A significant minority of non-union delegates appeared to question whether this is the best way for labour to assist the party, though perhaps their uncertainty simply reflected a lack of familiarity with such campaigns.

CONCLUSION

This chapter has explored the ideological and policy implications of the NDP's links with organized labour by focusing on the delegates to the 1987 federal convention. These data showed that the NDP is not controlled by organized labour, although union delegates form a significant minority lobby at its conventions. The strategists who designed the union link to the NDP in 1961 intended to prevent labour leaders from controlling the party. Perhaps they succeeded too well. As David Lewis (1981: 492) put it, with a twist of irony:

> Personally, I sometimes wished that labour would show a desire to dominate. I never had any doubt that we could defeat such an attempt, but it would have been evidence of a more earnest commitment to effective political action.

Data on the differences between union and non-union delegates presented quite mixed findings. In terms of socio-demographic background, the two types of delegates looked quite different. In general, union delegates were most likely to be blue-collar workers, with relatively low levels of education and a working-class self-image. Non-union delegates, in contrast, tended to be very well educated professionals, with a self-image as middle- or even upper-middle-class.

Yet despite these differences in outward appearance and class self-image, attitudes towards policy were remarkably consistent. When we compared union and non-union NDP delegates with Liberal and Conservative delegates on a series of policy indexes, we found that union delegates were almost always closer to their non-union NDP colleagues than to delegates of the other parties. Consistent with the argument put forward by some commentators that unions pull the NDP to the right—and despite their stronger working-class orientation—union delegates tended to take more centrist positions than non-union delegates. However, it is important not to over-state this finding, since with only one exception (bilingualism) the positions of union delegates were always closer to those of non-unionists within the NDP than to those of Liberal and Conservative delegates.

Furthermore, on some items, particularly related to labour relations, union delegates were not consistently more conservative than their non-union counterparts, although the tendency was certainly present. Perhaps one of the strongest issues of contention between union and non-union delegates was the party's policy on NATO and NORAD, a policy that historically has been particularly important and symbolic to many in the party. However, as we noted, changes in Eastern Europe have caused a re-examination of these alliances far beyond the NDP. It is too early to tell whether these changes will lead to a narrowing of the union–non-union gap in this area.

The question of labour's relationship with the NDP has given rise to increased debate in recent years. In the wake of both the 1988 and 1993 federal elections, several prominent labour leaders expressed dissatisfaction and disappointment with the party's performance; in fact, the 1993 results were so disturbing that they prompted the CLC to conduct a two-year reassessment of its relationship with the party (Whitehorn, 1993). And in the 1995 Ontario provincial election, many unionists and some important labour organizations, including the Canadian Auto Workers and several public-sector unions, showed their disapproval of the Rae government's 'social contract' by withholding their support for the party. Thus it is appropriate to ask whether this relationship can continue in its present form (see also Jenson and Mahon, 1995; Tanguay, 1995). Certainly the labour movement is quite different today than it was in 1961. Some international unions have declined, while others have been Canadianized. In addition, the growth of public-sector unions, which are less inclined than private-sector industrial unions to affiliate directly with the party, makes direct affiliation less promising than it once was as a means of promoting concerted collective action.

Thus a change in the party's formal relationship with labour is not inconceivable. However, the CLC concluded its review by reaffirming its commitment to the NDP. This conclusion, together with the very positive view that union and non-union delegates alike have expressed with respect to the party–labour link, the general compatibility of policy preferences, and the strong presence in the NDP of several important CLC officials, such as Nancy Riche and Bob White, suggests that the relationship will continue for the foreseeable future.

NOTES

An earlier version of this chapter, entitled 'Organized Labour in the New Democratic Party', was presented at the annual meeting of the Canadian Political Science Association, University of Victoria, Victoria, BC, 27–29 May 1990, and published as Archer and Whitehorn (1993).

1 There are many good accounts of the history of labour in Canada. See, for example, Brodie and Jenson (1988); Forsey (1982); Lipton (1966); Logan (1948); Morton (1980).

2 For example, at the provincial level labour overwhelmingly prefers the Parti Québécois to the NDP.

3 On the development of the CCF–NDP and the integration of organized labour, see Archer (1990); Caplan (1973); Horowitz (1968); Lewis (1981); MacDonald (1987); Morley (1984); Morton (1986); Wiseman (1983).

4 The NDP and the Reform Party provide for differential constituency representation based on the constituency's membership. Both the Liberals and Conservatives allocate equal numbers of delegates for each riding. See Archer (1991b); Whitehorn (1992); Courtney (1995).

5 For a more complete discussion of the various ways in which labour is linked to the NDP, see Archer (1990, 1991b).

6 At the 1987 NDP convention only 17.9% of delegates were 29 years of age or under; by contrast, delegates under 30 comprised 40% of Conservative convention delegates in 1983 (Perlin et al., 1988). In the Liberal Party, delegates under 30 were 30% in 1984 and 40% in 1990 (Perlin, 1991).

7 See Archer (1985).

8 In our analysis, union delegates are those specifically representing either central labour or affiliated unions; in addition, since some members of the NDP federal council represent affiliated unions, members of the federal council who were also members of a union executive are classified in this analysis as union delegates. All other delegates are included in the non-union category, even though some of them may belong to a union. (Membership in an affiliated union does not preclude joining the party at the constituency level, and vice versa.)

9 It may be that there were more double-income families in the union category, but this information is not available in our data set. In addition, most union representatives are by definition employed, whereas non-union members may not be; in 1987, for example, almost 1 in 10 of the constituency delegates was a student currently enrolled in university, while there were no students in the union category.

10 However, the examples of Shirley Carr's and Nancy Riche's leadership roles in the CLC suggest that in recent years unions have begun to make progress on this issue.

11 The predominance of men over women among union delegates might lead one to conclude that differences between union and non-union delegates are gender-based. The analyses in this chapter were repeated, controlling for gender (data not shown). Although there was some variation in responses from one item

to the next, in general the data for the larger response category of males reveals that male union versus male non-union delegates did not exhibit patterns dissimilar to that of the combined totals for males and females. Nor should the differences that did emerge detract from the more general conclusion that union and non-union delegates to NDP conventions are more notable for their similarities than their differences, which is one of the main conclusions of this study. Anyone wishing to review the analyses with the gender control may obtain copies directly from the authors.

12 Since these labels can overlap (see, for example, Lewis, 1981), the difference should not be overstressed.

13 Relatedly, female NDP delegates—who tend to represent ridings rather than unions—situate themselves further to the left than male NDP delegates (see Chapter 6).

14 This proportion is higher than in the Canadian population as a whole. See Pammett (1987: 277).

15 This provision already is in effect for federal council representatives elected by convention.

CHAPTER
5

Regionalism

The importance of regionalism in Canadian politics has long been a subject of scholarly dispute. Some view region of residence as central to the formation of political attitudes, claiming that Canada is made up of many regionally distinct cultures with a strong sense of particularism (Alford, 1963; Brodie, 1990; Brym, 1989; Dyck, 1986, 1991; Elkins and Simeon, 1980; Gibbins, 1980, 1982; Gibbins and Arrison, 1995; McCready and Winn, 1976; Phillips, 1982; Schwartz, 1974; Wearing, 1988). For others this description constitutes little more than 'hallowed nonsense' (e.g., Porter, 1965: 382). Instead, these critics argue that, with the exception of Quebec, region of residence has at best a marginal effect on attitude formation, and that any differences that do exist in the political orientations of Canadians across the regions of the country 'can be better explained by socioeconomic and demographic factors than by provincial residency' (Kornberg et al., 1982: 88).

The role that political parties play in defining and reinforcing the language and context of political debate (Brodie and Jenson, 1988) suggests that examining how regional considerations operate within them can shed some light on the political importance of territory more generally. A party can reveal something about territory in several ways. For example, regional aspects can be seen in the location of its electoral support, its membership composition, and its bases of legislative strength, as well as its ideological perspectives and policy positions. At times these may reinforce each other (e.g., when a party with a distinctive regional message obtains most or all of its support from one region, as was the case for the Reform Party and the Bloc Québécois in the 1993 election). At other times, regional support may be unrelated or even negatively related to the party's positions on issues.[1]

The first part of this chapter explores the regional composition of the NDP, highlighting the imbalance in regional representation at its conventions. The second part investigates the political attitudes of convention delegates towards issues at three territorial levels—subnational, national, and international[2]—to determine the extent of any regional differences in these

attitudes. We conclude with a discussion of the relationship between organizational structure and political divisions within the NDP, and of the
importance of territorial considerations in understanding the federal New
Democratic Party.

Regional Composition

Historically, the CCF–NDP as a third party has been linked with Western
regional protests against the Eastern-dominated politics of the two older
parties in Canada (Young, 1969). Not only has the CCF–NDP been a strong
voice for Western Canadian interests, but much of the party's representation
in Parliament has had a very heavy Western component (e.g., 89.3% for the
CCF years and 68.5% for the NDP period; Whitehorn, 1996a). As a number
of scholars have noted (Cairns, 1968; Seidel, 1989), the first-past-the-post
electoral system has perpetuated its image as a party of the West by ensuring that most of its MPs still tend to be elected to Western seats. The majority of the votes for the party, however, now come from the East (59.0% for
the NDP period, vs 40.7% during the CCF period; Whitehorn, 1996a), the
1993 federal election notwithstanding. This divergent pattern, in which
most of the party's votes come from one region while most of its elected
parliamentary representatives come from another, seems bound to create
strains within the party and can be accentuated when the leader comes
from one region and most of the MPs from another. This was the case for
much of the Broadbent era and is again the case under Alexa McDonough,
and at times (e.g., during the debate on constitutional reform in the early
1980s) it has made the task of leadership more difficult. Another important
regional factor for the CCF–NDP is the fact that most of the provincial governments it has formed have been in the West (British Columbia,

Table 5.1
Regional Profiles of Canadian Society and the NDP

Region	Canadian population, 1983 %[a]	Party membership (individual), 1987 %	Affiliated members, 1987 %	Convention delegates, 1971, 1979, 1983 %
British Columbia	11.3	23.4	10.5	15.7
Prairies	17.4	49.4	10.0	30.0
Ontario	35.4	22.6	76.0	47.0
Quebec	26.4	1.2	1.4	2.8
Atlantic	9.2	3.2	2.1	3.5
Northern territories	0.3	0.6	0.0	0.9

[a]Percentages may not add to 100 because of rounding.
SOURCES: Quick Canadian Facts (Surrey: Cannex Enterprises, 1985), 100; Whitehorn, 1988, 1995.

Saskatchewan, Manitoba, Yukon),[3] the Bob Rae government in Ontario from 1990 to 1995 being the notable exception.

As Table 5.1 shows, individual NDP memberships in 1987 had a decided Western tilt: 23.4% of the party's individual members came from British Columbia, virtually half (49.4%) from the Prairies (mostly from Saskatchewan), 22.6% from Ontario, only 1.2% from Quebec, and 3.2% from Atlantic Canada, with the Northern territories accounting for the rest. In contrast, only 10.5% and 10.0% of memberships through unions affiliated to the NDP came from British Columbia and the Prairies; Atlantic Canada accounted for 2.1%, Quebec for a minuscule 1.4%, and Ontario for an overwhelming 76.0%.[4] In the past, much has been made of the alleged differences between individual members of the party and affiliated members (see Chapter 4). Without overstating these differences, one could suggest that, where they do exist, they in part reflect activists' diverse regional backgrounds.

A regional breakdown of delegates at the three federal conventions before 1987 for which the survey data are available shows the following pattern for the period 1971 to 1983: Ontario 47.0%, Prairies 30.0%, British Columbia 15.7%, Atlantic 3.5%, Quebec 2.8%, and the North 0.9%.[5] Since the proportions of Quebec delegates attending past CCF–NDP conventions[6] were too small for meaningful statistical analysis, the 1987 convention, held in Montreal,

Table 5.2
Regional Breakdown of Surveyed Delegates, 1987

Province/Region	%[a]		N	
British Columbia	13.1		(96)	
Prairies	25.3		(185)	
Alberta		6.2		(45)
Saskatchewan		12.9		(94)
Manitoba		6.3		(46)
Ontario	45.1		(330)	
Quebec	7.8		(57)	
Atlantic	7.1		(52)	
New Brunswick		1.5		(11)
Nova Scotia		4.1		(30)
Newfoundland		1.0		(7)
Prince Edward Island		0.5		(4)
Northwest Territories	0.4		(3)	
Yukon Territory	1.1		(8)	
Total			(731)[b]	

[a] Percentages do not add to 100 because of rounding.
[b] 738 questionnaires were completed for the survey.

represented a milestone for the party. Not only was it the first federal NDP convention ever held in Quebec, but it took place at a time when the NDP was
leading in both national and Quebec popularity polls. With Quebec delegates
accounting for 7.8% of the convention (see Table 5.2), it provided a unique
opportunity for extended data analysis along regional lines. While Quebec's
representation was still smaller than desired by either party activists or political analysts, it was almost three times greater than in the past.

At any NDP convention, the overwhelming majority of delegates come
from riding associations. In 1987 the highest proportion of these delegates
came from British Columbia (see Table 5.3), while Ontario, with the highest absolute number of delegates, also provided the highest proportion of
delegates from affiliated union locals (see Table 5.4).

DELEGATES' ATTITUDES

We commence this analysis of attitudes among NDP activists by looking at
their perceptions of the different regional subsystems in Canada (see Table
5.5). Five items in the 1987 survey were devoted to Quebec and its status.
While no questions referred to the Meech Lake Accord per se, several tapped
elements related to the accord and contemporary debates on Quebec. For
example, an overwhelming majority (87.6%) of delegates agreed with the
statement 'Quebec is a unique province unlike the others'. More than two-
thirds (67.6%) favoured special status for Quebec (i.e., rejected the proposition that Quebec should not be granted such status). Solid majorities (61.4%
and 60.3% respectively) also agreed that Quebec has a right to self-determination and should be free to determine its own language legislation. On only
one important Quebec item, whether Quebec should have a veto in the

Table 5.3
Types of Convention Delegates By Province/Region, 1987

| Delegate Type | Province/Region | | | | |
	BC %	Prairies %	Ontario %	Quebec %	Atlantic %
Riding association	80.0	69.4	63.5	75.4	53.8
Affiliated union	4.2	5.5	21.5	12.3	7.7
Central labour	0.0	2.7	6.1	1.8	7.7
Federal council	6.3	13.7	3.7	1.8	25.0
Member of Parliament	3.2	1.1	1.2	0.0	0.0
Other	6.4	7.6	4.0	8.9	5.7
N	(96)	(185)	(330)	(57)	(52)

NOTE: Percentages may not add to 100 because of rounding.

Table 5.4
Regional Distribution of Delegates Surveyed from Affiliated Unions, 1987

Province/Region	%	N
British Columbia	4.2	(4)
Prairies	10.5	(10)
Ontario	73.7	(70)
Quebec	7.4	(7)
Atlantic	4.2	(4)
Total	100.0	(95)

Canadian constitution, did the majority of delegates not support an expansion of Quebec's rights. While a plurality (40.7%) favoured the proposition, a third (33.7%) opposed it and more than a quarter (25.6%) were uncertain. What is striking here is the NDP's sustained support overall for the aspirations of Quebec despite its lack of electoral success in that province and the risk that such support could cost it votes in the West. Of course, these trends in attitudes among NDP activists were reflected in the party's position on Quebec during the period of constitutional divisions in the late 1980s and early 1990s. Broadbent was an early and strong supporter of the Meech Lake Accord, even though a number of provincial NDP leaders were far less enthusiastic. Likewise, under the leadership of Audrey McLaughlin the federal party was a strong supporter of the Charlottetown Accord, despite reservations among many New Democrats across the country about some of its key elements. The Quebec issue remains problematic for the party.

Table 5.5
Attitudes towards Regional Entities: Subsystem Level, 1987

Topic Area/Statement	Agree/ strongly agree %	Disagree/ strongly disagree %	Uncertain %	Mean[a]
Quebec				
No special status for Quebec	21.7	67.6	10.6	3.62
Quebec has right to self-determination	61.4	23.1	15.6	2.50
Quebec should have constitutional veto	40.7	33.7	25.6	2.87
Quebec determines own language legislation	60.3	27.5	12.2	2.55
Quebec unique	87.6	10.3	2.1	1.99
Central Canada				
Central Canada has too much say	58.7	25.1	16.3	2.52

[a]The Likert scales are coded as follows: (1) strongly agree, (2) agree, (3) uncertain, (4) disagree, (5) strongly disagree. Thus a higher mean value indicates a higher level of disagreement with the statement.

No specific questions were asked about attitudes towards Atlantic Canada and the West—a serious omission. However, one question did ask about Central Canada. Not surprisingly for a party rooted in Western protest movements and populism (Brennan, 1984; Laycock, 1990; Lipset, 1968; Sharp, 1948; Young, 1969; Zakuta, 1964), a majority of delegates (58.7%) agreed with the statement that Central Canada has too much say in the federal system; even among delegates from Ontario, a plurality agreed.

A series of thermometer scales measured the coolness or warmth of respondents' feelings towards both their respective provinces and the country as a whole (for comparisons with the population as a whole, see Clarke et al., 1980, l984; Johnston, 1986); responses could range from 0 for very cool to 50 for neutral to 100 for very warm (see Table 5.6). Even though at that time the NDP was a third party, to some degree identified as an outgroup in Canadian politics, most delegates (87.6% and 93.9% respectively) indicated positive feelings about both their home province (mean = 75.1) and the country (mean = 82.8).[7]

Table 5.6

Attitudes towards Regional Entities: System vs Subsystem

Question/Statement	Positive %	Negative %	Neutral %	Mean %
Feel about province	87.6	5.5	6.9	75.10
Feel about gov't of province	26.9	63.9	9.2	34.30
Feel about Canada	93.9	2.2	3.9	82.80
Feel about gov't of Canada	9.0	86.5	4.5	22.30

	Federal %	Provincial %	Municipal %	None %
Level of gov't feel closest to	28.0	52.8	11.4	7.2
How much power?				
More	26.6	18.6	38.9	—
Less	14.1	23.9	7.8	—
Same	59.3	57.5	53.3	—

	Agree %	Disagree %	Uncertain %	Mean[a] %
Right to opt out of fed. programs	29.6	46.4	23.9	3.20
Fed. gov't has yielded too much power	30.8	45.5	23.8	3.20
Gov't services should be more decentralized	69.9	10.2	19.9	2.26
MPs soon lose touch	36.9	45.9	17.2	3.07
Gov't doesn't care	45.1	46.0	9.0	2.96

[a]The Likert scales are coded as follows: (1) strongly agree, (2) agree, (3) uncertain, (4) disagree, (5) strongly disagree. Thus a higher mean value indicates a higher level of disagreement with the statement.

As might be expected at a time when the only NDP government was the Yukon territorial administration, the attitudes of the majority of NDP delegates towards the existing governments, both federal and provincial, were quite negative (86.5%, mean = 22.3; 63.9%, mean = 34.3).[8] The literature on the apparent increase in alienation and cynicism regarding politicians, and on individuals' perceived lack of personal political efficacy, is extensive (Clarke et al., 1991, 1996; Dalton, 1988; Miller, 1974), and it has been suggested that protest movements and third parties in particular tend to attract people who feel alienated from both government and the society around them (Abcarian and Stanage, 1973; Gibbins, 1980). Although pluralities of NDP delegates (46.0% and 45.9%) disagreed with the twin assertions 'I don't think that the government cares much about what people like me think' and 'Generally those elected to Parliament soon lose touch with the people', significant minorities (45.1% and 36.9%) did agree, suggesting that even highly involved activists in a third party can in fact feel alienated on the level of government or 'regime'. On the community level, however, the thermometer scores showed high levels of support for and integration with society itself (see also Kenniston, 1971; Kornberg et al., 1979). Measuring attitudes towards both state and society enables us to distinguish lack of support for incumbent governments from lack of support for the community at large.

A majority of Canadians in recent years have reported feeling closer to their provincial governments than to the federal level (Johnston, 1986: 192),[9] and delegates to the 1987 federal NDP convention were no exception: a majority (52.8%) indicated that they felt closer to the provincial level of government. This finding may in part reflect the fact that the NDP has never placed higher than third in federal elections, while it has won or come second at the provincial level in the five most western provinces (BC, Alberta, Saskatchewan, Manitoba, and Ontario).[10] Another possible explanation, however, is the strong provincial orientation of the NDP's organizational structure. Except in Quebec, federal party members must simultaneously be provincial party members and in fact join through the provincial wing. Because there is no regular federal NDP newspaper, most New Democrats must rely on their provincial party newspaper (where there is one) to read about party matters—an arrangement that is more likely to encourage a regional than a pan-Canadian orientation.

In addition, a series of distinct questions explored the distribution of powers in the Canadian federation (Table 5.6; see also Chapter 8). Delegates were asked whether the federal, provincial, and municipal governments should have 'more power', 'less power', or 'about the same power'. In all three cases a clear majority of delegates opted for the status quo:

'about the same power'. Apparently delegates believed that social change does not necessarily require constitutional change. Among those favouring redistribution, more supported increasing the power of municipal governments (38.9%, to 26.6% for the federal government and 18.6% for provincial governments).

The socialist CCF, the NDP's precursor, has had an enduring image of favouring central government planning and increased power for the federal government at the expense of the provinces (Oliver, 1961, particularly chapters by Trudeau and Scott). While a majority of NDP delegates in 1987 did not appear strongly committed to a major redistribution of constitutional powers, a remnant of preference was evident for the federal level over the provincial. The curious element here was that the level of government to which NDP delegates felt closest (provincial) was the one to which they were least inclined to grant greater power. It seems that even political activists are not always consistent in their opinions.

Further complicating the picture was the finding that NDP convention delegates were divided on the question of whether the federal government had yielded too much power to the provinces (see Table 5.6). While a plurality (45.5%) disagreed, significant numbers agreed (30.8%) or were uncertain (23.8%).[11] On a related question, a plurality (46.4%) disagreed with the proposition that provinces should have the right to opt out of joint federal–provincial programs with full compensation. Nevertheless, almost one-third (29.6%) supported the notion and one-quarter (23.9%) were uncertain. Even in 1987, NDP members showed signs of opposition to features of the Meech Lake Accord. Although this opposition was constrained in 1988 for fear of alienating Quebec voters,[12] it certainly came to the fore in late 1989 and 1990, and again in 1992, with the failure to ratify the Meech Lake and Charlottetown constitutional accords. Despite their apparent concern over the erosion of federal power and their desire to maintain national standards in social programs, NDP delegates reflected the increased decentralist thrust of socialists from the 1960s onwards in their strong support (69.9%) for greater decentralization of government services to the local level.

Turning from domestic Canadian politics to the international level, a number of questions in the 1987 survey touched on Canada's relations with the United States and the NDP's nationalist orientation (see Table 5.7).[13] We noted earlier that on the thermometer scale the overwhelming majority of delegates (93.9%) gave a very high evaluation of Canada (mean = 82.8). In stark contrast, most (72.1%) projected a negative image of the United States (mean = 28.8). In the theoretical literature on nationalism (e.g., Smith, 1983), it has been suggested that nationalists tend to portray their in-group in a positive fashion while casting the out-group in a negative light (see also

Simmel, 1955). Our 1987 survey offers empirical confirmation of this theoretical proposition. The tendency to dichotomize into 'us versus them' along territorial lines seems pronounced.[14]

On several issue statements NDP activists showed concern about economic and cultural penetration of Canada by the US (Laxer, 1973; Mathews and Steele, 1969; Watkins, 1992).[15] An overwhelming majority (94.5%) felt that Canada must take steps to reduce American influence in its culture and mass media, and almost as many (86.0%) were opposed to the idea that Canada ought to seek greater American investment. More than two-thirds (67.7%) opposed the Mulroney government's policy of promoting freer trade with the United States,[16] and a commanding proportion (79.6%) rejected the idea that there should be no tariffs or duties between Canada and the United States.[17] Of all the policy issues under study in this chapter, these items seem to reflect the most intra-party consensus as evidenced by standard deviation scores (see Table 5.8 below). Although, in the 1988 election, the NDP was to give the free-trade issue less emphasis than perhaps it should have (see Whitehorn, 1989), its overall position in this area has proven to be both clearer and more lasting than that of the Liberal Party (see also Chapter 3; Goldfarb and Axworthy, 1988).

While defence and foreign policy have not usually attracted the sustained interest of the Canadian electorate at large (Fletcher and Drummond,

Table 5.7
Attitudes towards Regional Entities:
Other Systems and Transnational Entities

Topic area/Question/Statement	Positive %	Negative %	Neutral %	Mean %
United States				
Feel about US	13.9	72.1	14.0	28.80

	Agree %	Disagree %	Uncertain %	Mean[a] %
Free trade				
Reduce US cultural/media influence	94.5	2.3	3.1	1.55
Should seek more US investment	4.8	86.0	9.3	4.20
Should have freer trade with US	14.1	67.7	18.1	3.79
No tariffs between Canada and US	6.8	79.6	13.6	3.94
Alliances				
Canada should stay in NATO	28.3	56.5	15.1	3.50
Canada should stay in NORAD	22.5	58.3	19.2	3.56

[a]The Likert scales are coded as follows: (1) strongly disagree, (2) agree, (3) uncertain, (4) disagree, (5) strongly disagree. Thus a higher mean value indicates a higher level of disagreement with the statement.

1979), NDP conventions have devoted considerable attention to these sub-jects (see also Chapter 9). At the time when this survey was conducted, the NDP's official policy was to withdraw from both NATO and NORAD. Although the party's position on this issue was beginning to soften, in 1987 a clear majority of rank-and-file party members (56.5% and 58.3% respectively) still opposed Canada's involvement in the two US-based military alliances. While a solid majority of activists favoured leaving both NATO and NORAD, a significant minority opposed such a pull-out. The ratio of 2:1 favouring withdrawal was quite consistent over time,[18] although the end of the Cold War may have eased the intra-party differences on this issue.

In addition to exploring differences between parties (Blake, 1988; Goldfarb and Axworthy, 1988; Chapter 3), a number of studies have analyzed consensus and division within political organizations (Perlin, 1980; Whitehorn, 1988, 1992). In our study of regionalism and the NDP, 17 policy statements were scored with a 5-point Likert scale (see Tables 5.5–5.7). On two-thirds of these items (11), at least 20% of delegates disagreed with the majority position. This proportion was considerably higher than that found in the 1983 study of the NDP, which covered a more limited range of poli-cy areas and questions.[19] The failure of so many items from the 1987 survey to reflect a high level of consensus reinforces the impression that questions related to territoriality are among the more divisive issues for the party.

In specific topic areas, four of the five items on Quebec (five of the six items on regionalism) showed a divergence level of at least 20%, as did four of the five items relating to the federal system. On the international plane, however, consensus was somewhat greater. On all four of the statements dealing with the issues of free trade, foreign investment, and cultural pene-tration, dissent was less than 20%. And only two of the six items in the international relations area failed to meet the 20% criterion: these were the related questions on Canada's involvement in NATO and NORAD.

Table 5.8 shows regional differences in responses to the same items list-ed in Tables 5.5–5.7. Of the 17 policy statements coded on a Likert scale, 76% (13) produced no discord whatever in the overall direction of agree-ment for any of the regions (that is, for all regions either a majority or a plurality of respondents replied in the same direction). All regions replied in the same direction on all the items concerning defence and free trade, and the same was true with respect to four of the five items on Quebec (considerable regional differences were apparent on the question of whether Quebec should have a constitutional veto). Both items on alien-ation, however, revealed significant regional differences in the direction of the responses, as did the statement on opting out of joint federal–provin-cial programs. Overall, there seemed to be a fair degree of consistency in the responses across all regions. This may in part reflect the fact that the NDP was a third party with weak roots in two regions of Canada. It may also reflect the NDP's nature as a party with a stronger ideological base than its rivals and a greater emphasis on policy orthodoxy. Further analysis is need-ed to explore whether there are subtler regional differences even though responses tend in the same direction.

Determining with certainty the propensities of the various regions to dif-fer from the rest of the party is difficult because the regions differ so greatly in population size; this problem is compounded by the imbalance in regional representation of NDP delegates.[20] Nevertheless, for each of the 17 questions employing the Likert scale it is possible to identify the region locating itself at the greatest distance from the mean score for the party at large.[21] One region, Quebec, provided the overwhelming majority of these cases (11). On all items relating to Quebec, federal constitutional powers, and decentralization, Quebec delegates showed the greatest divergence from the overall response pattern. Quebec delegates were also out of phase on two of the four questions relating to free trade (anticipating their province's orientation in the 1988 election) and on one of the items (with a very close second on another) regarding alienation. These data suggest that in terms of attitudes Quebec del-egates (the great majority of whom were French-speaking) were the most estranged from the English-speaking majority within the NDP.[22]

As one would expect, Quebec delegates were the most likely to favour greater powers for Quebec—so much so that, even though the party as a whole also favoured those powers, they deviated the most from the pan-Canadian norm; not even Westerners, generally less sympathetic to expand-ing Quebec's rights, deviated so much as a group from the national average. These data, although preliminary, suggest that if the NDP were to make inroads into Quebec, intra-party differences on the province's status would likely become more critical. In short, any NDP growth in Quebec would like-ly be accompanied by increased regional differences within the party. Certainly the NDP's pre-election consensus on Meech Lake in 1988 collapsed the following year, and the Quebec provincial wing took the unique step of separating itself organizationally from its Quebec federal counterpart (*Globe and Mail*, 1 May 1989). These events and policy disagreements, coupled with the increase in regional fractionalization of the Canadian party system that has followed the 1993 federal election (see Frizzell et al., 1994), suggest that regional strains within the party will continue and perhaps increase.

The two regions next most often at odds with the NDP majority were those at the geographic peripheries: Atlantic Canada (four items) and British Columbia (two items). Atlantic Canada was the region most likely to believe that Central Canada had too much say in Canadian politics.

Table 5.8

Regional Differences in Attitudes of NDP Convention Delegates: 1987

Subsystem	BC %	Prairies %	Ontario %	Quebec %	Atlantic %	Canada	SD
Quebec							
No special status for Quebec							
Agree	23.4	26.0	21.2	5.3	36.4		
Disagree	68.1	60.8	68.3	91.2	54.5		
Uncertain	8.5	13.3	10.5	3.5	9.1		
Mean	3.6	3.5	3.6	4.5★	3.6	3.6	1.1
Quebec has right to self-determination							
Agree	62.8	59.1	56.0	87.7	67.3		
Disagree	20.2	22.1	29.4	8.8	13.5		
Uncertain	17.0	18.8	14.6	3.5	19.2		
Mean	2.4	2.6	2.7	1.7★	2.4	2.5	1.1
Quebec should have constitutional veto							
Agree	45.7	33.3	38.1	78.9	35.3		
Disagree	27.2	39.0	37.2	7.0	31.4		
Uncertain	27.2	27.7	24.7	14.0	33.3		
Mean	2.8	3.0	3.0	1.8★	2.9	2.9	1.1
Quebec determine own language legislation							
Agree	59.1	62.0	57.1	78.9	59.6		
Disagree	31.2	25.5	29.1	15.8	28.9		
Uncertain	9.7	12.5	13.8	5.3	11.5		
Mean	2.6	2.5	2.6	1.9★	2.7	2.5	1.1
Quebec unique							
Agree	89.4	89.1	85.3	96.4	86.2		
Disagree	8.5	8.7	12.0	3.6	13.8		
Uncertain	2.1	2.2	2.8	0.0	0.0		
Mean	1.8	2.0	2.1	1.5★	2.1	2.0	0.9
Central Canada							
Central Canada has too much say							
Agree	69.1	79.4	40.5	55.3	80.8		
Disagree	14.9	13.0	39.3	17.9	11.5		
Uncertain	16.0	7.6	20.2	26.8	7.7		
Mean	2.2	2.1	2.9	2.6	2.0★	2.5	1.1

System vs subsystem

Thermometer scores

Feel about province							
Positive	83.2	87.9	87.7	85.7	94.0		
Negative	10.5	8.2	2.8	7.1	4.0		
Neutral	6.3	3.8	9.6	7.1	2.0		
Mean	75.9	76.3	72.5	77.0	81.6★	75.1	18.7
Feel about government of province							
Positive	0.0	26.6	35.6	26.8	9.8		
Negative	98.9	71.7	48.6	62.5	80.4		
Neutral	1.1	1.6	15.8	10.7	9.8		
Mean	6.3★	28.9	44.8	39.3	24.7	34.3	28.1
Feel about Canada							
Positive	95.7	95.6	94.4	76.4	100.0		
Negative	2.1	1.6	1.9	9.1	0.0		
Neutral	2.1	2.7	3.7	14.5	0.0		
Mean	83.7	84.5	82.8	72.5★	85.8	82.8	16.2
Feel about government of Canada							
Positive	3.2	7.6	11.1	16.1	4.0		
Negative	94.7	87.5	85.5	73.2	90.0		
Neutral	2.1	4.9	3.4	10.7	6.0		
Mean	16.8★	19.6	23.7	30.2	21.7	22.3	21.4

Federal structures

Level of government feel closest to					
Federal	28.7	14.7	35.7	41.8	17.3
Provincial	48.9	73.4	41.1	36.4	65.4
Municipal	13.8	8.7	14.4	9.1	5.8
None	8.5	2.2	8.2	10.9	11.5
How much power: federal government					
More	26.9	25.6	30.9	10.9	22.4
Less	10.8	11.7	9.9	36.4	28.6
Same	62.4	62.8	59.2	52.7	49.0
How much power: provincial government					
More	6.5	21.0	13.2	45.5	30.6
Less	44.1	20.4	24.1	12.7	16.3
Same	49.5	58.6	62.7	41.8	53.1
How much power: municipal government					
More	50.5	30.7	39.3	47.2	36.7
Less	4.3	8.9	8.6	9.4	6.1
Same	45.2	60.3	52.1	43.4	57.1

Table 5.8 continued

		BC %	Prairies %	Ontario %	Quebec %	Atlantic %	Canada	SD
Right to opt out of federal programs	Agree	17.0	32.8	23.4	75.0	30.8		
	Disagree	63.9	41.0	49.8	14.3	46.2		
	Uncertain	19.1	26.2	26.7	10.7	23.1		
	Mean	3.6	3.1	3.3	2.1★	3.1	3.2	1.1
Federal government yielded too much power	Agree	36.9	34.8	31.8	12.3	21.6		
	Disagree	43.1	44.8	39.8	77.2	54.9		
	Uncertain	20.0	20.4	28.4	10.5	23.5		
	Mean	3.1	3.1	3.1	3.9★	3.3	3.2	1.0
Should decentralize government services	Agree	80.9	67.8	66.1	78.6	70.6		
	Disagree	7.4	11.7	11.9	7.1	5.9		
	Uncertain	11.7	20.6	22.0	14.3	23.5		
	Mean	2.1	2.3	2.4	2.0★	2.2	2.3	0.9

Government in general

		BC %	Prairies %	Ontario %	Quebec %	Atlantic %	Canada	SD
MPs soon lose touch	Agree	28.6	37.7	33.7	54.4	47.1		
	Disagree	54.9	44.8	48.5	31.6	37.3		
	Uncertain	16.5	17.5	17.8	14.0	15.7		
	Mean	3.3	3.1	3.1	2.7★	2.9	3.1	1.0
Government doesn't care	Agree	40.7	43.1	45.5	49.1	53.0		
	Disagree	50.5	46.5	47.1	42.1	33.4		
	Uncertain	8.8	10.4	7.4	8.8	13.7		
	Mean	3.0	3.0	3.0	2.8	2.7★	3.0	1.2

Other systems and transnational entities

United States

		BC %	Prairies %	Ontario %	Quebec %	Atlantic %	Canada	SD
Feel about US	Positive	9.8	13.1	14.9	16.4	13.7		
	Negative	72.8	73.2	71.1	74.5	68.6		
	Neutral	17.4	13.7	14.0	9.1	17.6		
	Mean	24.7	28.9	29.3	29.1	31.1	28.7	22.2

Free trade

Reduce US cultural/media influence							
Agree	93.7	94.5	95.7	89.4	96.2		
Disagree	3.2	1.6	2.5	3.6	0.0		
Uncertain	3.2	3.8	1.8	7.0	3.8		
Mean	1.6	1.5★	1.5★	1.6	1.6	1.6	0.7

Ought to seek more US investment							
Agree	5.3	1.1	3.3	15.8	7.7		
Disagree	86.3	94.0	86.6	70.2	82.7		
Uncertain	8.4	4.9	10.0	14.0	9.6		
Mean	4.2	4.4	4.2	3.7★	4.1	4.2	0.8

Should have freer trade with USA							
Agree	15.1	16.1	10.5	14.0	21.2		
Disagree	62.4	64.5	75.5	61.4	55.7		
Uncertain	22.6	19.4	14.0	24.6	23.1		
Mean	3.7	3.7	4.0	3.6	3.5★	3.8	1.0

No tariffs between Canada/US							
Agree	12.7	6.0	5.5	5.4	7.7		
Disagree	71.6	78.3	83.2	83.9	76.9		
Uncertain	15.8	15.8	11.3	10.7	15.4		
Mean	3.8	3.9	4.0	4.1★	3.9	3.9	0.9

Alliances

Canada should stay in NATO							
Agree	14.9	23.2	34.1	25.9	37.3		
Disagree	69.1	60.8	49.8	63.0	54.9		
Uncertain	16.0	16.0	16.1	11.1	7.8		
Mean	3.9★	3.6	3.3	3.6	3.3	3.5	1.2

Canada should stay in NORAD							
Agree	10.6	14.4	29.7	19.3	27.5		
Disagree	71.3	63.9	52.9	63.2	47.1		
Uncertain	18.1	21.7	17.3	17.5	25.5		
Mean	3.9★	3.7	3.4	3.6	3.3★	3.6	1.2

NOTE: Means are based on either a 5-point Likert scale (strongly agree, agree, uncertain, disagree, strongly disagree) or a 100-point thermometer scale. Figures may not add to 100 because of rounding.
★ Regions most deviant from overall NDP norm.

Echoing this theme of regional powerlessness, Atlantic delegates also scored highest on one of the alienation items, and second highest on the other. In addition, and perhaps reflecting their long tradition of ties with their fellow maritimers in New England, Atlantic Canadians were somewhat more favourable than others to freer trade with the US, and more uncertain about the NDP's policy of pulling Canada out of NORAD.

British Columbia reinforced its image as the most dovish region by registering both its deviant responses in the area of international affairs. Delegates from BC strongly opposed Canada's involvement in the NATO and NORAD alliances. Finally, Ontario and the Prairies were both the most deviant from the party norm on a single item, reducing American cultural and media influence in Canada. The range of opinion in all five regions on this item was very small indeed.[23]

Table 5.9 compares the attitudes of New Democrats from the various regions of the country across a range of policy dimensions. As Chapter 3 showed, New Democrats tend to be more consensual in their attitudes than either Liberals or Conservatives, and also to be more distinctive: that is, their

Table 5.9
Attitudinal Differences Between Regions (mean scores)

Index (range) (direction)	Region					
	BC	Prairies	Ontario	Quebec	Atlantic	Canada[a]
Continentalism (0–4) (pro-)	0.32	0.26	0.26	0.60	0.44	0.31
Hawkishness (0–6) (pro-)	0.78	0.64	1.04	0.63	1.10	0.87
Social security (0–5) (pro-)	4.30	4.04	4.11	3.54	4.10	4.07
Moral conservatism (0–3) (pro-)	0.51	0.75	0.51	0.56	0.52	0.58
Corporate power (0–3) (anti-)	2.56	2.76	2.63	2.34	2.68	2.64
Bilingualism (0–2) (pro-)	1.77	1.74	1.75	1.96	1.73	1.76
Civil liberties (0–3) (pro-)	1.95	1.75	2.02	1.95	1.88	1.92
Privatization (0–6) (pro-)	0.11	0.24	0.20	0.42	0.20	0.22
N	(96)	(185)	(330)	(57)	(52)	(738)

[a] Includes Yukon and Northwest Territories.

attitudes tend to be closer to the 'poles' of the various indexes. The most strik-ing feature of Table 5.9 is the overall consistency in the attitudes of delegates from across the country, and in particular between the three largest sections of the party (Ontario, the Prairies, and British Columbia). On the eight issue areas included in Table 5.9, the gaps between attitudes in each of the largest sections are at best modest, and in some instances virtually non-existent.

This is not to suggest that there were no regional differences in atti-tudes towards these policy areas. The differences are most noticeable in the case of Quebec delegates, who on 6 of the 8 indexes occupied a polar posi-tion. Whereas New Democrats as a whole tended to be strongly in favour of bilingualism (mean = 1.76 on a two-point scale), Quebec delegates were almost unanimous (mean = 1.96) in their support. They also tended to be slightly more continentalist, less hawkish, slightly less supportive of welfare policies, slightly less inclined to favour restrictions on corporate power, and slightly less opposed to privatization than their colleagues from outside Quebec. Yet in the main their attitudes were still much closer to those of the NDP as whole than to either the Liberals or the Conservatives.

The attitudes of New Democrats from the Prairies today tend to echo those of the agrarian activists who, in their opposition to Eastern business interests, played such an important role in the formation of the CCF. In 1987 the greatest distrust of corporate power was shown by Prairie New Democrats, whose view likely combined the socialist distrust of 'capitalists' with Prairie distrust of 'Eastern business'. In addition, the traditional orien-tation of Prairie NDPers can be seen in their stance on moral issues (more restrictive than that of other NDPers) and their greater willingness to accept restrictions on civil liberties.[24]

On the traditional vs non-traditional dimension, Ontario delegates pro-vided a counterpoint to those from the Prairies. New Democrats from the most urban and industrialized section of the country were the least inclined to favour restrictive positions on moral issues, and most strongly opposed to restrictions on civil liberties. Ontario delegates also scored higher than most other New Democrats on hawkish policies, and very low in support of con-tinentalist policies. (Ontario delegates' suspicions regarding continentalism would be confirmed in the early 1990s, when the negative, de-industrializ-ing consequences of the Free Trade Agreement hit the industrial heartland.)

The figures for delegates from Atlantic Canada should be interpreted with some caution because the party's weakness in that region means that these data are based on a relatively small number of cases. The one feature that stands out for New Democrats from the Atlantic region is their support for hawkish poli-cies. It seems likely that the more traditional culture and the relatively large reliance on military employment in the region promotes more favourable attitudes towards military spending. Even so, in general New Democrats from the Atlantic region were still more similar to New Democrats from elsewhere across the country than to Liberals or Conservatives.

The final province to examine is British Columbia. Table 5.9 indicates that New Democrats from BC tended to be more radical than others on policies that reflect a traditional left agenda—namely, support for social-security measures and opposition to privatization. In addition, BC New Democrats, like their counterparts in Ontario, tended to take a less restrictive position on moral issues. This finding reflects the fact that most BC New Democrats came from metropolitan Vancouver and Victoria. In summary, the overall pattern for New Democrats, whether in BC, Ontario, or the Prairies, shows remarkable consistency in attitudes across a wide range of policy areas. The strong ideological orientation of the party seems to promote inter-regional cohesion. That is, activists' commitment to social-democratic ideals and principles enables them to overcome the regional divisions that are so evident in the values and orientations of members of other Canadian political parties.

CONCLUSION

We will conclude this chapter's examination of regionalism within the NDP with a few general observations. First, with respect to Brodie and Jenson's thesis that political parties 'define the political', the NDP's experience with Quebec suggests that in fact there are limits on a party's ability to shape the context of political debate through the policies it adopts: as we have seen, even though the party strongly supports Quebec's aspirations, this policy has consistently failed to win electoral support.

Second, the argument has been made by John Wilson (1974) and others that cleavages based on territory are more difficult to resolve through the party system than are cleavages based on class. The instability in Canadian politics that has arisen over the 'Quebec issue'—in which the cleavages of language and territory overlap and reinforce one another—and the political strains produced by Western alienation attest to the difficulties posed by territorial cleavages. Although the NDP is not simply a party of the working class, in its appeal to 'ordinary Canadians' it comes as close as any party in Canada does to having a class appeal. Thus an obvious question is whether the NDP's class appeal has helped to blunt regional and territorial differences.

The data indicate that the regional cleavage is only partly blunted in the NDP. One complicating factor is the composition of the NDP membership. Quite simply, NDP conventions provide a skewed regional sample of Canadians: the party is strongest in Ontario and the West, and most of its convention delegates come from these regions. Regional representation is more varied at Liberal and Conservative conventions, and this diversity may be one reason that the attitudinal differences within those parties are greater than those found in the NDP. In addition, while the attitude diversity among New Democrats from the different regions was less marked than among their counterparts in the two older parties, delegates did tend to take distinctive regional positions when the questions related specifically to their region, and those positions often reflected regional self-interest. The best example was found among the Quebec delegates. Of the 11 issues on which they were the most distinctive, almost half (5) dealt specifically with Quebec, and most of the others concerned the relative power of the federal and provincial governments; on themes relating to military alliances, Quebeckers differed little from most other delegates.

With respect to the East–West cleavage, the data suggest that the NDP's class appeal may have at least partly blunted the regional differences. For example, on almost every Likert-scale question studied in this chapter, delegates from the Prairies and Ontario were more alike in their responses than were delegates from other regions. However, there is reason to suspect that important East–West differences persist. Many of the questions posed were not closely related to the issues that divide the electorates in these two regions. When such questions were posed, their different perspectives came to the fore (e.g., whether Central Canada had too much power, or whether the respondents felt closest to the federal or provincial government). When the questions posed did not touch directly on the self-interest of a region, the regional schisms declined. The existence of strong provincial caucuses within the party, together with the party's provincially-based federal structure, helps to ensure that regional perspectives always have an outlet within the NDP. Hence it appears that regional cleavages in Canada may be only partly blunted within a party. It also appears that in the party system as a whole, the importance of regionalism is on the rise. The strong regional nature of partisan support in Canada, together with the distorting effects of the first-past-the-post electoral system, usually means that it is in the interest of at least one of the major political parties to cast issues in a regional light. Such a strategy can be very effective for emerging parties as well, as the experiences of both the Reform Party and the Bloc Québécois in the 1993 federal election suggest.

Finally, it is difficult to organize political parties in a transcontinental state, particularly when the problem of geographic size is complicated by different regional economies, cultures, and ethnic-linguistic backgrounds. It should not be surprising, therefore, to find that ideological and policy differences reflecting diverse regional backgrounds exist not only between parties but within them. How serious these regional differences become depends in part on factors that are beyond any party's control—including the overall mood of the times—but also in part on the strategies employed by the parties to court the regional electorates. Political leaders must be highly skilled to accommodate the concerns of the various regions and to negotiate acceptable solutions. How the NDP addresses these regional differences and, in some cases, grievances may well determine the party's success in extending its support in all regions of Canada. The 1993 federal election resulted in a highly fragmented and regionally divided party system. The challenge for all parties is to find ways in which the regional and sectional interests of the country can be given effective voice so that parties do not become excessively balkanized and thereby accentuate the crisis of confederation.

NOTES

1 For example, the NDP is weak in Quebec despite its strong support for the province's right to self-determination see Johnston (1987).

2 For example, items on the status of Quebec, confederation, free trade, and NATO/NORAD each tap a different level of territorial social organization. The central federal government represents the system level; the provinces (e.g., Quebec) subsystems; and transnational entities (e.g., economic trading blocs and military alliances) the international environment.

3 See Whitehorn (1992); see also, on BC, Barrett (1995); Gawthrop (1996); Harcourt (1996), Kavic and Nixon (1979); on Saskatchewan, Lipset (1968); Tyre (1962); on Manitoba, McAllister (1984); Wiseman (1983); on Ontario, Ehring and Roberts (1993); Monahan (1995), Rae (1996), Walkom (1994). To date no book has been written on the Yukon NDP government experiment.

4 Data derived from Whitehorn (1995). See also Archer (1987), Archer and Whitehorn (1993).

5 In comparing the 1983 (Regina) and 1987 (Montreal) NDP conventions one notes a dramatic change in regional distribution of delegates; see Whitehorn (1988, 1992). As a result, caution is required in comparing conventions held in different regions of the country. It may well be that differences assumed to be caused by the passage of time are also a product of differing regional composition. This certainly complicates comparison, both within a single party and between parties.

6 The NDP's founding convention in 1961 endeavoured to break this pattern established through the CCF era, but unfortunately no survey was conducted at that time. See also Courtney (1973, 1995).

7 National election studies conducted between 1974 and 1980 reveal that Canadians gave scores of between 80 and 83 for the country and between 78 and 82 for their home province (Clarke et al., 1984: 42).

8 Here the NDP activists' rankings differ from those of the Canadian public at large, which has tended to rate both levels of government in a positive direction (1980

mean = 62 for both levels) and to prefer the government of Canada over that of the province (Johnston, 1986: 42).

9 For earlier findings on related questions see Schwartz (1974) and Wilson (1974); Blishen (1978) also posed similar questions while controlling for both region and language.

10 The lone incident in which the Nova Scotia CCF became the official opposition, in 1945, was a fluke, as the party received less than 14% of the vote and only two seats; it was a testament to the weakness of the other opposition party rather than the strength of the Nova Scotia CCF.

11 The Meech Lake Accord was officially signed on 30 April 1987, just a few weeks after the NDP federal convention (13–15 March).

12 The Quebec provincial NDP was also opposed to the Meech Lake Accord, though for different reasons.

13 While much has been written about the CCF–NDP's socialist ideology, relatively little attention has been paid to the party's nationalist orientation.

14 American multinational corporations no doubt understandably view the NDP as representing the twin evils of socialism and an anti-American form of Canadian nationalism (see Granatstein, 1996).

15 Some NDP activists would suggest that 'imperialism' is the appropriate term.

16 A comparable number (74.7%) responded the same way to the same question in the 1983 survey (Whitehorn, 1988: 290).

17 Of the activists in the three major political parties at that time, the NDP delegates indicated the strongest opposition to free trade. For comparisons see Goldfarb and Axworthy (1988: 33, 54, 73, 80, 99, 103, 113).

18 For results from earlier surveys see Whitehorn (1988, 1992).

19 In 1983 the proportion was just over one-third (38%, 20 of 52 items; Whitehorn, 1988, 1992).

20 Clearly Ontario, with 45.1% of the sampled delegates, will have a strong influence on where the Canadian mean score is located and thus will statistically be less likely to diverge from the Canadian norm. One way around this problem would be to weight each region equally and derive a modified 'mean' based on regional parity. The number calculated would of course cease to be the mean in the proper technical sense of the word. Such analysis was not done for this chapter.

21 On two items there was a tie for the greatest deviation by a region. Thus for the 17 survey questions 19 examples are cited.

22 It should be noted that 88.9% of NDP delegates reported using English as their language at home; only 6.7% reported using French and a paltry 1.1% reported using both languages.

23 Again, caution is required in interpreting these data, since statistically delegates from these two regions respectively account for 45.1% and 25.3% of the delegates.

24 Gun control is a notable exception to this pattern. The Saskatchewan section of the NDP, as well as all NDP federal MPs from Saskatchewan, voted against stiffer gun-control legislation in 1996.

CHAPTER
6

The Gender Gap

Throughout history, in political organizations no less than the societies in which they operate, one enduring form of social stratification has been that based on gender (see Anderson, 1991; Armstrong and Armstrong, 1978; Brodie, 1985b; Connelly, 1978; Lovenduski and Hills, 1981; McLaughlin, 1992; Prentice et al., 1988). Canadian women did not obtain the right to vote in federal elections until 1918, and progress in the election or appointment of women to important political posts has been slow: member of Parliament, 1921; senator, 1930; leader of a provincial party, 1951;[1] federal cabinet minister, 1957; Supreme Court justice, 1982; governor general, 1984; leader of a major federal party, 1989; premier, 1991; and prime minister, 1993.

Like so much in the area of women's studies, the topic of gender in politics has been a neglected area of research until recently (Bashevkin, 1985b, 1989, 1993; Brodie and Vickers, 1981; Vickers, 1989).[2] To what degree do political parties continue today past patterns of gender inequality? How significant are differences of opinion along gender lines within political parties today? This chapter examines those questions in relation to the federal NDP. Following a brief overview of women's participation at the various levels of the party hierarchy, it will examine selected data from two delegate surveys (1983 and 1987), which may provide some insights into the behavioural and attitudinal differences between female and male party activists. As befits a mass party, we will begin by looking at the extra-parliamentary wing.

WOMEN'S PARTICIPATION

Extra-parliamentary Wing
During the CCF era, only a small portion of the electorate (11.1% on average) voted for the party (Whitehorn, 1992: 3) and a disproportionate number of those who did were men.[3] Over the years, the party had various women's study clubs, auxiliaries, committees, and conferences (Bashevkin, 1985b: 85, 106–13; Beeby, 1982; Manley, 1980; Melnyk, 1989: 78–9, 95–103;

Sangster, 1989: 104–21, 209–22), but female members were heavily out-numbered by men.

This gender imbalance continued into the NDP era.[4] However, recent surveys have shown that today more women than men vote for the party (Brodie, 1991: 22; Pammett, 1989: 127; Wearing and Wearing, 1991).[5] And it appears that the numbers of women who are members of the NDP have increased as well, although few formal data have been available on the proportions of men and women members in any of Canada's federal parties. The only data we have on women's membership in the NDP come from the Ontario provincial section; they show that in September 1992 women made up just under half (46.7%) of that party's constituency (as opposed to affiliated union) members.[6]

Increasingly, information is available on women's participation at various levels of the party's management hierarchy. In the past, the participation of women in all Canadian political parties tended to decline as one moved up the levels of the party pyramid (see Figure 6.1; see also Bashevkin, 1985a, 1985b, 1989, 1991, 1993; Bashevkin and Holder, 1985; Brodie, 1985b; Brodie and Vickers, 1981). Although the 'pink-collar ghetto' still exists—that is, more women still occupy the support position of riding secretary than executive positions such as treasurer or president[7]—this situation seems to be improving (see Figure 6.2). For over two decades the NDP has had a Participation of Women (POW) committee intended to 'encourage women's participation in all forms of political activity' (Bashevkin, 1985b: 111), and similar committees now exist in all the provincial and territorial sections. The creation of the POW committees, together with the hiring of a women's organizer, has helped to encourage women members and fostered their promotion to more senior positions (Bashevkin, 1985b: 110–12; Brodie, 1991: 28; Brodie and Vickers, 1981: 334; Sangster, 1989: 224). The percentage of female delegates at the 1987 federal NDP convention rose to 42.5% from 36.9% in 1983, and a similar increase was recorded for provincial riding association executives (45.1% to 54.2%). In fact, at the 1987 convention more riding associations (federal and provincial) were represented by female than male executives.[8]

From 1988 to 1995, the next level in the organizational hierarchy was the 'councils of federal ridings', regional structures midway between the riding association executives and the federal council. These councils were promoted by outgoing leader Ed Broadbent in an attempt to give more vitality to the federal operations of the party between elections. Although the future of this structure is now in question, and the party's constitution made no provisions for gender parity on the councils themselves, a strong example was set in the constitutional requirement for parity in the selection of representatives from the councils of federal ridings to attend the national federal council.

Moving up the organizational hierarchy, the next level is the convention. Attendance at the early CCF conventions was overwhelmingly male, although a few women were prominent.[9] The most recent surveys show that growing proportions of delegates are women (see Table 6.2). However, men still predominate by about two to one (see Archer, 1991a; Bashevkin, 1985b: 64, 163; Bashevkin, 1989; Whitehorn, 1992).[10] One reason is that the second largest contingent of delegates comes from affiliated trade unions. While riding associations have made significant strides towards choosing equal numbers of male and female delegates, unions—whose members are still predominantly male[11]—have not moved so rapidly (Hayward and Whitehorn, 1991). For example, Bashevkin (1985b: 64) reports that in the early 1980s only 11% of affiliated union delegates were women, compared with 41% of

Figure 6.1
Women's Participation in Major Canadian Parties, 1980s

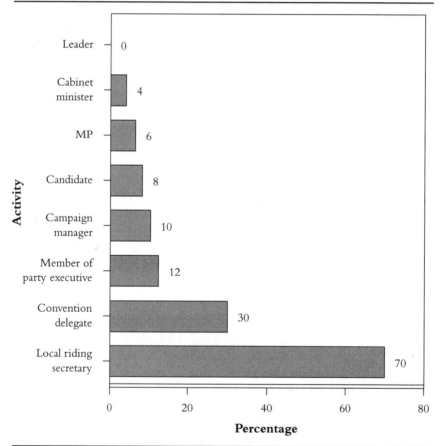

SOURCES: Bashevkin (1985b: 452: 1989: 452).

federal riding delegates. By 1987 the percentage of female union delegates had increased only slightly, to 16.5% (see Chapter 4).

Between conventions, the paramount decision-making body of the NDP is its federal council. The party's constitution in 1993 required that 10 of the 20 council members elected by the federal convention be women,[12] two of them aboriginal and another two from visible minorities. The councils of federal ridings also sent representatives to the federal council, and gender parity was required for those delegates. Similarly, at least one of the two representatives on the federal council elected by the provincial conventions had to be a woman, and as an official party committee, POW was also entitled to send one woman from each provincial/territorial section to the federal council.

Figure 6.2
Participation of Women in the NDP, 1989, 1990

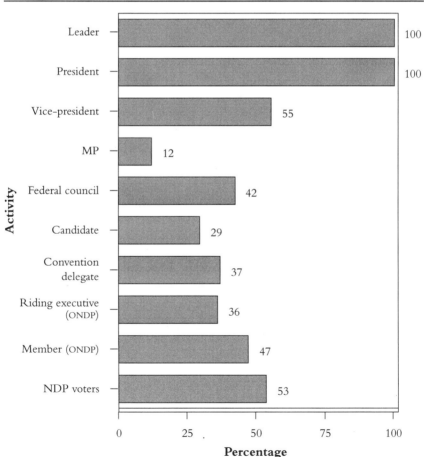

Table 6.1

Women Elected to Ontario Provincial NDP Riding Executives (% of positions filled by women)

Position	1973	1981	1985	1990
President	8.5	28.8	30.4	34.6
Treasurer or chief financial officer		41.6	36.8	29.2
Secretary		67.2	69.3	48.5

SOURCE: Bashkevin (1985a: 277; 1985b: 58; 1991).

All these measures have helped to increase the numbers of women on the federal council. For example, in March 1977, before the gender parity measures were implemented, women made up 20.8% of the federal council. Just over a decade later, in 1989–90, 41.5% of the council were women.[13] However, without provisions for gender parity in affiliated unions, which also send delegates to the council, full gender parity is not likely to be achieved. And, even if male and female representation were to become numerically equal, this would not necessarily guarantee equality in influence, as Pitkin (1967) and others (Gelb, 1989; Jennings, 1990: 246; Jennings and Farah, 1981: 469; Kornberg et al., 1979: 186) have pointed out: attitudinal factors such as vocational status and personal forcefulness, not to mention bias, can have a significant influence on the distribution of power. Still, a vast distance has been travelled since the first councils in the 1930s, when very few women were members.

Before a woman was first elected as federal party leader, important political gains were made in a number of executive posts. For example, since the early 1980s the federal party has 'balanced' its vice-presidents along gender lines (four to four in 1983; six to five in favour of women in 1995), and the party's constitution stipulates that either the party president or the associate president must be a woman. In addition, women occupy

Table 6.2

Percentages of Men and Women at Conventions, 1971–1989

	1971	1979	1983	1987	1989
Men	73.9	74.4	69.1	67.0	63.2
Women	26.1	25.6	30.9	33.0	36.8
N	(747)	(519)	(395)	(738)	(995)

SOURCES: Based on survey data. See Chapter 2; Whitehorn (1988; 1992); Archer (1991a).

many important positions that are not always included in formal charts of the party hierarchy. Election planning, for example, has always been a central task for political parties. In the age of mass advertising and public-opinion polling, the pivotal positions include principal secretary to the leader, chair of the election planning committee (SEPC), party pollster, caucus research director, and federal secretary. Even as recently as 1984, all these positions were filled by men. However, by January 1993, in the run-up to the October election, three of these five positions were held by women (Sandra Mitchell as principal secretary, Julie Davis as chair of SEPC, and Tessa Hebb as research director). This development stands in dramatic contrast to the NDP's earlier history and to the situation in other parties even today (Bashevkin, 1993: 76). The changes in the gender make-up of the principal federal NDP posts were no doubt influenced by the party's first female leader.

In the days of the CCF, all the party's national presidents and chairmen were men, although Thérèse Casgrain was elected vice-chair in 1948 (Engelmann, 1954). It was not until 1975, well into the NDP era, that a woman became president of the party. The election of Joyce Nash (Scotton) ended four decades of male dominance of this post. In keeping, to some degree, with the shift in the party's base of support and its desire to project a progressive image, four of the last five federal NDP presidents have been women (Marion Dewar, Joanna den Hertog, Sandra Mitchell, and Nancy Riche).

From the time of the party's founding in 1932 until 1989, almost six decades later, the CCF–NDP was led by men (see also Chapter 11). A first step towards the election of a female leader was taken in 1975, when Rosemary Brown (Brown, 1989; Roy, 1992) challenged Ed Broadbent and three other men for the party leadership. The fact that she came a close second, winning 41% of the vote on the final ballot, was a sign both of the growing power of the women in the party and of the increased acceptance both in the party and in Canadian society of women as political leaders. With the election of Audrey McLaughlin in 1989 the highest bastion of male ascendancy was finally breached.[14] Not surprisingly, the party's first female federal leader strongly advocated accelerating the pace of the party's commitment to gender parity and affirmative action. The adoption by the 1991 convention of a resolution to promote more female candidates for Parliament was one step in that direction. Perhaps another step was the January 1995 decision of the federal council to open up the leadership selection process to include a direct ballot of all party members (see Chapter 13); however, whether that democratized the political process still further or created new financial barriers to female leadership candidates remains open to question. In any case, the 1995 convention selected Alexa McDonough as its new leader.

Parliamentary Wing

From the founding of the party, CCF women ran as candidates at all three levels of government (Melnyk, 1989: 78; Roome, 1989: 106; Sangster, 1989: 208; Webster, n.d.). The numbers, however, were very small and for women success was more likely at the municipal level, where the prestige was lower and it was easier to combine family responsibilities and political activism (Bashevkin, 1989: 450; Brodie, 1985b: 20; Howard, 1992; Surrey-Newton, NDP 1994; Vickers and Brodie, 1981: 58).[15] Although the CCF–NDP has never had as many female as male candidates, the party has gradually made progress in both the numbers and the proportions of female candidates (see Table 6.3). From fewer than six CCF candidates, on average, in the 1940s, the NDP ran just over 60 in the 1980s, a tenfold increase, and in 1988 it nominated more female candidates than any other party (28.5%).[16] To encourage this trend, the party created the Agnes MacPhail Fund, which provides modest financial assistance to female candidates. The current NDP constitution calls for greater efforts towards 'affirmative action' and permits the federal council to promote greater female involvement in local nominations. One method employed to ensure that enough female candidates emerge is 'clustering', whereby nominations are frozen for an entire cluster of ridings in each region until a certain number of affirmative action candidates (e.g., women) have been nominated, or at least invited to run (McLaughlin, 1992: 220). As a result, in the 1993 federal election campaign the NDP nominated more female candidates than ever before (113), and more than any other party (Canada, 1993; Whitehorn, 1994).

The first woman elected to the Canadian House of Commons was Agnes MacPhail, in 1921 (Crowley, 1990; Pennington, 1990; Stewart and

Table 6.3
Women Candidates for the Federal CCF–NDP, by Decade

Decade	Number of women	Number of elections	Average per election
(CCF era)			
1930s	7	1	7.0
1940s	16	3	5.3
1950s	31	3	10.3
(NDP era)			
1960s	56	4	14.0
1970s	119	3	39.7
1980s	182	3	60.1
1990s	113	1	113.0
Total	524	18	

SOURCES: Correspondence with Abby Pollenetsky, former Director of Women's Organization, NDP; unpublished report by Diane Leduc.

French, 1959). Although she was elected as a member of the United Farmers of Ontario (UFO), more than a decade before the formation of the CCF, she became one of the pioneering figures in the CCF. Only a handful of women from any of the parties were elected to Parliament in the 1930s and 1940s. Macphail was defeated in her efforts at re-election in 1940, but she did run successfully for the CCF at the provincial level in 1943, when she and fellow CCFer Rae Luckock became the first women to sit in the Ontario legislature.

The CCF's record for electing women to Parliament, like that of other parties in the first half of the twentieth century, was abysmal (Brodie, 1991; Gotell and Brodie, 1991; Kome, 1985; Lazarus, 1983). Only one female CCF candidate (Gladys Strum, from Saskatchewan) was elected to Parliament in the entire CCF period (see Table 6.4). At the beginning of the NDP era there was a slight improvement, but not until the 1970s did the party have more than one woman in the House of Commons at the same time. One reason, of course, was that the CCF was a third party and never won more than 28 seats. As the NDP era progressed, so did the party's vote, numbers of seats, and numbers of women elected. In 1988 a record number of five women were elected for the party. Though still low (11.6%), the percentage of women in the caucus nevertheless represented an improvement over the average of 4.3% for the history of the CCF–NDP.[17] However, at the next election, in 1993, the NDP suffered a serious setback, and Audrey McLaughlin was the only female New Democrat elected. As of early 1997, party leader Alexa McDonough did not have a seat in the House of Commons.

Optimists might suggest that the overall record represents progress. Others would note that the gains came very late and that the numbers of women elected are still lamentably low (Brodie, 1991; McLaughlin, 1992: 218). In more than six decades, the number of women in the social-democratic caucus has averaged less than one per election—17 in 18 elections (see Table 6.4). Of course, the bias in the electoral system against third parties has made election even more difficult for female CCF–NDP candidates than for their counterparts in the leading parties.

Although women's participation rate at the higher levels of the party hierarchy has improved dramatically, and the party's 1993 election nomination plans sought to remove some of the remaining obstacles to gender equality, the results were disappointing. Not only was the party's showing, both in seats and in votes, its worst ever in the NDP era, but of the nine candidates elected only one was a woman. In general, does having more women candidates help or hinder a party's electoral chances? For a third- or fourth-place party, such as the NDP, are the risks even greater? Would more women have been elected if they had been candidates in stronger NDP ridings? Would more funding for women have helped?[18] Would matters improve if

Table 6.4
Women Elected as CCF–NDP Federal MPs, by Decade

Decade	Total seats	Number of elections	% of party's total
(CCF era)			
1930s	0	1	0.0
1940s	1	3	2.0 (1/49)
1950s	0	3	0.0
(NDP era)			
1960s	2	4	2.5 (2/79)
1970s	3	3	4.1 (3/73)
1980s	10	3	9.5 (10/105)
1990s	1	1	11.1 (1/9)
Total	17	18	
Mean			4.5

we had an electoral system based on proportional representation (Megyery, 1991)? In any case, while the number of female NDP MPs went down, the combined total of women elected by other parties went up.

GENDER AND CONVENTION DELEGATES[19]

Demographic Profiles

As we have seen (Table 6.2), men have always outnumbered women at federal NDP conventions. This section will examine the demographic differences between female and male delegates.[20]

While the overwhelming majority of all delegates in 1983 and 1987 were chosen from constituency associations, higher proportions of women (89.1% and 75.8%)[21] came to the conventions by this method than was the case for men (73.4% and 63.2%). The second largest category of male delegates at both conventions represented trade-union locals (9.6% and 16.7%); by contrast, only 1.7% and 5.8% of women represented unions, reflecting the fact that more men than women are union members. Perhaps the friction that has often been observed between delegates from union locals and those from constituency associations (Brodie, 1985a) has something to do with the gender imbalance between the two groups; this question is worthy of further research.[22]

While the great majority of NDP delegates said they had some higher education, at both conventions more women (81.1% and 85.5%) than men (63.7% and 74.6%) reported a university or college background.[23] One probable reason is that so many male delegates came from working-class backgrounds.

As might be expected from the findings on education, there were differences in the leading occupations listed by the female and male delegates. Of the occupations reported by 10% or more of the respondents in 1983, women were most likely to describe themselves as skilled white-collar (20.7%), followed by homemaker (18.2%), educator (11.6%), and retired (11.6%). In 1987 the women's rankings were similar: skilled white-collar first (28.3%), followed by homemaker (11.2%), and educator (11.2%). Reflecting the increasing proportions of women in the paid workforce, the skilled white-collar category grew while the homemaker category declined. By contrast, the most common occupations for male delegates in 1983 were skilled blue-collar (14.0%), retired (11.8%), skilled white-collar (11.2%), professional (11.1%), union administrator (10.0%), and student (10.0%). By 1987, more men listed skilled white-collar (20.0%), followed by skilled blue-collar (12.9%), and union representative (12.1%).

About two-thirds of the survey respondents said they could identify the social class to which they belonged. Women, as the data on education and occupation might suggest, were slightly more likely to describe themselves as middle-class (53.8% and 46.0%) than were men (40.4% and 40.3%), while a slightly higher percentage of men than women picked the working-class category (30.2% and 26.5% compared to 23.5% and 23.8%).

When asked whether they intended to run as NDP candidates in an upcoming election, most delegates answered no. But the rate was higher for women (77.6% and 68.6%) than for men (68.7% and 57.0%). Interestingly, the gender gap was greatest at the federal level.[24] Despite their higher levels of formal education, a larger percentage of women (33.3%) than men (20.5%) cited 'lack of experience' as their reason for not running. Though formal education is not an equivalent to experience, it is likely that part of the explanation can be found in a socialization process that often diminishes the importance and status of women's experience. This theme emerges even in the autobiography of then leader Audrey McLaughlin (1992: 199, 200, 214).

Attitudes Towards Gender Issues

All political questions, whether they relate to war and peace, the environment, or the constitution, are of interest to women as well as men. Yet there are certain questions (such as abortion and gender parity) that women have pointed to as being of more immediate relevance to them (see Tables 6.5 and 6.6). We will examine gender differences below, but to begin our analysis we will look at the replies of all delegates, men and women, to some of these questions.

The broadest survey question on gender issues asked delegates whether women are discriminated against within the NDP.[25] Even though, at both conventions, women were outnumbered by men by roughly two to one, most answers (77.9% in 1983 and 71.6% in 1987)[26] were negative. In both surveys, overwhelming majorities (86.5% and 88.2%) of delegates thought that more women should be candidates for the NDP. And when asked whether women are as effective as men as candidates, almost all (92.3% and 92.8%) answered in the affirmative.[27]

Large majorities (72.1% and 83.9%) of delegates at both conventions also agreed that the NDP should ensure that a significant percentage of its candidates and party officers are women. However, in 1983 many delegates were less likely to support the entrenchment of gender parity on the federal council (47.8% in favour, 36.7% opposed).[28] Even so, beginning at that convention, half the council members and vice-presidents elected by the convention were required to be women. Such measures certainly helped to raise the percentage of women at the executive levels of the party, and four

Table 6.5
Attitudes Towards Selected Issues by Gender, 1983

Statement	% Agree (A)/Disagree (D)[a]		
	Male	Female	Difference
Pornography should be banned	42.6A 41.1D	63.2A	20.6
Fifty percent of the federal council should be composed of women	38.9A 42.7D	66.9A	28.0
There should be no censorship of any kind	66.3D	78.8D	12.5
The NDP should ensure that a significant percentage of its candidates and Party officers are women	67.2A	82.5A	15.3
Women are discriminated against within the NDP	82.4D	65.5D	16.9
Abortion is a private matter which should be decided between the woman bearing the child and her doctor	79.7A	95.8A	16.1
On the whole, women are as effective as men as candidates for elected office	92.2A	93.4A	1.2
More women should be candidates for the NDP	83.2A	92.5A	9.3
Mean			15.0

NOTE: Average sample size = 385.
[a] Where no majority was found, both 'A' and 'D' percentages are shown.
SOURCE: Whitehorn (1992).

years later the opposition to parity provisions had declined to 23.4%, while a sizeable majority (62.3%) agreed with them.

Among the social issues of particular interest to women, abortion arouses strong feelings on both sides. The NDP has long supported the right of women to seek medical abortions,[29] and in 1983 an overwhelming number of delegates (84.6%) agreed with the statement that abortion is a private matter that should be decided between the woman bearing the child and her doctor. In 1987 a slightly different question (see Table 6.6) received virtually the same level of support (85.1%). Support for pro-choice positions has been somewhat higher among NDP delegates than among either Liberal or Conservative activists (Brodie, 1988; Blake, 1988; see also Chapter 3).[30] As might be expected, the overwhelming majority of NDP delegates, male and female alike (92.4% and 93.8%), believed that government-sponsored child care services should be greatly expanded. Again the rate seems to be higher than for Liberal and Conservative convention delegates (Brodie, 1988: 181).[31]

Many people believe that pornography fosters sexist and violent attitudes and behaviour towards women and perpetuates gender inequalities. While there are no survey data on NDP attitudes to censorship and pornography before the 1980s, our impression is that many NDP members have shifted their position in recent years away from a somewhat libertarian viewpoint to one more compatible with a radical feminist perspective. In the 1983 and 1987 surveys respectively, 69.8% and 55.8% of the delegates disagreed with the statement that there should be no censorship of any kind. Although the proportions supporting a ban on pornography were somewhat lower (49.0% in 1983 and 44.8% in 1987), this was still the dominant viewpoint.[32]

The Gender Gap

In earlier decades, when political parties in Canada, as elsewhere, were largely male organizations, any gender differences that did exist within them were treated as insignificant. However, as the numbers of women in political parties have grown, the question of intra-party gender differences has become increasingly salient.

Earlier reports on the 1983 survey (Whitehorn 1988: 289–91; 1992: 131–2, 135)[33] showed high levels of consensus within the party in some policy areas, such as issues of particular interest to women.[34] Of the 52 survey questions for which the replies were broken down by gender, only 17 showed a difference of 10% or more. Six of these 17 items involved issues seen by women as central concerns (see Table 6.5). In 1983, by far the most divisive of these was the question of gender parity on the federal council.

Women strongly supported the measure, whereas men were more inclined to disagree. Yet by 1987 the difference had fallen considerably (see Table 6.6). The second most divisive issue along gender lines in 1983 was the banning of pornography; while women strongly favoured a ban, men were split on the issue (see Table 6.5).

A similar analysis was made of a representative sample of 30 items from the 1987 survey (see Table 3.1). Again, the items targeted by women (see Table 6.6) were more likely to show disagreement along gender lines (mean

Table 6.6
Attitudes towards Selected Issues by Gender, 1987

Statement	% Agree (A)/Disagree (D)[a]		
	Male	Female	Difference
Pornography should be banned	38.2A 38.9D	61.1A	22.9
Fifty per cent of the federal council should be composed of women[b]	58.3A 57.4A	73.5A 75.2A	15.2 17.8
There should be no censorship of any kind	52.0D	64.6D	12.6
The NDP should ensure that a significant percentage of its candidates and party officers are women[b]	81.0A 83.4A	86.2A 88.7A	5.2 5.7
Women are discriminated against within the NDP[b]	81.6D 75.8D	63.6D 65.5D	18.0 10.3
Abortion is a private matter which should be decided between the pregnant woman and her doctor[c]	81.8A	94.1A	12.3
On the whole, women are as effective as men as candidates for elected office	92.4A	96.2A	3.8
More women should be candidates for the NDP	87.3A	93.3A	6.0
Government-sponsored child care services should be greatly expanded[d]	92.4A	93.8A	1.4
Overall, sexism is on the decline[d]	48.3A	35.2A 45.3D	13.1
Mean			11.1

NOTE: Average sample size = 722.

[a] Where no majority was found, both 'A' and 'D' percentages are shown.

[b] Three sets of statements were presented near the beginning of the questionnaire and repeated later. The twinned sets of responses thus provide an indication of the consistency in response patterns over the 300-item survey.

[c] Different wording than in 1983.

[d] Statement not included in 1983.

= 11.1) than were those 30 items (mean = 4.8). Not surprisingly, the most divisive issue of this cluster in 1987 was whether to ban pornography; women still favoured a ban, and men were still divided.

Interestingly, when the average gender differences on the eight targeted items in 1983 and 1987 were compared (see Tables 6.5 and 6.6), the gender gap proved to have narrowed. This suggests that the increasing participation and representation of women at NDP conventions and councils, and even in the leadership, has meant that issues of particular interest to women are being dealt with more satisfactorily than in the past. It also appears that greater numbers of men are now more willing to accept the policies and measures favoured by the majority of NDP women (such as gender parity). Table 6.7 records the changes in men's and women's attitudes between 1983 and 1987 on the selected issues and shows that, on average, men's attitudes shifted further. In addition, on six of the eight policy statements the men moved closer to the women's views.

Finally, it should be noted that the differences between men and women may not be the most significant ones within the NDP. When various demographic factors were explored to see which were associated with the greatest frequency of differences, gender was ranked third in 1983, behind education and community size (see Chapter 10; Whitehorn, 1992:

Table 6.7
Shifts in Attitudes by Gender, 1983 and 1987

| | % Agree (A)/Disagree (D) | | | | | |
| | Men | | | Women | | |
	1983	1987	Difference	1983	1987	Difference
Pornography ban	42.6A	38.2A	4.4	63.2A	61.1A	2.1
Women 50% of council	38.9A	57.9A[a]	19.0	66.9A	74.4A[a]	7.5
No censorship	66.3D	52.0D	14.3	78.8D	64.6D	14.2
Significant % women	67.2A	82.2A[a]	15.0	82.5A	87.5A[a]	5.0
Discrimination in NDP	82.4D	78.7D[a]	3.7	65.5D	64.6D[a]	0.9
Abortion	79.7A	81.8A	2.1	95.8A	94.1A	1.7
Women as effective candidates	92.2A	92.4A	0.2	93.4A	96.2A	2.8
More women candidates	83.2A	87.3A	4.1	92.5A	93.3A	0.8
Mean			7.9			4.4

NOTE: For full text of survey statements see Tables 6.5 and 6.6.
[a] In 1987 some survey items were duplicated; the percentage here is based on the average score for the duplicated items.

l34). On the other hand, as Chapter 12, will show, gender had a significant impact on Audrey McLaughlin's support.

Gender and Attitude Consistency

Another way of exploring gender differences is to build on the comparative work of Brodie (1988) and Blake (1988). In Chapter 3 we noted that NDP, Liberal, and Conservative delegates situated themselves at different points on the political spectrum. Is the gap between male and female NDP delegates greater than that between all NDP delegates and all Liberals, or between all NDP delegates and all Conservatives? Figure 6.3 suggests a hypothetical distribution on the political spectrum.

We postulate that internal party differences between male and female delegates (that is, the gap from 1 to 3 in Figure 6.3) are in general likely to be smaller than differences between the NDP and other parties (that is, between 2 and 4 or between 2 and 5) (see also Kirkpatrick, 1976). Thirty items were taken from the 1987 NDP survey to explore whether intra-party gender differences were smaller than inter-party differences (data not shown in tabular form). As expected, a smaller intra-party difference was found in 28 cases; this finding was similar to Brodie's (1988: 179, 182).[35] Since the inter-party differences were greater, it appears that the gender gap within the NDP was not large enough to cause excessive internal division.

This line of inquiry is pursued further in an examination of the levels of division and cohesion among men and women New Democrats in their attitudes towards the eight issue indexes introduced in Chapter 3 (see Table 6.8). Overall, and reflecting our findings on individual issues, women delegates proved to be somewhat more to the left ideologically, and somewhat more consistent as a group, than their male counterparts. Table 6.8 shows that on the continentalism, hawkishness, social security, moral conservatism, corporate power, bilingualism, and privatization indexes, the mean score for

Figure 6.3
Hypothetical Left–Right Positioning of NDP (Male and Female), Liberal, and Conservative Delegates, 1980s

left ----------+--+--+-------+--------+----------- right
      1 2 3   4   5

1   Female NDP delegates (1987)
2   All NDP delegates (both male and female) (1987)
3   Male NDP delegates (1987)
4   Liberal delegates (1984)
5   Conservative delegates (1983)

women was slightly closer to the pole and farther from the centre. In addition, on each of these measures the standard deviation was lower for women than for men, indicating greater consensus within the group. The one exception to this trend was on the issue of civil liberties, where men were slightly more likely to oppose restrictions than were women. On the whole, then, whereas in the past women were generally considered to be more conservative than men, today a greater role for women within the NDP would likely provide an impetus for greater radicalization.

However, it is important not to overstate this conclusion. The NDP is not an amalgam of conservative men and radical women. The data indicate clearly that although the gender differences in attitudes were consistent in direction, they were modest in size. The largest differences were on the hawkishness index, but even here women and men alike were well to the 'dovish' end of the index. In general, the data indicate that within the NDP men's and women's attitudes are characterized by greater consensus than division.

Table 6.8
Attitudinal Differences by Gender, 1987 (mean scores)

Index (range) (direction)	Men		Women		All Delegates	
	Mean	SD[a]	Mean	SD	Mean	SD
Continentalism (0–4) (pro-)	0.37	(0.63)	0.21	(0.47)	0.32	(0.59)
Hawkishness (0–6) (pro-)	0.94	(1.16)	0.74	(1.10)	0.87	(1.14)
Social security (0–5) (pro-)	4.03	(1.10)	4.14	(1.07)	4.06	(1.09)
Moral conservatism (0–3) (pro-)	0.59	(0.79)	0.55	(0.70)	0.58	(0.76)
Corporate power (0–3) (anti-)	2.62	(0.72)	2.68	(0.63)	2.64	(0.69)
Bilingualism (0–2) (pro-)	1.74	(0.67)	1.79	(0.61)	1.76	(0.65)
Civil liberties (0–3) (pro-)	1.95	(0.87)	1.88	(0.79)	1.92	(0.85)
Privatization (0–6) (pro-)	0.25	(0.85)	0.13	(0.59)	0.17	(0.78)

[a] SD = standard deviation.

CONCLUSION

The rise of the women's movement has left no political party, left or right, free of charges of gender bias and inequality. In the past, despite their commitment to cultural change, socialist parties worldwide have not been immune to male chauvinism (Whitehorn, 1992: 64, 250–1, 254–5). One way of reducing gender inequality has been to require parity in important party posts. Recent NDP constitutional amendments have ensured that this one obstacle to women's political equality has been significantly lessened. Although the gains in women's participation at other levels (for example, at conventions, as candidates, and as MPs) are less striking, there has been some progress in overall participation rates.

As to gender differences in attitudes among NDP activists, they appear to be less divisive than some other differences; the gender divide seems to be greatest on so-called targeted women's issues; the gender gap in attitudes seems to be lessening; and differences along gender lines within the NDP are smaller than those between members of the NDP and other parties. On the whole, a case can be made that the divisions and inequality along gender lines are lessening, at least in the NDP.

Lest we conclude on an excessively optimistic note, however, it may be useful to recall the replies of NDP delegates to the 1987 survey item asserting that 'overall, sexism is on the decline'. Men were more likely to agree, women to disagree (see Table 6.6).[36] Clearly, in some important respects, the gender gap has not closed.

NOTES

This chapter is a revised and expanded version of Whitehorn and Archer (1995). We wish to thank Leslie Kerr, Director of Organization, and Abby Pollenetsky, the former Director of Women's Organization of the federal NDP, and Ed Dale, the Director of Administration for the Ontario NDP, for providing data for portions of this paper. Comments on an early draft were gratefully received from Sylvia Bashevkin, Dawn Black, Sandra Burt, Wendy Hughes, Lynn Hunter, Joy Langan, Margaret Mitchell, and Dale Poel.

1 This was Thérèse Casgrain, elected leader of the provincial CCF in Quebec in 1951 (see Casgrain, 1972; Trofimenkoff, 1989). Alexa McDonough became the first female leader of the Nova Scotia NDP in 1980.

2 For example, two recent major election studies (Clarke et al., 1991; Johnson et al., 1992) do not list 'female', 'gender', 'sex', or 'women' in their indexes.

3 See various CIPO/Gallup reports available from the 1940s on, including no. 214 (October 1951); no. 230 (24 July 1953); no. 267 (March 1958); no. 282 (May 1961). We are indebted to the Carleton University data archives for help in

obtaining and processing these data. See also Bashevkin (1985b: 38, 40, 46, 48, 50, 51); Brodie and Vickers (1981: 334). Quebec may have been an exception, but the sample for the Quebec NDP is very small (Bashevkin, 1985b: 132–3).

4 See, for example, Canadian Institute for Public Opinion (CIPO; July 1974); Clarke et al. (1980: 88); Meisel (1975); Vickers and Brodie (1981: 62).

5 A number of commentators (Brackman et al., 1988: 223; Brodie, 1988: 174, 179; 1991: 20–3; Everitt, 1994; Gelb, 1989: 67–8) have suggested that one reason for this new gender gap in party support may be that women today are more pro-gressive than men on a number of social issues. One would expect this pattern of greater female support for the NDP to continue, if not increase, given the party's choice of women as federal leaders in 1989 and 1995. The long-term rea-sons for this shift in party support are beyond the scope of this chapter, but no doubt they include the rising education levels of women, the opening of more vocations to women, and the increasing numbers of women in the paid work force. It could also be argued that the party's commitment to sexual equality and feminism to some extent pre-dated the gender swing in membership and sup-port: 'it was the NDP, the party with the lowest proportion of women supporters in 1974, that developed the most aggressive and coherent campaign to attract women voters in 1979' (Brodie and Vickers, 1981: 334).

6 Correspondence from Ed Dale, Director of Administration of the Ontario NDP, 30 Sept. 1992.

7 Sangster (1989: 99, 101, 103,205) observes that this phenomenon could also be observed during the CCF era. Bashevkin and Holder (1985: 279) note that when a woman was president, it was often in a weak riding association. Nevertheless, Bashevkin (1991: 64, 68) has found that ghettoization of women is less evident in the NDP than in either the Liberal or the Conservative Party.

8 The corresponding federal riding executive rates for men were 39.6% in 1983 and 38.7% in 1987; for provincial riding executives, 52.7% in 1983 and 49.9% in 1987. Some caution is advised with respect to these data, however, since the many members of riding association executives who did not attend the conven-tions would not appear in the survey sample.

9 Sangster (1989: 247) states that 16% of delegates at the 1933 federal CCF conven-tion (21 of 131) were women (see also Roome, 1989: 106). Among those attend-ing was Grace MacInnis, the daughter of the first CCF leader, J.S. Woodsworth (Farrell, 1994; Lewis, 1993). In addition, Louise Lucas (Wright, 1965) and Agnes Macphail (Crowley, 1990; Pennington, 1990; Stewart and French, 1959), intro-duced two of the fourteen sections of the Regina Manifesto.

10 For a comparison with the Liberals and Conservatives, see Brodie (1988). According to Bashevkin and Holder (1985: 280), as early as 1982 the Ontario NDP approved affirmative action for the party's conventions and executive. An Ontario NDP provincial executive report (September 1992) on the provincial convention of that year noted that 52% of riding delegates (391 of 758) were women. However, these figures do not include union delegates. As of 1992, gender parity among NDP federal riding delegates was not required, but it was strongly encour-

aged. Certainly the features of mandatory parity at senior levels of the party set an important example for lower levels in the organizational hierarchy.

11 See White (1980, 1993). Given the decline in the economic sector of heavy industry and the rise in the service sector, one would expect the difference in rates of unionization of women and men should diminish. For an early episode in the history of women and unions, see the account (1983) by E. Sufrin, a long-time CCF–NDP activist.

12 A question on gender parity was posed at the 1983 convention, when the issue was debated and voted on (see Table 6.5).

13 When the names of the delegates at the 1977 and 1989 federal councils were being coded, it was not possible to determine the sex of two persons in 1977 and of 12 in 1989. Hence the data are based on a slightly smaller sample. While no detailed statistics are offered here on the gender breakdown of specialized committees of the federal council, the party has come close to achieving gender parity on these bodies as well (McLaughlin, 1992: 48; correspondence and data from Dawn Black to Whitehorn, 16 Nov. 1992). For data on the Ontario NDP provincial council, see also Bashevkin (1985b: 66; 1989: 457; 1991: 68); for partial data on other provincial sections, see Kornberg et al. (1979).

14 Although the final vote for Audrey McLaughlin in 1989 was the lowest to that date for a federal NDP leader, and the somewhat unorthodox 1995 convention saw an even lower vote for Alexa McDonough (see Chapter 13), it should be noted that there has been a steady decline in support for the winner in NDP leadership races. This is partly explained by the increase in the number of candidates, although one suspects another reason may well be the lower esteem in which political leaders are held today. In 1996, the NDP had three elected female leaders: Alexa McDonough at the federal level, Pam Barrett in Alberta, and Elizabeth Weir in New Brunswick. However, like Thérèse Casgrain in Quebec several decades ago, none of them had much chance of forming the government.

15 For historical data on the participation of women as candidates for Parliament and their success see Bashevkin (1985b: 72, 73); Brodie (1991); Brodie and Vickers (1981: 324); Gotell and Brodie (1991); Sharpe (1994: 226). For data on the Ontario NDP see Bashevkin (1985b: 73; 1991: 69); Bashevkin and Holder (1985: 283–4); Brodie (1991: 38). For data on Saskatchewan see Carbert (1997).

16 Of course many of the party's female candidates ran in regions where it had little electoral strength, such as Quebec (Brodie and Vickers, 1981: 329; Sangster, 1989: 208); in short, they were often sacrificial lambs.

17 Ten CCF–NDP women have won a total of 17 seats in general elections over seven decades: Gladys Strum, Grace MacInnis, Pauline Jewett, Margaret Mitchell, Lynn McDonald, Marion Dewar, Audrey McLaughlin, Dawn Black, Lynn Hunter, and Joy Langan. NDP provincial election victories in Ontario in 1990 and in Saskatchewan and British Columbia in 1991 saw record numbers of women elected and appointed to cabinets.

18 In 1991 the Royal Commission on Electoral Reform and Party Financing rec-
    ommended that parties receive financial compensation for recruiting female can-
    didates and having them elected. As yet the federal government has not acted on
    that recommendation.

19 The 1983 data and much of the commentary in this section are based on
    Whitehorn (1988; 1992). The 1987 data come from the delegate survey intro-
    duced in Chapter 3. For an earlier demographic profile of women in parties see
    Kornberg et al. (1979).

20 Since income was listed as family income only, no analysis is offered here on the
    gender differences in income.

21 Unless otherwise indicated, the first percentage given in each case is for 1983 and
    the second for 1987. The sample size in 1983 was 395; in 1987, 738 (see Table 6.2).

22 Regrettably, the index of Archer's (1990) study of unions and the NDP does not
    list 'female', 'gender', 'sex', or 'women'. However, Bashevkin (1985b: 48) does
    provide a gender breakdown among unionists supporting the NDP.

23 This finding is at variance with earlier observations by Brodie (1988: 177).

24 Note that very few people replied in the affirmative on this question, especially
    in the 1983 survey. See also Kornberg et al. (1979: 207).

25 The questions selected by political scientists for use in surveys are at times as inter-
    esting as the responses. For example, it is striking that social-science research drawn
    from the era when there were few female university professors paid very little
    attention to the gender question. Similarly, there were virtually no questions relat-
    ing to women's issues in the earliest surveys (1971 and 1979) of NDP delegates.

26 Because of changes in the research instruments, caution is required in comparing
    the delegates' responses over time. The 1983 survey asked respondents to reply to
    the policy statements with 'agree', 'disagree', or 'no opinion'. That format permit-
    ted more inter-party comparison but was less satisfactory for measuring the dis-
    tribution of opinions on any single item. Accordingly, in 1987, a five-point Likert
    scale was employed with the following responses: 'strongly agree', 'agree', 'uncer-
    tain', 'disagree', 'strongly disagree'. Clearly the 'uncertain' and 'no opinion' cate-
    gories are not fully equivalent, nor was the sequencing of response items the same.

27 Interestingly, women's election success rate has not been as high as men's (Brodie,
    1985b: 124; 1991, 7; Brodie and Vickers, 1981: 325; Sharpe, 1994: 226; Young,
    1991: 83). The reasons offered by commentators include lower winnability of
    ridings selected, lack of income and other resources, family duties, cultural bias
    (McLaughlin, 1992), and career background of the candidates.

28 Bashevkin (1985b: 87–9) reports that the responses of members of the Ontario
    NDP to a similar question were generally supportive of affirmative action.

29 Even in the CCF era, women were active on the issue of birth control (Farrell,
    1994; Lewis, 1993; Melnyk, 1989: 80; Sangster, 1989). As early as 1967 a resolu-
    tion was passed by an NDP convention favouring the legalization of abortion
    (Scotton, 1977).

30 Some caution is required in making comparisons because the coding of the questionnaires for the Liberal and Conservative surveys was different from that for the NDP study.

31 The question was worded differently in the NDP survey.

32 Significantly, 21.3% in 1987 said they were undecided.

33 For comparison, a similar analysis of areas of issue disagreement within the Conservative Party can be found in Perlin (1980: 154–5).

34 Some caution should be exercised with this assertion, since degree of controversy is also a function of the statements that are proposed.

35 The average inter-party score for Liberal/NDP differences was 26.3, for PC/NDP differences 42.6 (see Table 3.1), while the average intra-party difference for male and female members of the NDP was only 4.8.

36 Among men 48.3% agreed, 24.9% were uncertain, and 26.8% disagreed. In contrast, among women 45.3% disagreed, 19.5% were uncertain, and 35.2% agreed.

CHAPTER
7

The Age Gap

In virtually all parties, most of the active members are middle-aged or older (see Tables 2.2 and 7.2). Because they are numerically dominant, these individuals tend not to be organized as a distinct interest group along age lines. On the other hand, most parties do make provisions to reduce the age imbalance and facilitate the representation of young people at their conventions. Young people can constitute an important lobby within the party, and the youth caucus may become one of its key interest groups.

This chapter examines the generational divide in the NDP. Beginning with an overview of the CCF–NDP youth wing, it will explore the impact of age on ideological positions, attitudes towards public policies, and leadership preferences, as well as demographic changes over time in the age composition of NDP conventions. Finally, we will examine whether the age gap constitutes a serious division within the party.

YOUTH IN THE CCF–NDP

The youth wing of the federal NDP is called the New Democratic Youth of Canada (NDYC). The party has had a youth organization since its founding in 1961. Like other aspects of the NDP's structure and organization, the youth section was transferred intact from the CCF. Until very recently (see Goldstein, 1996), little was known about the history of the NDP's youth wing. In general, the party has not catalogued in depth the development of its youth section. However, it is possible to trace several key developments in its history and to assess, at least in part, its role in and impact on the party.

The youth movement began in the CCF with the creation of the Co-operative Commonwealth Youth Movement (CCYM) at the national convention of 1934, only two years after the party's founding (Goldstein, 1996: 10; McNaught, 1959: 282; Young, 1969: 261). A microcosm of the CCF, the CCYM had a federated structure, with most of its resources and activities focused on the provincial youth sections. As was the case with the party at large, the provincial youth sections varied in their organizational strength. The largest youth section was in Saskatchewan, which by the mid-1940s boasted more than two-thirds of all CCYM members across the country (McHenry, 1950: 97). The success of the 'youth rally', as it was popularly known, in Saskatchewan was a product of the provincial party's considerable efforts at developing the youth wing; it probably also reflected the fact that Tommy Douglas had been the CCYM's first national president. But Saskatchewan was the exception. Although there were periods of activity within the youth sections in other provinces, most notably in Ontario in the mid-1930s (see Caplan, 1973: 69), on the whole these experiences were sporadic, reflecting the fortuitous presence of strong individuals as leaders rather than sustained grassroots organizational support. As Leo Zakuta (1964: 115) has noted, in the 1930s the CCYM was perhaps most valuable as a recruiting ground for future leaders, rather than as a sustained organizational structure.

In addition to the CCYM, in 1946 the party organized a group of university students and young academics called the Co-operative Commonwealth University Federation (CCUF), in part as a replacement for the League for Social Reconstruction, which had ceased to exist in 1942; according to Goldstein (1996: 18), one of the CCUF's purposes was to provide research for the party. It lasted into the 1950s, when—like the CCYM itself—it was severely weakened by the pressures of the Cold War.

Although the CCYM has been described as representing little more than 'a faithful support group for the senior party' (Wiseman, 1983: 139), from time to time it attracted attention for its militancy and for its conflicts with party elders. Walter Young (1969: 261) has suggested that the CCYM, almost from its inception, indicated its radical posture within the party by adopting 'revolt' as its watchword, and by its members' insistence on addressing one another as 'comrade'. In addition, throughout the party's history, members of the youth movement have been the most likely to co-operate, or at least associate, with members or suspected members of revolutionary communist organizations. As early as 1935 the CCYM had affiliations with the League Against War and Fascism, a communist front organization (McHenry, 1950: 119). The CCF leadership, fearing that communists would begin to infiltrate the party, passed a resolution at the National Council prohibiting CCF organizations from entering into alliances with other political parties or groups (Lewis, 1981).

This prohibition has surfaced from time to time in the CCF–NDP's disciplining of youth members. For example, in the 1950s the BC youth section, known as the Socialist Fellowship, expelled a young radical named Rod Young (see Lewis, 1981: 385–7). And in 1963 ten members of the Ontario New Democratic Youth (OYND) were expelled from the party for having joined a Trotskyist organization (Goldstein, 1996: 23; Morley, 1984: 81). Four years later, at a meeting of the OYND executive, the political activities of sixty-eight OYND members were discussed, resulting in a recommendation to expel forty-seven of them for their membership in a Trotskyist organization called the League for Socialist Action (Morley, 1984: 207–10; O'Toole, 1977). However, because the loss of so many members would have decimated the OYND, the provincial council limited the expulsions to the twelve members thought to be the key Trotskyists (Morley, 1984: 210). In other cases the main party has responded to such revolutionary communist penetration by simply allowing the youth wing to wither for a time before permitting its resurrection.

One of the most famous internal challenges to the party's organization, ideology, and leadership emerged in the late 1960s and early 1970s in the form of the Waffle movement (see Brodie, 1985; Brodie and Jenson, 1988; Cross, 1974; Goldstein, 1996; Hackett, 1979, 1980; J. Laxer, 1996; R. Laxer, 1973; Lewis, 1981; Morton, 1986; Wiseman, 1983). Composed of academics, students, and, in general, younger party members (see Table 7.1), the Waffle was not officially tied directly to the NDYC. However, as Hackett (1980) points out, the Waffle drew heavily on the youth movement (see Table 7.1). Given that half the Waffle supporters at the 1971 leadership convention were under 30, and the NDYC drew all its members from the younger segment (under 26) of the same age group, the two groups shared a natural affinity and many of the same aspirations (but see Goldstein, 1996: 25). The Waffle heralded its appearance with the 1969 publication of a manifesto entitled 'For an Independent Socialist Canada'. Its major goals were to stress extra-parliamentary activity, to increase the party's ideological militancy on issues relating to socialism and economic nationalism, to

Table 7.1
Age of Delegates, Waffle and Other Voters, 1971

Age	Waffle %	Other[a] %
16–20 years	11.2	0.9
21–30 years	38.8	11.7
31–40 years	16.1	28.6
41–50 years	16.6	26.6
51–60 years	10.4	19.3
Over 60 years	5.8	10.7
Did not reveal age	1.2	2.4
N	(260)	(462)

[a] Excludes those who did not identify themselves as either pro- or non-Waffle.
SOURCE: Hackett (1980: 20 [Table 3]).

lessen Canada's dependency on the United States, and to re-evaluate the party's relations with labour unions, particularly the less radical multinational unions (Brodie, 1985: 210).

The Waffle achieved high visibility and some influence at the party's 1969 convention, and at the 1971 leadership convention it scored a dramatic symbolic success when James Laxer, its candidate for the party leadership, finished a surprisingly strong second to the veteran David Lewis. Soon, however, the party hierarchy began to question the Waffle's organizational activities and its highly critical voice within the party. The showdown occurred at the Ontario NDP's provincial council meeting in June 1972 (Morley, 1984: 218–19; Morton, 1986: 131–5). While affirming the general right of party members to form caucuses to influence party policies, as the Waffle had done, the provincial council demanded the formal disbanding of the Waffle on the grounds that it constituted a rival organization. Faced with this ultimatum, the Ontario Waffle held its last meeting within the NDP in August 1972, by which time the group had already fractured. Some left to form a new party, the Movement for an Independent Socialist Canada, while others grudgingly acceded to the decision of the provincial council and eventually returned to the party, in some cases to lead a new wave of radicalism (Morton, 1986: 135). The dismantling of the Ontario Waffle precipitated the group's collapse elsewhere in the country (see Wiseman, 1983: 138–9). The legacy of the Waffle continues to generate dispute. Some suggest that its 'purge' cost the party a number of potential future leaders and youth members with radical and sometimes innovative ideas (Brodie, 1985; Brodie and Jenson, 1988; Laxer, 1996). Others view the end of the Waffle as a boon for the party, citing the unwillingness of Waffle leaders to engage in constructive dialogue concerning the party's goals, strategies, and tactics (Morton, 1986: 135).

THE YOUTH MOVEMENT: ORGANIZATION AND STRUCTURE

The structure of the youth movement within the NDP is similar to that of the federal party. The federal organization, the NDYC, serves as a liaison for the various provincial sections, each of which is relatively autonomous. Thus most of the organizational and recruiting work of the youth movement takes place within the provincial and territorial units. Although the NDYC has the authority to charter a federal youth chapter in a province, it would do so only in the absence of a provincial youth organization. Furthermore, to date the party has provided relatively modest infrastructural support for the maintenance of a national youth organization. The NDYC has no permanent staff, and did not appoint a youth outreach officer to work out of the leader's office until January 1993.[1] In some provinces, particularly British

Columbia, the youth section is relatively well-organized and developed, and has included a paid staffer responsible for youth matters.

According to its constitution, the purpose of the NDYC is to

> provide a voice for New Democratic youth at the federal level through: (a) facilitating cooperation between provincial youth sections; (b) educating youth in the principles of co-operative socialism in a democratic society; (c) using the democratic process to decide on policy; (d) constructive criticism of the federal New Democratic Party's policies, programs, and/or organization; and (e) to encourage links with other young social democrats through the IUSY (International Union of Socialist Youth).

Thus, like the youth wings of the Liberal and Conservative parties, the NDYC sees its main purposes as educational and representative (Perlin et al., 1988: 190–2). To these, of course, may be added the important function of recruiting and training future activists and leaders for the parent party (1995 federal leadership candidate Svend Robinson is a notable example). The confluence of purposes emphasizing education, representation, and recruitment has ensured that much of the organization of the youth movement within the NDP has revolved around political clubs on university and college campuses across the country.

On the matter of representation of the youth wing, the NDP differs significantly from both the Liberals and the Conservatives. The Liberal Party defines a youth member as someone 25 years of age or under who belongs to a constituency organization or campus club. At the Liberal leadership convention in 1984, youth clubs were entitled to a number equivalent to 10% of constituency delegates; in addition, two of seven constituency delegate positions were reserved for youth delegates; and *ex officio* delegate status was provided for all members of the Commission of Young Liberals of Canada (Perlin et al., 1988: 191). In 1986 the Liberals dropped the 10% limit for campus clubs, providing instead four delegate spots for each campus club, while limiting each post-secondary campus to one Liberal Party club (Wearing, 1988: 203). In the Conservative Party, which usually draws most of its support from older voters, a youth member is someone under 30. At the 1983 convention, two of six constituency delegates were youth, three delegates were awarded to each Tory campus club, ten delegate positions were allocated to the National Youth Executive, and 20% of all at-large delegates were required to be youth (Perlin et al. 1988: 191–2).

As a result of these rules for youth representation, delegates under 30 made up 40% of the Conservative convention in 1983, 31% of the Liberal convention in 1984, and 36% of the Liberal convention in 1990 (Perlin et al., 1988: 192; Perlin, 1991: 61–2). In both parties, the resourceful use of campus club organizations by the major leadership candidates has proven to be contentious. The heights of resourcefulness appears to have been reached by the Conservatives at the 1983 leadership convention, when Quebec had 168 campus delegates to only 300 non-youth constituency delegates, and Newfoundland had 63 campus delegates but only 28 non-youth constituency delegates (Wearing, 1988: 203).

The large numbers of delegate positions awarded to their youth sections have raised a number of representational issues for the Liberals and Conservatives. As Perlin (1991: 62) notes, over-representation of the young means under-representation for the older and more experienced delegates within the party. This representational imbalance can at times shift the balance of power in crucial ways. During an era of fiscal restraint and cutbacks, for example, the choice between protecting programs to assist youth employment and preserving a universal pension program for the elderly can reveal a serious generational divide. A second representational concern is the degree to which young party activists themselves actually constitute a representative cross-section of young Canadians. More specifically, if youth delegates differ from the youth population as a whole in their socio-demographic attributes and their social and political attitudes, their increased numbers at conventions will not necessarily result in a more representative presence for youth. Concluding their study of youth activists in the Liberal and Conservative parties, Perlin and his colleagues (1988: 200–1) offer this warning:

> As they function at present, the youth organizations seem likely to produce a corps of future party leaders expert in the techniques of political manipulation but inexperienced in the substantive issues that face government. In short, not only do they fail as vehicles for the articulation of the issue concerns of young people, but they also fail as vehicles for the production of an informed, policy-concerned elite within the parties.

The NDP has been far more cautious than the Liberals and Conservatives in providing for youth representation at national party conventions. Given the radical proclivities of its youth wings in the past, this is a pattern not undesirable to senior party officials. However, it owes more to the general representational principles of NDP conventions than to a deliberate intention to limit the number of youth delegates. As we saw in Chapter 1, NDP convention delegates represent six categories: constituency associations, affiliated organizations, central labour, caucus, federal council, and the youth organization (NDYC). All members of caucus and the federal council are delegates, as are officials who hold key positions within central labour organizations (see Archer, 1990; Whitehorn, 1992). Most of these are middle-aged or older. The numbers of delegates from constituency associations, affiliated unions, and the NDYC are based on the size of each organization's membership. In the early 1990s, each federal constituency was allowed one delegate for 50 members or less, one for each additional 50 members up to a total of 200 members, and one for each additional 100 members or major fraction thereof (NDP Constitution, 1991:VI. 2). Affiliated locals were permitted one delegate for the first 1,000 members or less and one for each additional 1,000 members or major fraction thereof (VI. 4). NDYC organizations followed the same rules as constituency associations (VI. 7. l). Thus the NDP provides greater convention representation to those affiliated unions, constituency associations, and youth organizations with larger memberships. Because it sets earlier cut-off dates for membership and requires a relatively large number of members for each additional delegate allocated, the NDP has not experienced the problem of 'instant' members to the degree that the Liberal and Conservative parties have, especially in leadership contests (Archer, 1991a; see also Chapter 11).

Membership in the NDYC is restricted to people 25 years of age or younger (NDYC Constitution, IV. l). Together, this relatively low cut-off age and the large membership requirements for each delegate position have meant that representation of the NDYC at federal NDP conventions has been very limited: delegates from the NDYC comprised only 1.0% of total delegates in 1983, 2.7% in 1987, and 2.3% at the leadership convention in 1989 (Whitehorn, 1992; Whitehorn and Archer, 1994). Of course, youth members may also seek to attend conventions through other delegate categories (e.g., unions or constituency associations, provided they are members). Not surprisingly, however, relatively few have succeeded in doing so. For example, at the 1987 and 1989 NDP conventions delegates under 30 years of age were far less likely to belong to a union (27.7% in 1987, 24.4% in 1989) than were delegates aged 30 to 59 (52.5% and 43.9%). Furthermore, it is reasonable to assume that many union officials and party activists would regard attendance at the convention as a key responsibility earned only after years of service, and would not readily extend it to the newest, youngest, and least affluent members of the group. Indeed, it was recognition of the natural bias against selecting younger constituency members as delegates that led the Liberal and Conservative parties to provide youth quotas for each constituency. The absence of similar quotas in the NDP has contributed to the under-representation of youth members at its federal conventions. Thus, for example, the percentage of NDP delegates under 30 has been consistently low—and decreasing—in the time periods sampled (21.8% in 1979, 17.4% in 1983, 17.8% in 1987, 13.4% in 1989; see also Whitehorn, 1992: 108). Since approximately one-third of the Canadian population today is between 15 and 29 years of age (McDaniel, 1986; Sauvé, 1990; Wearing, 1988: 204), the New Democratic Party can be seen as significantly under-representing this group among its convention delegates[2]—perhaps even alienating the young people it needs if it is to be true to its name.

On the other hand, in addition to representation at conventions, the NDYC has several other avenues of representation within the party's policy-making bodies. In the early 1990s, the President of the NDYC was one of the 18 officers of the NDP (Constitution, VII. 1.4). The federal council included the NDYC president, secretary treasurer, both associate presidents, and one member from each provincial/territorial youth section (VIII. l.g). In addition, the president of the NDYC sat on the party's executive. Thus the youth wing is integrated into the NDP as one of its primary sections. This structure increases the probability that the interests and concerns of the NDYC will be brought to bear in the party's policy-making. However, those interests can also be counterbalanced by the presence of other sections at the pinnacle of the party hierarchy.

AGE AND POLICY ATTITUDES

The rest of this chapter will examine the impact of the age cleavage on the NDP by examining delegates to the 1987 and 1989 party conventions. The preceding chapters have suggested a number of hypotheses that can be tested empirically. First, it is possible that youth activists attending NDP conventions are not typical of young Canadians in general, particularly with regard to educational attainment. Second, incidents such as the Waffle episode, as well as the general literature on youth politics, suggest that young New Democrats will tend to situate themselves further to the left, and to be more critical of the party's stance on issues, than others. Third, the relatively small numbers of youth delegates, and the influence that the various caucuses have on all delegates, including youth, suggest that the NDYC may find it difficult to mobilize youth delegates to speak with one voice over a wide range of areas; youth delegates may be easily persuaded to unite when their position within the party is being debated, but on other policy matters their positions and support may be more diffuse (regarding Liberal and Conservative youth, see Perlin et al., 1988: 201). Given the very small number of convention delegates registered as NDYC delegates, the following statistical analysis defines youth delegates as those under 30 years of age.[3]

The expectations for delegates at the other end of the age continuum are less certain. We can test the common hypothesis that aging, even in a social-democratic party, is associated with increasing conservatism. But it must also be recognized that older delegates (those 60 years and over) do not possess any special intra-party status or formal organizational structure that can be used to represent the interests and issues of particular importance to them. Thus this group may display even greater variation in its policy positions and behaviour.

We begin by examining the demographic characteristics of NDP delegates, broken down by age. The most notable age variation according to province or region of residence was evident among delegates from Saskatchewan. More than one-quarter of all delegates aged 60 years or over at both the 1987 policy convention in Montreal and the 1989 leadership and policy convention in Winnipeg came from Saskatchewan (see Table 7.2). Much smaller percentages of delegates under 30 came from Saskatchewan, ranging from a low of 7.7% in 1987 to 12.3% in 1989. The disproportion-

Table 7.2
Selected Demographic Characteristics by Age, 1987, 1989

	1987 Age			1989 Age		
	<30 %	30–59 %	60+ %	<30 %	30–59 %	60+ %
Province of residence						
British Columbia	15.4	12.8	11.2	10.9	19.3	24.6
Alberta	5.4	6.1	7.9	12.3	10.9	8.9
Saskatchewan	7.7	11.8	25.8	12.3	14.3	26.2
Manitoba	6.9	6.5	4.5	7.2	10.3	9.9
Ontario	47.7	45.4	41.6	45.7	34.7	22.5
Quebec	9.2	8.4	2.2	2.9	1.9	2.6
Atlantic provinces	4.6	7.9	6.7	8.0	5.9	5.2
Northern territories	3.1	1.2	0.0	0.7	2.7	0.0
Sex						
Male	76.2	65.9	60.7	65.2	63.5	60.2
Female	23.8	34.1	39.3	34.8	36.5	39.8
Education						
High school or less	10.8	21.9	38.2	13.0	16.3	38.7
College	9.2	14.5	10.1	8.7	13.6	10.5
University	80.0	63.7	51.7	78.3	70.1	50.8
Total convention delegates						
	17.8	70.1	12.2	13.4	67.9	18.6
N[a]	(130)	(513)	(89)	(138)	(698)	(191)

NOTE: For 1983 age distribution see Table 2.2.
[a] Ns are approximate, and can change marginally for each question with changes in the numbers of missing responses.

ate number of older delegates coming from Saskatchewan likely reflects the fact that it was the first province to elect a CCF government (in 1944), and has had more CCF–NDP governments than any other. In addition, Saskatchewan has experienced a continuing out-migration, particularly of younger people. The demographic fact that the strength of the NDP in Saskatchewan is built on a foundation of increasingly older party activists is of continuing concern to party strategists.

At the 1987 convention delegates from British Columbia were some-what more likely to be under 30 and somewhat less likely to be over 60 than delegates in general, as were delegates from Ontario, although these trends were not very pronounced. More striking was the age distribution of Quebec delegates. The Montreal convention was the first ever held by the federal NDP in that province, and it represented an important symbolic overture to Quebeckers. Although this overture did have some success in attracting Quebec delegates to the convention, the greatest success was among the younger and middle-aged groups. However, by the time of the 1989 convention in Winnipeg, the attendance of Quebec delegates had receded to more typical levels—low in every age category.

The regional distribution of delegates in the different age groups changed in some respects from the 1987 policy convention to the 1989 leadership convention. The most stable age pattern was seen among dele-gates from Saskatchewan, which continued to have a large portion of those 60 and over in 1989. However, a substantial change occurred in the pro-portions of delegates from the two other large sections of the party, Ontario and British Columbia. Between 1987 and 1989 BC lost some of its share of the youngest delegates (15.4% to 10.9%), but gained substantially among the middle-aged (12.8% to 19.3%) and oldest groups (11.2% to 24.6%). In contrast, Ontario lost only a small proportion of young delegates (47.7% versus 45.7%), but its proportions of middle-aged (45.4% to 34.7%) and older delegates (41.6% to 22.5%) dropped significantly. The differences between policy and leadership conventions aside, one reason for this vari-ation was the smaller size of the subsamples of the data set (in 1989 only 13.4% of delegates were under 30, compared with 17.8% in 1987, and only 18.6% were 60 years and older; see also Whitehorn and Archer, 1994). In addition, delegate attendance by region varies considerably depending on the location of each convention (see Chapters 2 and 5), and this variation may have a particular effect on older delegates. Finally, British Columbians had two 'favourite son' candidates in the 1989 leadership race, Dave Barrett and Ian Waddell, and since Barrett had served as the province's premier almost twenty years before, he may well have had a particular appeal for older New Democrats from BC (see Chapter 12).

Table 7.2 also shows the gender composition of the various age groups at convention. As we saw in Chapter 6, men continue to outnumber women at NDP conventions. Somewhat surprisingly, the gender imbalance was even greater among the two younger age groups than among those 60 and over. In 1987 more than three-quarters (76.2%) of the under-30 delegates were men, compared with approximately two-thirds (65.9%) of the middle-aged and only three-fifths (60.7%) of older delegates. Although the gender gap between the youngest and oldest groups had narrowed by 1989, women remained more under-represented among the youngest delegates. The fact that younger women are more likely to be combining a career and primary child-rearing duties may make convention attendance more difficult for them (see, for example, Kay et al., 1987).

The most striking skew in the data on young delegates was evident in their levels of formal education. Previous studies of activists in the Liberal and Conservative parties at the federal level (Perlin et al., 1988), of provincial party activists in British Columbia (Blake et al., 1991: 24–9), and of all major parties at the federal level (Kornberg et al., 1979; Lele et al., 1979: 80) have demonstrated that activists tend to represent a socio-economic and educational élite. The survey data on educational attainment of NDP activists confirms at least the latter part of that finding, particularly among the younger delegates. About four-fifths of delegates under 30 at both the 1987 and 1989 NDP conventions had received at least some university education (see Chapter 2), compared with approximately two-thirds of the middle-aged group (63.7% in 1987, 70.1% in 1989) and about one-half of those aged 60 years and older (51.7% in 1987, 50.8% in 1989). It seems ironic that while the federal NDP has based its recent election campaigns on an appeal to 'ordinary Canadians', its own activists and leaders are anything but 'ordinary' when it comes to their educational qualifications (see also Whitehorn, 1992). This fact is particularly evident among the youngest party activists, and may explain why they might find it easier to relate to questions of the financing of post-secondary education than to other issues, such as the chronic un- or under-employment that plagues so many young people today.

Table 7.3 shows the types of delegate credentials held by delegates in the various age groups, as well as the number of previous conventions attended. In all age groups, the largest proportion of delegates came from constituency associations. Given that union delegates tend to be retired by age 65, it is not surprising that most delegates 60 or older (85.1% in 1987, 92.4% in 1989) came from constituency associations. Among the delegates under 30, only a minority were selected as representatives of the NDYC (16.5% in 1987, 27.8% in 1989). Thus, even among the youngest delegates, individuals are more likely to have an institutional tie to the constituency association than to the youth movement. This fact limits the ability of the NDYC to mobilize younger delegates at convention.

Whereas the Liberal and Conservative parties both engage in mass recruitment prior to leadership conventions, NDP conventions are marked by a very high degree of stability and consistency among delegates. As one would expect, this is particularly true for older delegates. For example, when asked whether they had attended a federal convention before, almost nine in ten delegates (88.8%) 60 and older in 1987 said that they had. Among those aged 30 to 59, more than six in ten (63.0%) said they had previously attended a convention. And, interestingly, the percentage decreased only marginally, to 51.2%, among those under 30 years of age. When delegates were asked whether they had previously attended a provincial convention, more than three-quarters of each age group said they had, with a peak of 92.0% for those 60 and older.

Table 7.3

Delegate Type and Convention Experience by Age, 1987, 1989

| | 1987 | | | 1989 | | |
| | Age | | | Age | | |
	<30 %	30–59 %	60+ %	<30 %	30–59 %	60+ %
Delegate type[a]						
Constituency	69.3	66.0	85.1	64.7	79.1	91.9
Affiliated union	6.3	16.2	8.0	4.5	9.3	2.3
ND Youth	16.5	0.8	0.0	27.8	0.0	0.6
Convention experience						
Attended federal convention before?						
(YES)	51.2	63.0	88.8	29.0	50.7	62.3
Number of previous federal conventions						
1–5	100.0	84.5	64.9	97.4	87.1	76.6
6–10	0.0	13.9	26.0	2.6	11.4	16.8
11+	0.0	1.6	9.1	0.0	1.5	6.5
Attended provincial convention before?						
(YES)	76.2	81.7	92.0	64.5	80.0	89.2
Number of previous provincial conventions						
1–5	88.8	67.0	39.0	83.1	61.6	49.3
6–10	10.2	23.1	37.7	16.9	26.1	22.7
11+	1.0	10.0	23.4	0.0	12.4	28.0
N[b]	(130)	(513)	(89)	(138)	(693)	(186)

[a] Percentages of delegates from federal council, central labour, and caucus excluded because of small sample sizes.
[b] Ns are approximate, and can change marginally for each question with changes in the numbers of missing responses.

Furthermore, many delegates, particularly in the older age group, had attended several previous conventions. For example, almost a quarter of delegates 60 and older in 1987 had attended 11 or more provincial conventions, and almost one in ten had attended more than 11 federal conventions. Even among the youngest age group in 1987, more than one-tenth had attended more than five provincial conventions. The data from the 1989 leadership convention also indicate striking levels of prior convention activity. Thus most delegates, even in the youngest age group, had considerable previous convention experience.

Central to the generational-divide hypothesis is the question of the impact of age on the political attitudes and orientations of convention delegates. If there are attitudinal differences among the age groups, should we expect the various age groups, especially youth and the elderly, to act as unified voting blocs within the party? In short, to what degree are NDP convention delegates motivated to act on the basis of their age?

To begin answering these questions, data on delegates' overall ideological and left–right ordering were examined (Table 7.4). Although there are some age-related differences in left–right placement, the various age groupings tend to be characterized more by consistency than by difference. For example, delegates in all age groups placed themselves further to the left than they placed the federal NDP. Much as Hackett (1980) found at the 1971 convention, the young NDP delegates were somewhat more likely to place themselves further to the left than their older counterparts (mean scores for self-placement were 2.6, 2.7, and 2.8 for the under-30, 30 to 59, and 60-and-over groups in 1987, and 2.2, 2.6 and 2.5 for the same groups in 1989). However, the younger delegates also tended to place all the political parties, including the Liberals and Conservatives, somewhat further to the left than did older delegates, although the differences were not pronounced. When rating Canadians or Americans in general, the differences largely disappeared.

Delegates to the 1989 convention were also asked to rate the leadership candidates on the seven-point left–right scale. In keeping with their tendency to score in a more polarized manner, younger delegates placed former BC Premier Dave Barrett further to the right than other delegates (4.0), while the oldest delegates placed him further to the left (3.3). This pattern was repeated for Howard McCurdy, placed at 3.8 by delegates under 30 and at 3.4 by delegates over 60. By contrast, younger respondents placed McLaughlin further to the left than did the oldest delegates. This pattern continued for Steven Langdon, Ian Waddell, Simon de Jong, and Roger Lagassé. Overall, the younger respondents placed McLaughlin considerably further to the left than Barrett (3.1 versus 4.0). Perhaps this perception was a factor in her appeal to youth.

Table 7.4

Left–Right Images and Ideological Self-description by Age, 1987 and 1989

	1987 Age			1989 Age		
	<30 %	30–59 %	60+ %	<30 %	30–59 %	60+ %
Left–right image (mean scores, seven-point scale)						
Self	2.6	2.7	2.8	2.2	2.6	2.5
Federal NDP	3.3	3.4	3.5	3.3	3.7	3.7
Provincial NDP	3.5	3.5	3.6	3.5	3.7	3.5
Dave Barrett				4.0	3.8	3.3
Simon de Jong				3.5	3.7	3.7
Roger Lagassé				2.9	3.5	3.7
Steven Langdon				2.7	2.9	3.2
Howard McCurdy				3.8	3.7	3.4
Audrey McLaughlin				3.1	3.4	3.3
Ian Waddell				3.2	3.2	3.4
Ideological self-description (%)						
Social democrat	39.1	51.5	56.3	N.A.		
Socialist	31.3	27.1	32.2			
Other	29.7	21.4	11.5			
N[a]	(130)	(513)	(89)	(134)	(652)	(165)

[a] Ns are approximate, and can change marginally for each question with changes in numbers of missing responses.
N.A.: not available.

We turn now to delegates' ideological self-description. Delegates from all age groups were most likely to describe themselves as social democrats, with a substantial percentage also describing themselves as socialists. The oldest age group were more likely to describe themselves as social democrats (56.3%) compared with 39.1% among those under 30. Interestingly, no clear pattern of age differentiation emerged for the 'socialist' label. This suggests that in 1989 the younger delegates were not dramatically more radical than their older counterparts.

The impact of age on political attitudes and orientations can extend beyond generalized ideological labels, such as 'socialist' or 'social democrat', or the summary ideological positioning represented by a left–right scale. In particular, if age does have an impact at party conventions, it should be evident in age-specific positions on policy issues or voting patterns in selecting a party leader. To assess the impact of age on policy, a variety of questions were asked about delegates' issue positions. For each question, respondents were scored on a five-point Likert index ranging from 'strongly agree' to 'strongly disagree'. Table 7.5 shows delegates' attitudes towards a number of issues—unions, cultural conservatism, gender, selected social issues, and the NDP in society—broken down by age.

Table 7.5

Selected Political Attitudes by Age, 1987

Issue Area/Statement/Attitude	<30	Age 30–59	60+
Unions			
Trade unions have too much influence in the NDP (agree)[a]	24.8	12.0	14.9
An NDP government should never interfere with free collective bargaining (agree)	39.5	40.3	53.5
The right to strike should never be restricted (agree)	46.5	49.0	56.3
Cultural conservatism			
Capital punishment should be reintroduced (agree)	3.8	5.7	6.8
People who are homosexuals should be permitted to teach school (agree)	88.5	85.1	71.6
The possession of marijuana should be legalized (agree)	61.5	52.1	36.4
Our society has become too permissive (agree)	7.8	16.7	33.7
Family and community disintegration are responsible for many social ills (agree)	54.7	48.7	69.8
The courts have been too lenient in handing out penalities to criminals (agree)	32.3	32.4	40.7
Crime is a growing problem in our society (agree)	53.9	58.0	67.8
Too many schools waste time and money on fads and frills (agree)	12.5	20.8	30.6
Children should show more respect towards their parents (agree)	29.6	42.7	56.1
Today's youth too often expect easy and high-paying jobs (disagree)	72.3	60.2	50.0
People are not willing to work hard enough (agree)	7.0	7.1	9.4
Pornography should be banned (agree)	36.7	45.3	62.4
Gender			
50 per cent of the federal council should be composed of women (agree)	76.0	61.7	54.0
The NDP should ensure that a significant percentage of its candidates and party officers are women (agree)	86.2	83.2	75.0
Other social issues			
Certain restrictions on civil rights would be acceptable if they would help police reduce crime (agree)	11.8	17.1	37.9
Compulsory retirement at age 65 should cease (agree)	53.1	49.0	43.2
We should be less concerned with the quantity of income and pay more attention to the quality of life (agree)	81.6	76.4	87.2
It is harder for young people to get a job today (agree)	90.6	91.3	88.8

Table 7.5 continued

Issue Area/Statement/Attitude	Age		
	<30	30–59	60+
The NDP in society			
The NDP is a socialist party (agree)	70.9	77.6	87.2
The NDP should seek to present a more moderate image to the general public (disagree)	66.7	61.7	73.8
The NDP should become more of a social movement and less of a political party (disagree)	55.1	75.0	78.2
The NDP should move more clearly to the left (agree)	37.0	39.3	48.2
NDP conventions are extremely democratic (disagree)	42.3	27.8	17.0
Resolutions passed at federal NDP conventions should be binding on the federal leader (agree)	77.5	64.1	56.2
The party leader should have the right to reject a candidate nominated by a constituency association if that candidate does not accept policies adopted by the party (agree)	54.3	66.4	67.8
The NDP is a nationalist party (agree)	85.0	80.2	64.7
N[b]	(130)	(513)	(89)

[a] (agree) indicates (agree or strongly agree); (disagree) indicates (disagree or strongly disagree).
[b] Ns are approximate, and can change marginally for each question with a change in the number of missing responses.

As we have seen, a period of pronounced disagreement within the NDP began in 1969 with the formation of the Waffle, a group of younger and more militant party activists who questioned the party's positions on various issues and challenged the role of organized labour within the NDP. Since labour was one of the founding groups of the NDP, the latter issue would prove to be pivotal. In studies of the NDP in the 1970s, Brodie and Hackett both found a high degree of disagreement among party activists at the polarized 1971 leadership convention on the question of labour's role within the party. In particular, Waffle supporters were much more likely than constituency delegates to agree that trade unions had too much influence in the NDP: 52.7% versus 22.4%, respectively (Brodie, 1985: 211; see also Hackett, 1980: 15). However, by 1979 the atmosphere had calmed and concern that unions had too much influence in the NDP had dissipated among all groups in the party (Brodie, 1985: 214). Similarly, the 1987 survey data in Table 7.5 indicate that the vast majority in all age groups disagreed with this statement, although younger delegates continued to be somewhat more likely than others to believe that unions had too much influence in the NDP. Younger delegates were also less sympathetic than others to key trade-union principles; for example, they were less likely to agree that an NDP government should never interfere with free collective bargaining, or that the right to strike should never be restricted.

Many have observed a revived conservative mood in the country in recent years. The Reform Party, as a right populist movement, has often struck a conservative chord among older voters; indeed, this has been a key component of its success to date. In our 1987 NDP survey, a number of items tapped a dimension that might be labelled 'cultural conservatism'.[4] While NDPers as a group tend to be more radical and culturally permissive than others, the data indicate a consistent pattern of greater conservatism among the older NDP delegates. For example, older NDP delegates were less likely than their young or middle-aged colleagues to agree that homosexuals should be permitted to teach school, or that marijuana should be legalized. Older delegates were also more likely to agree that society has become too permissive, that family and community disintegration are responsible for many social ills, that pornography should be banned, that the courts have been too lenient in handing out penalties, that crime is a growing problem, that children should show more respect towards their parents, and that schools waste time and money on fads and frills. In view of the overall level of consistency with which New Democrats as a whole regard questions of policy (see Chapter 3), the persistence of age-related differences on issues such as these is striking. It also lends credibility to the proposition that older NDP activists and voters were potentially vulnerable to a right-populist message of cultural conservatism such as that offered by the Reform Party. The results of the 1993 election, when a significant number of former NDP voters defected to the Reform Party, provide further evidence for this hypothesis (see Archer and Ellis, 1994; Pammett, 1994; Whitehorn, 1994).

On policy questions concerning gender representation within the NDP, those in the youngest age group were most supportive of affirmative action and those in the oldest group were least supportive. For example, 76.0% of delegates under 30 agreed that half the federal council should be composed of women, compared with 54.0% of those 60 and older. Similarly, while delegates from all age ranges agreed that a significant percentage of NDP candidates and party officers should be women, support was strongest among the youngest group (86.2%) and weakest among the oldest (75.0%) —even though women made up a smaller percentage of delegates in the under-30 group than in the 60 and older range.

On other social issues the age effect was less clear. Delegates 60 and over were much more supportive than those under 30 of restrictions on civil liberties to reduce crime (37.9% vs 11.8%). In addition, members of the oldest group were somewhat less supportive of putting an end to compulsory retirement than were those in the youngest group (43.2% vs 53.1%). However, on the two other items selected (that people should be less concerned with the quantity of income and more concerned with the quality of life, and that it is harder for young people to get a good job today) there were no consistent age-related trends.

The last set of policy questions included in Table 7.5 concerns views on the role of the NDP in society (for an earlier period see Hackett, 1980: 15, 41, 46). Here there are several age-related trends. The oldest delegates were most likely to see the NDP as a socialist party. Interestingly, and in contrast to the tendency in the 1970s, older respondents were more likely to disagree that the NDP should present a more moderate image to the public. The older delegates were also more likely than those under 30 to agree that the NDP should move more clearly to the left. Curiously, the weakest support for this position was found among the youngest age group. However, older respondents, as veteran activists, were also more likely to disagree that the NDP should become more of a social movement and less of a political party; they appear to have been more focused on electoral success. Perhaps reflecting the under-representation of youth at the convention and the limited economic and political resources available to them, younger delegates tended to be more critical of the convention process itself, with a significantly higher percentage opposing the suggestion that NDP conventions are extremely democratic (42.3% versus 17.0% among delegates 60 and older). Young delegates were also more likely to agree that the party leader should be bound by resolutions passed at convention, and correspondingly less likely to agree that the leader should have the right to reject a candidate nominated by a constituency association. Echoing the Waffle almost two decades earlier, the younger delegates are also more likely to agree that the NDP is a nationalist party.

We can conclude that in a number of policy areas the different age groups varied in their attitudes. Younger delegates were somewhat more likely to question the role of unions in the party and to agree with limits to collective bargaining and strikes. Older delegates, on the other hand, tended to be more conservative in their cultural attitudes than their younger counterparts. Younger delegates, raised amidst the feminist revolution, tended to favour increasing provisions for greater gender representation in the party. In the area of perceptions of the NDP itself, older activists seemed more leftist, but the young had more reservations about democracy within the party.

To provide a comparative context for examining the issue positions of the various age groups among party activists, these attitudes were measured on the eight issue indexes introduced in Chapter 3 (see Table 7.6; for Liberal and Conservative delegates, and the NDP as a whole, see Table 3.2).

The most notable finding here is the overall consistency in attitudes of the various age groups in the NDP, at least when compared with Liberals and Conservatives. For example, on the important issue of continentalism, the mean scores of all age groups within the NDP were almost identical, with very similar levels of consistency within each group. To the extent that the NDP age groups differed on this issue, the oldest delegates were the most opposed to continentalism, and internally the most consistent. Similarly, on the indexes of hawkishness and social security the age-related differences were modest, with the older delegates less hawkish and more in favour of social security. On corporate power and privatization older delegates were the most likely to take a more militant socialist position. On cultural matters, however, a different pattern emerges. Whereas the youngest age group, growing up in a more secular and relativist age, tended to take a tolerant position on moral issues (mean = 0.39), delegates 60 years and over favoured the most restrictive position (mean = 0.87). It should also be noted, howev-

Table 7.6
Attitudinal Differences Between Age Groups in the NDP, 1987

Index (range) (direction)	<30		30–59		60+	
	$\overline{x}$	SD	$\overline{x}$	SD	$\overline{x}$	SD
Continentalism (0–4) (pro-)	0.32	0.56	0.33	0.61	0.26	0.47
Hawkishness (0–6) (pro-)	0.88	1.04	0.90	1.20	0.71	0.93
Social security (0–5) (pro-)	3.98	1.16	4.08	1.04	4.07	1.24
Moral conservatism (0–3) (pro-)	0.39	0.60	0.57	0.74	0.87	0.98
Corporate power (0–3) (anti-)	2.48	0.81	2.64	0.69	2.85	0.45
Bilingualism (0–2) (pro-)	1.88	0.48	1.76	0.65	1.60	0.81
Civil liberties (0–3) (pro-)	1.95	0.81	1.97	0.83	1.62	0.91
Privatization (0–6) (pro-)	0.28	0.77	0.21	0.79	0.15	0.72

NOTE: For data on Liberal and Conservative delegates, and on the NDP as a whole, see Table 3.2.

er, that even the oldest group of New Democrat delegates remained far less restrictive than the Liberal (mean = 1.65) or Conservative delegates (mean = 2.16). A similar pattern among the NDP age groups is evident on the question of civil liberties, although in this case older New Democrats adopted positions closer to Conservative delegates (mean = 1.62 versus 1.51, respectively) than their fellow New Democrats. Bilingualism was the only issue on which the positions of the NDP age groups actually overlapped the mean of another party (the Liberals). Young New Democrats were the most in favour of bilingualism (mean = 1.88), and older New Democrats (mean = 1.60) the least. The oldest group was closer to the average position of Liberal delegates on this issue (mean = 1.71) than to that of younger New Democrats. On the whole, however, Table 7.6 shows a high level of consistency on issue and policy indexes among the various age categories in the NDP.

Clearly there is some indication of a generational divide within the NDP. For example, older delegates were more likely to favour restrictions on corporate power, to oppose privatization, and to adopt conservative positions on cultural issues; they were less sympathetic to bilingualism and not as strong as younger delegates in their commitment to gender equality. However, in general the differences between young and old New Democrats were not as great as those between New Democrats and activists in other parties.

Although the age-specific differences in policy positions could lead to the development of a politically relevant age cleavage in the NDP, such a cleavage would be more likely to develop if it were provided with some institutional support. NDP conventions provide the possibility for such sup-

Table 7.7

Convention Caucus Attendance by Age, 1987 and 1989

	1987 Age			1989 Age		
Caucus	<30 %	30–59 %	60+ %	<30 %	30–59 %	60+ %
Youth	54.6	1.6	0.0	42.0	1.0	1.1
Women's	13.8	23.2	21.8	13.8	15.9	11.3
Left	10.8	7.8	6.9	8.0	8.1	6.5
Gay–lesbian	N.A.			10.9	2.6	1.1
Environment	N.A.			10.9	14.6	13.4
Labour	11.5	27.9	19.5	10.1	21.0	9.1
Provincial	65.4	57.4	51.7	52.9	48.6	46.2
Regional	10.8	7.6	10.2	8.7	8.4	6.5
Municipal	0.8	1.0	4.6	1.4	1.7	2.7
N[a]	(130)	(513)	(89)	(138)	(693)	(186)

[a]Ns are approximate, and can change marginally for each question with changes in numbers of missing responses.

port through the caucuses that operate both at and between conventions. Table 7.7 shows attendance by age at NDP convention caucuses.

As we have noted elsewhere, the most popular caucuses for all age groups are the provincial ones, which are generally attended by at least half of all delegates. This high level of attendance reflects the provincial and sectional structure of the NDP's organization and suggests that for many delegates the provincial section remains their primary group attachment within the federal party. The youth caucus also holds a strong appeal, with slightly more than half (54.6%) of the delegates under 30 attending it in 1987 and slightly less than half (42.0%) doing so in 1989.[5] However, the attendance of younger delegates at other caucuses is generally quite low (none greater than 15%). For delegates over 60, the absence of an age-specific caucus such as that available to youth means that they are without an obvious institutional vehicle to promote collective action.

There is some disagreement as to the overall impact that caucuses have at NDP conventions, although it has been argued that the women's caucus

Table 7.8
Leadership Voting by Age, 1989

Ballot	Age			Attended Youth Caucus	
	<30	30–59	60+	Yes	No
First					
McLaughlin	29.7	32.2	24.3	17.4	31.1
Barrett	11.6	17.5	28.6	10.1	19.5
Langdon	15.9	15.6	9.5	20.3	13.9
de Jong	13.8	12.1	20.6	14.5	13.7
McCurdy	13.0	9.1	3.7	14.5	8.2
Waddell	11.6	11.3	10.6	17.4	11.3
Lagassé	4.3	2.2	2.6	5.8	2.3
Second					
McLaughlin	38.7	39.6	31.6	27.9	38.4
Barrett	18.2	25.7	39.6	25.0	28.0
Langdon	28.5	23.0	11.2	32.4	20.5
de Jong	14.6	11.7	17.6	14.7	13.1
Third					
McLaughlin	51.1	51.2	45.7	36.2	50.7
Barrett	24.1	30.9	44.6	29.0	33.4
Langdon	24.8	17.9	9.8	34.8	15.9
Fourth					
McLaughlin	71.0	63.0	51.6	63.6	61.4
Barrett	29.0	37.0	48.4	36.4	38.6
N[a]	(138)	(692)	(189)	(69)	(972)

[a] Ns are approximate, and can change marginally for each question with changes in numbers of missing responses.

played an important role in Audrey McLaughlin's victory at the 1989 leadership convention (Thomlinson, 1993; Whitehorn, 1992). Our data do not allow for a complete examination of this question. However, they do permit a more limited analysis, comparing the leadership voting patterns of the various age groups as well as those of the delegates attending the youth caucus in 1989 (see Table 7.8; for further analysis of leadership voting in 1989, see Chapter 12).

There appear to have been a number of important age effects in leadership voting at the 1989 convention. On the first three ballots, Audrey McLaughlin drew roughly equal levels of support from each age group, although her support was consistently lowest among delegates 60 and older. The age variation in support for Dave Barrett was far greater. Barrett's support was much weaker among the youngest delegates and stronger among the oldest delegates. In fact, the latter group typically provided Barrett with twice as much support as the younger group. Both Steven Langdon and Howard McCurdy drew more heavily from younger delegates, and when McCurdy withdrew from the contest after the first ballot, throwing his support to Langdon, the latter's appeal among the younger delegates was reinforced. After Langdon's elimination following the third ballot, most of his supporters moved to McLaughlin; thus in the end the support she received was very high among the youngest delegates and high among the middle-aged.

Table 7.8 also shows the voting patterns of youth delegates according to their attendance at the youth caucus. Among those who attended the youth caucus, first-ballot support for both front-runners was markedly lower than among the delegates as a whole. In fact, Langdon received more first-ballot support than any other candidate among delegates attending the youth caucus, a pattern that persisted into the second ballot. By the third ballot, youth caucus attendees were almost evenly split, with approximately one-third voting for each of the three remaining candidates. By contrast, delegates as a whole favoured McLaughlin far above Barrett and Langdon. Finally, by the fourth ballot there was no measurable effect of attendance at the youth caucus: delegates attending the caucus were as likely to support McLaughlin as those who did not. Thus in the process of voting across the four ballots, attendance at the youth caucus was related to patterns of support for the various candidates. But in the end, on the fourth ballot, the choice was between two candidates for whom attendance at the youth caucus had no effect.

While Chapter 13 will explore more fully the 1995 federal leadership campaign, it is worth noting that the age issue was used quite effectively by one of the candidates. A key component of Svend Robinson's strategy was to tap the youth wing of the party and to recruit new young members into the party as a means of attracting support in the leadership race. As a former member of the youth wing, Robinson reminded delegates and party members of the fact that he was a 'child of the party', and a member of a new generation ready to take power.

CONCLUSION

This chapter has examined youth and older members of the New Democratic Party. We found that, at various times in the history of the CCF–NDP, youth activists have been a source of some militancy and division over the party's issue positioning and organizational structure. At other times the youth section has been relatively weak and less disruptive. If too little has been written about the youth wing, almost nothing has been written about the more elderly group within the NDP despite the rising average age of Canada's population (Bibby and Posterski, 1992; Dyck, 1993: 124; McDaniel, 1986: 36, 113; Sauvé, 1990: 19–27). The older members of the party have never had a formal institutional embodiment, either in the form of a 'grey' movement with specific party representation or as a 'grey' caucus at convention.

When one examines both the youth and the elderly party activists, it seems that an age cleavage has not become a major feature in the party's internal politics. Yet the attitudinal data indicate that there is some room for a politics of age to emerge in the NDP, particularly as the competition for scarce resources increases. A number of possibilities present themselves. Members of 'generation X' may become more militant as the economic recession continues, or if their standard of living lags behind that of their parents. The older generation of baby-boomers may become more preoccupied with protecting their past economic gains. To date, the NDP has not witnessed any serious gulf between the generations. However, the 1993 election defections of many former NDP supporters, particularly older voters, to the Reform Party may suggest that the NDP is vulnerable to generational issues.

NOTES

1 Interview with Kerry Brinkert, NDP Youth Outreach Officer.

2 The record for under-representing youth may have been set by the Reform Party at its 1992 assembly, where only 4.3% of the delegates were under 30, compared with 38.6% aged 60 and over (Archer and Ellis, 1996).

3 Technically, the older portion of this group cannot be members of the party's youth wing.

4 The inclusion of these survey items in the data set was inspired by Wendy Hughes.

5 Although attendance at the youth caucus is restricted to delegates under 26, the youngest age category in our data includes delegates up to the age of 30.

Part III

Key Domestic and Foreign Policy Areas

CHAPTER
8

The State, Public Ownership, and Social-Welfare Policy

The 1980s and 1990s have witnessed changes of historic proportions across much of the advanced industrial world. The collapse of communism throughout Eastern Europe significantly altered economic, military, and cultural relations between what used to be known as the First and Second worlds. Economic restructuring, globalization, and trade liberalization have become the hallmarks of the capitalist economy as the twentieth century draws to a close.

These powerful market forces have placed considerable pressure on political leaders to reduce the size and scope of government. Public debt and deficit levels that were allowed to escalate in the 1970s and 1980s placed governments in highly vulnerable positions because in many countries much of the money was owed to foreign lenders. International financial agencies gained increasing leverage to influence government fiscal policy by lowering, or threatening to lower, credit ratings (and thereby increasing the cost of servicing the debt). Politically, parties of the right repeated the mantra of 'living within our means', and governments of all political stripes felt considerable pressure to reduce and even eliminate their deficits and debts. Increasingly, the welfare state has been challenged both pragmatically, as too costly, and philosophically, as an unjustified state interference in the market economy.

These recent changes in the global political economy have created challenges for all parties and perhaps especially for those of the left. In a study of European social-democratic parties, Kitschelt (1994) found increasing support for a mixed economy, and for a more clearly defined regulatory role for the state in the current political and economic climate. In addition, there have been increasing efforts to link social-democratic parties to 'new social movements', particularly those oriented towards peace and disarmament, women's groups, gay and lesbian organizations, and ecological organizations.

This section examines the responses of NDP activists to changes in the international political economy. The present chapter focuses on attitudes towards the role of the state, public ownership, and social-welfare policy. In short, it examines how New Democrats have reacted to the neo-conservative and neo-liberal policy agendas, and whether they continue to see a positive and essential role for an interventionist state. In addition, to the extent that New Democrats do continue to view government in a positive light, we wish to explore the relative priority they attach to various areas of government spending and government regulation. Chapter 9 will examine NDP activists' attitudes towards defence and foreign policy in an era of globalization, while Chapter 10 will investigate the 'new politics' theme by examining the degree to which NDP activists support 'postmaterialist' values, and the groups linked to those values (e.g., environmentalists and feminists).

THE ROLE OF THE STATE

The modern state is a pivotal entity in the realm of politics. Representing the supreme or sovereign power in a society, it claims the right to make and administer the laws of the land. For both the liberal and the socialist, the state represents the efforts of society at large to pursue the public good. The classic liberal saw the individual as the key unit in politics and thus defined the public sphere narrowly and sought to minimize state activity (i.e., interference with individual freedom). The socialist, by contrast, focused on the social (i.e., group) nature of humans. Thus the classic socialist believed in a greater need for collective action, whether through the state or by some other means. Socialists have long championed the idea of an interventionist state to provide a helping hand to the 'have-nots'. The assumption of socialists is that many members of the working class cannot cope in a capitalist market society. Accordingly, the state must provide key social services to the community at large, particularly the poorest strata, to ensure fair and adequate access to the 'common wealth'.[1]

In general, the attitudes of NDP activists in 1987 towards the role of government in Canada were still markedly positive, as one might expect from classic socialist theory. This is in marked contrast to the increasing distrust with which Canadians as a whole regard their government (see for example, Blais and Gidengil, 1991; Whitehorn, 1996a). Table 8.1 demonstrates that more than half of the NDP convention delegates disagreed or strongly disagreed that 'big government increasingly is a major problem' (52.9%). Slightly fewer than one-third, on the other hand, either agreed or strongly agreed that big government is a problem. The fact that a significant minority of delegates saw government as a major problem indicates some concern, even within the NDP, over the size and scope of government.[2] However, one should be careful not to read too much into these data: the question asked respondents to reflect on 'big' government, not on government *per se*. Most delegates believed that government has an important and legitimate role to play in a modern society as it pursues collective solutions to the community's problems.

A number of the 1987 survey questions explored the size and scope of government, and the answers to them suggest that New Democrats continued to see a positive and significant role for government. Socialists in general believe the state can be used to regulate the excessive economic power of large corporations. Our survey indicated that about 4 in 5 respondents (80.5%) agreed that stronger measures should be taken by the government to break up monopolies and create competition. Delegates' support for an interventionist government extends beyond a regulatory role, and includes direct state participation in the economy in the form of public ownership as a counterweight to excessive private ownership. In 1987, 9 in 10 NDP respon-

Table 8.1

Attitudes Towards the Role of Government, 1987

Statement/Question	Strongly agree/ agree %	Uncertain %	Strongly disagree/ disagree %
Big government increasingly is a major problem	29.5	17.6	52.9
The government ought to take stronger measures to break up monopolies and create competition in the economy	80.5	13.1	6.4
There is too much government ownership in the Canadian economy today	5.2	4.9	89.8
Today public ownership is less required than it was during the 1930s Depression	9.1	12.4	78.6
Canada should nationalize key foreign-owned resource industries	74.0	16.0	10.0
The government should require that a significant proportion of the directors of Canadian corporations be selected by workers	73.7	18.1	8.2
An NDP government should never interfere with free collective bargaining	41.8	18.4	39.8
	More %	About the same %	Less %
Overall, with regard to public ownership, how much should there be?	79.1	17.2	3.6

dents (89.8%) disagreed that there is too much government ownership in the Canadian economy, and almost 4 in 5 (78.6%) disagreed that public ownership is less necessary than it was during the 1930s Depression.

The strong socialist commitment of NDP activists to public ownership has extended beyond a resolve to protect and preserve the industries that have already been nationalized. Indeed, there has been a strong consensus within the party in favour of further nationalization of important industries. For example, in 1987 almost 4 in 5 respondents (79.1%) believed there should be more public ownership in Canada. Similarly, about three-quarters (74.0%) agreed or strongly agreed that Canada should nationalize key foreign-owned resource industries.

Many New Democrats see government planning, regulation, and intervention as means towards public direction of the economy. Increasingly, however, there are socialists who believe that government action alone is not enough. Public control can be exercised without state intervention through public enterprises such as co-operatives and worker-owned factories. Many radical socialists favour more local input by workers in factory co-ops and workers' self-management (Cole, 1918; Garson, 1977; Hunnius, 1970, 1971; Hunnius et al., 1973; Whitehorn, 1974, 1978, 1979a, 1979b). The 1987 data indicate substantial support for the principle of industrial democracy among party activists. For example, almost 3 in 4 respondents (73.7%) agreed or strongly agreed that government should require that a significant proportion of directors of Canadian corporations be selected by workers. The strength of this response suggests the continuing importance of industrial democracy—a key plank in socialist doctrine—to an overwhelming majority of NDP activists and undercuts the suggestion by some commentators that the party is composed merely of 'liberals in a hurry' (Teeple, 1972). This is a party composed of activists with a collectivist and working-class orientation who believe in and are committed to public ownership and workers' self-management.

The one area where attitudes towards the role of government were divided concerned government commitment to the collective bargaining process. For example, 41.8% of delegates felt that an NDP government should not interfere with free collective bargaining, while 39.8% believed that sometimes it should. As we saw in Chapter 4, there was a predictable split on this item, with union representatives more likely to oppose government interference in collective bargaining. Unfortunately, in 1993 the Ontario NDP government found itself directly enmeshed in this complex web when it imposed the so-called 'social contract' on provincial public-sector employees (see Ehring and Roberts, 1993; Panitch and Swartz, 1993; Schwarz, 1994; Walkom, 1994). Although it is difficult to calculate the full cost of this policy in terms of political support for the NDP, at the very least it alienated significant portions of the labour movement, especially among the party's supporters in the CAW and public employees' unions (see Archer, 1995; Gindin, 1995; Laxer, 1996; McBride, 1996; Monahan, 1995; Rae, 1996).

Despite the divisions within the party on the matter of government interference with the collective bargaining process, in general Table 8.1 shows that NDP activists were overwhelmingly in favour of a strong interventionist government. They saw the state as having a positive role to play in regulating the private sector, in becoming involved in economic management through public ownership, and in supporting workers' participation in management. This can be seen in the fact that almost 90% of the delegates believed that 'the best hope for our economic development is a mixed economy with both private and public sector participating' (see Table 8.2). The overwhelming majority (89.8% and 78.6% respectively) rejected assertions that 'there is too much government ownership in the Canadian economy today', and that 'today public ownership is less required than it was during the 1930s Depression' (see Table 8.2). Interestingly, the support for the latter statement was a little lower.

To further explore attitudes towards public ownership, respondents were given a list of twelve industrial sectors and asked how much public ownership there should be in each one (see Table 8.2). Perhaps the most notable pattern to emerge from the data was the dearth of support among New Democrat activists for decreasing public ownership in any sector. Levels of support for decreasing public ownership were less than 10% across all twelve sectors, and as low as 2% in some. Furthermore, even in those economic sectors that were characterized as having significant levels of public ownership in 1987 (e.g., radio-television, railroads, airlines, and, to a certain extent, oil and gas through Petro-Canada), there was little discernible support for decreasing levels of public ownership. Clearly delegates did not favour privatization.

When one compares across the various sectors, however, differences emerge as to the amount of public ownership desired. It is significant that the three sectors most highly favoured by New Democrats for increased public ownership were resources (oil and gas), finance (banking), and culture (radio-television).[3] There was also majority support for increasing the level of public ownership in the area of transportation, including railroads, shipbuilding, and the airline industry. NDP reactions to more recent instances of privatization by the federal government (e.g., Petro-Canada in the resource sector and Air Canada in the transportation sector) indicate that the party still strongly defends public ownership. The table indicates that support for increased public ownership was lowest for the chemical, computer, and automobile industries, but was still far greater than support for decreasing it. In these three sectors, however, the majority opinion favoured maintaining about the same (i.e., very low) levels of public ownership. Overall, the data in Tables 8.1 and 8.2 indicate substantial support among NDP activists for public ownership in key sectors of the Canadian economy. Here we have empirical confirmation of the NDP's socialist commitment.

SOCIAL SPENDING

In addition to believing that government has an important and positive role to play in economic management, New Democrats maintain strong commitments to government spending on social programs. For example, socialists have long held that all citizens have a right to decent housing. Table 8.3 indicates a near unanimous view among delegates (97.4%) that the government should ensure that everyone has adequate housing. In an age when

Table 8.2
Attitudes Towards Public Ownership, 1987

Industry/Sector[a]	More %	About the same %	Less %
Oil and gas	82.3	15.8	2.0
Banking	82.0	15.9	2.1
Radio-television	61.2	35.0	3.8
Railroads	59.1	38.7	2.3
Shipbuilding	53.4	41.7	4.9
Airplane construction	53.3	39.7	7.0
Airlines	49.9	46.8	3.4
Chemical industry	41.6	50.2	8.2
Computer industry	41.1	52.1	6.9
Auto industry	34.8	56.9	8.3

Statement	Strongly agree/ agree %	Uncertain %	Strongly disagree/ disagree %
The best hope for our economic development is a mixed economy with both private and public sector participating	89.7	5.6	4.7
There is too much government ownership in the Canadian economy today	5.2	4.9	89.8
Today public ownership is less required than it was during the 1930s Depression	9.1	12.4	78.6

[a] Question: 'With regard to public ownership in different sectors, how much do you think there should be?'

growing numbers of women participate in the paid work force (see Chapter 6), child care becomes increasingly important. In 1987 New Democrats agreed almost unanimously (92.6%) that government-sponsored child-care services should be greatly expanded. Apparently many New Democrats view public support for housing and for child-care services as central to a modern welfare program and see the provision of such services as a key part of government's role in providing for the common good. This view of the role of government is reinforced by the finding that almost 9 in 10 delegates (88.1%) agreed that more money should be spent on social services. Support levels dropped when it cames to subsidizing the cost of some essential foods, such as milk and bread—a finding that is a little surprising. But even here supporters outnumbered opponents by three to one. On the issue of state support for religious schools—a controversial issue for many Canadians— even the NDP has been divided (e.g., Saskatchewan in the early 1960s and Ontario in the mid-1980s). When asked in 1987 whether they supported such funding, 54.8% of the delegates were in favour and 32.3% opposed. The relative lack of support for public funding of religious schools likely reflects both the secular belief system of many New Democrats (approximately 40% of delegates indicated no religious affiliation[4]) and a commitment to state funding focused on the public education system. Support for the public education system can also be seen in the negative responses to the statement 'too many schools waste time and money on fads and frills', an opinion often supported by those on the political right and those intent on reform-ing the system of public education (e.g., through the introduction of vouch-er systems, putting funding in the hands of parents, 'charter schools', the removal of school boards, etc.). Among NDP activists the ratio of those dis-agreeing to those agreeing was three to one, illustrating their continuing commitment to the current system of public education.

For the past decade the twin issues of debt and deficit have increasing-ly set the parameters for much of the economic and political discourse in Canada and the world. It is a divisive debate, even among social democrats. For example, we may observe the differences in priorities expressed by such prominent New Democrat academics as John Richards and Mel Watkins, or premiers Roy Romanow and Bob Rae. So too at the level of activists we see significant differences of opinion. For example, nearly half the respondents (49.7%) in 1987 agreed that the government should seek to reduce the public deficit as much as possible, compared with 30.0% who disagreed. As one might expect, there is an important regional dimension to attitudes towards deficit reduction. Whereas almost 3 in 4 Saskatchewan delegates (72.0%) agreed that an NDP government should reduce the deficit, the figure dropped to 60.8% in the Atlantic region, 54.3% in British

Columbia, approximately 45% in Alberta, the northern territories, Manitoba, and Ontario, and reached a low of 34.5% in Quebec (data not shown in tabular form). Thus it would appear that NDP governments across the provinces have different degrees of latitude to implement deficit reduction policies. Furthermore, activists were quite divided on whether governments had been spending too much (40.8% agreed; 40.6% disagreed). Even though significant proportions of delegates would have liked to see the deficit reduced and thought the government had been spending too much money, these attitudes co-existed with continued support for an activist government and for government spending in a variety of areas.

The orientation of New Democrats with respect to macro-economic management is clearly on the side of increasing employment over decreas-

Table 8.3

Attitudes Towards Government Spending, 1987

Issue Area/Statement	Strongly agree/ agree %	Uncertain %	Strongly disagree/ disagree %
Spending on social programs			
The government should see that everyone has adequate housing	97.4	2.0	0.5
Government sponsored child care services should be greatly expanded	92.6	4.2	3.1
More money should be spent on social services	88.1	10.1	1.8
Government should subsidize the cost of some essential foods such as milk and bread	58.0	22.9	19.1
There should be no government funding for religious schools	54.8	12.9	32.3
Too many schools waste time and money on fads and frills	20.5	17.7	61.8
Government spending: deficit and debt			
An NDP government should seek to reduce the government deficit as much as possible	49.7	20.3	30.0
Governments have been spending too much	40.8	18.6	40.6
If given a choice between increasing employment or decreasing inflation, the government should always opt for more jobs	85.1	12.0	2.9

ing inflation (see Levitt, 1996). For example, in 1987 over 85% of respondents agreed that, if given a choice between increasing employment and decreasing inflation, the government should always opt for more jobs. This position is consistent with the strategy of parties of the left, which draw their support disproportionately from those with little capital to invest, and who are either without work or most at risk of losing their jobs during difficult economic times.[5] New Democrats are significantly less likely than other Canadians to express concern about 'big government' and 'welfare dependency'.

To further explore attitudes towards public spending, respondents were presented with a list of eleven policy areas and asked whether government spending in each area should be greatly increased, slightly increased, kept about the same, slightly decreased, or greatly decreased. The data for the eleven policy areas are summarized in Table 8.4, with the 'greatly' and 'slightly' categories combined on each side of the 5-point Likert scale.

The data confirm that New Democrats continue to strongly support an activist state; they also confirm the 'big spender' image of the party. NDP delegates overwhelmingly supported increased spending in eight of the eleven policy areas. The highest levels of support were for increased spending on education, housing, welfare, and health, with 5 of every 6 respondents in favour. In addition, large majorities of respondents supported increased spending on foreign aid, technology, the arts, and transportation/roads.

The data also provide empirical confirmation of the theoretical literature on the left-wing bias against the 'military–industrial complex', to use the phrase made famous by former US general and president Dwight

Table 8.4

Attitudes Towards Government Spending in Various Policy Areas, 1987

Policy Area	Greatly/slightly increase %	Keep about the same %	Greatly/slightly decrease %
Education	91.0	8.0	1.0
Housing	89.3	9.7	1.0
Welfare	87.0	11.5	1.5
Health	83.1	16.2	0.7
Foreign aid	76.6	16.6	6.8
Technology	75.8	18.5	5.7
Arts	65.5	26.7	7.8
Transportation/roads	63.5	32.3	4.2
Industry	27.7	23.7	48.6
Defence	21.9	18.5	59.6
Police/prisons	21.8	47.4	30.8

NOTE: Question: 'Looking at the amount of government spending on various areas, how much do you think should be spent (greatly increase; slightly increase; keep about the same; slightly decrease; greatly decrease)?'

Eisenhower. Almost 60% favoured decreased spending on defence,[6] and a near majority (48.6%) favoured decreased government spending on industry. On the matter of spending for police and prisons, more delegates favoured cuts than increases, although most preferred to keep spending about the same.

Regarding the coercive side of the state (defence and police), therefore, social democrats in 1987 were more inclined to cuts. However, in 'nurturing' areas such as education, housing, health and welfare, the party strongly favoured spending increases. NDP activists' commitment to a strong and interventionist state was thus focused on social policy. This suggests that New Democrats favour a more co-operative and less conflictual model of politics.

GOVERNMENT AS EMPLOYER

In view of the strong support among NDP activists for high levels of public ownership and management of the economy and for extensive public services in many policy areas, an important role for government is that of employer. New Democrats hold relatively high expectations of government when it performs that role. For example, more than three-quarters of respondents in 1987 agreed or strongly agreed that government should be a model employer, irrespective of the economic cost (see Table 8.5). Furthermore, respondents strongly disagreed with the view that government-run corporations are less efficient than privately operated ones.

While the public increasingly sees big government as a problem and tends to be receptive to civil-service freezes (Gallup data cited in Whitehorn,

Table 8.5
Attitudes Towards Government as Employer, 1987

Statement	Strongly agree/ agree %	Uncertain %	Strongly disagree/ disagree %
Irrespective of economic cost, government should be a model employer	75.9	12.7	11.4
Government-run corporations are less efficient than privately operated ones	11.2	11.6	77.3
The federal government should impose a freeze on civil-service hirings	7.6	16.9	75.5
The federal government should limit civil-service wage increases	17.1	22.1	60.8
NDP government should never interfere with free collective bargaining	41.8	18.4	39.8

1992, 1996a), there was little support among New Democrats in 1987 for freezes on civil-service hiring (75.5% were opposed). On the matter of civil-service wages, however, opinions shifted somewhat. While a strong majority (60.8%) disagreed or strongly disagreed that the federal government should limit civil-service wage increases, almost 20% agreed with such limitations, and about 20% were uncertain. When the Ontario NDP government imposed wage freezes on provincial civil servants as part of its 'social contract' legislation, the immediate response of many NDP affiliated unions was quite negative and no doubt contributed to the defeat of the Rae government in the 1995 provincial election.[7]

POLITICAL REPRESENTATION AND INSTITUTIONAL CHANGE

One of the enduring themes in the socialist literature concerns the alienation of the workers and citizens in capitalist society. From Marx to contemporary New Left radicals, the rise of alienation and loss of a sense of community is a persistent message (Geyer and Schweitzer, 1976, 1981; Oldenquist and Rosner, 1991). Among the dimensions of alienation that have been discussed by theorists both normative (Marx) and empirical (Dean, 1961; Seeman, 1959; Whitehorn, 1974, 1979a), the question of powerlessness versus efficacy may be particularly telling. Given the high socio-economic status of many convention delegates (see Chapter 2), it is not surprising to learn that NDP activists had relatively high levels of internal political efficacy (see Kornberg and Clarke, 1992): that is, many believed that they were able both to understand and to influence the political process. In 1987, for example, about 3 in 4 respondents disagreed that 'politics seem so complicated that a person like me can't really understand what's going on', and a similar proportion disagreed with the statement that 'people like me don't have any say about what the government does' (see Table 8.6). In short, the vast majority of delegates believed in their ability both to understand and to influence politics.

In view of the strong support that NDP delegates gave to the state and government programs, it is interesting to find that nevertheless many had significant concerns about the effectiveness of political representation. The 1987 survey data demonstrate much lower levels of external political efficacy—that is, the belief that government is actually responsive to the public's attempts to influence policy. For example, nearly half of the respondents believed that 'many people in government are dishonest' (42.6%), and that 'the government doesn't care what people like me think' (45.0%). In addition, more than 1 in 3 (36.9%) believed that in general those elected to Parliament soon lose touch with the people. Despite their high levels of

support in principle for activist governments, therefore, significant proportions of New Democrats appear to have felt alienated from their actual governments. These alienated responses may in part reflect the fact that the NDP
has never formed the government at the federal level; thus delegates'
responses reflect alienation from Liberal or Conservative governments.
However, they are also likely due in part to a lack of what Hanna Pitkin
(1967) called 'descriptive representation'—the reflection of one's own characteristics in the representative legislative body. For example, almost half the
respondents (45.9%) agreed that there were not enough working-class MPs
in the NDP parliamentary caucus in Ottawa. Thus it appears that even NDP
activists lacked descriptive representation.

Feelings of alienation can be directed towards individuals, governments,
and state institutions at large. The survey data indicate that NDP activists were
far from content with Canada's current arrangement of political institutions
(see Table 8.7). Most delegates supported the abolition of the Senate.
Although appointments to the 'red chamber' are highly partisan, and usually involve veteran Liberals and Conservatives, over the years a few high-profile CCF and NDP figures have been offered Senate seats, including Eugene
Forsey and Thérèse Casgrain (who accepted the offer), and Frank Scott
(who turned it down). Given the dominance of Liberal and Tory patronage
appointments to the Senate, it seems fair to say that the vast majority of NDP

Table 8.6

**Attitudes Towards Political Representation and Personal Political
Efficacy, 1987**

Statement	Strongly agree/ agree %	Uncertain %	Strongly disagree/ disagree %
People like me don't have any say about what the government does	22.4	6.5	71.2
Generally, those elected to Parliament soon lose touch with the people	36.9	17.2	45.9
Many people in government are dishonest	42.6	15.0	42.3
Sometimes politics seems so complicated that a person like me can't really understand what's going on	19.4	5.3	75.3
I don't think the government cares what people like me think	45.0	9.0	46.0
There are not enough working-class MPs in the NDP parliamentary caucus in Ottawa	45.9	26.0	28.1

activists would welcome its abolition. More important, most would also welcome significant changes to the representative character of the House of
Commons. For example, in 1987 almost 70% of delegates agreed that Canada
should opt for some element of proportional representation in federal elections. A number of studies (Archer et al., 1995; Cairns, 1968; Gibbins, 1982;
Seidel, 1989; Whitehorn, 1989, 1996a) have demonstrated that over time the
New Democrats have been seriously penalized in the translation of votes in
federal elections into seats in the House of Commons. This distortion could

Table 8.7

Attitudes Towards Canada's Political Institutions, 1987

Statement	Strongly agree/ agree %	Uncertain %	Strongly disagree/ disagree %
The Senate of Canada should be abolished	72.7	14.0	13.2
Canada should opt for some features of proportional representation in federal elections	69.2	19.2	11.6
The monarchy is an essential part of the Canadian Constitution	22.4	14.9	62.7
On the whole, the benefits of the new Canadian Charter of Rights outweigh the disadvantages	49.5	34.1	16.4
The federal government has yielded too much power to the provinces	30.8	23.8	45.5
Government services should be decentralized more to the local level	69.9	19.9	10.2

Looking at the distribution of political power in Canada, how much power would you
like to see the different levels of the government have?

	Federal %	Provincial %	Municipal %
More	26.6	18.6	38.9
About the same	59.3	57.5	53.3
Less	14.1	23.9	7.8

Which level of government do you feel closer to?

Federal	28.0%
Provincial	52.8
Municipal	11.4
None	7.2

be rectified through an electoral system that would allocate legislative seats on a more proportional basis, but while this proposal drew considerable support from delegates in 1987, historically CCF–NDP premiers and federal NDP leaders (such as Broadbent) have opposed it.

An interesting division of opinion appeared in 1987 over the monarchy. Although a substantial majority of delegates disagreed with the proposition that the monarchy is an essential part of the Canadian Constitution (62.7%), almost a quarter agreed that it is essential—a surprisingly high figure for a party that traditionally has placed little stock in hereditary positions of power. Attitudes towards the monarchy vary in several predictable ways. Age is an important predictor of the perception that the monarchy is essential, with 40.2% of those 60 and over, and 27.7% of those 50 to 59, holding that view, compared with approximately 22% for the sample as a whole. In addition, those born in the United Kingdom were more likely to view the monarchy as essential than were those born either in Canada or in the United States (33.9% versus 22.4% and 23.5%, respectively).

In 1987, nearly half the respondents (49.5%) agreed that the benefits of the Charter of Rights and Freedoms outweighed its disadvantages; this may have reflected a belief that minority rights would be best preserved if supervised by the courts. The responses also display a marked degree of uncertainty: fully one-half of respondents either admitted they were uncertain whether the Charter had been advantageous on the whole or believed that it had been disadvantageous. Historically, both the CCF and the NDP supported the constitutional entrenchment of a charter of rights, an initiative advocated many decades ago by Frank Scott (see Djwa and Macdonald, 1983; Scott, 1977, 1986). However, concerns seem to have persisted that the constitutional package engineered by Prime Minister Trudeau, a former colleague of Scott's, had not delivered the benefits that might have been expected. Allan Blakeney, premier of Saskatchewan at the time of the Charter debate, expressed such misgivings, but to no avail (Gruending, 1990).

Division of powers is an important element in any federal polity, and it is particularly important in Canada because the provinces have primary jurisdiction over several significant social areas (such as education and health), whereas the federal government has primary responsibility for taxation and managing the national economy. Given the importance of education and health to social democrats, one would expect them to express greater interest in provincial than in federal politics. In addition, the fact that the NDP, like the CCF before it, has had greater electoral success provincially than federally might lead one to expect high support among NDP activists for decentralization within the Canadian federal system. To a considerable extent the data confirm these expectations. Almost half the respondents

(45.5%) at the 1987 convention disagreed that the federal government had yielded too much power to the provinces, and almost 7 in 10 (69.9%) favoured greater devolution of responsibility for government services to the local level.[8] It is notable that the size of the respondent's community had no significant effect on support for decentralization. In particular, residents of large urban centres were no more likely to favour decentralization than were residents of smaller cities and towns. This suggests that the preference for decentralization was a matter of principle or philosophy rather than a reflection of the capacity of local governments to provide services.

Respondents were also asked whether they would like each of the three levels of government (federal, provincial, and municipal) to have more power, about the same amount of power, or less power. In each instance a majority (ranging from 53.3% to 59.3%) chose the status quo. However in keeping with their tendency to support decentralization, almost 40% of delegates favoured giving the municipal level of government more power. Interestingly, though, that preference for the more local level did not extend to the level of the province: only some 20% said they would like to see the provinces have more power. Slightly more, about 25%, would have reduced the provinces' power. Federal NDP delegates were more likely to support an increase in power for the federal government (26.6%) than for provincial governments (18.6%). It would be interesting to know whether provincial NDP convention delegates felt the same way, but unfortunately our data do not permit this.

This preference for expanding federal power may stem from the realization that provinces vary widely in the financial resources available to support social programs, and that the federal government plays an important role in equalizing services across the confederation. The 1987 data on the institutional ties and preferences of NDP activists appear to support this interpretation. When asked which level of government they felt closer to, the percentage replying 'provincial' was almost twice as large as that saying 'federal' (52.8% versus 28.0%). A much smaller percentage (11.4%) said they felt closest to the municipal level. That federal convention delegates should wish to grant more institutional powers to municipal and federal governments yet indicate feeling personally closer to provincial governments points to a considerable gap between structural observations and personal perceptions.

The current period has been characterized by profound shocks to the state, both in Canada and in other developed economies. The optimism that accompanied the growth in state activity and the creation of the welfare state in the post-war period has been supplanted by increasing wariness of 'big government'. In a global context, the dual problems of government deficits and debts have limited governmental autonomy and flexibility in providing funds for social policies. For example, the March 1996 budget of the

Canadian federal government projected that in fiscal 1997–98 spending on interest on the public debt would be almost half as large as total program spending ($49 billion versus $106 billion), and the net public debt would hit $619.7 billion (*Globe and Mail*, national ed., 7 March 1996: A1). Fiscal pressures resulting from a generation of budget deficits, together with the ideological commitments of some 'new right' governments, have led many people to favour privatization and downsizing of government services. In Canada these trends are also reflected in demands for more decentralization of government services, and in calls for Ottawa to vacate areas of provincial responsibility, particularly in matters of social policy. The role of the state in Canada has been further challenged by the increased globalization of trade, including the adoption of anti-interventionist policies and international trading agreements such as the Canada–US Free Trade Agreement and NAFTA. To all of these challenges is added the perennial issue of the role of Quebec within Canada, particularly in light of the near-victory of the *yes* forces in the 1995 Quebec referendum and the election in January 1996 of Lucien Bouchard to the leadership of the Parti Québécois and his appointment as premier of Quebec. These challenges make the future direction and indeed the survival of the Canadian state highly uncertain. In the midst of this uncertainty, however, New Democrats have the distinction of continuing to see a positive and constructive role for an active federal state in managing a market economy and alleviating the inequalities to which it gives rise.

SOCIAL CLASS AND SOCIAL STATUS

Social class has long been viewed as one of the primary determinants of support for political parties in advanced industrial societies (see, for example, Alford, 1963; Lipset and Rokkan, 1967). Much of the comparative analysis on the role of class in party systems has viewed Canada as an 'exception', arguing that the class element in our politics is less pronounced than elsewhere because of the importance of cultural, linguistic, and regional differences among Canadians (Alford, 1963). A lively debate has emerged as observers of Canadian parties attempt to account for the weakness of class-based parties in general, and for the weak working-class base of the New Democrats in particular (see, for example, Brodie, 1985a; Brodie and Jenson, 1988; Horowitz, 1968; Teeple, 1972; for an excellent overview see Pammett, 1987).

An examination of the class character of the Canadian electorate, and hence of the costs and benefits to the NDP of attempting to mobilize the electorate along class lines, is beyond the scope of our analysis (but see Johnston et al., 1992: 89–101). However, to understand the role that class plays in structuring the opinions and beliefs of New Democrats, and the role it might play in the future, we can examine the class character of NDP delegates. First we examine the 'subjective' dimension of class: how did New Democrats in 1987 view their personal class position? Next we briefly examine the 'objective' dimension of class: that is, the occupational and income characteristics of delegates. We then turn to an examination of delegates' attitudes towards social and economic inequality and towards the government's role in responding to such inequality in Canada.

When asked whether they thought of themselves as belonging to a social class, almost two-thirds of respondents (63.4%) answered in the affirmative (see Table 8.8). However, almost 4 in 10 (36.6%) said they did not think of themselves as belonging to a social class. These data suggest that although class may be an important characteristic for New Democrats, it is certainly not the only, nor perhaps even the most important, component of their self-image.

This view finds further support when one examines the class to which delegates felt they belonged. Although parties of the left traditionally find disproportionate support among the working class, activists in the NDP were more likely to view themselves as members of the middle or even upper-middle class than the working or lower class. For example, 57.7% of the 1987 delegates stated their class position as middle-class or higher, whereas only

Table 8.8
Social–Class Perceptions of NDP Delegates, 1987

Do you think of yourself as belonging to a social class?

Yes	63.4%
No	36.6

If you had to choose one, to which of the following six social classes would you say you belonged?

Upper	0.3%
Upper middle	15.2
Middle	42.2
Lower middle	15.0
Working	25.6
Lower	1.7

To which class did your parents belong when you were growing up?

Upper	0.3%
Upper middle	9.5
Middle	26.1
Lower middle	19.7
Working	39.4
Lower	5.0

Do you ever consider yourself a member of the working class?

Yes	77.2%
No	22.8

42.3% answered lower-middle, working-, or lower-class. The data also indicate an interesting inter-generational rise in class status, with 64.1% of respondents reporting that they had grown up in a lower-middle, working-, or lower-class household; thus for many activists their class position has risen. The portrait that emerges from these data on class is a mosaic, with activists representing the full range of class categories from working to upper-middle class. Yet there appears to be a persistent affinity for the working class, with 77.2% of respondents answering that they sometimes considered themselves to be members of the working class. However, it should be acknowledged that this self-perception appears especially weak and open to change. While the party's appeal to the working class may continue to have resonance among NDP activists, for most it is not the primary class orientation.

At least part of the explanation for the weakness of working-class self-images among New Democrats can be found in their 'objective' class experiences: that is, in their occupational and income levels. For example, Table 8.9 shows that delegates were equally likely to describe their occupation as 'white collar' or 'blue collar' (14.4% versus 15.1%). But if one adds to the 'white collar' group the respondents describing themselves as 'professional employees', 'self-employed professionals', or farm- or factory-owners, that category increases to 57.8%. Thus a relatively small percentage of delegates worked in what might be called traditional working-class occupations, and a relatively large percentage worked in areas traditionally associated with the middle class.

Similarly, the income levels of NDP activists in 1987 were relatively high, with 42.9% earning a family income of at least $45,000 per year, and 69.7% earning $30,000 or more. These relatively high income levels are associated with fairly high levels of home ownership. Nearly 3 in 4 NDP activists (73.0%) owned their homes, compared with 27.0% who rented. Thus many measures of 'objective' class position affirm the relative affluence of NDP delegates, who possessed many of the characteristics associated traditionally with the middle class. However, it also appears that this group had experienced a certain amount of economic hardship, as 57.6% reported having been unemployed at some point.

It appears, then, that class has an ambiguous impact within the NDP. Delegates reported self-perceptions, levels of income, types of occupations, and rates of home ownership more typical of the traditional middle class than the working class. Yet despite these general self-perceptions and personal economic circumstances, a relatively large percentage reported sometimes thinking of themselves as part of the working class. It is in this way, through empathy and in some cases even self-identification with the working class, that class comes to play an important role for New Democrats.

Table 8.9
Employment, Income, and Home Ownership of NDP Delegates, 1987

Occupation[a]

Factory owner	0.5%
Farm owner	3.3
Self-employed professional	8.5
Professional employee	31.1
White collar	14.4
Blue collar	15.1
Homemaker	3.4
Student	7.3
Retired	5.8
Unemployed	2.9
Other	7.8

Family income

0–$15,000	9.8%
$15,001–$30,000	20.5
$30,001–$45,000	26.8
$45,001–$60,000	21.4
$60,001–$80,000	14.7
$80,001 or more	6.8

In the home in which you live at the present time, do you or your family

Rent	27.0%
Own	73.0

Have you ever been unemployed since first seeking a full-time job?

Yes	57.6%
No	42.4

[a] Closed-ended question; see Table 2.2 for open-ended results.

This empathy and sense of working-class solidarity can be seen in delegates' attitudes towards broader issues of class and inequality in Canadian society (see Table 8.10). Indeed, New Democrat activists showed a strong tendency to view Canadian society as characterized by significant economic inequalities. For example, 94.9% agreed that the difference between the rich and the poor is too great, and approximately 85% agreed that despite efforts to reduce social inequalities, Canada is still basically divided between the rich and the poor. A full 90% disagreed with the statement that really severe poverty no longer exists in Canada, and only slightly fewer (84.9%) disagreed that there is no ruling class. As we noted in Chapter 4, the concept of class struggle is a key divide within the labour and socialist movements. While a majority of NDP delegates (53.9%) agreed that 'the central question of Canadian politics is the class struggle between labour and capital', a significant minority (33.5%) disagreed (see Table 8.10). Union delegates, some of whom were veterans of historic labour–management conflicts, were more likely to portray Canadian politics in terms of a class struggle than were non-union delegates (see Table 4.4). Delegates were somewhat divided on the question of whether social inequality is inevitable. In response to the statement 'no matter what steps are taken, the poor will always exist', almost 6 in 10 (58.1%) disagreed; only half as many (24.8%) agreed. Although we do not have data on this question across the parties in Canada, it seems likely that the level of disagreement on this item would be very high in a comparative context. However, it is in the belief that such social inequalities can be reduced and alleviated that many socialists find their deepest commitment to politics. New Democrats are also likely to see individuals, including younger members of society, as not personally responsible for their poor economic status. For example, 81.5% of delegates in 1987 disagreed with the statement that 'too many of the unemployed are not trying hard enough to find jobs'. In addition, 91% agreed that it is harder for young people to get a job today.

For many New Democrats, at least part of the explanation for the persistence of inequality and poverty can be traced to the performance of the welfare state. Slightly more than half of the delegates (50.9%) in 1987 agreed that the welfare state has accomplished less than expected. There are two possible explanations for this finding. It could be that their expectations of the welfare state were unrealistic. Alternatively, the perceived 'failure' of the welfare state might reflect dissatisfaction with the way in which welfare policies have been designed and implemented. Responses to other items in the survey indicate that the latter is the more likely explanation. The strong disagreement with the statement that 'no matter what steps are taken, the poor will always exist' suggests that many delegates believed poverty can be reduced and perhaps eliminated altogether. Thus the finding that a majority agree the welfare state has accomplished less than expected should be read not as an indictment of the principle of a strong and active welfare state, but rather as an indication of dissatisfaction with the actual performance of the welfare state in Canada.

In fact, delegates' views on responses to economic inequality and the principles governing access to social programs demonstrated their commitment to a strong and active welfare state (see Table 8.11). New Democrats were almost unanimous in the view that the rich should pay more taxes (97.9%), and only slightly less unanimous in the view that full employment is a realistic goal (90.2%). A similar percentage (87.9%) believed that consumer protection laws are too weak. In addition, the data seem to suggest a general concern for the welfare of others and an emphasis on the non-material aspects of life. For example, almost half the respondents (46.9%) agreed that during difficult economic times, workers should be willing to share jobs, although one-third disagreed (33.0%). Perhaps those disagreeing believed that salaries are already too low, and that governments or corpo-

rations have a responsibility to ensure sufficient opportunities for employment. Many more—almost 8 in 10 (78.6%)—believed we should be less
concerned with the quantity of income and pay more attention to the
quality of life. One suspects that this latter view reflected the opinion of
those at the middle and upper levels of the income and occupational
ranges. Certainly delegates showed a strong commitment to increasing the
quantity of income among those at the lower end of the range. However,
they also appeared to recognize that other social goals and objectives may
be more important. This theme is pursued further in Chapter 10 in our discussion of materialist and postmaterialist attitudes.

As for the principles that New Democrats believe should underlie the
welfare state, universality of access to social programs appears to have been

Table 8.10

**Attitudes Towards Economic Inequality and the Role of Government,
1987**

Area/Statement	Strongly agree/ agree %	Uncertain %	Strongly disagree/ disagree %
Inequality in Canada			
The difference between the rich and the poor is too great in Canada	94.9	2.0	3.0
Despite all the efforts to reduce social inequalities, Canada in the 1980s is still basically divided into the rich and the poor	84.0	5.1	10.9
There is no ruling class in Canada	9.4	5.8	84.9
The central question of Canadian politics is the class struggle between labour and capital	53.9	12.6	33.5
Really severe poverty no longer exists in Canada	6.1	3.8	90.0
No matter what steps are taken, the poor will always exist	24.8	17.1	58.1
Too many of the unemployed are not trying hard enough to find jobs	8.4	10.1	81.5
It is harder for young people to get a job today	91.0	3.4	5.6
Government and economic inequality			
The welfare state has accomplished less than expected	50.9	20.6	28.5

one of the most important. Over 9 in 10 (91.8%) agreed that unemployment insurance should be a fundamental right for all. A similar proportion (88.6%) agreed that all Canadians should have the right to receive a guaranteed annual income. However, support for universality, while strong

Table 8.11
Attitudes Towards the Role of Government and Social Policy, 1987

Area/Statement	Strongly agree/ agree %	Uncertain %	Strongly disagree/ disagree %
Responses to inequality in Canada			
The rich should pay more taxes	97.9	1.0	1.1
Full employment is a realistic goal	90.2	4.6	5.2
Consumer protection laws are too weak	87.9	8.9	3.2
During difficult economic times, workers should be willing to share jobs	46.9	20.1	33.0
We should be less concerned with the quantity of income and pay more attention to the quality of life	78.6	11.5	9.9
Principles of access to social programs			
Unemployment insurance should be a fundamental social right for all	91.8	3.7	4.5
All Canadians should have the right to receive a guaranteed annual income	88.6	8.4	3.0
Social security programs, like old age pensions and family allowances, should be based on family income needs, and people who don't need this type of assistance should not receive it	23.4	6.2	70.5
A means test may be necessary in some social programs	28.6	12.1	59.3
The welfare state makes people nowadays less willing to look after themselves	11.0	12.5	76.5
Government regulation of social progams			
Doctors and hospitals should not be allowed to extra-bill	96.6	0.5	2.8
Rent controls are often necessary in large cities	93.8	4.0	2.2
Crime and punishment			
The courts have been too lenient in handing out penalties to criminals	33.4	20.3	46.3

across a wide range of issues, is tempered in certain instances. For example, while approximately 7 in 10 disagreed with the statement that 'social programs, like old age pensions and family allowances, should be based on family income needs, and people who don't need this type of assistance should not receive it',[9] almost one-quarter agreed. In addition, almost 3 in 10 agreed that 'a means test may be necessary in some social programs'. Even among New Democrats, the commitment to universality of access to social programs is not universally shared. Still strong defenders of the welfare state, more than 3 in 4 NDP respondents disagreed or strongly disagreed that welfare makes people less willing to look after themselves.

As we have already noted, the state plays an important regulatory role in shaping the contours of the welfare system. Not only does it provide public goods and services, but in many cases it regulates how they are delivered. New Democrats tend to support an activist role for the state in regulating social programs. In 1987, for example, an overwhelming number of respondents (96.6%) believed that doctors and hospitals should not be allowed to extra-bill.[10] Similarly, a very high proportion (93.8%) agreed that rent controls are often necessary in large cities. The NDP's positive view of government regulation is not only an important defining feature for the party; it is also the feature that sets its activists apart from those in other Canadian parties.

Finally, one social policy that has gained increased salience recently concerns the criminal justice system, and in particular the degree to which the courts have been 'soft on crime'. While New Democrats are far more divided on this matter than are supporters of, for example, the Reform Party (see Archer and Ellis, 1994), there is a significant pocket of concern about this issue. While almost half (46.3%) of the delegates in 1987 disagreed, approximately one-third did agree that the courts have been too lenient on criminals, and 20.3% were uncertain.

CONCLUSION

The Canadian state is facing significant challenges. The consensus that existed among all parties in the post-war period regarding government support for social programs has begun to break down. Virtually all governments, regardless of political stripe, have become increasingly concerned with balancing their budgets, although their approaches to this task have differed.

As socialists and social democrats, NDP activists strongly support a continuing role for government social programs. Their collectivist principles give an important role to the state in lessening the inevitable inequalities generated in a capitalist market economy. Socialists view social programs not as a temporary luxury to be provided only during periods of relative economic prosperity, but as a public responsibility to the poor that must be fulfilled regardless of economic circumstances. The social democrat differs from the liberal and the conservative in showing a greater sensitivity to the social ills caused by economic inequality. Whereas both classic liberals and all conservatives accept social inequality as a necessary consequence of the economic market, socialists view such inequality as fundamentally unjust and unacceptable. In their view, a social-democratic government has an obligation to work proactively to lessen inequality. The NDP, like the CCF before it, offers a unique political perspective. To a significant degree, it is the party's distinctiveness on the role of the state and social programs that has enabled the federal NDP to retain its *raison d'être*, despite its limited electoral success.

NOTES

1 This idea was embedded in the name of the NDP's predecessor, the Co-operative Commonwealth Federation.

2 In this regard they echo the British socialist George Orwell, the author of *1984*.

3 These are key areas for the Canadian polity and identity. Each of these sectors has been heavily influenced by international markets and cultural trends, particularly those emanating from the US. Many New Democrats believe that Canada can preserve its economic and cultural independence from the United States only through an interventionist state. An activist state thus can be an essential tool not only for the working class but also for a weaker nation in a relationship of dependency on a larger imperial state (Laxer, 1973).

4 Several methods can be used to calculate the percentage of delegates with no religious affiliation. The largest response category in 1987 was 'none' (19.9%). However, an additional 6.1% indicated they were 'agnostic', 5.1% replied 'atheist', and 1.2% indicated 'no formal religion'. A further 11.2% did not respond to the question. If these 'non-responses' are included in calculating the 'non-religious', a total of 43.6% are classified as having no religious affiliation. If the non-responses are excluded, 36.5% are classified as 'no religious affiliation'. In either case, the percentage of delegates with no religious affiliation was very large.

5 However, it should be noted that the NDP has not consistently benefited at the polls during times of high unemployment. For example, in 1984 the first Mulroney government was elected on a platform of 'Jobs, Jobs, Jobs'—even though, once in power, it focused instead on maintaining low rates of inflation (see Archer and Johnson, 1988; Happy, 1986; Monroe and Erickson, 1986).

6 For a comparison with the British Labour Party see Whiteley (1983).

7 It is difficult to determine with any certainty how high a political price the Rae government paid for implementing its 'social contract'. Although the party lost some of its core union supporters, especially among the Auto Workers and some

of the public-service unions, other unions, such as the Steelworkers, the United Food and Commercial Workers, the Service Employees International Union, and the Communications, Energy and Paperworkers, increased their support for the party (see Archer, 1995; Gindin, 1995). In any case, difficulties with public-sector workers were not unique to the Rae government: over the years other CCF and NDP governments have had trouble in this area as well. In contrast, the Conservative government in Alberta was able to increase its popular support when it imposed a 5% wage rollback on civil servants (including teachers and health-care workers) in 1994 (see Archer and Gibbins, 1997).

8 Our intention was for respondents to focus on the municipal level in answering this question, and although some may have done so, others may have equated 'local' with provincial. In either case, there was substantial support for devolution of political authority.

9 The family allowance was replaced in 1990 with a system of child tax credits.

10 An earlier conflict between doctors and state socialism led to the doctors' strike in Saskatchewan in the early 1960s; see Badgley and Wolfe (1967) and Tollefson (1963).

CHAPTER 9

Defence, Foreign Policy, and Canadian Nationalism

Since its inception, the CCF–NDP has often pursued a distinctive path in the realm of defence and foreign policy. Favouring neutrality in the mid-1930s, the CCF opposed exports of Canadian resources (e.g., nickel) for foreign war industries, and when the Second World War began, CCF leader J.S. Woodsworth voted against Canada's participation; after the war, the party took a skeptical view of the rearmament of West Germany, and for many years called on Canada to withdraw from the NATO and NORAD military alliances; in the 1960s the NDP criticized US involvement in the Vietnam War; and more recently, under Audrey McLaughlin, it opposed Canada's participation in the 1991 Gulf War. The party's tradition of socialist idealism stands in sharp contrast to the 'real-politik' that dominates so much of international politics. As a party document entitled *Peace, Security and Justice* stated in 1981:

> . . . the democratic socialist alternative depends upon two major initiatives: an urgent effort to reverse the arms race and reduce tension between the nuclear powers and, secondly, an effective assault on worldwide poverty. As socialists, we believe that there needs to be a reordering of the world's economic institutions to transfer a share of power to the poorer nations. Significant steps are necessary to bring multinationals under public control at the community and international levels.[1]

On matters of defence and foreign policy the CCF–NDP has often taken stands in direct opposition to those of Canada's other political parties (see Chapter 3).[2] Despite the importance of these events, however, relatively little has been written about the party's position on them.[3] Thus it may be useful, before proceeding to the survey data from the 1970s and 1980s, to briefly review the party's historical stands on defence and foreign policy. Historical and archival information are taken from two key sources: CCF–NDP manifestos (1933, 1956, 1961, 1983) and federal election pamphlets.[4]

DEFENCE AND FOREIGN POLICY

The CCF Era

Throughout the history of the CCF–NDP, the Regina Manifesto (1933) has been considered the touchstone for the party's policies. Stressing the twin goals of disarmament and peace—and commencing a long tradition in the party of distrust of military entanglements—the manifesto asserted the CCF's opposition to 'all participation in imperialist wars', pronounced capitalism to be incompatible with 'genuine international cooperation', and proposed to 'rescue' the League of Nations from domination by the 'capitalist Great Powers'. Interestingly, however, the party had not yet taken the strong economic nationalist stance that was to become one of its hallmarks. The manifesto condemned what it called 'insane protectionist policies' and suggested that 'the old controversies between free traders and protectionists are now largely obsolete'. In the CCF's view, Canada needed to enter into trade agreements with other foreign countries to stabilize prices.

In the 1935 election, the CCF denounced all imperialist wars and expressed its support for neutrality in the abstract. However, when war finally began in 1939, the party was divided between pacifists (including federal leader J.S. Woodsworth) and those who volunteered for military service (including Saskatchewan CCF leader George Williams). Outvoted by the party's national council on war policy, Woodsworth was the only MP to vote against Canada's entry into the global conflict. However, the party's support for the war effort was conditional, and this position, combined with its socialist ideology, made the CCF all the more suspect to many Canadians. Later the party opposed the compulsory conscription of manpower/labour introduced by the Liberal government and called for a more effective war effort through limits on war profits and increased state economic planning and public ownership of wartime industries.

The end of the war brought a new focus on building a better world. However, the wartime alliance of Britain, the United States, and the Soviet Union was soon shattered by events, including the 1945 defection, in Ottawa, of the Soviet cipher clerk Igor Gouzenko, the 1948 coup in Czechoslovakia, and the Berlin blockade of 1948–49. The hardening of the Cold War divisions of Europe into Western and Eastern blocs was cemented by the communist takeovers in Eastern Europe, the Marshall Plan, and the formation of NATO and later the Warsaw Pact. The global division into a capitalist West and communist East was completed by the military victory of Mao Zedong and the communists in China.

As early as the 1949 election, addressing the growing concern about the Cold War, the CCF counselled that the 'developing Western European Union [i.e., NATO] is not and should not be a mere military alliance'.

Despite the reluctance of some party members, criticism was also directed at the USSR, and the CCF stated that it would 'fight against totalitarian dictatorship of every kind'. In addition, twenty years before the Waffle Manifesto, the party expressed a clear nationalist message in its warning against the 'wanton alienation of vital Canadian resources to powerful private interests . . . controlled outside Canada'.

By 1953 the CCF, like many other social-democratic parties, was also caught up in the Cold War. Although it continued to support NATO in principle, it criticized the military emphasis of the treaty and urged greater stress on joint economic objectives. Endeavouring to stake out a middle path in a rigidly bipolar world, the CCF condemned 'world communism' and 'world capitalism' alike and expressed its idealistic and internationalist hopes in calling for Canadians to play a more dynamic role in the United Nations.

In 1956 the party's new statement of principles, the Winnipeg Declaration, pointed to the 'oppressive fear of nuclear destruction' and called for prohibition of nuclear weapons. While it condemned imperialism, 'whether of the old style or the new totalitarian brand', it also cautioned against excessive reliance on military spending to meet 'the threat of communist aggression'; instead, greater effort should be directed towards the United Nations and aid to underdeveloped countries. In the election campaign of the following year, the CCF continued to warn that American corporations 'threaten our economic, and even our political independence'. It proposed a national energy policy and public ownership of all trans-Canada pipelines. A year later the party called for 'Canadian resources for Canadians' and blamed the Liberals for allowing the Canadian economy to 'fall increasingly under the control of American corporations'.

The NDP Era

In 1961 the New Party Declaration, issued to mark the birth of the NDP, noted that in the 'struggle between democracy and totalitarianism' Canada must stand for freedom. However, it also warned of the danger 'of relying on military strength as the chief means of settling international disputes'. While welcoming the formation of the Common Market, the new party expressed concern that NATO had concentrated too much on a military role.[5]

Opposing the provision of nuclear weapons for Canadian troops, the Declaration urged 'an immediate ban on nuclear tests' as a first step towards disarmament and proposed the establishment of 'a non-nuclear club of nations' in which Canada would 'play a much more dynamic role'. It also stated that if NATO increased its nuclear orientation, Canada should not remain in the alliance. To relieve tensions in Europe, the party suggested a demilitarization of central Europe and the simultaneous disbandment of both the Warsaw Pact and NATO. In addition, the party questioned the value of the NORAD agreement to the defence of Canada, and asserted that it had 'outlived its usefulness'.

Again the United Nations was seen as the best hope for peace. The NDP urged the creation of a permanent international police force and suggested that in the interim Canada should establish a 'mobile force' ready for UN service. It also expressed the hope that Canada would cease voting as part of the Cold War blocs, pointing to the Commonwealth as a positive alternative.

Calculating that Canadians were spending billions of dollars a year on defence but less than five per cent of that amount on economic aid, the party called for a drastic alteration of this ratio. Canada's 'agricultural and industrial potential' should be put to use to relieve global famine and Canada's youth mobilized to work as overseas volunteers. Finally, like the CCF before it, the new party expressed concern over foreign corporate control of Canadian industry and resources, which if unchecked would 'endanger Canada's political independence'. Accordingly, the NDP called for legislation repatriating Canada's resources and industries. Yet at the same time it criticized tariffs as 'out-moded, patchwork attempts to protect domestic industry' and proposed a closer economic association with West European states and trade with the Third World.

In the election of 1962 the NDP was similarly inconsistent. Although it called for reductions in foreign control of Canadian industries, in the same breath it recommended freer trading arrangements. The party urged 'universal disarmament' but opted for the middle ground with respect to NATO, stating that it encouraged efforts to reappraise and change the alliance's policies and objectives.

Defence issues and the question of American interference in Canadian domestic affairs received unusual prominence in the 1963 election. The NDP's position on nuclear weapons, unlike that of the Liberals and Conservatives, was clear-cut. Strongly opposing any nuclear weapons for Canadian forces either in Canada or overseas in Europe, the party continued to stress that a permanent mobile force of Canadian troops should be available to the United Nations for peacekeeping operations throughout the world. It also urged that Canada increase its foreign aid to 2% of the GNP.

Against the backdrop of escalating conflict in Southeast Asia, the NDP's 1965 election pamphlet called for an end to the Vietnam War and admission of communist China to the United Nations. Calling, yet again, for a reappraisal of NATO's role, the party also reiterated its suggestion that Canada's armed forces become more mobile and more involved in UN peacekeeping operations. In addition, it pointed out that the problems of foreign ownership were becoming 'more serious'.

By the end of the 1960s Canadian nationalism was emerging as a major public issue as concern grew over foreign investment and the rise of the Marxist-inspired New Left. Once more the NDP warned about the risks of excessive foreign ownership and economic domination of Canada. Party leader T.C. Douglas criticized the escalation of the Vietnam War and called for a cessation of US bombing of North Vietnam. The NDP also urged the dismantling of both the NATO and Warsaw Pact military alliances in favour of a common European security system.

In the first federal election following the NDP's heated 1969 Winnipeg convention (see Cross, 1974), the party's 1972 election platform stressed the need for Canadians to recover their economic independence, called for an end to the plundering of Canadian resources to fuel US industry, and opposed any continental energy deal (see Laxer, 1970). One of the first steps the party proposed was to achieve public ownership in the oil and gas industry. Calling for a ban on all nuclear testing, the NDP now favoured the more radical position of withdrawal from both NATO and NORAD. This militancy was largely a reaction to the absence of democratic government in the NATO states of Portugal and Greece and the continuing US involvement in Vietnam.

In the early 1970s yet another war in the Middle East triggered an explosion in oil prices and, as a consequence, inflation. Among the items introduced in Canada's minority Parliament were plans for a government-owned national oil company and a foreign investment review agency (FIRA). In the 1974 campaign, the NDP reiterated its opposition to a continental energy deal and instead suggested that Canada should become self-sufficient in oil by the end of the 1970s.

Over the next decade the main plank of the NDP's foreign policy was its opposition to NATO and NORAD,[6] although in its election pamphlet of 1984 it also pointed out that the NDP was the only major party opposed to Cruise missile testing and seeking to turn Canada into a nuclear-free zone. Finally, in the spring of 1988, on the eve of a national election, the party's federal council issued a report on defence options entitled *Canada's Stake in Common Security*. While formally retaining the long-term goal of Canada's withdrawal from NATO, the report added the promise that an NDP government would not actually withdraw from NATO during its first term in office. Although this was an ingenious attempt at closing the internal divisions on this issue and conveying the image of a party ready to govern, some strategists worried that it might not appeal to voters concerned about the party's adherence to its principles.

In the end, of course, the party's NATO policy had very little effect on the election, which focused almost exclusively on the Canada–United

States free-trade agreement. Although the NDP seemed well-positioned to carry the banner of opposition to free trade (Whitehorn, 1989, 1992), to the surprise and anger of many activists the leadership chose to mute the party's nationalist commitment during much of the campaign.

In the 1993 election, although continental trade was once again an issue (this time in the form of the North American Free Trade Agreement, or NAFTA), it lacked the impact among the electorate that the Free Trade Agreement had had in 1988. Now Canadians as a whole appeared more concerned with domestic issues—ousting the Tories, the role of Quebec in Canada, the politics of regionalism, government spending—and with the personalities of the party leaders (and former leaders). Although the NDP clearly opposed NAFTA, the issue was not important enough to provide much political gain.

DELEGATES' ATTITUDES ON DEFENCE AND FOREIGN POLICY

Having briefly set the historical context, we will now turn to the second focus of this chapter, NDP convention delegates' attitudes. The sole question on defence posed in the 1971 NDP convention survey concerned defence spending. In the context of continuing American involvement in the Vietnam conflict and the ongoing Cold War between the United States and the Soviet Union, the overwhelming majority (85.3%) of delegates replied that they favoured a reduction in military spending. Even by 1987, when Canadians were more involved in peacekeeping, the majority (54.7%) of activists supported spending less on defence.[7] (Regrettably, no questions were asked on the subject of peacekeeping.) Many on the left link the notion of spending less on defence with a corresponding increase in funding for foreign aid. When delegates were asked whether Canada should devote more effort and aid to underdeveloped countries, large majorities (74.1% in 1971; 79.7% in 1987) replied in the affirmative.[8]

Almost all NDP delegates agreed (97.6%) with the suggestion that Canada should pursue an independent foreign policy; 59.2% strongly agreed, and not a single delegate strongly disagreed. As we shall see, this desire for independence was also reflected in delegates' attitudes towards involvement in the NATO and NORAD military alliances.

Most of the delegates (71.6%) also believed that Canada should shift its defence priorities towards the North.[9] Whether this reflected an isolationist desire to stay out of European affairs or simply a desire for better allocation of resources is unclear. Finally, a majority (64.5%) of NDP delegates rejected the notion that the British Commonwealth connection was unimportant.

Military Alliances and Weaponry

Since the Second World War Canada's involvement in the NATO and NORAD military alliances has often provoked debate among social democrats. In general, however, the idea of a world polarized by opposing military alliances has been an alarming one for most party members. As a result, the proportions of delegates supporting the party's official position that Canada should withdraw from NATO and NORAD were relatively stable: 58.6% and 59.9% respectively in 1983 (Whitehorn, 1992: 124) and 56.5% and 58.3% in 1987 (see Table 9.2). Nevertheless, significant minorities disagreed (31.1% and 24.4% in 1983; 28.3% and 22.5% in 1987). While no federal convention surveys have been administered since 1989, it seems likely that the collapse of the Soviet Union at the end of the decade has increased support, particularly within the NDP, for Canada's withdrawal (see Fortmann and Cloutier, 1991).

In a party that has strongly opposed the international preoccupation with the arms race and reliance on deadly weaponry, very high proportions (91.3% in 1983 and 92.8 in 1987) of delegates opposed the bringing of

Table 9.1

Attitudes Towards Defence and Foreign Policy, 1987

Statement/Question	Strongly agree/ agree %	Uncertain %	Strongly disagree/ disagree %	N
Canada should spend less on defence	54.7	20.2	25.1	(722)
Canada ought to devote much more effort and money to aiding the underdeveloped countries	79.7	11.9	8.5	(731)
Canada should pursue a foreign policy more independent of the United States	97.6	1.8	0.7	(730)
Canada should shift its defence priorities from Western Europe to protecting Canadian sovereignty in the North	71.6	22.3	6.1	(718)
The Commonwealth connection is no longer important for Canada	20.2	15.3	64.5	(734)

	Increase/ greatly increase	Keep the same	Decrease/ greatly decrease	N
How much spending?				
Defence	21.9	18.5	59.6	(720)
Foreign aid	76.7	16.6	6.8	(719)

Table 9.2
Attitudes Towards Military Alliances and Weaponry, 1987

Statement/Question	Strongly agree/ agree %	Uncertain %	Strongly disagree/ disagree %	N
Canada should remain in NATO	28.3	15.1	56.5	(720)
Canada should remain in NORAD	22.5	19.2	58.3	(720)
No nuclear weapons should be permitted on Canadian territory	92.8	2.7	4.5	(736)
Canada should refuse to permit the testing of the Cruise missile on Canadian soil	94.0	2.3	3.6	(736)
Canada should disarm unilaterally	41.4	17.8	40.9	(721)

nuclear weapons into Canada; the intensity of feeling can be seen in the fact that 63.3% selected the 'strongly agree' response. Agreement was similarly high (94.0%; 71.6% 'strong') that the federal government should have refused to allow testing of the Cruise missile—which many regarded as a potential first-strike weapon—in Canada.[10]

A major finding in both 1983 and 1987 was that relatively high proportions of delegates favoured unilateral disarmament for Canada (59.2% in 1983 and 41.4% in 1987).[11] While this was no longer the majority view in 1987, it was still the largest category of reply, at least by a slim margin (40.9% disagreed). Certainly J.S. Woodsworth, the former Methodist minister who became the first federal leader of the CCF, was an unequivocal proponent of non-violence and pacifism at the time of the Second World War, but his voice was in the minority (Horn, 1980). Although the party has been critical of defence spending and military alliances, it was nevertheless surprising to find such a level of support for unilateral disarmament. (In follow-up interviews, several activists suggested that some respondents might have interpreted this question as referring specifically to nuclear weapons. This may be so, although Canada is not officially a nuclear power. In any case, the proportion supporting unilateral disarmament was dramatically lower (41.4% vs 92.8%) than that supporting the exclusion of nuclear weapons, and this suggests that at least a majority of delegates perceived a difference between the two questions.)

The Cold War[12]
A relapse in superpower relations occured during the Brezhnev/Reagan era as both superpowers made increasingly bellicose statements about the

militarization of space, the Soviet Union invaded Afghanistan, and the United States invaded Grenada. Perhaps as a result, when delegates at the 1987 convention were asked their opinion on the likelihood of nuclear war within twenty years, only 30.1% rejected the possibility entirely; 30.6% did expect such a war, and 39.3% were 'uncertain'.[13] Nevertheless, a majority (52.0%, up from 47.5% in 1983) of delegates disagreed with the notion that détente was an illusion, and the proportion agreeing declined from 35.4% in 1983 to 22.7% in 1987. By the end of the decade, the progress of the reforms introduced during the Gorbachev era no doubt fostered new hope for an end to the Cold War, but unfortunately no questions on defence or foreign policy were posed at the 1989 leadership convention.

When delegates at the 1983 and 1987 conventions were asked which of the two superpowers presented the greater threat to world peace, the highest proportions (65.1% in 1983 and 48.3% in 1987) suggested that the US and the USSR were about equal in blame. This response was consistent with the party's long-standing desire to see Canada pursue a path independent of the military alliances of the two superpowers. However, among those delegates who did point to one of the two as more of a threat, the great majority selected the US (by almost 5 to 1 in 1983, and 15 to 1 in 1987).[14] Presumably a key factor in this response pattern was the Canadian nationalist—in some cases, even anti-American—orientation of many New Democrats (see Granatstein, 1996). This theme will be explored in more

Table 9.3

Attitudes Towards the Threat of War and the Soviet Union, 1987

Statement/Question	Strongly agree/ agree %	Uncertain %	Strongly disagree/ disagree %	N
A nuclear war is likely within the next 20 years	30.6	39.3	30.1	(720)
Détente is an illusion	22.7	25.4	52.0	(698)
Soviet communism is no longer a threat to Canada	53.2	19.3	27.4	(724)
Canada should seek closer relations with communist countries	56.2	23.1	20.6	(723)

Which of the two superpowers is the greater threat to world peace?

US	46.9%
USSR	3.4
About equal	48.3
Neither	1.4
N	(731)

detail below. Finally, as early as 1971, most NDP delegates (66.8%; 53.2% in 1987) did not perceive the Soviet Union as a threat to Canada, and increasing numbers of delegates over the years (36.5% in 1979, 57.8% in 1983, and 56.2% in 1987) favoured closer ties with communist countries.

Canada–US Relations

Among the industrialized nations of the world, Canada for many decades had an unusually high proportion of foreign-owned industry (Levitt, 1970). The CCF was an early critic of this pattern of dependency, and the NDP has continued the critique. Not surprisingly, overwhelming majorities of delegates at NDP conventions (95.8% in 1979, 96.3% in 1983, and 95.8% in 1987) agreed that Canada's independence is threatened by the large percentage of foreign ownership in key sectors of its economy. The intensity of feeling on this subject can be seen in the fact that in 1987 53.5% selected the 'strongly agree' response. With regard to the cost of proposed remedies for excessive foreign ownership, more than three-quarters of the delegates at all the NDP conventions surveyed (76.0% in 1971, 76.7% in 1979, 81.0% in 1983, and 76.8% in 1987) agreed that Canada should ensure its independence even if that meant accepting a lower living standard. By contrast, Liberal and Conservative delegates in the mid-1980s expressed much lower support for these positions: only 51.5% of Liberals and 27.3% of Conservatives agreed with the former; 58.1% of Liberals and 33.3% of Conservatives with the latter (Blake, 1988; for comparisons on continentalism see Chapter 3).

The influence of the US on Canada is not limited to the economic realm (see Godfrey and Watkins, 1970; Hurtig, 1992a, 1992b, 1996; Laxer, 1973; Mathews and Steele, 1969). Thus very high proportions of NDP delegates (92.5% in 1971; 91.6% in 1983; and 94.5% in 1987, 53.2% 'strongly') also agreed that Canada must reduce American influence on its culture and mass media. Even the trade unions—a key building block in the NDP alliance—have been targets of nationalist fervour. Delegates at all four conventions showed increasing support (79.0% in 1971, 78.5% in 1979, 79.9% in 1983, and 94.5% in 1987) for the position that Canadian affiliates of international unions should have full autonomy.

The key issue in the 1988 federal election was the Canada–US Free Trade Agreement (Clarke et al., 1991; Johnston et al., 1992; Whitehorn, 1989; 1992). In the years preceding that election, nearly three-quarters of NDP delegates disagreed with the statements that there should be no tariffs or duties between Canada and the United States (74.7% in 1983, 79.6% in 1987) and that Canada should have freer trade with the United States (72.5% in 1979, 67.7% in 1987). In contrast, majorities of both Liberal and

Conservative delegates (63.9% and 53.7% respectively) favoured free trade in the 1980s (Blake, 1988; Goldfarb and Axworthy, 1988; Chapter 3 of this book). Despite Liberal leader John Turner's strong opposition to the proposed Free Trade Agreement in the 1988 federal election, the attitudes of Liberal delegates in general suggest that, over the long term, the Liberal position on this issue might weaken, and in fact, after four years in office, the Liberal government had not rescinded the agreement. Apart from Mel Hurtig's short-lived National Party (Hurtig, 1992a, 1992b, 1996), the NDP has remained the Canadian party most opposed to continentalism. Finally, 79.1% of the delegates in 1987 agreed with the assertion that the NDP is a nationalist party. These survey items point to the increasing importance of nationalism within the NDP. Although, like socialism, nationalism is a collectivist ideology, the two do not necessarily complement one another: where socialism is inclusionary, nationalism can be strongly exclusionary. Whether the two can continue to coexist in the NDP will remain a topic of debate (Mathews, 1988; Whitehorn, 1992).

Table 9.4
Attitudes Towards Canada–US Relations, 1987

Statement/Question	Strongly agree/agree %	Uncertain %	Strongly disagree/disagree %	N
Canada's independence is threatened by the large percentage of foreign ownership in key sectors of our economy	95.8	1.6	2.6	(733)
We must ensure an independent Canada even if that were to mean a lower standard of living for Canadians	76.8	12.0	11.2	(723)
Canada must have freer trade with the United States	14.1	18.1	67.7	(722)
There should be no tariffs or duties between Canada and the United States	6.8	13.6	79.6	(730)
We ought to seek greater American investment in Canada	4.8	9.3	86.0	(735)
Canada must take steps to reduce American influence on its culture and mass media	94.5	3.1	2.3	(731)
Canadian affiliates of international unions should have full autonomy	86.4	8.0	5.6	(735)
The NDP is a nationalist party	79.1	11.1	9.8	(714)

The Third World and Immigration Policy

We have already seen that most New Democrats have called for less spending on defence and a corresponding increase in foreign aid to Third World countries. Not surprisingly, in 1987 most delegates agreed (87.3%; 52.5% 'strongly') that Canada should stop selling arms to developing states; among those who did disagree, not one disagreed 'strongly'. In addition, a majority (69.5%) of delegates called for recognition of more Third World liberation movements.

Although, strictly speaking, immigration is a matter of domestic rather than foreign policy, delegates' attitudes in this area reflect the traditional socialist emphasis on internationalism and working-class solidarity. The overwhelming majority of delegates (90.8%) agreed that Canada should accept immigrants from all ethnic and racial groups, and almost half (45.2%) 'strongly' agreed. Activists also showed a commitment to multiculturalism in their strong opposition (81.6%) to the idea of reducing the rate of immigration to Canada.

INTRA-PARTY CLEAVAGES

What, if any, differences are there in the attitudes towards defence, foreign policy, and nationalism of the various demographic groups within the NDP? Of the 29 variables explored in Table 9.6, only 5 showed gender differences of 10% or more (see also Chapter 6). The greatest gender gap was found on the issue of defence spending (a difference of 24%), followed by unilateral disarmament (22%). Women delegates were more likely than men to call for reductions in defence spending and to favour unilateral disarmament. In addition, women were more likely than men to oppose freer trade with the United States (a finding consistent with 1988 election surveys). Presumably a factor contributing to this pattern was the concern expressed by many women that free trade would jeopardize social programs.

Almost half the items in Table 9.6 (13) showed differences of 10% or more by delegate type (constituency/union).[15] It has often been suggested that Canadian trade unions, in many cases influenced by American parent unions, have acted as a conservative influence within the CCF–NDP. Partial support for this view can be seen in the paired items on NORAD and NATO membership. While constituency delegates favoured withdrawal from these military agreements by about a two-thirds majority, affiliated union delegates tended to support the alliances (see also Chapter 4). Constituency delegates in 1987 were also more inclined to believe that détente was an illusion, while union delegates tended to choose the 'uncertain' reply. (With less formal education, perhaps they understood the term 'détente' less well.) Finally, union delegates were less likely to take progressive stands on issues such as aid to Third World countries and accepting immigrants from all groups. These findings, which echo earlier work by Lipset (1960), appear to be correlated with the lower educational levels of union delegates (see below and Chapter 4).

Of all the variables explored, region provided the greatest number of differences of 10% or more (17).[16] The greatest differences along regional lines appeared on the two items concerning spending on defence. Even though Quebec was a major beneficiary of defence contracts, delegates from that province were the most inclined to favour cuts in defence spending. Such a stance, one would suspect, might be attractive to Quebec nationalists, a group the NDP has frequently sought to court. Delegates from Atlantic Canada, where a significant number of military bases are located and the cultural milieu is somewhat conservative, were the least likely to agree with such cuts. Regional differences were also apparent on the issue of unilateral disarmament. A majority of Quebec delegates favoured this option, while the second highest level of support came from the West and the lowest from Atlantic Canada. The same regional pattern was evident on a number of other issues, including NORAD. On the issue of free trade the opposition was lowest among delegates from Atlantic Canada and Quebec and highest among those from Ontario and the West.

Only eight items showed differences of 10% or more according to age.[17] The greatest gap concerned willingness to ensure Canada's indepen-

Table 9.5
Attitudes Towards the Third World and Immigration Policy, 1987

Statement/Question	Strongly agree/agree %	Uncertain %	Strongly disagree/disagree %	N
Canada should stop selling military weapons to countries in the Third World	87.3	8.3	4.4	(732)
Canada ought to devote much more effort and money to aiding the underdeveloped countries	79.7	11.9	8.5	(731)
Canada should give recognition to more national liberation movements in the Third World	69.5	24.9	5.6	(715)
When Canada admits immigrants, it should take them from all ethnic and racial groups	90.8	5.2	4.1	(735)
We should dramatically reduce the rate of immigration to Canada	7.2	11.2	81.6	(731)

Table 9.6

The Impact of Demographic Characteristics on Attitudes Towards Defence and Foreign Policy, 1987

Statement	Gender M.	Gender F.	Del.Type const.	Del.Type union	Region BC	Region Pra.	Region Ont.	Region Que.	Region Atl.	Age Yng	Age Mid.	Age Old	Education[a] Sec.	Education[a] Univ.
Canada should spend less on defence	47	71			64	65	48	70	35					
Canada ought to devote much more effort and money to aiding the underdeveloped countries			82	65									65	84
Canada should pursue a foreign policy more independent of the United States*														
Canada should shift its defence priorities from Western Europe to protecting Canadian sovereignty in the North			73	60	84	67	70	69	75					
The Commonwealth connection is no longer important for Canada					68D	70D	63D	46D	71D				54D	67D
Defence spending should be decreased or greatly decreased	53	74	64	50	68	69	53	77	44				51	62
Foreign aid spending should be increased or greatly increased			80	58									59	82
Canada should remain in NATO			63D	26D	69D	61D	50D	63D	55D	71D	55D	52D	36D	62D
Canada should remain in NORAD			66D	25D	71D	64D	53D	63D	47D				34D	65D
No nuclear weapons should be permitted on Canadian territory					96	96	92	93	83					

Statement											
Canada should refuse to permit the testing of the Cruise missile on Canadian soil*	34	56									
Canada should disarm unilaterally	45	47	38	52	22						
A nuclear war is likely within the next 20 years*											
Détente is an illusion	56D	33D	51D	52D	54D	60D	39D	39D	56D		
Soviet communism is no longer a threat to Canada	58	38	66	53	49	60	43	41	57		
Canada should seek closer relations with Communist countries	59	49	58	41	63	59	53	63	50	44	60
Which of the two superpowers is the greater threat to world peace (response: US)	50	32	62	50	41	44	52	56	47	46	
Canada's independence is threatened by the large percentage of foreign ownership in key sectors of our economy*											
We must ensure an independent Canada even if that were to mean a lower standard of living for Canadians	79	64	78	79	77	68	79	63	75	90	
Canada should have freer trade with the United States	64D	76D	62D	64D	76D	61D	56D	69D	72D	58D	
There should be no tariffs or duties between Canada and the United States	81D	85D	69D								

Table 9.6 continued

	Gender		Del. Type		Demographic Characteristic — Region					Age			Education[a]	
Statement	M.	F.	const.	union	BC	Pra.	Ont.	Que.	Atl.	Yng	Mid.	Old	Sec.	Univ.
We ought to seek greater American investment in Canada					86D	94D	87D	70D	83D					
Canada must take steps to reduce American influence on its culture and mass media*														
Canadian affiliates of international unions should have full autonomy*														
The NDP is a nationalist party					77	74	82	75	88	85	81	71		
Canada should stop selling military weapons to countries in the Third World*														
Canada should give recognition to more national liberation movements in the Third World			73	52	77	72	65	76	70				55	74
When Canada admits immigrants, it should take them from all ethnic and racial groups			92	81						93	94	84	83	94
We should dramatically reduce the rate of immigration to Canada										90D	83D	72D	62D	87D
Total cases with statistically significant differences (10% or more)	5			13			17				8			12

NOTES: 'D' indicates disagreement with statement; * indicates statistically insignificant differences (not presented).

[a] Sub-sample with only primary education too small for inclusion.

dence even at the cost of a lower standard of living (a difference of 27%, with young people the least likely to agree). Perhaps reflecting a greater pride in Canada's heritage, older delegates were the most likely to support independence regardless of the cost. While no age group actually gave NATO an endorsement, the older delegates, more likely to recall the brutal Stalinist regimes imposed on Eastern Europe in the early days of the Cold War, were the least inclined to pull out of the alliance. Finally, while on balance all age groups opposed the idea of reducing the rate of immigration, older delegates were the most likely to support such cuts, perhaps reflecting more traditional images of Canada.

Twelve items showed differences of 10% or more when controlling for education. The most educated delegates were almost twice as inclined as those with only a secondary-school education to favour withdrawal from NORAD and NATO. The fact that the same two items topped the list of differences according to type of delegate, with union members (who tend to have less education than other delegates) favouring these military alliances, suggests that more progressive attitudes are strongly linked with higher education. Similarly, delegates with more formal education were more likely to take a liberal view of immigration, opposing cuts.

Of the five demographic variables, region was correlated with differences on the most items (17), followed by delegate type (13), education (12), age (8), and gender (5). The largest differences were by type of delegate and concerned participation in NORAD (41% difference) and NATO (37% difference); the third largest difference was by region on the issue of defence spending.

The issues that revealed the most demographic differences of 10% or more were NATO (delegate type, region, age, education) and defence spending (gender, delegate type, region, education), followed by NORAD (delegate type, region, education).

CONCLUSION

The data from the 1987 convention survey echo the CCF–NDP's historical record on issues of defence and foreign policy. The NDP's response to the Gulf War in 1991, when it opposed Canada's involvement and advocated reliance on trade sanctions (McLaughlin, 1992), offers further confirmation of the party's preference for non-violent common-security solutions in international relations.

No doubt the issues of Canada's involvement in NATO and NORAD and appropriate levels of defence spending will continue to be debated and differences of opinion associated with various demographic groups will remain significant. Canada's role in peacekeeping and/or peacemaking is destined to have a higher profile and also greater risks, both military and political. The CCF–NDP repeatedly called for an end to the bipolar East–West confrontations of the Cold War, but today the international left–right division seems to have receded in the face of competing nationalisms. The NDP, as both a socialist and a nationalist party, may find the issue of nationalism much more of a double-edged sword in the future.

As to Canadian nationalism and Canada's unique relationship with the United States, the NDP will likely continue to be wary of the superpower's embrace, whether economic or military. While the NDP's nationalist flag wavered during the 1988 federal election, it was raised once again during the 1993 federal election campaign in the debate over NAFTA. The continuing globalization of the economy and the increasing dependence of Canada's economy on trade with the US will undoubtedly heighten anxieties among Canadian economic and cultural nationalists. The NDP will play an important role in providing a political home for such concerns.

NOTES

1 On the theme of idealism vs realism in foreign policy see Carr, 1964.

2 Joel Sokolsky (1989) writes: 'There is no disagreement on the need to increase Arctic capabilities, air defence, or the requirement for additional land forces to support civil authority in Canada in the event of an emergency. . . . But there is a profound difference between the NDP approach to defence and that of the Conservatives and even the Liberals, particularly in regard to relations with the United States.' See also Coulon (1991: 154).

3 But see Groome (1967); Sims (1977); Thorburn (1986). In addition, several edited readers on social democracy in Canada have chapters on defence/foreign policy: Oliver (1961); Richards et al. (1991); Rosenblum and Findlay (1991); Wilson (1985).

4 Much of this section is based on Whitehorn (1992).

5 Thorburn (1986) describes the NDP's stand as at times reflecting a policy of 'semi-alignment' similar to that adopted by several social-democratic governments in Scandinavia.

6 Broadbent's attempts in 1980 to soften the party's official position on NATO brought an angry rebuke from BC New Democrat MP Pauline Jewett.

7 Unless stated otherwise, percentages cited are those from the 1987 survey.

8 For differences between NDP and Liberal and Conservative delegates on defence and foreign policy, see Chapter 3. For data on the Canadian public's attitude to defence spending, see Fortmann and Cloutier (1991).

9 Even some Department of National Defence studies echoed this theme. See 'Defence department think tank echoes NDP proposals', *Ottawa Citizen*, 10 Aug. 1987.

10 The Persian Gulf War confirmed its first-strike capability.

11 A similar position was officially adopted by the British Labour Party.

12 Readers should be cautioned to note that the survey was taken in the spring of 1987—well before the dramatic events of the late 1980s that saw the withdrawal of Soviet troops from East European satellite states and the collapse of the Soviet Union itself.

13 For an overview of Canadian public opinion on this topic, see Fortmann and Cloutier (1991); for data on youth, see Bibby and Posterski (1985: 150; 1992).

14 Comparative data on party supporters and members reveal that NDP voters take a more critical attitude to the United States than do other voters (CBC Research, 1985: 66; see also Chapter 3).

15 While there are several types of delegates, only the two largest categories were selected for study because the other categories offered too small a sample size.

16 This finding may in part reflect the large number of categories for region, although the multiple categories of age did not reveal a similar pattern.

17 As was noted in Chapter 7, the youngest age category includes all delegates aged 29 and under.

CHAPTER 10

A 'New Politics'? Materialism and Postmaterialism

The Canadian party system has undergone profound changes in recent years. The issue of Quebec's role in the confederation, never far from the centre of Canada's political stage, has gained new vigour within the emergence of the Bloc Québécois, while concerns about regional representation, as well as honesty and integrity in government, have been strongly expressed by the Reform Party. The rapid growth of these new parties illustrates the capacity of the party system to recompose itself in response to the emergence of new political issues.

There has been speculation that the linguistic and regional divisions that have dominated the party system may be joined by other, even more far-reaching cleavages involving the so-called 'new politics' (Amyot, 1986; Phillips, 1996). The term 'new politics' usually describes a collection of issues related to the environment, political equality, and quality of life that cluster together under the heading of postmaterialism (Inglehart, 1977, 1990; Kitschelt, 1989, 1994). Postmaterialist values are usually seen as a challenge to parties of the left because they represent an even more radical alternative to the materialist orientation of capitalism than does the traditional left, with its emphasis on jobs and wages. This chapter will examine where and to what degree postmaterialist issues have emerged in the New Democratic Party. Are these issues fostering new divisions among various groups within the party? If so, will they lead to a realignment of group relationships in the NDP?

POSTMATERIALISM IN CANADA

A growing number of analysts today suggest that the changing value systems in industrial democracies are making traditional political alignments obsolete. They posit that whereas, in the past, political alignments in most industrial democracies were based on two competing models of economic distribution, debated under the ideological markers of 'left' and 'right' and organized by class-based parties, a new political alignment is emerging that is based more on the quality of life (Inglehart, 1990; Milbrath, 1984; Morris, 1979) than the quantity of income—that is, postmaterialist values—and that centres on ecological or 'green' parties (Bookchin, 1990; Dobson, 1991; Gorz, 1980; Hulsberg, 1988; Kemp and Wall, 1990; Porrit, 1984). According to this model, the relevant opposition today is between the 'old' materialist industrial orientation, whether of the left or the right, and a 'new' postmaterialist orientation (Inglehart, 1977; 1990).

The *prima facie* evidence suggests that Canada may be relatively immune to these trends, or at least to their most obvious manifestations. For example, survey evidence over at least a generation indicates that economic issues, far from receding in importance, have remained at the forefront of the concerns of Canadian voters from the early 1970s through the 1990s (Clarke et al., 1991: 69–87; Clarke and Kornberg, 1992; Fletcher and Drummond, 1979). From inflation in 1974 to unemployment in 1984 (Archer and Johnson, 1988) to free trade in 1988 (Johnston et al., 1992) and the pervasive uncertainties of the 1990s, the fact that economic concerns have remained high on the political agenda and in voters' perceptions as the most important issues in elections seriously challenges the claim that political debate and divisions are increasingly about postmaterialist concerns centring on the environment and quality of life. To date, no significant increase in support for ecological or green parties in Canada has emerged to lend weight to the postmaterialist thesis. Although the Green Party of Canada was formally registered in 1984, it has never won a seat in the House of Commons or a provincial legislature; it has never received even one per cent of the national vote; and as late as 1990 it had an annual operating budget of less than $60,000—less than one per cent of the operating budgets of the Liberals, Conservatives, or New Democrats at that time (Elections Canada, 1991).

Nevertheless, some researchers have suggested that postmaterialist values are evident among a key segment of the electorate. For example, in their study of Canadian youth élites, Nevitte, Bakvis, and Gibbins found that the postmaterialist–materialist divide rivalled left–right ideology in its explanatory power, and that in some policy domains—notably foreign affairs—postmaterialism was a superior predictor of attitudes (1989: 488–9). In addition they reported that the NDP was unique among the major parties in receiving disproportionate support from people espousing postmaterialist values. However, they also noted that this support may face the party with a serious conundrum:

> can parties of the left simultaneously hold their traditional bases of support and satisfy postmaterialists? . . . the difficulties emerge over attempts to resolve the tradeoffs between such issues as economic growth and environmental protection. (1989: 500–1)

Nevitte et al. note that an important fault line may emerge within the NDP as it endeavours to appeal to voters with postmaterialist values and at the same time maintain its links with organized labour. They speculate that, with unionists (and blue-collar workers) anchoring the materialist side of the cleavage, any attempt to increase the party's postmaterialist constituency is likely to create conflicts. The argument that unionists act to stifle the emergence of new and more creative lines of political debate within the NDP is not novel (see, for example, Brodie, 1985; Brodie and Jensen, 1988; Hackett, 1979; but see also Chapter 4). In the past, the typical critique was that labour prevented the party from adopting a more radical socialist agenda. The new critique, in contrast, while acknowledging the link between postmaterialism and political ideas on the 'left' (Flanagan, 1987; Milbrath, 1984: 24; Nevitte et al., 1989), suggests that the labour caucus may prevent the party from adopting a postmaterialist agenda—which, as an emerging 'mainstream' of political thinking, may represent an opportunity for growth in partisan support.

Although the argument of Nevitte et al. is intriguing, their data were not well-suited to test their speculations about the NDP, particularly with respect to labour's role in opposing the emergence of the new politics, because their sample of university students did not adequately represent members of organized labour. This chapter will pursue empirically some of their more speculative hypotheses with the help of data taken from surveys of NDP convention delegates.

MEASURES AND METHODS

A key feature of the Nevitte, Bakvis, and Gibbins analysis was a comparison of the explanatory strength of two indexes: postmaterialist versus materialist and left versus right (1989; for more on such indexes, see Inglehart, 1977, 1990; Milbrath, 1984). In part, they were interested in examining which of the two measures played a more prominent role in organizing political thought and in structuring attitudes towards political issues. In this chapter we will explore some of the lines of division, both attitudinally and organizationally, within the NDP by using data from the 1987 and 1989 federal convention surveys. This analysis differs from a full replication of the Nevitte et al. study because of several important differences in data bases.

First, the focus on convention delegates emphasizes the views of party activists and decision-makers as opposed to those who simply identify with the party. Parties, of course, mean different things to different people, and it is well known that party activists tend to have a more structured set of political attitudes than the mass public (see, for example, Converse, 1964;

Kornberg et al., 1975). Thus a party can be seen as representing quite different political beliefs, or levels of ideological coherence, depending upon which strata of the party hierarchy are studied: the parliamentary caucus, party conventions, party members in general, or party identifiers. Although the Nevitte et al. study of youth élites attempts to control for features such as age and level of education, the convention samples contain a richness and diversity of party activists that is not replicated in youth élite studies.

Second, the structural linkage between organized labour and the NDP, and the crucial role that labour is seen to play in anchoring the materialist end of the postmaterialist scale makes it difficult to assess the degree to which postmaterialism represents either a significant departure or a major ideological divide for the NDP without including a measure of unionism in the data. In short, if one is to ask whether unions and their members present an obstacle to the adoption of a new political agenda, it is necessary to assess the extent to which trade unionists anchor the 'old' political agenda. The NDP convention data are well suited to this purpose because they include a sufficiently large number of union delegates.

A third difference in the two data bases is that our NDP surveys do not rely on the standard battery of questions used in the construction of post-materialist scales (see for example Milbrath, 1984: 133). They do, however, include a number of items that can serve as surrogates: items measuring attitudes towards issues—women, minorities, youth, the environment, and quality of life—that are typically associated with postmaterialist concerns. In turn, these attitudes can be explored according to a number of criteria, such as union membership, gender, age, and left–right placement, to see how well the postmaterialist hypothesis fits. In addition, the fact that NDP conventions are organized in such a way that individuals with similar interests can join together in informal caucuses to share concerns and perspectives and to plan strategic behaviour (Whitehorn, 1992) makes it possible to explore the extent to which attendance at 'new politics' caucuses indicates a unique set of political attitudes or policy preferences, and to examine the behavioural consequences of such attendance.

OPINION STRUCTURE AMONG NEW DEMOCRATS

Chapter 3 demonstrated that, over a broad range of issue areas, New Democrats are more ideologically distinctive in the positions they take than are Liberals and Conservatives, and that they tend to show considerably more consensus on policy than their counterparts in the two older parties. In general, however, New Democrats still show substantial diversity in their views on a wide range of issues. In an analysis of attitudes towards various issues, Whitehorn (1992: 130–3) found evidence of both consensus and diversity of views: the highest levels of consensus were evident on women's issues, defence and foreign affairs (issues that Nevitte et al. associate with postmaterialism), the lowest on matters pertaining to internal party affairs, labour, government's role, and the welfare state.

Table 10.1 presents the attitudes of delegates to the 1987 convention on issues relating to the environment and quality of life, and towards minorities and immigration. Although the following discussion will refer briefly to attitudes towards women, class, the economy, social policy, youth, defence, and foreign affairs, readers are directed to earlier chapters for more detailed data on these issues. Most policy areas showed a high level of consensus on some specific items and considerably more diversity on others. For example, we saw in Chapter 6 that delegates were nearly unanimous in agreeing that women candidates for public office are as effective as men. There was also a very high level of agreement that a significant percentage of candidates and officers of the NDP should be women. However, consensus declined when respondents were asked whether women were discriminated against in the party, and as the questions moved from general attitudes to specific proposals to lessen gender-based differences, consensus was further reduced. Thus one in four delegates did not agree that women should have 50% of the seats on the party's federal council. Nevertheless, taken together, these data suggest that there is considerable support within the NDP for the 'new politics' issue of gender equality.

Likewise, Table 10.1 shows that NDP delegates appeared to hold positions consistent with 'new politics' perspectives on the environment (see also Whitehorn, 1992: 128–9) and on minorities and immigration. For example, they agreed almost without exception (99.2%) that there should be tougher laws for environmental polluters. Nearly 8 in 10 delegates (78.7%) believed that more attention should be paid to the quality of life than to the quantity of income, and 7 in 10 (70.6%) agreed that industrial society pollutes. In addition, more than 8 in 10 delegates favoured a moratorium on building nuclear reactors (83.4%), and a ban on the export of nuclear materials (81.7%). However, significant divisions emerged in delegates' assessments of the impact of technology: while roughly 40% thought its effects on the whole beneficial, almost 25% disagreed, and about 36% were uncertain. This division was likely influenced by perceptions of a trade-off between technology and jobs: to the extent that technological advances result in fewer jobs, New Democrats as a whole, and the party's labour section in particular, view technology more negatively.

On policies relating to minorities and immigration, delegates were nearly unanimous in the view that immigrants should be taken from all groups (90.7%), and they were almost equally united in opposing restrictions to immigration (81.5%) (see also Chapters 3 and 9).

Attitudes towards issues of defence and foreign affairs—closely related to postmaterialism, according to Nevitte, Bakvis, and Gibbins—also indicated

Table 10.1

Attitudes Towards Selected Policy Issues, 1987

Area/Statement	Strongly agree/agree %	Uncertain %	Strongly disagree/disagree %
Women (see Chapter 6)			
Environment/Quality of life			
Canada should take a tougher stand on environmental polluters	99.2	0.4	0.4
Industrial society is essentially a polluting society	70.6	10.4	19.1
We should be less concerned with the quantity of income and pay more attention to the quality of life	78.6	11.5	9.9
There should be a moratorium on building nuclear reactors	83.4	9.9	6.7
The export of nuclear materials should be banned	81.7	8.7	9.6
The good effects of technology outweigh its bad effects	39.4	36.6	24.0
Class (see Chapter 8)			
Economy (see Chapter 8)			
Minorities/Immigration			
When Canada admits immigrants, it should take them from all ethnic and racial groups	90.7	5.2	4.1
We should dramatically reduce the rate of immigration to Canada	7.3	11.2	81.5
Social policy (see Chapter 8)			
Youth (see Chapters 7 and 8)			
Defence and foreign policy (see Chapter 9)			

a range of views. Although delegates were nearly unanimous in opposing nuclear weapons, they were almost evenly divided over whether Canada should disarm unilaterally (Table 9.2). There were also significant differences in opinions on defence spending, with slightly more than half the delegates supporting cuts and almost one-quarter opposing them (Table 9.1). On foreign affairs the greatest consensus emerged on the propositions that Canada should pursue an independent foreign policy (Table 9.1), that American cultural and media influence in Canada should be reduced, and that foreign ownership threatens Canadian independence (Table 9.4).

The 'old politics' issues of the economy and social class (Chapter 8) provided evidence of both consistency and diversity. Delegates showed high levels of agreement on the statement that business has too much influence in Canada (Table 3.1), on the merits of a mixed economy (Table 8.2), and on the appropriateness of increasing employment over reducing inflation as a policy goal (Table 8.3). But they were clearly divided over the importance of reducing the deficit. Interesting variations were evident in the evaluations of class: almost all the delegates agreed that the rich should pay more taxes (Table 8.11), and almost all disagreed with the statement that there is no ruling class (Table 8.10). However, the importance of class was ambiguous: although slightly more than half the respondents agreed that the central question in politics is the class struggle, nearly one-third disagreed (see Table 8.10, and earlier data in Whitehorn, 1992: 131).

Thus delegates' attitudes towards individual policy areas showed both consensus and dissent within each area, 'new' and 'old' alike. To a considerable degree, the level of consensus depended on the particular question being answered, rather than the general policy area under examination. This suggests there is space for consistent differences to emerge among delegates, according to their age, gender, union connection, or left–right ideological position. Whether such differences do in fact emerge is the focus of the rest of this chapter.

The postmaterialist thesis leads to a number of expectations about the effects of delegates' age, gender, union connection, and left–right ideological position. For the purposes of this discussion the age variable compares those born after 1947 (post-war) with those born earlier.[1] One of the major assumptions of the postmaterialist thesis is that in advanced industrial democracies the value shift is most prevalent among the generations raised during the period of post-war prosperity. Thus we would expect the post-war generations to exhibit stronger postmaterialist concerns than their elders. The gender variable is included to measure the degree to which women's issues—also considered to be postmaterialist—divide the sexes. The union variable indicates whether the respondent is or is not an accredited union delegate (from an affiliated union, from central labour, or a union representative on the federal council). The expectation based on the postmaterialist thesis is that union delegates will be more materialist in orientation and take positions on issues consistently at odds with those of other party activists. The left–right variable refers to a standard seven-point scale, scored left (1) to right (7), and is included as a benchmark for the degree to which postmaterialism and materialism may be replacing left and right as the primary ideological poles. The expectation is that left–right differences will be greatest on issues such as perceptions of class and of the economy, and least on issues relating to the environment, women's issues, and attitudes towards minorities. The findings of Nevitte et al. would also suggest a decrease in the importance of left–right ideology in the area of defence and foreign affairs.

Table 10.2 examines the fit between delegates' issue positions and their union connection, gender, age, and left–right ideology. Cell entries are zero-order correlation coefficients.[2] Several features of the table warrant comment. The most consistent ideological divide in the NDP is between those who situate themselves on the party's left and those further to the right.[3] Left–right ideology was significantly related to issue positions on all but one of the 33 items included in the table. Furthermore, in most issue areas (the exceptions were women's issues, foreign affairs, and social policy), left–right ideology remained consistently powerful and the most significant predictor of political attitudes. Even in the policy areas where it was not the strongest predictor of issue positions, its importance rivalled that of any other predictor variables. Thus left–right ideology retains a generalized and pre-eminent importance in organizing issue positions within the NDP.

Each of the other predictor variables had an importance that was confined to specific policy areas. For example, unionism was an important predictor of attitudes in the areas of women's issues, immigration, defence, and foreign affairs (areas often associated with postmaterialism), but was less consistently related to attitudes towards the environment (another key postmaterialist issue). Furthermore, unionism showed no relation at all to the materialist area of the economy, and its effect on assessments of the importance of class was mixed. Finally, unionism had almost no effect on attitudes towards social policy—one of the pillars on which the NDP has built its electoral appeal.

The gender variable was associated with the smallest total of differences in delegates' attitudes. However, the differences between men and women on issues relating to women were large and significant. In addition, women were more favourable than men towards unilateral disarmament and reductions in defence spending, but for all other policy areas there were few significant differences. Thus the male–female divide in the party was not

Table 10.2

Attitudes Towards Policy Issues By Union, Sex, Age, and Left–Right Ideology, 1987 (zero–order correlations)

Area/Statement[a]	Non–union/ union	Men/ women	Post–war/ pre–war	Left/ right
Women				
Fifty per cent of the federal council should be composed of women	.23★★	−.20★★	.23★★	.21★★
The NDP should ensure that a significant percentage of its candidates and party officers are women	.21★★	−.14★★	.14★★	.24★★
Women are discriminated against within NDP	.17★★	−.22★★	.07	.22★★
On the whole, women are as effective as men as candidates for elected office	.12★★	−.18★★	.14★★	.14★★
Environment/quality of life				
Canada should take a tougher stand on environmental polluters	.07	−.03	.09★	.11★★
Industrial society is essentially a polluting society	.04	−.08	−.07	.11★
We should be less concerned with the quantity of income and pay more attention to the quality of life	.12★★	−.03	−.06	−.01
There should be a moratorium on building nuclear reactors	.11★★	−.14★★	.04	.23★★
The export of nuclear materials should be banned	.07	−.11★★	.08★	.18★★
The good effects of technology outweigh the bad effects	.00	.11★★	−.04	−.08★
Class				
The central question of Canadian politics is the class struggle between labour and capital	−.09★	.00	.00	.14★★
There is no ruling class in Canada	−.16★★	.00	−.15★★	−.22★★
The rich should pay more taxes	−.03	−.05	.11	.19★★
Economy				
Big business has too much influence in Canadian politics	−.05	−.05	.04	.13★★
An NDP government should seek to reduce the government deficit as much as possible	−.08	.00	−.15★★	−.22★★
If given a choice between increasing employment or decreasing inflation, the government should always opt for more jobs	−.03	−.01	.00	.11★

Table 10.2 continued

Area/Statement[a]	Non–union/ union	Men/ women	Post–war/ pre–war	Left/ right
The best hope for our economic development is a mixed economy with both private and public sector participating	.01	.00	−.05	.16★★
Minorities/immigration				
When Canada admits immigrants, it should take them from all ethnic and racial groups	.17★★	−.05	.21★★	.19★★
We should dramatically reduce the rate of immigration to Canada	−.16★★	.02	−.16★★	−.24★★
Social policy				
The government should see that everyone has adequate housing	−.04	−.04	.20★★	.15★★
Full employment is a realistic goal	.00	.08	.11★★	.11★
All Canadians should have the right to receive a guaranteed annual income	.00	.02	.10★	.15★★
Unemployment insurance should be a fundamental social right for all	.01	.00	.11★	.13★★
More money should be spent on social services	.03	−.10★	.11★★	.26★★
Government–sponsored child care services should be greatly expanded	.10★	−.08★	.22★★	.22★★
Youth				
Today's youth too often expects easy and high paying jobs	−.15★★	.05	−.19★★	−.21★★
It is harder for young people to get a job today	−.02	.00	.06	.09★★
Defence and foreign policy				
Canada should disarm unilaterally	.07★	−.24★★	.01	.15★★
No nuclear weapons should be permitted on Canadian territory	.21★★	−.07	.09★	.28★★
Canada should spend less on defence	.11★	−.21★★	.00	.22★★
We should ensure an independent Canada even if that were to mean a lower standard of living for Canadians	.15★★	−.07	−.15★★	.14★★
Canada must take steps to reduce American influence on its culture and mass media	.12★★	−.13★	.01	.09★
Canada ought to devote much more effort and money to aiding the underdeveloped countries	.20★★	.05	.06	.28★★

NOTE: The non-union/union variable is coded (1) for constituency, federal council, caucus, and youth delegates, and (2) for delegates from affiliated unions and central labour. The gender variable is coded (1) men and (2) women. The age variable is coded (1) for those born in 1947 or later, and (2) for those born before 1947. The coding of the original age variable precluded a cut-off of 1945. The left-right variable ranges from (1) left to (7) right.
[a] Responses coded as follows: (1) strongly agree, (2) agree, (3) uncertain, (4) disagree, and (5) strongly disagree.
★ p ≤ .01; ★★ p ≤ .001.

among the more powerful predictors of issue positions in 1987 except on specific gender issues. As we shall see, however, its importance was to increase dramatically two years later, in leadership voting.

Our findings with respect to the age variable were consistent with some expectations of the postmaterialist thesis and inconsistent with others. For example, on women's issues the younger (post-war) delegates were significantly more supportive of increasing female representation on the federal council and among candidates and party officers; they were also more likely to agree that women candidates are as effective as men. On social policy, the younger delegates were more favourable towards spending on housing, child care, and all other social policies. They were also more likely to support acceptance of immigrants from all groups and to oppose reductions in immigration. Predictably, the younger delegates were more likely to oppose the idea that the expectations of youth are too high. They were also more likely to favour a ban on nuclear weapons. Surprisingly, in the area of foreign affairs younger delegates were less inclined to support an independent Canada at the cost of lower income; this suggests that economic security may continue to play a role in structuring the political beliefs of the so-called postmaterialist generation. On the two free-trade items the younger delegates were more likely to oppose free trade with the US.

As the postmaterialism thesis would suggest, the younger delegates were indistinguishable from their older counterparts on most of the 'old politics' economic issues, and the differences that did exist were slight. A significant age-related difference appeared on only one of three issues in the class area: the younger delegates were more likely to dispute the suggestion that no ruling class exists in Canada. However, contrary to the postmaterialist thesis, the younger delegates' views on the environment and quality of life generally did not differ significantly from those of the older delegates. Although younger people were somewhat more likely to support the introduction of laws that are tough on polluters, they did not differ significantly on the belief that industrial society pollutes or on the need to place greater emphasis on quality of life over quantity of income.

The data in Table 10.2 can also be analyzed from another perspective, to see which issues generated the greatest divisions within the party and which generated the greatest consensus. Here the greatest differences emerged over policies relating to women. The attitudes most sympathetic to women's issues were found among non-unionists, women, younger delegates, and those on the left of the party. These groups could become an increasingly important coalition in support of women's issues within the NDP.

On the classic 'old politics' issues of economic policy and class there were few systematic differences between the groups. Even on the 'new politics' issue of environmental concern, delegates are marked more by consensus than by division. On the other hand, there appeared to be considerable division in the areas of defence and foreign policy, with the possibility of considerable cohesion within the two polarized groups. Thus, to the extent that a postmaterialist division is developing, and there is some evidence to suggest that it is, the division appears largest on women's issues and foreign policy and defence, moderate on immigration and minorities, and smaller on matters relating to the environment.

The relative weakness of an environmental basis for a 'new politics' in Canada is reinforced by the labels that delegates chose to describe their ideological positions (see Chapter 2). When asked (in a closed-ended question) which label best described their ideology, approximately half chose 'social democrat', and more than one-quarter chose 'socialist' (see Table 2.3). Well down the list, at slightly more than 2%, was 'ecologist'.[4] This is not to suggest that concern for the environment and ecological issues is inconsistent with a 'social-democratic' or 'socialist' self-image. But it does seem that such concern was not the top priority for most delegates—for many, their perspective on the environment appeared to be part of a broader view of the social and political landscape, with the general orientation being of greater importance than the particular. As recently as 1987, then, concern for the environment and ecology was not particularly divisive in the federal NDP—at least on the broad questions posed in the survey. (It is worth noting that considerable division exists within the BC NDP on issues where environmental concerns threaten jobs.) These concerns did not appear to divide labour delegates from other delegates, and with very few exceptions did not constitute the central principle or ideological identification of NDP delegates.

There is some indication, however, that concerns over the environment did increase in importance between 1987 and 1989.[5] This change was most noticeable in the caucuses held during the conventions, at which delegates who share particular concerns can discuss issues and develop appropriate strategies. The size of the various caucuses gives some indication of the importance—at least the numerical importance—of each group at the convention. As we noted in Chapter 2, and as Table 10.3 shows, the provincial sections of the party remain its major organizational building blocks; approximately half the delegates in both 1987 and 1989 attended a provincial caucus. When one recalls that only about two-thirds of delegates were accredited constituency delegates and hence were directly connected to their provincial organization (Chapter 2), the percentage attending the provincial caucuses is even more impressive. The second and third most popular caucuses in both 1987 and 1989 were the labour and women's caucuses, and here again the data may underestimate the importance delegates attached to these.

Table 10.3

Attendance at Caucuses During Convention, 1987 and 1989

Caucus Type	Attended Caucus[a]	
	1987 %	1989 %
Provincial	58.1	48.8
Labour	24.0	17.6
Women's	21.4	14.6
Environment	0.9	13.6
Regional	8.6	8.3
Left	8.2	7.7
Youth	10.9	6.6
Gay/lesbian	1.8	3.3
Municipal	1.4	2.0
N	(738)	(1060)

[a] Percentages do not add to 100%, since delegates may attend multiple caucuses.

Recalling that accredited union delegates numbered only 22.5% and 23.0% of delegates in 1987 and 1989, respectively, it becomes clear that almost all union delegates (and in 1987 even some who came without union accreditation) attended the labour caucus (see Chapter 4). A similar, though less pronounced, trend was found among women. The proportions of delegates in 1987 and 1989 who were women were 33.0% and 36.8%, respectively, while the proportions of delegates who attended the women's caucuses were 21.4% and 14.6%. Although the appeal of the women's caucus was less general than that of the labour and provincial caucuses, it was seen by many as an important instrument for the pursuit of women's issues. And, as we shall see, it was particularly important in the 1989 leadership race.

The greatest change between 1987 and 1989 was evident in the environment caucus. A relatively new caucus, it went from the position of the smallest in 1987 to the fourth largest in two years, rivalling the labour and women's caucuses for attendance. The increasing awareness of environmental issues that the growth of this caucus indicates could help to lead the NDP in a more postmaterialist direction. However, to date the environmental cleavage has not developed in a way consistent with the postmaterialist thesis.

To what extent is caucus attendance within the NDP related to delegates' characteristics? Is a postmaterialist coalition emerging? These questions are explored in Table 10.4. The data suggest that, in general, attendance at the caucuses in 1987 and 1989 was predictable. Union delegates were highly likely to attend the labour caucus, women the women's caucus, young delegates the youth caucus, and so on. In addition, women were less likely to attend the labour caucus—largely because the vast majority of union delegates are male (see Chapter 4)—and the younger delegates were more likely than others to attend the gay–lesbian caucus. One of the striking features of Table 10.4 is the apparent absence of a relationship between any of the criterion variables and attendance at the environment caucus. One could infer that instead of dividing the delegates, environmental issues and concerns may serve to unite them.

CAUCUSES, POSTMATERIALISM, AND LEADERSHIP VOTING

As we noted at the beginning of this chapter, our data sets lack a direct measure of postmaterialism using the standard indexes developed by Inglehart and Milbrath. In its absence, attendance at key caucuses was used as a surrogate measure to test the effect of postmaterialist views on leadership voting in the NDP (for more on leadership selection in the NDP see Chapters 11 to 13). Our analysis focuses on the leadership voting behaviour of those attending the labour, women's, and environment caucuses. These three were chosen because each had sufficient attendance for meaningful analysis and because each related in important ways to the postmaterialist thesis. The expectations are that labour will anchor the materialist end of the scale, that environmentalists will anchor the postmaterialist end, and that women will stand in between but lean more towards the postmaterialist end. The following analysis will explore the degree to which these groups act as cohesive blocs in leadership voting, which may shed some light on the likelihood that postmaterialist coalitions will emerge. In addition, focusing in particular on those attending the environment caucus, we will ask whether environmentalists, as strong postmaterialists, pursued a

Table 10.4

Caucus Attendance by Union, Sex, Age, and Left–Right Ideology, 1989 (zero–order correlations)

Caucus	Non-union/union	Men/women	Post-war/pre-war	Left/right
Provincial	−.04	−.03	−.05	.00
Labour	.48★★	−.14★★	.00	.02
Women's	−.07	.49★★	−.01	−.16★★
Environment	−.06	.01	.00	−.04
Regional	−.03	−.03	−.02	−.03
Left	−.07	.00	−.02	−.20★★
Youth	−.40	−.03	−.18★★	−.03
Gay–lesbian	−.03	−.07	−.10★	−.02
Municipal	−.01	−.05	.04	.05

NOTE: For the scoring of predictor variables see note to Table 10.2. The caucus-type variable is dichotomous, indicating did not (0) or did (1) attend caucus.
★ p ≤ .01; ★★ p ≤ .001.

consistent leadership voting strategy that might represent a significant departure from other delegates.

Table 10.5 presents delegates' voting behaviour across four leadership ballots according to their attendance at the labour caucus. Those attending the labour caucus differed systematically in their behaviour from those who did not, with the most significant difference appearing in support for Audrey McLaughlin and Dave Barrett. As the female candidate, McLaughlin was more likely than Barrett to tap the postmaterialist orientation. And Barrett was more likely to attract the materialist-oriented labour vote. Throughout all four ballots, Barrett received more support from those who attended the labour caucus than any other candidate. In contrast, McLaughlin consistently received less support from labour-caucus delegates. Thus although labour can act with relative cohesion when its leadership is in agreement over policies or leadership candidates (as in 1971), in 1989 the union leadership was more divided in its support for leadership candidates; as a result labour voted with considerably less unity than might have been expected. Nevertheless, it did indicate a consistent preference for Barrett.

The effect of attendance at the women's caucus is examined in Table 10.6. The 1989 convention was the first federal convention to elect a woman party leader. Given this result, one might expect that McLaughlin (the only female candidate) would have received disproportionate support from those attending the women's caucus, and the data confirm that expectation. As early as the first ballot, McLaughlin received over half the votes of those attending the women's caucus, a percentage that rose consistently until by the fourth ballot she received the votes of over 80% of those attending the women's caucus. To a considerable extent, then, the 1989 leadership vote

Table 10.5
Convention Voting by Attendance at Labour Caucus, 1989

	Attended Caucus (Yes/No)							
	Ballot 1		Ballot 2		Ballot 3		Ballot 4	
	Y	N	Y	N	Y	N	Y	N
Candidate	%[a]	%	%	%	%	%	%	%
McLaughlin	16.8	33.0	20.0	41.6	29.7	54.1	42.4	65.7
Barrett	33.3	15.9	41.1	24.9	50.8	29.2	57.6	34.3
Langdon	19.0	13.3	30.3	19.3	19.5	16.7		
de Jong	8.7	14.8	8.6	14.2				
McCurdy	16.3	7.0						
Waddell	3.8	13.4						
Lagassé	2.2	2.6						
N	(184)	(857)	(185)	(851)	(185)	(846)	(184)	(835)

[a] Does not add to 100% because of rounding.

represented a contest between a strong, united women's caucus and a strong but far less united labour caucus. It is less clear, however, whether this contest should be characterized as one between 'old' and 'new' politics. Those looking for evidence that such an alignment is developing within the party might well interpret these data as indicative of an important shift. But the relationships between caucus attendance and leadership voting in 1989 appear too weak and tentative to signal a definitive realignment. At most they are suggestive of new possibilities for intra-party realignments.

The need for caution in interpretation is underlined when the voting behaviour of those attending the environment caucus is examined (Table 10.7). These data can be read in two ways. One way (reading the table by columns) suggests that on each of the four ballots, the largest number of delegates attending the environment caucus supported McLaughlin—by the third and fourth ballots, a majority of such delegates. Barrett's support among those attending the environment caucus was much lower than McLaughlin's, and on most ballots those attending the environment caucus favoured McLaughlin over Barrett by a margin of two to one. Reading the table the other way (by rows), however, suggests that attendance at the environment caucus alone explains little of the support for McLaughlin: except, perhaps, on the fourth ballot, those attending the environment caucus were not significantly more likely to support McLaughlin than were those not attending that caucus. Thus once again we are faced with a tentative conclusion: data from the 1989 leadership convention suggest that environment caucus attendance had only a modest impact on leadership voting. If a postmaterialist cleavage has emerged in the NDP, it was in a nascent stage in the late 1980s.

Table 10.6
Convention Voting by Attendance at Women's Caucus, 1989

Candidate	Ballot 1 Y %[a]	Ballot 1 N %	Ballot 2 Y %	Ballot 2 N %	Ballot 3 Y %	Ballot 3 N %	Ballot 4 Y %	Ballot 4 N %
McLaughlin	53.9	26.1	62.0	33.6	71.3	46.1	82.3	58.0
Barrett	6.6	21.0	14.0	30.1	15.3	36.1	17.7	42.0
Langdon	12.5	14.6	15.3	22.2	13.3	17.8		
de Jong	7.9	14.7	8.7	14.0				
McCurdy	6.6	9.0						
Waddell	9.2	12.1						
Lagassé	3.3	2.4						
N	(152)	(889)	(150)	(886)	(150)	(881)	(147)	(872)

Header spanning: Attended Caucus (Yes/No)

[a] Does not add to 100% because of rounding.

Table 10.7

Convention Voting by Attendance at Environment Caucus, 1989

| | Attended Caucus (Yes/No) | | | | | | | |
| | Ballot 1 | | Ballot 2 | | Ballot 3 | | Ballot 4 | |
Candidate	Y %[a]	N %	Y %	N %	Y %	N %	Y %	N %
McLaughlin	28.2	30.5	37.9	37.7	52.9	49.3	66.2	60.8
Barrett	12.7	19.9	22.1	28.7	27.9	33.9	33.8	39.2
Langdon	12.7	14.6	18.6	21.7	19.3	16.8		
de Jong	23.2	12.2	21.4	11.9				
McCurdy	5.6	9.1						
Waddell	12.7	11.6						
Lagassé	4.9	2.1						
N	(142)	(889)	(140)	(896)	(140)	(891)	(136)	(883)

[a] Does not add to 100% because of rounding.

CONCLUSION

This chapter has sought to examine the role of 'new politics' in the federal NDP in the late 1980s. The data suggest that while in some key areas, notably the environment, policies associated with 'new politics' had been incorporated into the NDP with a high degree of consensus, on other issues there was considerable division. On the consensual side, we note that policies and political attitudes related to environmentalism had apparently been integrated with little, if any, systematic dissent. Contrary to the speculation of previous research (Nevitte et al., 1989), no major division had emerged between unionists and non-unionists on issues relating to the environment; there was no significant difference in attendance at the environment caucus between unionists and non-unionists; and the leadership voting behaviour of those attending the environment caucus did not differ from that of other delegates. When one adds to this the findings that very few delegates labelled themselves primarily as ecologists, and that most delegates were highly supportive of environmentalism, at least in principle, the conclusion is that this area is not the most divisive one in the federal NDP.

By contrast, gender does appear to have become politicized and more divisive than environmentalism within the federal party. Although in general there was high support for policies accommodating of women's representational demands, the differences that did exist were the most systematic of those we found. Across the range of women's issues, support was less strong among unionists, men, older delegates, and those on the party's ideological right. Thus there are several issues on which a gender-issue coalition could develop among non-unionists, women, younger delegates, and those on the left of the party (see also Whitehorn, 1992). Furthermore, the data showed that attendance at the women's caucus in 1989 was an unusually strong predictor of support for Audrey McLaughlin; this suggests that such a coalition may well have been crucial to her success.

The labour element within the NDP was not so distinguishable on the 'old politics' issues of economic development as the postmaterialist thesis would suggest; nor was it consistently different from other elements in the party on environmental issues. To that extent, it would be inaccurate to claim that labour invariably anchors the materialist pole within the party. However, across a number of other 'new politics' issues, labour does appear to occupy a distinctive—perhaps oppositional—position. As we saw in Table 10.2, it is less supportive than other groups of women's issues, of an open immigration policy, and of the new left positions on defence and foreign affairs. On these issues, labour is more closely associated with the right wing of the party.

Is the NDP becoming more divided with the emergence of 'new politics'? The data suggest that in some areas it is. The left–right division has always been the major fault line within the party, and the emergence of 'new' issues has not reduced its importance (see also Nevitte and Gibbins, 1990). In fact, it seems that new issues are incorporated into the old left–right ideological divide. While environmental issues have been accommodated with relative ease in the federal party, this is less true of gender issues. On defence, the old left–right divide is reinforced by an important gender gap, and on foreign policy and immigration it is joined by a youth cleavage. As new divisions emerge and are given organizational form through new party caucuses, further divisions may arise, creating more scope for intra-party coalitions. For example, a coalition of 'new politics' interests could rival the position of organized labour, one of the party's founding partners and an important interest in the policy-formulating process. Such a coalition could pressure the party to change party policies in ways that the unions may not support. Although to date such coalitions appear to be in a nascent stage, the possibility exists for them to grow. Whether the 'new politics' will provide such an impetus remains to be seen.

NOTES

1 In the 1987 survey the age variable was collected in 10-year intervals, making 1947 the closest war-time cutoff.

2 This is a standard statistical technique used to examine bivariate relationships (i.e., not controlling for other variables). It is a way of looking at the strength of association between the two variables. An asterisk indicates that the relationship is statistically significant (i.e., did not occur by chance), and the number indicates the strength of the relationship: the farther it is from zero, the stronger the relationship is.

3 Almost all delegates placed themselves left of centre, and some placed themselves farther left than others. For left–right placement in 1983 see Whitehorn (1992: 120).

4 The figure has risen only slightly from the 1.3% of delegates who called themselves ecologists in 1983 (Whitehorn, 1992: 118).

5 For an earlier comparison see Whitehorn (1992: 128–9).

Part IV

Leadership

CHAPTER 11

Leadership Selection and Campaign Financing

BACKGROUND

As a mass party, the CCF–NDP has always invested its conventions with the powers of leadership review and selection,[1] and all its leaders have been chosen at conventions. In theory, each federal convention tests the mandate of the leader, who is elected for only two years and hence needs to renew her/his term at each subsequent convention, should she/he choose to run again. While the specific details for nomination have varied over the years, the general principle has remained unchanged. Any party member can run for the leadership simply by gaining the required number of signatures of convention delegates. At the last of the old-style conventions, in 1989, a would-be candidate needed the signatures of 50 delegates from at least 8 different ridings or affiliated organizations,[2] and in 1995, a candidate for the party primaries (see Chapter 13) required the signatures of 50 party members from 10 ridings or affiliated organizations (New Democratic Party, 1995). If two candidates are so nominated, a leadership contest ensues. If no rival is nominated, the incumbent leader wins by acclamation. In practice, however, few meaningful leadership contests have emerged in the history of the federal CCF–NDP (see Courtney, 1995).

One possible explanation for the relative rarity of leadership contests is Robert Michels's 'iron law of oligarchy' (1962), according to which a leader always dominates the party structure regardless of democratic mechanisms. With greater access to party funds, staff, information, and media exposure, a leader is usually able to prevail over any would-be rivals. This is often enough to deter competitors from even entering the fray.

The possibility of changing the method of leadership selection, from a convention of several thousand delegates to a direct ballot of all party members and affiliated union members, was a subject of debate within the party for several years (Carty et al., 1992; Courtney, 1995; Latouche, 1992; Woolstencroft, 1992; see also Chapter 13); in the mid-1990s direct voting could involve as many as 400,000 individual and affiliated members. Although the 1989 leadership convention passed a resolution to study the constitutional and procedural reforms necessary to alter the selection method (Archer, 1991a; Hayward and Whitehorn, 1991),[3] at the 1991 federal convention there still seemed little urgency for such a move; delegates seemed more concerned with debate and formulation of policy on the Canadian constitution and North American free trade. However, after the calamitous 1993 federal election, the mood altered dramatically, and by the time the federal council met in January 1995, the party was ready to adopt a hybrid process consisting of a 'primary' mechanism and a party convention (see Chapter 13).

The CCF–NDP has had only eight leaders—J.S. Woodsworth (1932–42); M.J. Coldwell (1942–60); Hazen Argue (1960–61); T.C. Douglas (1961–71); David Lewis (1971–75); Ed Broadbent (1975–89); Audrey McLaughlin (1989–95); and the current leader, Alexa McDonough (1995–present)—of whom the first seven served an average of nine years. Even though it has had a more formally democratic mechanism in place for a longer time than either the Liberals or the Conservatives, the CCF–NDP has not shown a significantly greater tendency to change its leaders; this is in keeping with Michels's observation regarding the strong oligarchic tendencies in socialist parties (Michels, 1962). In fact, the first three leaders of the CCF were elected unanimously by convention, and it was only in the NDP era that the leadership contest actually became a significant phenomenon.

Despite the party's working-class base, its leadership has been decidedly white-collar and professional. Of the eight leaders, two were originally clergymen, two were teachers, one was a lawyer, two were social workers, and only one was a farmer (albeit a university graduate). By the time of their selection as party leader, each was an experienced politician. Six were members of Parliament, and three had been provincial party leaders, including T.C. Douglas who had served as premier of Saskatchewan. Their average age at election as leader was over 50.

Although at least two retired for reasons related to their health (Woodsworth and Coldwell) and two in part because of age (Douglas and Lewis), in three cases the leader had also lost his seat in the House of Commons; given the paucity of safe CCF–NDP seats, this was a significant factor in the decision to step down. Hazen Argue was the only leader who was, in a sense, challenged and subsequently defeated; technically, however, he was never challenged because he had been the leader of another party, the CCF.[4] In two cases devastating election setbacks, one in 1958 in the CCF era and the other in 1993, precipitated the leader's retirement (Coldwell and McLaughlin).

All three federal CCF leaders were Westerners, as was the NDP's first leader. The next two leaders, Lewis and Broadbent, came from Ontario, giving strength to suggestions that the Western farmer-based socialist CCF was transformed over the years into a more Eastern, labour-oriented and pragmatic party, the NDP (see Whitehorn, 1985, 1992). The two most recent leaders, Audrey McLaughlin and Alexa McDonough, came from the Northwest and Atlantic peripheries of the country. The more pragmatic emphasis of the NDP can be seen in the outcome of the five leadership contests. In each case, left-versus-right labelling between the final two candidates has been common, and it has usually been the so-called 'right-wing' candidate who has defeated the more left-wing one (Douglas over Argue, Lewis over Laxer, Broadbent over Brown,[5] McDonough over Robinson). In regional terms, the final two candidates in 1961 were both Westerners; in 1971 they were both Easterners; and in 1975 the contest was inter-regional, with the Easterner winning over the Westerner. The 1989 leadership contest saw two Westerners, or to be more precise one Westerner and one Northwesterner, on the final ballot, with the candidate from the sparsely populated Yukon victorious. In 1995, by contrast, only one ballot was held among three candidates—one from the Maritimes and two from the West. Alexa McDonough, the winner, was the first federal NDP leader from the Maritimes.

Although the number of leadership contests form a very small base on which to generalize, several observations can be made. Until 1995 and the introduction of the new hybrid process, the number of candidates (seven in 1989), and thus the competitiveness, had been increasing (Whitehorn, 1992). Correspondingly, the percentage vote for the eventual winner on both the first and final ballots had been declining. Some have speculated that this trend also may show increasing dissatisfaction with the final leadership choice. In each of the four NDP leadership contests from 1961 to 1989, four ballots were required for a clear winner to emerge. Nevertheless, those individuals leading on the first ballot won, and the final margin of victory was large enough to be definitive. However, in 1995 the first-ballot leader (Svend Robinson), anticipating his probable defeat, withdrew in a dramatic fashion and Alexa McDonough, the second-place candidate on the first ballot, won without going to a second round.

In contrast to earlier NDP leadership conventions, which were clearly male-dominated, the past three contests (1975, 1989, and 1995) have included women and/or visible-minority candidates. With Audrey McLaughlin's victory in 1989 a woman finally won the federal leadership of a major national party in Canada, and Alexa McDonough's victory in 1995 continued the advance for women.

DELEGATE SELECTION

Reflecting the importance of leaders to modern political parties, leadership conventions receive considerable attention, and, in general, the competition to be a delegate at a leadership convention is usually greater than for a policy convention. Delegates to leadership conventions are selected by different methods, depending on the category to which they belong. Two categories of *ex-officio* delegates, federal council and caucus, have delegate status by virtue of their positions. The delegates of central labour and its affiliated organizations are selected by whatever method the organization (i.e., the union or central labour body) chooses to employ. The party sets no rules for the method of selection, only the numbers allowed. Most union delegates are chosen by a method selected by the officials responsible for maintaining a union's liaison with the party. For the affiliated unions, the delegate positions are allocated to relatively small bodies, such as the union local that chooses to affiliate. Since approximately 600 union locals affiliate with the party, most affiliates have only one or two positions to fill (Archer, 1990). Thus the decision-making process by which union delegates are selected to go to the federal convention is highly decentralized.

Delegates from the two remaining categories, constituency and youth, are selected through elections (Wearing, 1988). Whereas the selection process for delegates to Liberal and Conservative leadership conventions has often been controversial, involving 'instant' members recruited through last-minute (and sometimes pre-paid) deals, the use of delegate slates (where two or more potential delegates identify themselves as a group), and the creation of entirely new campus and youth organizations for the purpose of claiming additional delegate positions (Courtney, 1986: 98; 1995; Wearing, 1988), the NDP has largely been spared these problems. This probably reflects a combination of factors. Quite significantly, the NDP has a relatively early cut-off-date (120 days before the convention) both for joining a riding association and for choosing to stand as a candidate for selection as a delegate. In addition, the fact that NDP riding associations tend to select long-time members as delegates, coupled with the party's open, democratic culture, has the effect of making efforts to subvert the process highly counter-productive. NDP candidates' spending limits ($150,000 in 1989, $250,000 in 1995; discussed in more detail below) also make it more difficult for them to finance the kind of mammoth organizational team that can reach into the local constituency to mount mass recruiting drives. Finally, the federal NDP's constitutional requirement of joint federal/provincial membership lessens the likelihood that members will be supporters of another party.

All these factors help to deter NDP leadership candidates from mounting party recruitment drives in an attempt to 'pack' delegate selection meetings. Not only are the costs of doing so relatively high, given the large number of recruits necessary (50 members for each delegate position for the first 200 members, then 100 members for each delegate thereafter), but the pay-offs, factoring in the resentment and alienation of long-time party workers, seem relatively modest. In most areas of Canada, therefore, NDP delegate selection meetings are relatively small events. As Table 11.1 shows, in 1989, 64% of all constituency delegates were chosen at meetings attended by fewer than 50 people. Most of the remainder (29.9%) were chosen at meetings of 50 to 100 people. Only 6.1% of the delegates surveyed reported having more than 100 people at the riding nomination meeting.

Not surprisingly, the largest nomination meetings were held in areas where the party was strongest. In Saskatchewan, the province with the greatest membership per riding and the greatest numbers at nomination meetings, over half the meetings were attended by 50 to 100 party members, and another 13.9% of meetings had more than 100 members. By contrast, the entire province of Quebec has fewer NDP members than some Saskatchewan ridings; thus all the delegates from Quebec were chosen at meetings attended by fewer than 50 members. In the case of the North, however, it is the region's sparse population, rather than the NDP's performance (the party has formed the government in the Yukon), that accounts for the small size of the meetings.

The NDP's 1989 selection meetings differed from those of the Liberal and Conservative parties in degree of competition, in the incidence of identification with leadership candidates prior to selection, and in the use of slates (see Table 11.2). For example, whereas only one-quarter of Liberal and Conservative constituency delegates in the mid-1980s were elected without a contest (Carty, 1988: 86), fully half of the NDP's constituency delegates were unchallenged. In addition, whereas some 41% of Liberal delegates and 48%

Table 11.1
Size of Delegate Selection Meeting by Province/Region, 1989

Province/Region	Less than 50 %	50–100 %	More than 100 %	N of riding delegates
British Columbia	53.8	35.0	11.3	160
Alberta	66.7	28.9	4.4	90
Saskatchewan	32.8	53.3	13.9	137
Manitoba	80.5	19.5	0.0	77
Ontario	76.9	21.0	2.1	238
Quebec	100.0	0.0	0.0	16
Atlantic	71.4	26.2	2.4	42
North	100.0	0.0	0.0	13
Canada	64.0	29.9	6.1	773

of Conservative delegates identified themselves as supporters of one of the leadership candidates, this was the case for only 31% of New Democrats. Thus more than two-thirds of the NDP's constituency delegates were elected without identifying their choice for leader in advance. Our data do not permit us to know whether this has been the case in other NDP leadership races; however, we do note that on the eve of the 1989 convention there was speculation that party activists at all levels were unenthusiastic about the declared candidates. This factor may partly account for the number of delegate-selection meetings at which no preference was declared.

Even more pronounced were the differences between the NDP and the two other parties in the use of slates. Whereas almost 40% of Liberal and Conservative delegates in the 1980s were elected as part of a slate, only 10% of New Democrats followed that route to election. Instead, New Democrats appeared to rely much more on an individual's personal service, and commitment to the party, than on how the individual ranked his or her preferences for party leader. Furthermore, although it has been a common practice among Liberals and Conservatives to run on a slate identified with a particular leadership candidate—approximately one-quarter in each party did so—in the 1989 NDP contest only 6% of delegates claimed to have used that approach. Carty (1988) describes as 'trench warfare' situations in which a slate identified with one candidate is pitted in all-out battle against a slate identified with another. In the selection of constituency delegates for the 1989 leadership convention, very few New Democrats (2%) reported that they had engaged in a contest of this kind.

Thus, although there has been some use of slates and candidate preferences in choosing NDP convention delegates, these tended not to be the norm in the 1989 contest. Instead, when there was a nomination contest it

Table 11.2

Constituency Delegate Selection in the Liberal, Conservative, and New Democratic Parties, 1980s

	Party/Year		
	PC (1983)	Liberal (1984)	NDP (1989)
Selection contested	77	75	51
Prior identification as supporting a candidate	48	41	31
Ran as part of slate	39	38	10
Ran as part of slate identified with a candidate	26	24	6
'Trench warfare' (candidate slate vs candidate slate)	10	12	2

NOTE: Data are based on percentages of constituency delegates.
SOURCE: Data on Liberal and Conservative conventions are from Carty (1988: 86).

tended to focus more on the individual party members than the leadership candidates.

The practices employed in the selection of delegates to Conservative and Liberal conventions—including signing large numbers of new party recruits in the final days before the contest, recruiting heavily on campuses and in ethnic communities, bringing busloads of supporters to the selection meetings, and the widespread use of slates—have contributed to Canadians' growing cynicism about the political process. Some commentators have even suggested that these practices have led to a governability crisis. Would it help matters for the state to become more involved in regulating the internal affairs of political parties in areas such as the selection of delegates to party conventions? The short answer is no.

The benefits of state regulation in the selection of convention delegates range from minimal to non-existent. The parties differ across the full range of delegate-selection criteria, often deliberately.[6] As noted above, each of the three major parties has sizeable numbers of delegates not chosen by constituency associations. At NDP conventions, union delegates are a significant minority of delegates, but each union local has only one or two delegate positions. Imposition of state-regulated selection criteria would centralize a process that was explicitly intended to be decentralized (Archer, 1990; Lewis, 1981). It was a matter of political choice—a choice to depart from the centralized model of the British Labour Party, which encourages affiliation of national rather than local labour bodies—and such choice is still best exercised by the party, not the state. Likewise, the selection of *ex-officio* delegates is one with little room for useful state regulation.

The regulation of delegate selection is problematic for several reasons. Perhaps most important, the fact that every biennial convention of the NDP includes the election of the party leader implies that the NDP does not make as strong a distinction as the Liberal and Conservative parties do between policy conventions and leadership conventions. Thus it would not be possible to devise one series of regulations for leadership conventions and another for policy conventions, and expect them to apply equally to all parties: the NDP would always fall under the leadership convention regulations. Few would argue that the state should regulate how parties formulate their policies, or who may participate in the policy-making process. The very idea of such state control seems repugnant in a pluralist democracy.

Nor should the state attempt to establish a cut-off date for new members to participate in the delegate-selection process. An early cut-off date (such as 90 or 120 days preceding the convention) makes a large membership recruiting drive more difficult, whereas a late date simplifies the task. Parties differ in the purposes of their conventions, and hence in their preferred cut-off dates: parties that view the leadership convention mainly as an exercise in public relations or as a forum for the recruitment of new members are more likely to favour a later date, while parties more interested in membership knowledge and expertise in debating policy—both signifying a longer-term commitment to the party—tend to favour an early date. In either case, it is simply not a matter that requires state regulation.

The delegate-selection practices used by some of the parties may well have contributed to public cynicism about the political process. However, there are no solutions to the most problematic features of those practices that can be applied uniformly and neutrally. The conflicting goals of party conventions—which include membership recruitment, policy development, rewards for the party faithful, strengthening of personal networks, representation of specific groups, and public relations, in addition to selecting a new party leader—increase the likelihood that there will be conflicting demands over the process of delegate selection. However, it is in the very resolution of those conflicting demands that parties define their character and their image. The growing movement towards direct election of party leaders represents one possible solution to the problems of delegate selection. This will be discussed in more detail in Chapter 13, when we analyze the 1995 NDP leadership race.

FINANCING LEADERSHIP CONTESTS

Money has been called the mother's milk of politics (Jesse Unruh, quoted in Stanbury, 1996). The analogy suggests that a well-financed political party or candidate, like a well-nourished baby, possesses the necessary conditions for good health and strong growth. The analogy, however, ends there. Between a mother and her nursing child, the balance between supply and demand is usually almost perfect in that the mother rarely produces too much or too little milk. There is, after all, a fixed amount of milk that any baby can consume, and the mother's supply usually adjusts to provide the amount demanded. Such is not the case with political parties.

The financing of political parties and candidates is somewhat unstable. For one thing, there appears to be no definite point at which a party's or candidate's appetite for funds is sated. By way of illustration, between 1977 and 1986, total expenditures by the Liberal Party increased from $4.2 million to $11.1 million; by the Conservative Party from $4.2 million to $14.1 million; and by the NDP from $3.1 million to $15.2 million (Stanbury, 1989: 358; note that in the case of the NDP this figure includes federal party transfers to the provincial parties). Likewise, there has been tremendous growth in the funds spent by candidates seeking the leadership of the parties, although the increase has been significantly smaller for the NDP than for the Liberals and Conservatives. The parties have responded to these increases in different ways; the NDP is more likely to set limits on expenditures and the others, particularly the Conservatives, are less likely. Consequently, the rules for the financing of leadership contests are quite different in each party, with the greatest difference being between the NDP and the others.

The Liberal Party established a spending limit of $1.65 million per candidate in 1984 (Wearing, 1988: 73), a limit that was adjusted to $1.7 million in 1990. In the 1984 contest, candidates were required to file financial statements to party headquarters, but these figures were not released to the public. John Turner spent $1.6 million in 1984, compared with $1.5 million for Jean Chrétien, $900,000 for Don Johnston, and $700,000 for John Roberts (Courtney, 1995: 315). For the 1990 leadership contest, the limit of $1.7 million related only to the official campaign period itself, and most of the candidates spent considerable sums both within and outside that period. Total spending reported by Jean Chrétien and Paul Martin was $2.4 million each, and by Sheila Copps $800,000 (Courtney, 1995: 316). The Conservatives in 1976 asked candidates to submit accounts of expenditures and receipts. All complied except Brian Mulroney. In that year Mulroney's expenditure was estimated at between $343,000 and $500,000, compared with a reported expenditure of $168,000 for Joe Clark (Courtney, 1995: 315). In the 1983 contest, the Conservatives had no internal regulations regarding either limits or reporting of expenditures (Wearing, 1988: 78). However, it has been estimated that expenditures by both Clark and Mulroney may have been as high as $1.9 million, and John Crosbie's were estimated at $1.5 million (Courtney, 1995: 315). Spending by Conservative candidates continued to skyrocket in 1993: Kim Campbell spent an estimated $3 million to win the party leadership, and Jean Charest spent $2.3 million in his unsuccessful bid (Courtney, 1995: 316). Both parties claim to have observed a limit on individual contributions of $10,000, although without public reporting of individual contributions, this claim is impossible to verify.

Historically, money has been less plentiful, if not less important, in NDP leadership contests. Canada's social-democratic party, seeking to represent the less affluent, has been much more inclined then the other parties to regulate, or at least impose guidelines on, campaign expenditures. For example, prior to the 1975 leadership contest the party outlined its set of rules (New Democratic Party, 1975). Leadership candidates could spend a maximum of $15,000, of which $1,000 would be reimbursed by the party for the all-candidates' tour and for mailings. Thus NDP leadership hopefuls could spend only a fraction (between one-tenth and one-twentieth) of the amount likely spent by Conservative candidates the following year. In addition, NDP candidates were required to appoint official agents responsible for filing both an interim report (due during the convention) and a final report that would disclose all revenues and expenditures and identify all contributors of $10 or more.

For the 1989 convention the party issued a more elaborate statement of rules governing the leadership contest (New Democratic Party, 1989). The new rules called for the appointment of a chief electoral officer (Donald C. MacDonald), and candidates were again required to appoint an official agent who would file an interim financial statement at the time of the convention and a final statement by 1 July 1990. The party established a modest spending limit of $150,000 per candidate, less than one-tenth of the limit set by the Liberal Party six months later. The NDP limit included candidates' spending on the party-organized all-candidates' tour. Since the party reimbursed candidates' spending on the tour to a maximum of $5,000, candidates' net fund-raising was limited to $145,000.[7] Contributions from individuals, unions, or other organizations were limited to $1,000, and disclosure was required for contributions of all kinds, including services, exceeding $100.

All the candidates stayed well below the spending limit (see Table 11.3). The largest expenditures were by McLaughlin ($129,000) and Barrett ($114,000): 85.7% and 76.0% of the allowable limit, respectively. None of the remaining five candidates spent as much as half the allowable amount. Nor did any of the candidates emerge from the contest with a surplus: even with the tour rebate, the funds raised did not cover total expenditures as of 1 July 1990, when final statements were filed. Langdon came closest to covering all his expenses (within $50). However, Waddell, McLaughlin, Barrett, and de Jong had substantial shortfalls, which the candidates had to make up either by prolonged post-convention fund-raising or by personally absorbing the costs.

Table 11.3
Leadership Campaign Revenues and Expenditures, 1989

Candidate	Campaign expenditures $	Campaign revenues $	Surplus (deficit) $	Expenditure as % of limit
Barrett	113,986.98	94,505.15	(19,481.83)	76.0
de Jong	42,516.85	42,515.85[a]	(26,935.73)	28.3
Lagassé	11,891.62	10,300.39	(1,591.23)	7.9
Langdon	52,461.91	52,426.44	(35.47)	35.0
McCurdy	72,891.54	68,364.08	(4,527.46)	48.6
McLaughlin	128,575.50	111,051.46	(17,524.04)	85.7
Waddell	39,256.00	30,048.00	(9,208.00)	26.2

SOURCE: New Democratic Party, 'Final Financial Statement of Candidates for Leadership' (to 30 June 1990).
[a] Includes personal loan of $26,935.73 to candidate.

Financing rules for the 1995 NDP leadership contest were similar to those used in 1989 (New Democratic Party, 1995), except that the spending limit for candidates was increased to $250,000—a small fraction of the $3 million spent by Kim Campbell to win the Conservative leadership in 1993. Candidates were required to submit interim statements on revenues and expenditures by 1 October 1995, two weeks before the leadership vote, and these reports were made available to delegates at the convention. The interim reports also included the names of individuals, unions, or organizations contributing $100 or more to a candidate. The maximum contribution by individuals, unions, or organizations to each candidate was increased to $10,000 in 1995 (from $1,000 in 1989). However, since the candidates were required to declare only the names of contributors of $100 or more, not the amount contributed, it is not possible to know how many donors made contributions that approached the limit.

In addition to the interim financial statements, candidates were required to file final statements within 75 days of the conclusion of the convention (i.e., by 29 December 1995). However, by January 1997 most candidates who were still trying to raise funds had failed to file their official statements. Hence the most complete data we have are the candidates' interim reports. These indicate that with two weeks remaining in the campaign, spending totalled $129,000 for Svend Robinson, $128,000 for Alexa McDonough, $37,000 for Herschel Hardin, and $29,000 for Lorne Nystrom (see Table 13.2). Although additional expenses would have been incurred before the campaign ended, the relatively modest expenditures by these leadership hopefuls generally point to an important difference between the NDP and the two older parties.

Following a favourable ruling by Elections Canada, the party was able to accept tax-creditable contributions for individual candidates in the 1989 leadership contest (New Democratic Party, 1989).[8] Under this arrangement, contributions made to the federal party on behalf of a particular candidate would be transferred from the party to the candidate, minus a 15% 'revenue-sharing' fee (administrative charge; in 1995 this fee was reduced to 10%). Since making such contributions tax-creditable meant that they had to be included in the financial statements filed by the party, this represented an important step towards greater public accounting in the financing of NDP leadership contests.

The party enforces its regulations governing the financing of leadership contests mainly through the reporting process itself. The chief electoral officer monitors expenditures through examination of the two (interim and final) statements submitted by each candidate and reports his findings to the convention, so that, when they vote, delegates are apprised of the candidates' reported expenditures. At that time the delegates in effect decide on the propriety of each candidate's expenditures.[9] Apart from the vote at the convention itself, the party has two ways of ensuring that candidates abide by its spending limits and disclosure requirements. The first sanction is financial: although the party is committed to paying the costs of the all-candidates' tour, to a maximum of $5,000, these funds can be withheld if candidates fail to comply with the spending and disclosure rules. The second and more significant sanction is moral suasion from party officials and members. To date, these have been sufficient, although in the 1995 contest it was still common for candidates to delay filing final statements beyond the deadline in the hope of raising more funds to retire any outstanding debt.

Since, as recent history shows, the leader chosen by a party can become prime minister without a general election, the financing of leadership contests is clearly one area that could benefit from greater public accounting and documentation. The system used by the NDP in 1989, and modified in 1995, could serve as a model for public disclosure in the financing of all parties' leadership campaigns. The party has shown that full public disclosure of all revenues and expenditures, identification of contributors of $100 or more, and provision of receipts for income-tax purposes generally work well. However, some problems do exist.

For example, the experience of the NDP in 1989 and 1995 suggests that fund-raising drives are likely to fall short, leaving some candidates with high levels of personal debt; the problem is most severe for optimistic candidates who borrow heavily in anticipation of success. Another problem is that candidates may both raise and spend money in the pre-campaign period, thus bypassing any limits set on contributions or expenditures (as was done by Glen Clark in the BC NDP leadership contest in 1996).

Many people would agree that it is only fair to set a reasonable limit on the amount of money that any candidate can spend. However, Canadian parties differ dramatically in their perceptions of what constitutes a reasonable amount. In 1989 the NDP felt that $150,000 was sufficient, yet six months later the Liberal Party permitted ten times that amount. Similarly, in 1995 the NDP allowed spending of $250,000, whereas two years earlier the Conservatives had approved an amount more than ten times greater. Clearly different parties have different socio-economic profiles, and these are reflected in their expenditures. Historically, as a mass party with working-class roots, the NDP has had considerably less to spend than parties with more affluent supporters. Despite these differences in income profiles, it seems appropriate to encourage all parties to set and enforce spending limits, with the NDP's format as a possible model.

CONCLUSION

The NDP's mass-based organization and social-democratic ideology seem to have had an important impact on its approach to leadership selection. NDP leaders have had relatively long tenures and have generally enjoyed quite high levels of support and solidarity within the party. Indeed, even though the party has never moved beyond third-party status, NDP leaders to date have not experienced the unrelenting internal divisions and conflict over their performance that Conservative leaders have (on the 'Tory syndrome' see Perlin, 1980). It has also been far less costly for candidates to compete for the leadership in the NDP than in the Liberal and Conservative parties. The NDP has pioneered a more open and egalitarian approach to the financing of leadership campaigns. Overall, we have seen that the NDP's approach to leadership selection is significantly influenced by the fact that it is a mass-based social-democratic party.

The next two chapters examine in detail the two most recent federal NDP leadership conventions. Chapter 12 focuses on the 1989 contest, in which the party, still using a traditional convention format, made the historic decision to elect Canada's first female federal party leader. Chapter 13 explores the 1995 contest, which combined regional and union primaries with a national convention. Of particular interest is the question of whether different formats produce different outcomes. Both the 1989 and 1995 conventions illustrate the importance of the forces for change that exist today both within the NDP (e.g., the women's and other caucuses) and in society at large (e.g., increasing demands for a more open and participatory political process).

NOTES

Portions of this chapter were previously published in Whitehorn (1992), Archer (1991a), and Whitehorn and Archer (1994).

1   For the first two CCF leaders, the procedure was actually a more complex two-step process involving first a vote within the caucus of MPs and then election/ratification by the convention of the caucus leader as party president (Lewis, 1981: 499).

2   In the past, nominations were easier in that they required nomination signatures from fewer ridings or affiliated organizations. The result was that from time to time fringe candidates appeared with no chance of mounting a serious contest. Tommy Douglas, David Lewis, and Ed Broadbent, as incumbents, all experienced such token challenges at some point.

3   Respondents to the 1989 survey were asked 'Are you in favour of a change to a "one member—one vote" system to choose party leaders?'; 52.4% were in favour, 35.8% were opposed, and 11.9% were uncertain.

4 Elected leader of the CCF only in its twilight year of 1960, during its transformation into the NDP, Argue was the youngest leader of the old and dwindling party. Perhaps he was not politically mature enough to lead the new party; in any event, the first-ballot landslide for T.C. Douglas at the NDP's founding convention suggested that the delegates felt as much.

5 It should be noted that in 1971, when Broadbent was not among the final two leadership aspirants, he could have been labelled as 'centre-left'; it was in comparison with Rosemary Brown that he appeared more to the right in 1975. For a discussion of the Brown campaign see her memoirs (Brown, 1989). The 1989 leadership convention, discussed in more detail below, was characterized by many observers as being influenced less by ideology than by other factors.

6 In 1992, when the provincial Conservatives in Alberta used two ballots, held two weeks apart, to elect Ralph Klein as leader, party memberships were even sold between the two ballots.

7 Any surplus funds were required to be donated to the party's national office.

8 Interview with Dick Proctor, 15 Aug. 1990.

9 Interview with Donald C. MacDonald, 21 Sept. 1990.

CHAPTER
12

Leadership Selection: 1989

Leadership contests are often pivotal moments in the lives of political parties. The choice of a new leader can set the tone and, to a certain degree, the direction the party will take in the years ahead. A leadership contest can foster debate among activists about the nature of the party, its goals, and even its composition. It also provides one of the few occasions when activists indicate which section of the party they feel closest to. In the months before the convention, delegates are selected to represent constituency associations, affiliated unions, and the youth section (see Chapter 11), and are joined by *ex-officio* delegates from the caucus, federal council and central labour bodies. By the time they arrive at the convention, the atmosphere is often electric (Courtney, 1995). The candidates are put on display in policy debates, in 'bear-pit' question-and-answer sessions, and in their formal speeches the night before the balloting. Since normally a winner is not declared on the first ballot, the drama is heightened as defeated candidates either 'release' their supporters to vote as they choose or declare their support for another candidate and in so doing encourage their own supporters to follow their lead. Finally, the climax comes with the announcement of the winner on the final ballot.

This chapter examines voting at the 1989 federal NDP leadership convention. It begins by briefly discussing the campaigns of the seven candidates and examining the patterns of voting across the four ballots, paying particular attention to trends that may have been associated with strategic voting on the part of delegates. We then turn to the question of whether the rules used for balloting (that is, a multi-ballot, majority voting system in which the candidate with the lowest vote total is dropped after each ballot) affected the results of the election—in other words, whether Audrey McLaughlin was really the delegates' most preferred candidate. We conclude with an examination of why delegates voted as they did, expanding on Chapter 10's discussion of intra-party caucuses to provide a more complex model of the determinants of leadership voting.

THE CANDIDATES

Much of the early press coverage of the 1989 NDP leadership campaign suggested that the candidates were a relatively weak group. Unlike three of the 1971 candidates (David Lewis, Ed Broadbent, and James Laxer), none of the 1989 candidates had published books. Nor had any of them attracted a reputation as a strong leadership prospect. When, in 1987, respondents to our NDP convention survey had been asked who they would like to see replace Ed Broadbent when he stepped down, the only eventual candidate to finish in the top ten had been Dave Barrett, who tied for tenth place with the generic response of 'a woman'. None of the top nine named in 1987 (Bob White, Lorne Nystrom, Marion Dewar, Nelson Riis, Stephen Lewis, Alexa McDonough, Bob Rae, Roy Romanow, and Svend Robinson) opted to run for the leadership in 1989, although Nystrom, McDonough, and Robinson were to run six years later. Audrey McLaughlin, the eventual winner in 1989, was a virtual unknown in 1987[1] and received not a single mention as a possible replacement for Broadbent. In fact, the perceived weakness of the existing field was one of the reasons behind the candidacy of Barrett, a former BC premier and then member of Parliament, who decided to enter the contest only on the eve of the cross-country leadership tour.

The bear-pit session and candidates' speeches revealed the key themes pursued by each of the candidates. Roger Lagassé, a teacher and political neophyte operating on a $10,000 budget for his cross-Canada campaign, gently spoke of the need to make politics more consensual. Urging delegates to redirect their efforts towards the environment, he reaffirmed the appeal of idealism for New Democrats when, although a long-shot candidate, he received several standing ovations.

Simon de Jong, at the time a Saskatchewan MP, offered a fresh mix of ideas. He urged Canadians to move away from the élitist pattern of constitution-making by first ministers; called for a special constitutional assembly, an idea particularly attractive to Prairie populists; and advocated the adaption of proportional representation to lessen the distortions in the electoral system (see, for example, Cairns, 1968). He also put forward the proposal—still relatively unpopular in 1989—that NDP governments should devote more attention to balancing the budget, a prescription that was to become a hallmark of Canadian politics in the 1990s.

Ian Waddell, then a British Columbia MP, called for greater democracy within the party. Howard McCurdy, a former university professor and at the time an Ontario MP, suggested the need for a more inclusionary party and country. Stephen Langdon, another former professor then sitting as an Ontario MP, called for a new radicalism culminating in a general strike against the GST, recalling the historic Winnipeg General Strike of 1919.

Although Langdon had a minor speech impairment, and the unenviable task of being the last candidate to speak, virtually all delegates and commentators agreed that his presentation was by far the best.

Dave Barrett reminded the delegates that natural resources are a public trust for all generations and thus should not be controlled exclusively by private corporations. His populist style was as effective as ever, but many suspected that his late entry into the race was too great a handicap to overcome.

Audrey McLaughlin, the sole female candidate and for that reason the expected front-runner, talked about the need for a revolutionary change and alluded to the groundbreaking possibility of electing a female federal leader. While in the past she had been accused of being somewhat vague on issues, her convention speech contained a surprisingly high number of references to socialism and suggested a conscious attempt to appear more ideologically and intellectually precise. Many delegates and media commentators felt that her formal speech, like her earlier performances, was uninspired and might cost her some votes.

VOTING RESULTS

Table 12.1 charts the voting results over the four ballots held. McLaughlin finished slightly ahead of Barrett on the first ballot, with 26.9% of the vote to his 23.6%. The other major candidates were 10 percentage points or more behind the leaders. The convention rule requiring the candidate with the lowest vote total and/or those with less than 75 votes to withdraw forced Roger Lagassé out of the race, and both Ian Waddell and Howard McCurdy withdrew voluntarily after the first ballot. Lagassé freed his delegates, McCurdy moved to support Langdon, and Waddell supported Barrett.

Table 12.1
Voting Results Over Four Ballots, 1989

| | Ballot | | | | | | | |
| | 1 | | 2 | | 3 | | 4 | |
Candidate	N	%	N	%	N	%	N	%
McLaughlin	646	26.9	829	34.3	1,072	44.4	1,316	54.7
Barrett	566	23.6	780	32.3	947	39.2	1,072	44.6
Langdon	351	14.6	519	21.5	393	16.3		
de Jong	315	13.1	289	12.0				
McCurdy	256	10.7						
Waddell	213	8.9						
Lagassé	53	2.2						
Spoiled	3	0.1	0	0.0	3	0.1	18	0.7
Total	(2,403)		(2,417)		(2,415)		(2,406)	

The second ballot saw McLaughlin maintain her lead at 34.3% of the vote, although the gap between her and Barrett narrowed slightly to 2%. Langdon's support grew in step with that of the two front-runners, and de Jong was forced off the ballot. In a moment charged with excitement, and later with controversy, de Jong moved to support McLaughlin even though minutes earlier a live wireless microphone had recorded de Jong pledging to move to Barrett in exchange for a valued appointment in caucus. However, de Jong chose not to act on that commitment. His support helped McLaughlin to make gains on Barrett on the third ballot, and after Langdon was forced off the ballot, McLaughlin secured victory on the fourth ballot by a comfortable 10-point margin.

Previous research into leadership selection has shown that considerable proportions of delegates (as many as 25%) engage in 'strategic voting' at conventions (Krause and LeDuc, 1979: 102–5; LeDuc, 1971: 100), voting for candidates other than their first preference in order to prevent the election of a least-favoured candidate. Table 12.2 indicates that a considerable amount of strategic voting took place at the 1989 NDP convention, although the proportion engaging in this activity was smaller than at previous Liberal and Conservative conventions. Delegates' preferences were determined from a question asking them to rank-order the seven candidates from their most (1) to their least (7) preferred.[2]

Most of the strategic voting that occurred on the first ballot was at the expense of the two front-runners. Among those who ranked Barrett as their most preferred candidate, only 73.6% voted for him on the first ballot. Of those who ranked McLaughlin first, 80.8% gave her first-ballot support. For each of the other candidates except Lagassé (for whom the sample size was very small), those ranking the candidate as most preferred were very likely to be first-ballot supporters. Levels of support ranged from 90.1% for Langdon to 97.8% for Waddell.

It appears that the only way for candidates to ensure the continued allegiance of their supporters is to continue to perform up to expectations and to project an image of forward momentum (Krause and LeDuc, 1979). Once this momentum stops, some supporters will begin looking elsewhere to cast their vote. For example, on the second ballot both Barrett and McLaughlin were able to get the support of about 90% of those who ranked them first, as was Langdon, buoyed by McCurdy's support. However, de Jong received no such endorsement, and there was no visible movement to his camp. Consequently, the movement that did occur was away from him, and his support among those naming him as their first preference dropped to 80.5%.

Similarly, on the third ballot Barrett and McLaughlin both increased their support among those who ranked them first, whereas Langdon's support

Table 12.2
Vote on Each Ballot by First Preference on Rank Order, 1989

Vote	Barrett	de Jong	Lagassé	Langdon	McCurdy	McLaughlin	Waddell
			Rank-order First Preference (%)				
Ballot 1							
Barrett	73.6	0	0	1.4	0	1.3	0
de Jong	8.1	96.6	6.7	3.5	1.4	7.8	2.2
Lagassé	2.3	0	80.0	1.4	2.7	1.0	0
Langdon	3.9	0	6.7	90.1	0	3.1	0
McCurdy	3.1	0	6.7	2.1	94.5	2.6	0
McLaughlin	1.6	0	0	0	1.4	80.8	0
Waddell	7.4	2.3	0	0.7	0	3.1	97.8
Spoiled	0	1.1	0	0.7	0	0.3	0
Ballot 2							
Barrett	93.4	6.9	6.7	1.4	11.0	0.8	31.5
de Jong	3.1	80.5	26.7	5.0	20.5	5.0	16.9
Langdon	3.1	5.7	53.3	90.1	45.2	4.4	25.8
McLaughlin	0.4	5.7	13.3	3.5	21.9	89.0	25.8
Spoiled	0	1.1	0	0	1.4	0.8	0
Ballot 3							
Barrett	97.3	26.4	6.7	7.1	27.4	1.6	38.2
Langdon	2.0	16.1	46.7	73.0	26.0	2.1	23.6
McLaughlin	0.8	55.2	46.7	19.1	43.8	95.6	38.2
Spoiled	0	2.3	0	0.7	2.7	0.8	0
Ballot 4							
Barrett	97.7	30.7	0	30.7	33.3	1.3	47.7
McLaughlin	2.3	67.0	100	60.7	64.0	97.9	51.1
Spoiled	0	2.3	0	8.6	2.7	0.8	1.1
N	(258)	(87)	(15)	(141)	(73)	(385)	(89)

among those ranking him first dropped to 73.0%. By the fourth ballot, Barrett and McLaughlin had secured all but a handful of those ranking them first.

When a candidate who has withdrawn from the ballot moves to endorse one of the remaining candidates, it is widely assumed that the first candidate's supporters will change their votes accordingly, and that the newly endorsed candidate will retain that support. To what degree were these assumptions validated in the 1989 NDP leadership convention? Table 12.3 maps delegate movement across the four ballots. Panel A, which shows the relationship between first- and second-ballot voting, shows that both Barrett and McLaughlin retained almost all their first-ballot support on the second ballot, while Langdon lost only 10%. Those who left Langdon split almost evenly between Barrett and McLaughlin. The remaining second-ballot candidate, de Jong, managed to hold only two-thirds of his first-ballot support, and once again Barrett and McLaughlin picked up roughly equal proportions of the slippage. When Lagassé freed his supporters to vote as they wished, the largest proportion of them went to Langdon, although the margin was not substantial. Between the ballots both McCurdy and Waddell voluntarily withdrew, moving to support Langdon and Barrett respectively. However, both met with mixed success in delivering their supporters' votes. Fewer than half of McCurdy's supporters followed him to Langdon; almost one-quarter joined McLaughlin, and roughly one-sixth voted for Barrett and one-sixth for de Jong. Waddell was even less successful in delivering votes to Barrett: only 36.9% went to Barrett, while 28.7% went to McLaughlin.

On the third ballot both Barrett and McLaughlin were able to maintain their supporters, including those acquired following the second ballot, losing only a handful. In contrast, Langdon maintained only two-thirds of his supporters, with the remainder moving to McLaughlin over Barrett by a margin

Table 12.3

Vote Movement Across Ballots, 1989

Second-ballot Vote	First-ballot Vote (%)						
	Barrett	de Jong	Lagassé	Langdon	McCurdy	McLaughlin	Waddell
Barrett	99.0	14.5	23.1	4.0	15.4	0.6	36.9
de Jong	0.0	66.9	23.1	1.3	16.5	.0	14.8
Langdon	0.0	4.8	30.8	90.0	45.1	1.6	19.7
McLaughlin	1.0	13.8	19.2	4.7	23.1	97.1	28.7
Spoiled	0.0	0.0	3.8	0.0	0.0	0.6	0.0
N	(198)	(145)	(26)	(150)	(90)	(315)	(122)

Cramer's V = .71

Third-ballot Vote	Second-ballot Vote (%)			
	Barrett	de Jong	Langdon	McLaughlin
Barrett	99.0	23.2	10.9	0.5
Langdon	0.0	21.0	65.9	0.8
McLaughlin	0.7	55.1	22.3	98.7
Spoiled	0.3	0.7	0.9	0.0
N	(289)	(138)	(220)	(395)

Cramer's V = .75

Fourth-ballot Vote	Third-ballot Vote (%)		
	Barrett	Langdon	McLaughlin
Barrett	96.8	32.8	0.4
McLaughlin	3.2	59.3	99.2
Spoiled	0.0	7.9	0.4
N	(343)	(177)	(519)

Cramer's V = .70

of two to one. When de Jong moved to McLaughlin, he was accompanied by 55.1% of his second-ballot supporters, while 23.2% of them went to Barrett. The large movement of de Jong supporters to McLaughlin had an important effect on the final outcome, enabling McLaughlin to extend her lead over Barrett and to maintain her momentum. Following the third ballot, Langdon was able to deliver his votes to McLaughlin by a two to one margin, and McLaughlin won on the fourth ballot. Thus there appears to be more than rhetoric in the importance ascribed to candidate movement, although those departing early were somewhat less successful in delivering their supporters than those who stayed in the race longer.

Overall, more than half the delegates changed their vote at least once over the four ballots (see Table 12.4). On the other hand, more than five in six delegates (84.5%) either did not change at all or changed only once. Since Barrett and McLaughlin together received just over half (50.5%) of the votes on the first ballot, the other half of the delegates had to move at least once, even if the move was to spoil their ballot. Most chose to move once and to stay there. Frequency of movement seems to have varied depending on which candidate the delegates supported on the first ballot. Almost all Barrett's and McLaughlin's first-ballot supporters continued to vote for them across the four ballots (see Table 12.4, Panel B). Among the first-ballot supporters of other candidates, only Langdon's were almost universal in moving only once (96.0%), though five in six (83.6%) of de Jong's

Table 12.4
Number of Vote Changes by Delegate Type and First-ballot Vote, 1989

	A. Delegate Type (%)						
Number of Vote Changes	Constituency	Federal council	Caucus	Youth	Affiliated unions	Central labour	Total
None	45.7	68.6	56.3	28.9	45.9	55.2	47.0
Once	38.5	25.5	37.5	50.0	32.4	34.5	37.5
Two	13.0	5.9	6.3	18.4	21.6	10.3	13.2
Three	2.8	0.0	0.0	2.6	0.0	0.0	2.3
N	(794)	(51)	(13)	(38)	(74)	(29)	(1002)

		B. First Ballot (%)					
	Barrett	de Jong	Lagassé	Langdon	McCurdy	McLaughlin	Waddell
None	96.0	0.0	0.0	0.0	0.0	95.3	0.0
One	3.0	83.6	34.6	96.0	37.4	1.9	61.5
Two	1.0	15.8	53.8	2.7	56.0	2.8	28.7
Three	0.0	0.7	11.5	1.3	6.6	0.0	9.8
N	(199)	(146)	(26)	(150)	(91)	(317)	(122)

supporters did likewise. Among Waddell's first-ballot supporters, three in five changed their vote only once, but for supporters of Lagassé and McCurdy the figure dropped to about one in three. Well over half of Lagassé's and McCurdy's first-ballot supporters changed twice, as did almost three in ten of Waddell's.

There was also a difference between party insiders and outsiders in the likelihood of vote switching (see Table 12.4, Panel A). The greatest stability was found among members of federal council, followed by caucus and central labour. Less stable were the constituency delegates and those from affiliated unions. The greatest instability was evident among the less experienced members of the youth wing, of whom almost three in four changed their votes across the four ballots.

DID THE MOST PREFERRED CANDIDATE WIN?

Theoretical research on voting has suggested that elections may be as heavily influenced by the rules of the contest as by voters' attitudes and preferences with respect to the candidates (Arrow, 1961). The so-called voting paradox was applied to Canadian politics in Terrence Levesque's (1983) controversial analysis of the 1983 Progressive Conservative leadership convention (see also the responses by Woolstencroft, 1983, and Perlin, 1983). Levesque argued that John Crosbie was preferred by more Conservative delegates than either Joe Clark or Brian Mulroney. The argument was that those who favoured Clark first generally preferred Crosbie to Mulroney, whereas those who favoured Mulroney first generally preferred Crosbie to Clark. Thus Levesque speculated that Crosbie could have won in a two-person contest over either Clark or Mulroney. However, since Crosbie finished behind both Clark and Mulroney on the third ballot, he was dropped from the fourth and final ballot and thus was denied the chance to go head-to-head with either Clark or Mulroney. Levesque concluded that the best (that is, the most preferred) candidate lost the leadership election.[3]

Is it possible that someone other than Audrey McLaughlin might have been the preferred candidate in the 1989 NDP leadership? Table 12.5 shows each candidate's preference ranking relative to that of every other candidate. Focusing on the relative ranking of row (r) and column (c) candidates, the table shows the hypothetical outcome of a two-candidate contest between each of the candidates (r) and the three strongest candidates (c), Barrett, Langdon, and McLaughlin. Thus each cell entry shows first the proportion of delegates ranking the row candidate higher and then the proportion ranking the column candidate higher. For example, 42.6% of respondents ranked de Jong higher than Barrett, and 57.4% ranked Barrett

Table 12.5

Outcome of Two-Person Contests Based on Ordinal Preference Ranking, 1989

		Column Contestant	
Row Contestant	Barrett	Langdon	McLaughlin
Barrett		43.3/56.7	38.2/61.8
de Jong	42.6/57.4	27.0/73.0	19.4/80.6
Lagassé	19.5/80.5	8.7/91.3	6.4/93.6
Langdon	56.7/43.3		34.2/65.8
McCurdy	40.9/59.1	26.5/73.5	20.1/79.9
McLaughlin	61.8/38.2	65.8/34.2	
Waddell	43.2/56.8	31.5/68.5	23.4/76.6

higher than de Jong. In a two-person contest between Barrett and de Jong, Barrett would have won by 57.4% to 42.6%.

A Condorcet winner is one who can defeat every other candidate in a series of two-person contests. Table 12.5 indicates that the eventual winner, McLaughlin, was also the clear Condorcet winner of the NDP contest. She was preferred over Barrett by 61.8% to 38.2%,[4] over Langdon by 65.8% to 34.2%, and over every other candidate by a margin of at least three to one. For Barrett, on the other hand, the margin of victory was large only when facing Lagassé, and was less than six to four for all others. Furthermore, not only was Barrett preferred less than McLaughlin, but he was also preferred less than Langdon. In addition, Langdon's margin of victory over the remaining candidates (other than McLaughlin) exceeded Barrett's. Thus these data suggest that, contrary to the results of the third ballot, which placed McLaughlin first, Barrett second, and Langdon third, in fact the delegates' preference ordering placed Langdon ahead of Barrett. However, since McLaughlin would have defeated Langdon by an even greater margin than she did Barrett, the final outcome would not have changed.

These results can be explained by examining the second-preference rankings of all delegates. Table 12.6 compares the first-preference rankings of all candidates with the second-preference rankings for Barrett, Langdon, McLaughlin, and all others combined. These data suggest that Barrett's major weakness was that he was not a strong second preference of many delegates. In contrast, McLaughlin was not only the most popular first choice, but a strong second choice as well. To illustrate, half of de Jong's and Langdon's first-preference supporters saw McLaughlin as their second choice, compared with 21.6% and 23.9%, respectively, for Barrett. Langdon's strength relative to Barrett was evident mainly among those whose first preference was McLaughlin: they favoured Langdon over Barrett by a margin of three to one. Although these delegates gave Langdon the advantage over Barrett,

Table 12.6

Second-Preference Rankings for Top Three Candidates by First Preference, 1989

Second Preference	First Preference Rankings (%)						
	Barrett	de Jong	Lagassé	Langdon	McCurdy	McLaughlin	Waddell
Barrett		21.6	0.0	23.9	13.9	16.8	33.0
Langdon	22.7	19.8	20.0		38.4	52.6	19.8
McLaughlin	38.5	50.0	26.7	50.0	37.8		29.9
All others	33.8	8.6	53.3	26.1	9.9	30.6	17.3

they obviously would not have had that effect in a contest between Langdon and McLaughlin. Furthermore, even those preferring Barrett as their first choice tended to favour McLaughlin over Langdon (38.5% versus 22.7%).

The conclusion that McLaughlin was the most preferred candidate, followed by Langdon and then Barrett, is confirmed by a Borda count of the preferences of delegates. In a seven-person contest, a Borda count assigns a value of 7 for each time a candidate is mentioned as first preference, 6 for second preference, and so on through to 1 for the least-preferred candidate (Brams, 1985). These values are then added across the population to produce a total preference rating for each candidate. Table 12.7 presents the complete candidate rankings and the Borda count.

Note that McLaughlin received 387 first-preference rankings, compared with 259 for Barrett and 141 for Langdon. However, Langdon was the most popular second choice, with 328 mentions to 149 for Barrett. The factor ensuring that McLaughlin's campaign would not stall was her strong second-preference total of 267, behind Langdon but substantially ahead of

Table 12.7

Borda Count of Rank-Order Preferences, 1989

Preference Ranking	Candidate						
	Barrett	de Jong	Lagassé	Langdon	McCurdy	McLaughlin	Waddell
First	259	89	15	141	75	387	89
Second	149	90	13	328	77	267	106
Third	134	134	31	213	151	171	178
Fourth	106	162	63	167	195	114	194
Fifth	84	185	98	95	241	55	222
Sixth	140	228	169	52	201	26	156
Seventh	141	105	589	21	56	19	54
Total Borda count	4,474	3,579	1,811	5,098	3,703	5,858	3,957

NOTE: Borda formula (seventh × 1) + (sixth × 2) + (fifth × 3) + (fourth × 4) + (third × 5) + (second × 6) + (first × 7) = total.

Barrett. Applying the Borda count procedure, McLaughlin again emerges as the overall preference of delegates (5,858), followed at some distance by Langdon (5,098). Barrett finishes a very clear third (4,474). The voting rules used at the convention did alter the standings of the top three candidates. However, the major effect was on the second- and third-place finishers, not the first-place McLaughlin. Thus, in a winner-take-all system, the most preferred candidate did win.

DETERMINANTS OF VOTING

The preceding analysis examined both the observed and the hypothetical movement of voters based on their preference ranking of the candidates. How do these preferences develop? What factors lead delegates to support one candidate over his or her rivals? Are those supporting a particular candidate doing so for the same reasons, or is there a wide range of interests, strategies, and evaluations that account for the voting behaviour of individual delegates?

Richard Johnston developed a sophisticated multivariate model to answer similar questions in his analysis of Liberal and Conservative conventions (1988). Focusing on the decision structure underlying individual choices, Johnston posited a model featuring five determinants of voting, three direct and two indirect. He hypothesized that each of the three direct determinants—social-background factors, organizational factors, and policy and/or ideological beliefs—is a function of a distinctive dynamic underlying the process of convention voting. If the vote is best explained by social-background characteristics, such as the delegates' age, gender, religion, language, and region of residence, Johnston suggests (1988: 207) that their motivations were similar to those of mass electorates in general elections (Courtney, 1986: 101; Krause and LeDuc, 1979: 102). If, on the other hand, organizational factors, particularly the distinction between 'insiders' and 'outsiders', appear to have dominated, the vote may be later perceived as the result of delegate manipulation along the lines suggested by Power (1966; but see Courtney, 1986). Finally, evidence supportive of policy/ideological factors would suggest that a market analogy—minimizing costs and maximizing benefits—is the most appropriate explanation of delegates' voting behaviour (Downs, 1957; Johnston, 1988: 206). In addition, Johnston postulates that two of these direct factors, social-background and organizational characteristics, also have indirect effects on policy and ideology.

Such a model is a very helpful in evaluating the relative effects of a wide range of potentially important determinants of attitudes and voting behaviour. Its major deficiency is that it fails to examine the full range of potential voting dynamics. For example, Johnston's use of the mass-electorate analogy is restricted to social-background characteristics. However, a substantial body of literature has demonstrated the importance of attitudes towards party leaders in Canadian elections, and the relative weakness of socio-demographic characteristics (see LeDuc et al., 1984; Archer, 1987a). Many voters base their decisions on their like or dislike of the party leaders, independent of their ideological views or policy positions. This is not to deny the potential significance of socio-demographic, organizational, or ideological determinants of leadership voting; however, if convention voting is to be likened to mass voting behaviour, measures of attitudes towards the candidates should be included.

In this section the model that Johnston developed for Liberal and Conservative conventions is extended to the NDP. The specifications of the model have been altered to include attitudes towards candidates as another independent variable. The voting-behaviour analogy thus has two separate branches: the group effect, based on socio-demographic characteristics and emphasizing the mobilization of identifiable groups, and the candidate affect model, stressing delegates' attitudes towards the candidates. The first stage of analysis highlights the importance of attitudes towards the candidates; the second stage then estimates attitudes towards candidates using social background, organizational position, policy positions, and ideology as the independent factors.

This model was used to generate estimates of the effects of social background, organization, policy/ideology, and candidate attitudes on a preference-ranking measure and on the four ballots in voting for Barrett, Langdon, and McLaughlin (see Figure 12.1). In addition, estimates were generated of the effects of background, organization, and policy/ideology on attitudes towards the candidates. We will begin by examining the determinants of candidate ranking and the vote.

The patterns that emerge in the data tend to be unique to each candidate (see Tables 12.8–12.10).[5] In addition to his support among British Columbians, Barrett found disproportionately high support among older delegates,[6] and on the final ballot he received disproportionately low support among the university-educated. The gender variable emerges as important in Barrett's relative preference ranking. Men were more likely to rank Barrett positively relative to the other candidates. Barrett was less likely to be supported by women than men on each of the last three ballots, with the relationship in the final two bordering on statistical significance at the 95% confidence level. If women were less likely to vote for Barrett— and they were—it was not simply because they were mobilized to support other candidates. As we shall see below, their gender had a powerful impact

Figure 12.1
Determinants of Convention Voting

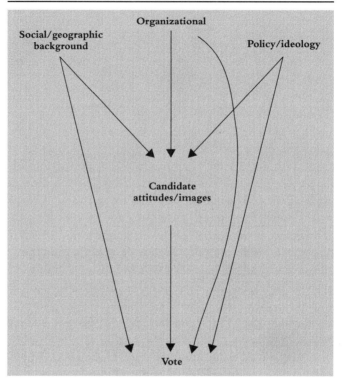

on their assessment of candidates' characteristics. In other words, women were not blindly led away from Barrett and towards McLaughlin: they were convinced that McLaughlin was the more suitable candidate for the party.

As with Barrett, support for McLaughlin was not strongly influenced by social background. Her fourth-ballot support came disproportionately from the younger delegates, and she was more likely to be supported by women than by men on all four ballots, although the difference on the final ballot does not achieve statistical significance at the .05 level. Her final ballot support also appears to have been greater among delegates from rural areas and New Brunswick, and lower among those from British Columbia. In addition, while de Jong was still in the race, Saskatchewan residents were less likely to support McLaughlin; but when de Jong moved to support her following the second ballot, the negative impact on McLaughlin's support from Saskatchewan delegates disappeared.

The social-background determinants of Langdon's support had a number of interesting features. Women were more likely than men to rank

Table 12.8

Determinants of Support for Barrett

Independent variable	Preference ranking	Ballot 1	Ballot 2	Ballot 3	Ballot 4
Social background					
Age	0.01(0.004)★	0.001(.001)	0.002(0.001)★	0.001(0.001)	0.002(0.001)★
Female	−0.42(0.11)★★	0.02(0.02)	−0.02(0.02)	−0.04(0.02)	−0.04(0.02)
University	0.001(0.12)	0.06(0.02)★★	0.04(0.02)	−0.03(0.02)	−0.07(0.03)★★
Rural	0.14(0.16)	−0.02(0.03)	−0.03(0.03)	−0.04(0.03)	−0.06(0.03)
Metropolitan	−0.18(0.13)	−0.04(0.02)	−0.05(0.02)★	−0.02(0.03)	0.01(0.03)
Francophone	−0.40(0.45)	−0.10(0.08)	−0.06(0.08)	−0.08(0.09)	−0.08(0.09)
Working class	−0.22(0.14)	0.03(0.02)	0.02(0.03)	−0.02(0.03)	0.001(0.03)
Upper class	−0.06(0.13)	−0.03(0.02)	−0.01(0.02)	−0.01(0.03)	−0.03(0.03)
Public sector	−0.04(0.11)	−0.03(0.02)	−0.01(0.02)	−0.01(0.02)	−0.01(0.02)
Catholic	0.24(0.16)	−0.05(0.03)	−0.005(0.03)	0.01(0.03)	0.02(0.03)
British Columbia	0.28(0.16)	0.10(0.03)★★	0.16(0.03)★★	0.10(0.03)★★	0.004(0.03)
Alberta	0.10(0.18)	0.03(0.03)	0.12(0.03)★★	0.07(0.04)★	−0.01(0.04)
Saskatchewan	−0.47(0.17)★★	−0.03(0.03)	0.001(0.03)	0.04(0.03)	−0.03(0.04)
Manitoba	0.12(0.19)	0.03(0.03)	0.06(0.03)	0.02(0.04)	0.01(0.04)
Quebec	−0.35(0.40)	0.04(0.07)	−0.05(0.07)	−0.09(0.08)	0.05(0.09)
New Brunswick	−0.87(0.42)★	−0.003(0.07)	0.02(0.08)	−0.01(0.08)	−0.01(0.09)
Nova Scotia	−0.28(0.30)	0.01(0.05)	−0.05(0.06)	−0.04(0.06)	0.03(0.06)
Prince Edward Isl.	−0.68(0.79)	−0.13(0.14)	−0.20(0.14)	−0.20(0.16)	0.02(0.17)
Newfoundland	0.40(0.59)	0.01(0.10)	−0.02(0.11)	−0.03(0.12)	−0.08(0.12)
Territories	−0.57(0.46)	0.01(0.08)	−0.03(0.08)	−0.08(0.09)	−0.12(0.10)
Immigrant	−0.14(0.15)	−0.0001(0.03)	−0.01(0.03)	−0.01(0.03)	−0.03(0.03)
Delegate status					
Affiliated union	0.42(0.23)	0.10(0.04)★	0.10(0.04)★	0.12(0.05)★★	0.11(0.05)★
Federal council	0.05(0.27)	0.08(0.05)	0.17(0.05)★★	0.12(0.05)★	0.04(0.06)
Central labour	0.004(0.32)	0.16(0.06)★★	0.19(0.06)★★	0.13(0.06)★	0.04(0.07)
ND Youth	−0.08(0.28)	−0.04(0.05)	0.03(0.05)	0.01(0.06)	−0.02(0.06)
Small meeting	0.12(0.12)	−0.01(0.02)	0.03(0.02)	0.04(0.02)	0.04(0.03)
Policy position					
NATO	−0.12(0.05)★	−0.01(0.01)	−0.01(0.01)	−0.004(0.01)	−0.01(0.01)
Free trade	−0.13(0.06)★	0.01(0.01)	0.01(0.01)	0.003(0.01)	0.01(0.01)
Meech Lake	−0.01(0.05)	0.01(0.01)	0.001(0.01)	−0.0004(0.01)	−0.02(0.01)
Distinct Quebec	−0.006(0.04)	−0.02(0.01)★★	−0.01(0.01)	−0.02(0.01)★	−0.02(0.01)
Leader cut off	0.02(0.05)	0.02(0.01)★★	−0.001(0.01)	−0.01(0.01)	−0.02(0.01)
Left–right	0.02(0.05)	0.001(0.01)	0.01(0.01)	0.02(0.01)	0.001(0.01)
Attitudes toward candidate					
Likeable	0.68(0.14)★★	0.11(0.03)★★	0.07(0.03)★★	0.06(0.03)★	0.06(0.03)★
TV image	0.23(0.12)	−0.01(0.02)	−0.03(0.02)	0.02(0.02)	0.07(0.03)★★
Policy positions	0.52(0.17)★★	0.19(0.03)★★	0.21(0.03)★★	0.17(0.03)★★	0.09(0.04)★
Competence	0.84(0.17)★★	0.11(0.03)★★	0.17(0.03)★★	0.20(0.03)★★	0.18(0.04)★★
Unite party	−0.12(0.21)	0.14(0.04)★★	0.04(0.04)	−0.02(0.04)	0.003(0.04)
Tough decisions	0.53(0.14)★★	0.10(0.02)★★	0.11(0.03)★★	0.11(0.03)★★	0.11(0.03)★★
Respect from leaders	0.34(0.16)★	0.06(0.03)★	0.09(0.03)★★	0.12(0.03)★★	0.12(0.03)★★
Regions	0.22(0.19)	0.06(0.03)	0.10(0.04)★★	0.06(0.04)	0.04(0.04)
Win elections	0.88(0.16)★★	0.08(0.03)★★	0.20(0.03)★★	0.25(0.03)★★	0.31(0.03)★★
Labour ties	0.06(0.11)	−0.01(0.02)	−0.01(0.02)	−0.02(0.02)	−0.002(0.02)
Intercept	3.53(0.41)	−0.08(0.07)	−0.09(0.08)	0.05(0.08)	0.22(0.09)
R^2	.55	.58	.64	.62	.59
N	(901)	(901)	(901)	(901)	(901)

NOTE: Standard error in parentheses.
★p<.05; ★★p<.01.

Table 12.9

Determinants of Support for Langdon

Independent Variable	Preference Ranking	Ballot 1	Ballot 2	Ballot 3
Social background				
Age	0.0004(0.003)	−0.0001(0.001)	−.002(0.001)★	−0.001(0.001)
Female	0.24(0.09)★★	0.003(0.02)	−0.06(0.02)★	−0.04(0.02)
University	0.05(0.10)	−0.03(0.02)	−0.05(0.03)	−0.02(0.03)
Rural	0.16(0.13)	−0.01(0.03)	0.002(0.03)	−0.03(0.03)
Metropolitan	0.03(0.10)	0.02(0.02)	0.02(0.03)	0.01(0.03)
Francophone	−0.36(0.36)	0.13(0.08)	0.20(0.10)★	0.15(0.09)
Working class	0.02(0.11)	0.04(0.02)	−0.01(0.03)	0.06(0.03)★
Upper class	−0.15(0.11)	−0.03(0.02)	−0.06(0.03)★	−0.05(0.03)★
Public sector	0.07(0.09)	0.02(0.02)	0.02(0.02)	0.03(0.02)
Catholic	0.11(0.13)	−0.01(0.03)	0.02(0.03)	0.02(0.03)
British Columbia	−0.37(0.12)★★	−0.12(0.03)★★	−0.19(0.03)★★	0.11(0.03)★★
Alberta	−0.29(0.14)★	−0.08(0.03)★	−0.09(0.04)★	−0.02(0.04)
Saskatchewan	−0.82(0.14)★★	−0.11(0.03)★★	−0.21(0.04)★★	−0.09(0.04)★
Manitoba	−0.30(0.16)	−0.06(0.03)	−0.13(0.04)★★	0.02(0.04)
Quebec	0.52(0.33)	−0.005(0.07)	−0.08(0.09)	0.10(0.08)
New Brunswick	0.18(0.34)	−0.04(0.08)	−0.08(0.09)	−0.12(0.09)
Nova Scotia	0.10(0.24)	−0.01(0.05)	0.20(0.06)★★	0.17(0.06)★★
Prince Edward Isl.	0.47(0.64)	0.15(0.14)	0.04(0.17)	0.08(0.16)
Newfoundland	−0.84(0.45)	−0.18(0.10)	−0.29(0.12)★	−0.15(0.11)
Territories	0.14(0.36)	−0.10(0.08)	−0.22(0.09)★	−0.14(0.09)
Immigrant	0.004(0.12)	−0.02(0.03)	0.03(0.03)	0.07(0.03)★
Delegate status				
Affiliated union	0.13(0.18)	0.02(0.04)	0.03(0.05)	−0.01(0.05)
Federal council	0.20(0.21)	−0.004(0.05)	−0.02(0.06)	−0.001(0.05)
Central labour	−0.27(0.27)	−0.01(0.06)	−0.03(0.07)	0.01(0.07)
ND Youth	0.14(0.23)	0.04(0.05)	−0.03(0.06)	0.06(0.06)
Small meeting	−0.09(0.10)	0.01(0.02)	−0.002(0.03)	0.05(0.02)★
Policy position				
NATO	0.04(0.04)	−0.003(0.009)	−0.01(0.01)	−0.003(0.01)
Free trade	0.03(0.05)	−0.02(0.01)	−0.01(0.01)	0.004(0.01)
Meech Lake	0.01(0.04)	0.001(0.01)	0.004(0.01)	−0.01(0.01)
Distinct Quebec	0.03(0.03)	0.001(0.01)	0.004(0.01)	−0.001(0.01)
Leader cut off	0.003(0.04)	0.002(0.01)	−0.01(0.01)	−0.01(0.01)
Left–right	0.11(0.04)★★	−0.01(0.01)	0.0001(0.01)	−0.003(0.01)
Attitudes toward candidate				
Likeable	0.51(0.16)★★	0.29(0.04)★★	0.15(0.04)★★	0.11(0.04)★
TV image	0.25(0.22)	−0.10(0.05)★	−0.06(0.06)	0.01(0.06)
Policy positions	0.69(0.11)★★	0.11(0.02)★★	0.12(0.03)★★	0.10(0.03)★★
Competence	0.37(0.14)★★	0.15(0.03)★★	0.20(0.04)★★	0.14(0.04)★★
Unite party	0.32(0.18)	0.04(0.04)	0.04(0.05)	0.05(0.05)
Tough decisions	0.37(0.16)★	0.14(0.03)★★	0.14(0.04)★★	0.10(0.04)★
Respect from leaders	0.05(0.15)	0.04(0.03)	0.04(0.04)	0.17(0.04)★★
Regions	−0.01(0.19)	0.02(0.04)	0.003(0.05)	−0.07(0.05)
Win elections	0.24(0.23)	0.15(0.05)★★	0.23(0.06)★★	0.21(0.06)★★
Labour ties	0.12(0.11)	0.04(0.02)	0.02(0.03)	−0.004(0.03)
Intercept	4.64(0.34)	0.14(0.07)	0.35(0.09)	0.20(0.09)
R^2	.35	.47	.43	.39
N	(910)	(910)	(910)	(910)

NOTE: Standard error in parentheses.
★$p<.05$; ★★$p<.01$.

Langdon high, but that attitude did not translate into more votes. On the contrary, women were less likely than men to vote for Langdon on the second and third ballots, a tendency that achieved statistical significance for the second ballot, and bordered on significance for the third. One suspects that had McLaughlin not been a candidate, Langdon would have received disproportionate votes from women. In this particular contest, however, the support of women delegates was drawn away from Langdon to McLaughlin. The strongest social-background determinants of Langdon's support were found in measures of the province of residence. Residence in the three western-most provinces had a negative impact on his support, especially in British Columbia and Saskatchewan. Nova Scotians, in contrast, were firm Langdon supporters over the second and third ballots.

The most important organizational factor as measured by type of delegate in the 1989 NDP convention was union membership. Union delegates (affiliated union and central labour) were more likely to support Barrett than were constituency delegates. Interestingly, the results are stronger for central labour on the first two ballots and for affiliated unions on the fourth. Union delegate status had a negative effect on McLaughlin's support, although the effects for both Barrett and McLaughlin were tempered when the two candidates went head to head on the fourth ballot. The strong effect of union membership illustrates that the mobilizational capacity of unions as a group is substantial. The fact that these coefficients were not even larger is important, and reflects divisions in the labour movement over candidate endorsements. For example, Shirley Carr, then president of the Canadian Labour Congress, supported Barrett, whereas Leo Gerard (Steelworkers) and Bob White (Auto Workers) endorsed McLaughlin.

In addition to his support from labour, Barrett was able to secure disproportionate support from the federal council, a group that, overall, was somewhat unfavourable to McLaughlin. Once again it is worth noting that, while the coefficients remain in the same direction on the final ballot (i.e., negative for McLaughlin, positive for Barrett), they lose their statistical significance. In fact, the organizational factors tended to have their strongest effect early in the contest. By the final ballot, most had decreased in statistical significance beyond the critical value.

The data indicate that left–right ideological placement had a very weak direct effect on voting, and that the effect of policy positions was mixed. Ideology had no significant impact on any of the ballots for McLaughlin, and had a positive effect for Barrett on only one of the four ballots. Those on the left of the party were more likely than those on the right to give Langdon a high preference ranking, but those attitudes had no significant effect on the likelihood of voting for Langdon. In addition, none of the

Table 12.10

Determinants of Support for McLaughlin

Independent Variable	Preference Ranking	Ballot 1	Ballot 2	Ballot 3	Ballot 4
Social background					
Age	0.004(0.003)	−0.001(0.001)	−0.001(0.001)	−0.001(0.001)	−0.003(0.001)★★
Female	0.10(0.08)	0.08(0.02)★★	0.07(0.02)★★	0.06(0.03)★	0.03(0.03)
University	−0.003(0.09)	0.01(0.03)	0.02(0.03)	0.05(0.03)	0.04(0.03)
Rural	−0.03(0.11)	−0.04(0.03)	−0.04(0.03)	0.05(0.04)	0.10(0.04)★★
Metropolitan	0.005(0.09)	0.01(0.03)	0.06(0.03)★	0.04(0.03)	0.03(0.03)
Francophone	−0.27(0.32)	−0.08(0.09)	−0.15(0.10)	−0.03(0.10)	0.13(0.10)
Working class	0.02(0.10)	0.01(0.03)	−0.01(0.03)	−0.02(0.03)	0.01(0.03)
Upper class	0.001(0.09)	0.01(0.03)	0.02(0.03)	0.06(0.03)★	0.02(0.03)
Public sector	0.06(0.08)	0.01(0.02)	−0.01(0.02)	−0.003(0.02)	0.01(0.03)
Catholic	−0.05(0.11)	−0.02(0.03)	−0.02(0.04)	−0.06(0.04)	−0.05(0.04)
British Columbia	0.06(0.11)	0.07(0.03)★	0.02(0.03)	−0.05(0.03)	−0.16(0.04)★★
Alberta	0.08(0.12)	−0.01(0.04)	−0.01(0.04)	−0.02(0.04)	0.004(0.04)
Saskatchewan	−0.20(0.12)	−0.11(0.04)★★	−0.11(0.04)★★	0.05(0.04)	−0.05(0.04)
Manitoba	−0.04(0.13)	−0.03(0.04)	−0.03(0.04)	−0.03(0.04)	−0.04(0.04)
Quebec	0.001(0.28)	0.20(0.08)★	0.10(0.09)	−0.02(0.09)	−0.03(0.09)
New Brunswick	0.28(0.30)	0.05(0.09)	0.16(0.09)	0.19(0.10)★	0.20(0.10)★
Nova Scotia	−0.56(0.21)★★	−0.05(0.06)	−0.08(0.07)	−0.09(0.07)	−0.06(0.07)
Prince Edward Isl.	−1.48(0.55)★★	0.03(0.16)	0.04(0.18)	0.02(0.18)	−0.21(0.18)
Newfoundland	0.002(0.39)	−0.01(0.12)	0.18(0.12)	0.01(0.13)	−0.02(0.13)
Territories	0.13(0.28)	0.16(0.08)	0.13(0.09)	0.05(0.09)	−0.09(0.09)
Immigrant	0.10(0.11)	0.0003(0.03)	0.04(0.03)	−0.03(0.03)	0.05(0.04)
Delegate status					
Affiliated union	−0.32(0.16)	−0.06(0.05)	−0.12(0.05)★	−0.10(0.05)	−0.09(0.05)
Federal council	0.09(0.18)	0.05(0.05)	−0.04(0.06)	−0.14(0.06)★	−0.04(0.06)
Central labour	−0.14(0.23)	−0.14(0.07)★	−0.21(0.07)★★	−0.17(0.07)★	−0.12(0.08)
ND Youth	−0.10(0.20)	−0.04(0.06)	−0.06(0.06)	−0.08(0.06)	−0.02(0.07)
Small meeting	−0.17(0.08)★	−0.03(0.03)	−0.05(0.03)	−0.09(0.03)★★	−0.05(0.03)
Policy position					
NATO	−0.08(0.04)★	−0.004(0.01)	0.01(0.01)	0.01(0.01)	0.01(0.01)
Free trade	−0.01(0.04)	−0.01(0.01)	0.02(0.01)	0.01(0.01)	0.02(0.01)
Meech Lake	0.05(0.04)	−0.006(0.01)	0.01(0.01)	0.03(0.01)★★	0.02(0.01)
Distinct Quebec	0.07(0.03)★	0.01(0.01)	0.001(0.01)	0.01(0.01)	0.01(0.01)
Leader cut off	0.07(0.03)★	0.003(0.01)	−0.002(0.01)	0.01(0.01)	0.01(0.01)
Left–right	−0.02(0.03)	−0.01(0.01)	−0.01(0.01)	0.001(0.01)	−0.001(0.01)
Attitudes toward candidate					
Likeable	0.31(0.10)★★	0.12(0.03)★★	0.06(0.03)★	0.06(0.03)★	0.06(0.03)
TV image	0.19(0.09)★	0.02(0.03)	0.02(0.03)	0.01(0.03)	0.03(0.03)
Policy positions	0.37(0.11)★★	0.17(0.03)★★	0.14(0.03)★★	0.08(0.03)★	0.04(0.04)
Competence	0.36(0.12)★★	0.22(0.03)★★	0.23(0.04)★★	0.21(0.04)★★	0.11(0.04)★★
Unite party	0.24(0.10)★	−0.02(0.03)	0.03(0.03)	0.07(0.03)★	0.10(0.03)★★
Tough decisions	0.17(0.11)	0.12(0.03)★★	0.15(0.03)★★	0.16(0.04)★★	0.12(0.04)★★
Respect from leaders	0.35(0.11)★★	0.05(0.03)	0.05(0.03)	0.08(0.03)★	0.05(0.03)
Regions	0.20 (0.10)★	0.04 (0.03)	0.03 (0.03)	−0.04 (0.03)	0.05 (0.03)
Win elections	0.54(0.10)★★	0.10(0.03)★★	0.17(0.03)★★	0.25(0.03)★★	0.30(0.03)★★
Labour ties	−0.18(0.10)	−0.005(0.03)	−0.02(0.03)	−0.03(0.03)	−0.04(0.03)
Intercept	4.31(0.29)	0.04(0.09)	0.08(0.09)	0.002(0.09)	0.23(010)
R^2	.50	.56	.55	.56	.51
N	(926)	(926)	(926)	(926)	(926)

NOTE: Standard error in parentheses.
★$p<.05$; ★★$p<.01$.

policy questions had a significant impact on Langdon's support. Barrett's support was measurably reduced among those who believed that Quebec constitutes a distinct society, since during the campaign Barrett had argued that both the party and the country should turn their attention away from Quebec and towards other matters. McLaughlin's support increased among those agreeing that the Meech Lake Accord was 'unacceptable in its present form'. Again, however, on the important fourth ballot no issue divided the supporters of McLaughlin and Barrett, and delegates' left–right ideological self-placement had no independent effect.

In view of the fact that the NDP is often described as a programmatic (as opposed to brokerage) party, the idea that policy and ideology would play only a minimal role in the selection of the party leader may appear counterintuitive. Previous leadership contests, such as the showdown between Lewis and Laxer in 1971, suggest that when there are significant differences between the candidates on major issues of policy (Hackett, 1980: 15), the delegates will respond by casting their ballots according to their positions on those issues, a finding that has been corroborated by research on mass publics (Archer and Johnson, 1988). When leadership candidates do not differ measurably on policy, then delegates will choose according to other criteria. At the 1989 convention, the most compelling criteria were more generalized attitudes towards the candidates.

Tables 12.8 to 12.10 illustrate the marked effect on voting choice of attitudes towards the candidates. Furthermore, the coefficient emerging particularly strongly for each of the candidates, and especially for Barrett and McLaughlin, was their perceived ability to win the next federal election. The belief that a candidate could help win elections was the most important factor attracting support. The delegates were not looking for someone necessarily on the left or right of the party, or someone who would champion one issue position over another: they wanted a winner. From that perspective, leader selection in the NDP in 1989 was similar to that in the Conservative and Liberal parties (Goldfarb and Axworthy, 1988; Martin et al., 1983).

Other attitudes towards the candidates also had a significant effect on voting. The perception that he or she was competent and able to make tough decisions was important for all the candidates. But there were also areas in which the candidates, particularly McLaughlin and Barrett, differed. For example, the perception that the candidate had a positive television image did not differentiate McLaughlin supporters, and barely achieved significance for Barrett on the last ballot—a curious finding, given the importance attached to winnability. Candidate likeability was more important on the earlier than the later ballots, as were the candidates' policy positions. Across the four ballots, likeability and policy positions decreased in importance for Barrett and McLaughlin, and by the fourth ballot were no longer significant predictors of McLaughlin's support.

There was an important difference between McLaughlin and Barrett in the delegates' perceptions of their ability to unite the party. Even though Barrett's first-ballot supporters believed that he could unite the party, this did not strengthen his position. Apparently many delegates thought that a Barrett victory, particularly in the later ballots, would be divisive for the NDP. Just the opposite was true for McLaughlin. Her perceived ability to unite the party became more important across the four ballots, and by the fourth, when she went head to head with Barrett, it had a strong positive effect on her support. Barrett, on the other hand, was perceived as capable of gaining the respect of international leaders, apparently because of his long career in British Columbia as premier and opposition leader. Perceived ability to appeal to all regions of the country, and the likelihood of strengthening party ties with organized labour, had no measurable effect on the support for the major candidates. Thus, to reiterate, it was the perception of McLaughlin as a winner for the party in federal elections, combined with her perceived competence and ability both to make tough decisions and to unite the party, that propelled her to victory.

DETERMINANTS OF ATTITUDES TOWARDS CANDIDATES

Why did some delegates perceive McLaughlin as more likely than Barrett to help win a federal election, and rate her high on the competency variable?[7] Were there any characteristics of delegates that systematically led them to develop positive images of some candidates and negative (or at least less positive) images of others? To answer these questions, estimates were generated of the effects of social background, organizational position, and policy and ideology on delegates' perceptions of the attributes of Barrett, Langdon, and McLaughlin (data not presented in tabular form).

Delegates' backgrounds, in terms of their gender and regional roots, had the strongest influence on candidate preference. For example, women were much more likely than men to give McLaughlin a positive evaluation on all attributes; Barrett, by contrast, was favoured by men, although less strongly. Also, McLaughlin received strong support from residents of the territories, while Barrett received strong support from British Columbians.

Among organizational factors, the union variable once again emerged as an important predictor. Overall, labour delegates had a more negative perception of McLaughlin than did non-labour delegates, whereas for Barrett the union effect, when it was present, was positive. Union delegates were not substantially more negative towards McLaughlin in all areas, but those areas in which their evaluations were less positive are instructive. For example, they were less likely than others to perceive McLaughlin positively with respect to helping win the next election, uniting the party, and leading it competently. By contrast, labour, especially central labour, took a positive view of Barrett in the areas of policy stands, competence, ability to make tough decisions, and ability to gain the respect of international leaders.

The policy issue with the greatest positive effect for McLaughlin was the view that Quebec constitutes a distinct society. This important concept, central to the ill-fated Meech Lake Accord, was not complicated by other aspects of the Accord such as Senate reform and changes in federal transfer funding provisions. Those agreeing on the distinctiveness of Quebec were less likely to support Barrett; the issue had no effect on Langdon's support. Perhaps surprisingly, delegates' positions on free trade and Canada's participation in NATO also had very little impact. Attitudes on these issues did not seem to affect delegates' perceptions of the candidates' attributes.

Although ideology had a role to play in 1989, it was not a profoundly important one; nor, as we have seen, did it persist to the final ballot. Barrett tended to be favoured by delegates who placed themselves further towards the right of the party, although it must be noted that the NDP's right does not extend to the right of centre. Langdon, on the other hand, received disproportionate support, and positive evaluations, from delegates who placed themselves on the left. McLaughlin's support suggests that she could be placed at the position of the Downsian median voter. Thus ideology had almost no measurable impact, whether directly, on her support, or indirectly, on attitudes towards her.

CONCLUSIONS

In 1989 the NDP, like the other major parties in Canada, chose its leader with a simple-preference, non-transferable vote, with candidate elimination and a majority election system. Such a system may encourage delegates to vote strategically, rewarding and penalizing candidates differently. In particular, a candidate who is the second preference of many voters may be penalized under such a system (although Joe Clark's election in 1976 illustrates that such candidates can be victorious). Conversely, those who polarize a party—those who are either loved or hated—are favoured by the simple-preference system.

The 1989 NDP leadership convention was marked by both these features of simple-preference rules for aggregating delegates' preferences. Langdon's support was understated because he was more often a second choice than a first. By contrast, Barrett's support was overstated. Although he was preferred by many delegates, there were also many delegates who ranked Barrett low on the list of candidates. The simple-preference ballot distorted the relative rankings of both Barrett and Langdon. However, McLaughlin was strong as both a first and a second preference, and was a Condorcet winner. Thus she would have won under any voting system.

The survey data demonstrated that leadership contests offer a parallel to general elections, albeit with some important distinctions. Most important, attitudinal determinants of voting outweighed socio-demographic, organizational, or ideological factors. To the extent that the latter features influenced voting behaviour, they tended to do so indirectly, through their effect on attitudes towards the candidates. It would appear that there is considerably less mobilization of group activity behind various candidates than might be expected. NDP delegates appear to have been more individually than collectively oriented in their decision-making than might be expected in a party with so many caucuses at convention.

The 1989 leadership convention was a milestone in Canadian national party politics. More than a century and a quarter after Confederation, the federal NDP became the first party at the national level to elect a female leader. At last a woman had entered the convention with considerable delegate support, been able to avoid the 'Flora syndrome' (Perlin, 1980), and win the party leadership. Audrey McLaughlin had achieved an important electoral breakthrough. Three and a half years later, the Conservative convention selected Kim Campbell as party leader, making her Canada's first woman prime minister.

McLaughlin, however, would not become prime minister. In view of the events to follow, it is paradoxical that one of the chief reasons for her victory at the 1989 convention was the perception that she would improve the party's showing at the polls. In her quest for the party leadership she was able to translate her relative inexperience in politics into an asset: she was a fresh face on the political stage. But under the intense and sustained scrutiny that accompanies national party leadership, McLaughlin did not excel. She did not inspire the general public, nor did she offer dynamic direction either to her party or to the country. Her performance was judged harshly by electors, and the more they saw of her, the less positive their evaluations became.[8] In the 1993 election, the federal NDP had its worst showing ever in both popular vote and seats, dropping below the twelve seats needed for official party status in the House of Commons.

Thus although there are parallels between general elections and party leadership conventions, in the end the two are entirely separate events. Delegates at conventions operate within the context of the party's organizational structure and culture. They forge alliances, they form caucuses, and they attempt to represent a variety of intra-party interests. Convention delegates often have a keen eye on the potential 'electability' of leadership candidates, but they evaluate a candidate's electability through their own partisan, ideological, and group-influenced lenses. General elections, in contrast, involve a much broader spectrum of society, which is less united by party membership (i.e., less communal) and hence more individualistic. The characteristics that lead to success in one setting do not necessarily carry the same value in another.

It is sometimes said that nothing builds party cohesion like the taste of electoral success. Conversely, few things can more effectively sour a political party on its leader than severe electoral defeat. Even for a party that was accustomed to placing third, the 1993 election was a devastating shock. As the person at the pinnacle of the party pyramid, McLaughlin took responsibility for the setback. Accordingly, in 1995 she stepped down and opened the door for the selection of a new leader who might rebuild the party. As the next chapter will show, the 1995 leadership contest would mark an important innovation in the NDP's procedures for leadership selection.

NOTES

This chapter is a revised version of Archer (1991a). The data reported in Tables 12.8–12.10 are re-analyzed versions of Tables 1.13–1.15 in the original publication. The re-analysis produced small changes in several intercepts. On the whole, the results of the two analyses are either identical or very similar.

1 McLaughlin was first elected to the House of Commons in a by-election in 1987.

2 The data in Table 12.1 are the official results of the convention, whereas the data in the remaining tables are taken from the survey of delegates. In general, the survey data conform well to observed convention data, although in several cases there are small differences. For example, the official data show 18 spoiled ballots on the fourth round of voting (Table 12.1), whereas the survey indicate that 20 people reported spoiling their fourth ballot (Table 12.2). This small difference may be due to misreporting of actual behaviour; or perhaps some who chose not to vote interpreted this action as spoiling the ballot (note that 2,417 ballots were cast on the second vote, but only 2,406 on the fourth). In either case, the discrepancy is well within the expected margin of error. For a discussion of the error in under-reporting Barrett's support, see note 4.

3 Both Woolstencroft (1983) and Perlin (1983) argue that Levesque's conclusions are incorrect, although for different reasons. Woolstencroft argues that the rules of the contest are 'endogenous' to the process of leadership selection: that is, the strategy used by the candidates to garner support assumed a simple-preference, adversarial system. If a plurality rather than a majority voting system had been used, the candidates would have approached the contest differently. While acknowledging the *prima facie* arbitrariness of the rules, Woolstencroft maintains that once the rules of the election are set, they become an integral part of the strategy of delegate recruitment

and candidate appeal. Perlin's (1983) critique is more empirical. Examining the preferences of delegates through a survey questionnaire, Perlin argues that Levesque overestimated second-preference support for Crosbie. Finding that a substantial proportion of Clark supporters preferred Mulroney to Crosbie, he claims that Mulroney would have prevailed in a two-person contest with Clark.

4   Note that these data overestimate support for McLaughlin and underestimate that for Barrett. In general, Barrett's support in the survey was about 6 percentage points less than at the convention. McLaughlin's support was over-stated in the survey by a similar amount (about 6%), but the other candidates' support was accurately mapped. The discrepancies reflect the relatively low response rate of union delegates, who were disproportionately supportive of Barrett, as well as the more generalized finding that post-convention or post-election studies tend to overstate the support for the winning candidate. However, the size of the difference, and the fact that it applies only to McLaughlin's and Barrett's support, reinforces the reliability of the data on relative voter preferences, particularly with respect to the standings of Barrett and Langdon.

5   Many of the variables included in Tables 12.8 to 12.10 are 'dummy variables'. A dummy variable has two values: a score of (1) corresponding to the value listed in the table, and a score of (0), the absence of that characteristic. For example, the gender variable is coded as (1) female and (0) not female, and is identified in the table as 'Female'. A negative coefficient indicates that women are less likely than men to rank a candidate highly or to vote for the candidate. However, when a variable, such as province of residence, has many categories, several dummy variables are created. To generate reliable estimates, one of the categories must be suppressed (i.e., coded '0' for all of the variables). In this instance the largest category, Ontario, was the suppressed value, and each of the province coefficients was interpreted in relation to Ontario delegates. Thus the figures for BC represent the degree to which they differed from Ontario delegates. For the social-background variables, the suppressed categories are males, individuals without university education, individuals living in small towns and mid-sized cities, anglophones, the middle class, non-public-sector workers, non-Catholics, residents of Ontario, and non-immigrants. The suppressed categories for the delegate's status variables are delegates from constituency associations and those selected at large meetings. The variables measuring policy positions are based on Likert-type questions ranging from (1) strongly agree to (5) strongly disagree. The attitudes towards the candidates are dummy variables, based on whether the candidate was ranked first on the variable.

6   The age variable is measured as age in years. Because it ranges up to approximately 90 years, compared to a dummy variable with a range of 0 to 1, the age variable produces smaller coefficients and is therefore taken to the third decimal. However, in interpreting the importance of age effects, one still compares the regression coefficient with the standard error (in parentheses). In general, a coefficient twice the size of the standard error indicates a statistically significant relationship, which in Tables 12.8 to 12.10 is indicated by an asterisk.

7   McLaughlin was not unique in this regard. Barrett supporters tended to give him a high ranking on the competency variable as well.

8   See Gallup data for the years 1989 to 1993.

CHAPTER 13

The 1995 Leadership Campaign

BACKGROUND

The period 1988 to 1993 was 'the best of times and the worst of times' for the NDP. The 1988 federal election had produced the party's best electoral results ever (20.4% of the vote and 43 seats); but more had been expected, and Ed Broadbent, the party's popular leader, resigned, partly in response to unfavourable evaluations of his performance. Still, there were several reasons for renewed optimism. In December 1989 the NDP became the first federal party in Canada to elect a woman, Audrey McLaughlin, as its federal leader (see Chapter 12), and initially she and the party did well in the polls. The electrifying victory of the provincial NDP in the industrial heartland of Ontario in 1990 was followed by similar victories in British Columbia and Saskatchewan in 1991, with the result that, at the provincial level, half the country's population was governed by social democrats. For the federal party, these provincial victories at first appeared to be assets, though later they would prove otherwise.

The victories of Brian Mulroney's Conservatives in 1984 and 1988 had been in significant part based on an unlikely alliance of Western Canadian neo-conservatives and Quebec nationalists. The fracturing of the Tory's electoral alliance in the 1990s had negative implications for the federal NDP. The newly created right–populist Reform Party challenged not only the Conservatives but also the NDP in the West, and it portrayed the NDP as one of the traditional, Ottawa-based parties.

In the lead-up to the 1993 federal campaign, organizationally the NDP appeared to be in increasing disarray. There was a steady exodus of senior party personnel, and even the leader offered to resign, just weeks before the campaign began. The 1993 campaign strategy had been drafted when the new leader was doing well in the polls, but by the last days of the campaign itself, the NDP was fighting for its very survival.

The reasons for the NDP's precipitous decline were many, and most are beyond the scope of this chapter (for further details see Whitehorn, 1994).

However, the major reasons included (1) a backlash by rank-and-file NDP members, particularly in the West, who disapproved of the party's efforts to appease Quebec nationalists and its support for the failed Charlottetown Accord; (2) the unpopularity of Bob Rae's NDP government in Ontario (over the 'social contract' legislation) and Mike Harcourt's NDP government in BC; and (3) strategic voting by the centre–left segment of the Canadian electorate, which, after the 1988 election, was so determined to get rid of the Conservative government that in 1993 many social democrats voted Liberal; in fact, among the voters who in 1988 had supported the NDP, more voted Liberal in 1993 than NDP (Whitehorn, 1994; Pammett, 1994).

From its best-ever results in the previous election the NDP fell to fourth place, with its worst showing ever both in number of seats (9) and in percentage of the vote (6.9%). Perhaps most significantly, the loss of seats took the NDP below the threshold number required (12) to be recognized as an official party in Parliament. The party was left with only a Western rump of two MPs from British Columbia, five from Saskatchewan, one from Manitoba, and one from the Yukon. In terms of votes received, the party stood at a dismal fifth place. Most ridings had given the NDP less than 15% of the vote—the crucial level required to receive riding financial reimbursement. Every single province had seen a decline in the NDP vote.

The NDP had been created to correct the problems of the CCF, notably its limited appeal and skewed regional profile. Had it now failed? Many party activists began to reconsider the NDP's future. The leader and her staff were criticized extensively. Many staff members at party headquarters were immediately laid off and urgent meetings were held by senior party officers to discuss the party's grave financial status. Declining party income and membership were growing problems across the country. The CLC, a key partner in the creation of the NDP, began a post-mortem of the election and set out to re-evaluate the relationship between the party and the labour movement (see Whitehorn, 1993).

The very survival of the federal NDP was in doubt. The party faced challenges on three fronts: leadership, organization, and policy. Audrey McLaughlin, as federal leader, bore major responsibility for the election fiasco; inevitably she would have to resign and a leadership race ensue. But should a party in such dire straits explore a new format, as had been suggested in a 1989 NDP convention resolution? Nor was it clear whether the NDP could successfully rebuild in Central Canada. The Rae government, with its controversial social-contract legislation, had seriously alienated its trade-union allies and precipitated major divisions within the labour movement. Ultimately, the experiences of both the federal party and the NDP provincial governments raised the question of what policy direction social-democratic parties should take in the 1990s. As the new century approached, social democrats needed to reflect on their policy priorities and ideological course.

Contrary to the NDP's written constitution, by 1995 no convention had been held for four years. Certainly activists needed to re-organize and meet in convention. But after such a long hiatus and such a serious electoral setback, what form should it take?

There was near-universal consensus that the federal NDP was in crisis (McLeod, 1994), and that any possible political recovery would require major reassessment. Accordingly, a number of broadly based renewal conferences (the first in Ottawa, 27–28 August 1994)[1] and research papers were launched to discuss public policy, socialist ideology, compatible doctrines, and the organizational future of the party. Among the major topics of discussion were the development of a new statement of principles, 'party mission', 'party structure', 'party relations' (with other social movements and groups), 'globalization', 'economy' (mostly domestic) and 'social policy'.[2] These conferences were intended to provide the ideological and policy underpinnings for the drafting of a new party manifesto at the 1995 federal convention.[3] As part of the renewal process, vigorous debate recommenced on various methods of leadership selection, culminating in the decision to use a new hybrid, two-step process.

Throughout 1994, a number of renewal conferences had discussed policy options and the nature of social democracy. These deliberations were expected to produce a cluster of new resolutions and a revised platform to be presented at the long-delayed federal convention scheduled for Ottawa in October 1995. As important as policy and ideology might have been to the renewal process, however, they were to yield centre stage to the task of selecting a new leader by a new method. It is to this new mechanism of leadership selection that we now turn.

PRIMARY DIRECT BALLOT VS CONVENTION FORMAT

Although New Democrats had been content with the existing leadership selection process, which had fostered increases in both the number and the diversity of candidates over the years (see Chapter 11), others felt that after 1993 a dramatic change was needed to jolt the party back to life and capture the imagination of the public. Earlier in the century, Canadian parties had shifted away from the élitist method of leadership selection by a small parliamentary caucus to the more democratic forum of a national convention attended by several thousand delegates. However, since it is the more affluent citizens and activists who are most likely to be able to travel to a convention, and parties of various ideological stripes were experimenting with new forms of leadership selection procedures (Courtney, 1995: 233–53; MacIvor, 1994, 1996; Preyra, 1996), some New Democrats felt the time was ripe for a more participatory system of leadership selection in Canada's social-democratic party.

The debate over the possibility of adopting a new leadership selection process had acquired some momentum at the 1989 leadership convention in Winnipeg. A resolution was approved to explore the feasibility of a new selection method and to report to the next convention two years later. The 1989 NDP survey gauged delegate support on this topic. When the delegates were asked '. . . Are you in favour of a change to a "one member, one vote" system to choose party leader?', just over half of the respondents (52.4%) agreed, while slightly more than one-third (35.8%) disagreed; the remaining 11.9% either were undecided or did not answer. Although the question did not refer directly to the term 'primary' or suggest how the affiliated members would be involved, if at all, there seemed to be considerable support for a new system of leadership selection. The survey, however, suggests that support was perhaps not high enough to be passed with a two-thirds vote, as required for a constitutional amendment.

Concurrent with the party's review, a research paper was commissioned by the Douglas–Coldwell Foundation (Hayward and Whitehorn, 1991) to analyze the academic literature on leadership selection methods and summarize the pros and cons of different formats. The study suggested that a convention format and a direct primary method both had advantages and disadvantages. Drawing on early drafts of the pioneering work by Latouche (1992) and Woolstencroft (1992) on the experiences of the Parti Québécois and the Ontario Conservatives with a direct ballot, the report indicated that recent NDP conventions had produced higher levels of participation, competitiveness, and media exposure than earlier conventions, and in addition were perceived as forums for inter-regional debate and possible pan-Canadian integration. On the negative side, convention attendance was still limited to the more affluent and powerful in the party. A direct ballot would certainly enable more people to participate directly, and thus might increase the legitimacy of any leader selected. On the other hand, the members participating would tend to be less experienced than convention delegates, and since they would be voting in their respective regions, they would be isolated from party members in other regions. Whereas virtually all convention delegates could be expected to vote, a direct ballot would likely mean a much lower participation rate, and the challenges facing a candidate trying to reach hundreds of thousands of individual and affiliated members might prove daunting, both organizationally and financially (see Tables 13.1 and 13.2). The Hayward and Whitehorn report was widely circulated

Table 13.1
Eligible Voters Based on Individual Membership, 1995

Region/Province	Regional Membership	Provincial Membership
Quebec	418	
Atlantic	4,011	
New Brunswick		863
Nova Scotia		2,413
Newfoundland		308
PEI		427
Ontario	19,814	
BC/North	18,398	
BC		18,121
Yukon		248
NWT		29
Prairies	36,174	
Alberta		2,890
Saskatchewan		26,648
Manitoba		6,636
Total	78,815	

SOURCE: NDP.

among a number of social democrats, including those on the NDP's constitutional affairs committee and federal council.

Both the 1991 federal council meeting in Montreal and the federal convention in Halifax later that year decided not to alter the leadership selection process. The party might well have continued for several years along the same course had it not been for the 1993 electoral fiasco. The status quo no longer appeared adequate. In the midst of interrelated financial, organizational, and intellectual crises, urgent measures were needed. A new leadership selection method was seen by some sections (e.g., Saskatchewan)

Table 13.2
Spending by the Leadership Candidates, 1995

	Amount			
	Interim Report		Final Report	
Candidate	Income	Expenses	Income	Expenses
Robinson	$119,892	$128,688	$206,318	$209,534
McDonough	66,210	127,507	N.R.	203,050[b]
Nystrom	45,443	29,131	79,856	79,856[b]
Hardin	N.R.[a]	37,426	N.R.	39,493[b]

[a] Not reported.
[b] These data are not official; provided in correspondence with authors.
SOURCES: NDP; correspondence with authors.

and some key figures in the party, including McLaughlin and Svend Robinson, as one of the more promising ways of revitalizing the party.[4]

Many felt that the NDP's populist image had faded badly. It was time for the party that had long seen itself as Canada's most democratic party and the champion of the ordinary citizen to choose a system of leadership selection that would be less élitist and more participatory for the rank and file. In so doing, perhaps it could recapture a sense of dynamism and renewed populism. A new system might also help to obtain much-needed publicity and attract new party members.[5]

Unfortunately, the window of opportunity for major constitutional change in the method of leadership selection had already closed. Any constitutional changes were supposed to have been completed at least one convention prior to any leadership race. Since the 1991 Halifax convention had opted for the status quo, and the 1993 national convention had been postponed because of the federal election that year, it was too late and too costly in 1995 (an unprecedented four years after the last convention; see McLeod, 1994), to call a convention just to change the constitution.[6] It was unconstitutional to abandon outright the convention format for selecting a new leader. However, grafting a new mechanism onto the existing convention format might provide an interim solution. How well a hybrid of the new and old formats would hold up remained to be seen.

To complicate matters still further, would-be leadership candidates were already active in preliminary organizing for their campaigns. The philosophical debate over the selection process and the jostling for position by potential candidates were increasingly intermingled, and made it difficult to discuss principles without candidates' electoral tactics clouding matters. To some degree, the emergence of campaign tactics amid the debate over organizational principles delegitimized the future candidates' critiques of the current system and suggested that proposals for reform were not necessarily altruistic.

THE TWO-STEP FORMAT

After several months of intense discussions, a delicate compromise was worked out at the federal council meeting in January 1995. The Vancouver meeting approved a unique two-step approach, grafting onto the constitutionally enshrined convention process a non-binding direct ballot by all party members. The first step would involve a series of five regional ballots open to all constituency members—perhaps as many as a hundred thousand (see Table 13.1). These primaries[7] would be held over four weeks from mid-August to mid-September. All individual party members in good standing as of 1 July were eligible to vote by mail-in ballot. To include affiliated union members in the new direct ballot, one national primary of affiliated union members[8] was also scheduled to take place in September, by a method still undecided at the January meeting. The five regional primaries and one ballot for affiliated members were to provide a preliminary, but not binding, threshold to determine which candidates could continue in October to the next level in the leadership race, the convention in Ottawa. To qualify for the second round, a candidate needed either to win one of the primaries (regional or union) or to take more than 15% of the combined total vote in all the primaries.

On the convention side there remained much that was familiar. Delegates were to be selected by the usual methods from either riding associations or affiliated unions, with the majority coming from the former (see Chapter 2). In theory, the delegates at the Ottawa convention were free to nominate and select any candidate, whether or not he or she had entered any of the primaries, let alone met the criteria set for continuing in the race. But such a scenario was unlikely, particularly if another candidate had received more than 51% of the total vote in the primaries. Thus the constitutional power of the NDP convention had in fact been curtailed, albeit informally, by the introduction of the first-round, non-binding, direct ballot.

Few if any party members knew in advance how this complex format would operate in practice. Among the questions confronting the candidates was whether to focus on the primaries to win, perhaps even on the first round, or to organize in the usual way, with an eye to influencing delegates attending the national convention. One thing, however, was clear: the four candidates—Herschel Hardin, Alexa McDonough, Lorne Nystrom, and Svend Robinson—would make history, regardless of who won. The new leader would be selected by a format never before attempted at the national level in Canada. It was a gamble by a party fighting for its life.

THE CANDIDATES

The 1995 leadership contest was unique in NDP history[9] in involving two hurdles, primaries and a convention. This extra obstacle, along with the party's dismal electoral prospects, was an important reason that only four candidates entered the race. By contrast, five candidates had run in 1971 and 1975, and a record seven in 1989.

As was the case in 1989, this race was notable in part for those who did not run. None of the former NDP premiers—Dave Barrett, Allan Blakeney, Ed Schreyer, Howard Pawley, and Bob Rae—entered the race in 1995. Dave Barrett, who had come second in 1989, chose instead to finish his memoirs (Barrett, 1995). Nor did Stephen Lewis, the high-profile former Ontario NDP leader, throw his hat into the ring. In contrast to the last three contests (1971, 1975, 1989), in each of which at least two Ontario candidates had run, this time there was no candidate from Canada's most populous province,[10] the heartland of union affiliation to the NDP and the province with the largest number of delegate entitlements (see Table 13.8). This was another sign[11] that the Ontario section of the party was still suffering the demoralizing and divisive effects of the social-contract legislation enacted two years earlier by the Rae government. Curiously, despite the party's ties with the labour movement, no union leader has ever run for the NDP leadership, and 1995 was no exception. Would a Bob White have made a difference in strengthening the link between the unions and the party?

From the CCF–NDP's founding, it had always selected as federal leader either a sitting or a former MP. J.S. Woodsworth, M.J. Coldwell, Hazen Argue, Tommy Douglas, David Lewis, Ed Broadbent, and Audrey McLaughlin had all served in Parliament. If that yardstick had been applied to the 1995 leadership contestants, only Robinson and Nystrom would have qualified. Of the seven federal leaders from 1932 to 1995, three had come from Saskatchewan, two from Ontario, and one each from Manitoba and the Yukon. The federal CCF–NDP had never selected a leader from either Atlantic Canada or British Columbia. Three of the candidates (McDonough, Robinson, and Hardin) hoped this would change in 1995.

Not surprisingly, the four candidates reflected diverse backgrounds and bases of support. Svend Robinson, from British Columbia, sought to build bridges with the Quebec section and form a winning coalition around the youth wing of the party, the gay caucus, labour, and new social movements. Lorne Nystrom, a former long-time MP from Saskatchewan, would endeavour to revive the more traditional roots of the party, while the Nova Scotian Alexa McDonough would draw on the extensive women's network in the NDP and attempt to build up her profile in the more populous regions of the country, particularly Ontario. As was noted in Chapter 11, the selection of party leader conveys a message as to the direction in which a party intends to travel. In 1995, the NDP's options included a return to the Saskatchewan heartland and a more traditional male leadership; an experienced but youthful radical from the West Coast who was openly gay; a woman and former provincial leader from the poorest region in Canada; and an articulate, unorthodox, and relatively unknown left intellectual.

Svend Robinson

Vancouver MP Svend Robinson was one of only a handful of NDP MPs to survive the 1993 federal election. He was charismatic, young, and energetic.

Some felt he was just the tonic needed by a party that increasingly appeared anything but new to the public. Robinson was photogenic and his name was recognized across the country. He had a capacity for generating publicity, a trait not unimportant for a party so low in the polls and often neglected by a corporate-owned press. As a former youth activist (he called himself 'a child of the party'), Robinson had obvious appeal for the young, dispossessed members of 'generation X'.

Robinson, like retiring leader Audrey McLaughlin, strongly favoured the change to a direct ballot. Both believed that a system of membership primaries would be more democratic and make the party more inclusive. In addition, with his high national visibility, Robinson believed he had a better opportunity to win in a series of primaries, which would appeal to youthful new party members, than in a convention, which would draw more heavily from older party veterans.

Well aware of the party's poor electoral prospects, Robinson called for a grand coalition of environmentalists, students, socialists, unionists, feminists, nationalists, and gays and lesbians. Under his leadership, the NDP would perhaps become even more of a rainbow coalition, embracing a broad range of interest groups, than in the past. Robinson's strategy was to bring into the party disgruntled greens and nationalists. Having gone to jail in British Columbia over the issue of clear-cutting, he had high visibility on the environment. In addition, his fluency in French made Robinson one NDP leadership figure who could speak directly to francophone Quebeckers at a critical moment for the confederation.[12] Declaring himself a candidate early on, and before a woman had entered the race, he hoped to receive strong support from feminists in the party. Robinson, who liked to portray himself as a radical and principled outsider, was expected to do well among the more militant left-wing party members, such as Dan Heap and John Rodriguez, a group that historically has done better than many expected at leadership conventions (e.g., James Laxer in 1971 and Rosemary Brown in 1975). After two moderate leaders, McLaughlin and Broadbent, Robinson appealed to many activists who longed for a greater sense of radicalism in the party.

But several potential weaknesses emerged in Robinson's candidacy. Although political idealism has been a hallmark of CCF–NDP history, sometimes it can also suggest a lack of realism.[13] Robinson's strategy of seeking to open the decision-making circle and making the NDP perhaps even more a coalition of coalitions troubled some party veterans who saw it as similar, if not identical, to the one espoused by Audrey McLaughlin. The 1993 federal election, when too many interest groups proved to be 'fair weather friends' and abandoned the party during the tough campaign, had revealed the weakness of this strategy.[14] In addition, while the urbane Robinson had appealed to voters in metropolitan Vancouver, some wondered how well he would do as a leader in more traditional and rural communities,[15] where his openly declared homosexuality might prove problematic for older, more traditional party supporters.[16]

Despite Robinson's well-planned[17] and early entry into the leadership race, no sitting MP publicly supported him, nor did many past MPs or sitting BC MLAs.[18] As one party member put it, 'Their silence was deafening.' Was Robinson, in their eyes, too much a grandstander and too little a team player? The lack of support from caucus colleagues suggested that Robinson's Achilles heel may have been not so much his ideological stance as various perceived personal characteristics.[19]

Lorne Nystrom

In the history of the CCF–NDP, the greatest number of federal leaders have come from Saskatchewan (M.J. Coldwell, Hazen Argue, and T.C. Douglas). No doubt Lorne Nystrom hoped he would add to the list. The youngest individual ever to sit in Parliament at that time, Nystrom was first elected in 1968, at the age of 22, and had served for two and a half decades as a Saskatchewan MP (Whitehorn, 1992: 88–100). In many ways he reflected the party mainstream in his wish to focus on bread-and-butter economic issues. He hoped to bring back to the NDP many of its traditional supporters (e.g., older male voters, particularly those from smaller communities). Coming from Saskatchewan, he could draw, at least initially, on the strong support of that province's powerful party machine and most of the sitting MPs (the majority of whom were from Saskatchewan).[20] In addition, he presented a tall, handsome figure on television, and thus might appeal to voters in an age when the leader's image seems as important as the party's ideological orientation.

Perhaps Nystrom's greatest weakness was the fact that he, like so many of his fellow New Democrats, had been defeated in the 1993 federal election. This lowered his public profile and made the mailings and travel required in a leadership contest more costly for him. It was probably a factor in his initial reluctance to run for the leadership, particularly when Saskatchewan NDP MP Chris Axworthy was also beginning preliminary campaigning. Some believed Nystrom was too cautious a figure to lead the party through difficult times and a new age; relatedly, some felt he lacked intellectual depth. Another personal issue, largely unspoken, was the fact that he had been charged (and later acquitted) with shoplifting on the eve of the 1989 leadership contest.[21] On a more strategic level, some pundits wondered whether a candidate drawing on the less populous and more traditional rural base of Saskatchewan could be the best leader for a national party looking to the future. The whole purpose of founding the NDP in 1961 had been to break out of the old CCF heartland of Saskatchewan and move into Central Canada. Despite his relative youth, Nystrom seemed to many delegates to be a voice from the past.

Alexa McDonough

Alexa McDonough was an experienced and highly respected provincial leader from Nova Scotia. Her family's political roots dated back to the early CCF era. Her father had been a legendary figure, a factory owner supporting the socialist movement in Atlantic Canada. As a feminist, Alexa McDonough represented one of the most vibrant movements of the second half of the twentieth century and one that has had a profound intellectual impact on the NDP. In addition, there was the key electoral fact that today more women than men support the NDP (see Chapter 6).[22] Many party veterans and strategists had hoped that McDonough would be a candidate in the 1989 leadership race; had she won, the party's fate might have been different. For personal reasons she had declined to run at that time, but by 1995 she was prepared to leave Nova Scotia and move onto the national stage.

Despite McDonough's long legislative career (14 years as provincial NDP leader), the harsh reality was that she had no experience in the federal Parliament, a fact underlined by the absence of public endorsement for her campaign from any of the nine sitting MPs. She was also handicapped in coming from one of weakest sections of the party. As the region with Canada's highest levels of unemployment and poverty, Atlantic Canada was perhaps a potential area of growth for the NDP, but so far that potential had been largely unrealized.[23] After Audrey McLaughlin's tenure as leader, many activists, particularly men, wondered whether the party would be willing to embrace another female leader. The poor showings of other female political leaders, most notably Ontario Liberal leader Lyn McLeod in 1995 and federal Conservative leader Kim Campbell in 1993, did not help McDonough's case. Instead of ignoring this potential problem, her campaign team took the issue head on with the slogan 'Two is not too many'. Her late entry into the race also meant that some women had committed themselves to other candidates (notably Robinson). In addition, the Participation of Woman (POW) committee officially remained neutral. Even McDonough's endorsement from former Ontario Premier Bob Rae was a mixed blessing. Her late entry into the leadership contest meant that McDonough's organization got off to a slow start, and initially she did not seem to appreciate the importance of the direct-ballot stage in establishing momentum in a campaign. She and her strategists just hoped to do better in the second stage, with the veteran convention delegates. It was a gamble that she could easily lose.

Herschel Hardin

Herschel Hardin is an accomplished author and playwright currently living in Vancouver (Hardin, 1973, 1974, 1991). As a left-wing, nationalist intellectual, he had a strong vision for Canada in the new world economy. If sheer intellectual ability and eloquence were sufficient, he should have won a place at the convention with ease. But he had no legislative experience (although he had run for the party in at least one election) and had never held an executive post within the party, federal or provincial. Although his political profile and support grew as his campaign progressed, his campaign organization had a quixotic quality. His campaign funds were extremely limited (see Table 13.2), and he was clearly a long shot. His articulate presence, however, would enliven the campaign.

ROUND ONE

In general, the primaries were scheduled to proceed from the smallest to the largest section of the party,[24] in the hope of building momentum and excitement. The plan also had the advantage of enabling party officials to learn gradually about the new and untested format. But it did carry some risks. For a party almost obliterated in the 1993 federal election, starting the regional primaries with Quebec, the NDP's weakest section, could convey a negative message to the media, highlighting the party's weakness in that province. It also meant that the time available for counting late ballots was shortest for one of the largest sections (i.e., Saskatchewan). The sequence of primaries could also significantly affect the visibility and image of some of the candidates. For example, the major bilingual candidates, Robinson[25] and Nystrom,[26] were likely to get a real boost, while McDonough, who was then largely unilingual, would not be seen at her best.

Primary Results

To commence our analysis of the primary voting (see Tables 13.3, 13.4, 13.5), we start with a brief summary of the results.

Robinson won the primaries in Quebec, Ontario, and BC—the three most populous provinces. However, the voting was weighted by party membership, not provincial population (see Table 5.1; for a discussion of this issue, see Courtney, 1995). Given the minuscule size of the Quebec section, Robinson's victory, while symbolic, contributed little to his total vote figure.

Nystrom was victorious in the Prairies and in the labour primary. His total from the former—almost 7,200 votes—was especially impressive: more than any other candidate received in total for the entire country. Robinson, his closest rival in the region, received just over 1,800 votes. In

Table 13.3
Primary Vote by Region, 1995 (number of mailed votes received)

			Candidate		
Regional Primary	Robinson	Nystrom	McDonough	Hardin	Total
Quebec	111	86	25	21	245
Atlantic	268	92	870	40	1,273
Ontario	1976	1184	1035	330	4,592
BC/North	2640	1524	625	408	5,265
Prairies	1806	7183	560	447	10,067
Late ballots	281	289	226	74	870
Total (column)	7082	10,358	3341	1320	22,312

SOURCE: NDP.

fact, Nystrom's margin of victory on the Prairies far surpassed Robinson's in Quebec, Ontario, and BC combined, and this accounted for his strong showing overall.[27] Nystrom's victory on the Prairies was due in large part to strong support from his home province of Saskatchewan and the backing of the Romanow government.[28] McDonough was able to carry only the Atlantic region—not one of the party's larger sections. Hardin did not receive the required 15% of the national vote, let alone win any of the primaries, and thus technically did not qualify to be on the ballot at the upcoming convention. Whether the delegates would choose to exercise their full constitutional power and suspend this regulation, allowing him on the ballot after all, remained to be seen.

As we noted earlier, the sequence of the primaries was roughly based on the size of the group voting. As expected, Robinson did well in the first

Table 13.4
Primary Vote by Region, 1995 (percentage)

			Candidate		
Regional Primary	Robinson	Nystrom	McDonough	Hardin	Total
Quebec	45.7	35.4	10.3	8.6	245
Atlantic	21.1	7.2	68.5	3.2	1,273
Ontario	43.7	26.2	22.9	7.3	4,592
BC/North	50.8	29.3	12.0	7.9	5,265
Prairies	18.1	71.9	5.6	4.5	10,067
Late ballots	32.3	33.2	26.0	8.5	870
Total (column)	32.0	46.9	15.1	6.0	

SOURCE: NDP.

Table 13.5

Primary Vote by Labour, 1995[a] (number of votes received)

Labour Primary	Candidate				
	Robinson	Nystrom	McDonough	Hardin	Total[b]
CAW, Toronto	52	7	4	0	63
East, Toronto[c]	33	81	92	2	208
West, Vancouver	52	87	16	4	159
Total					430
	Weighted percentage of votes[d]				
Total	32.1	38.2	28.5	1.2	

[a] In order of balloting dates.
[b] Totals include ballots spoiled, but percentages do not.
[c] Includes Manitoba.
[d] Weighted voting for unions based on size of union membership.
SOURCE: NDP.

rounds, winning three of four regional primaries, and in general his support was relatively steady (he was one of the top two in each case). By contrast, McDonough's support peaked early, in the Atlantic primary, and declined quite significantly thereafter. Relatedly, Lorne Nystrom seemed to do better as McDonough faltered.[29] Hardin, the distant fourth-place finisher, gained greater publicity as time went on, but his support was too small to present a major challenge to any of the other candidates.

Regionalism is a major fact in Canadian politics (see Chapter 5), affecting voting patterns in general elections, conventions, and regional primaries. When we analyze who won which regional primary, we find that, as in primaries in the United States, candidates usually did quite well in their home regions at the expense of others. Thus the Nova Scotian Alexa McDonough won the Atlantic primary with 68.3% of the vote, and the Saskatchewan candidate Lorne Nystrom won on the Prairies with 71.9% of the vote. While there were two candidates from British Columbia, only one was considered a major contender. As expected, Svend Robinson won in British Columbia, but by the smallest majority (50.8%) of the regional winners. Hardin's BC vote, at 7.9%, was a factor, but clearly BC party members did not endorse Robinson as strongly as members in other regions did their local candidates. This was a serious blow to the Robinson campaign.

Is regionalism a greater factor in primaries than at national conventions? One of the risks in opting for a primary ballot is that individuals in each region vote in isolation from individuals in other regions (Hayward and Whitehorn, 1991: 7, 14). This may well accentuate a voter's tendency to be indifferent to other regions; it certainly provides little opportunity for the development of a pan-Canadian perspective.[30] At a convention, by contrast, delegates from the different regions meet in both working and social contexts, and this gives them an opportunity to interact before voting. Of course this does not ensure that individuals from the different regions will change their voting patterns, but at least it provides the opportunity for such change.

At the January federal council meeting, the detailed format for the labour ballot was still largely undecided, but several key principles had been established. The labour results would be combined with the results of the five regional primaries at a ratio of 1:3. This gave labour 25% of the final tally, whereas labour's delegate entitlements at a convention would have been closer to 35% (825 of 2,325; see Table 13.8).[31] A large number of trade-union members are affiliated indirectly to the NDP. However, instead of encouraging tens of thousands of unionists to participate in the primaries, the trade unions opted to involve only several hundred individuals (430), delegated by their locals and union national offices, in the voting (see Table 13.5).[32] No doubt the novelty and uncertainty of the format, along with the limited time and money available to reach all union members, were also among the reasons that such a small number participated. Another was the fact that rank-and-file union members generally show only lukewarm support and low rates of participation in the activities of the party.

The labour primary was broken into three stages: first the CAW voted separately in Toronto; then unionists from Eastern Canada and Manitoba voted in Toronto; and finally Western union activists voted in Vancouver. Since all the votes were cast at these three meetings, union members outside the two major urban centres were at a clear disadvantage. Robinson won convincingly, with 82.5% (52 of 63 votes), in the CAW ballot. McDonough, with 44.2%, won a narrow victory over Nystrom (92 votes vs 81) in the Eastern union ballot; Robinson came a distant third in this contest. Nystrom's surprisingly strong showing in the Eastern union vote provided a momentum that carried over to the Western meeting, where he topped the polls with 54.7%. Robinson was a strong second, and McDonough a very distant third; her candidacy seemed to be faltering among the union rank and file, while Nystrom's was growing (see Table 13.5).

Labour's voting patterns were as varied as those of the regions, with the three sections selecting three different candidates.[33] In fact, whereas in percentage terms the regional vote had placed McDonough a distant third, with 15.1% to Nystrom's 46.9% and Robinson's 32.0% (see Table 13.4), reducing the field to the two men, the labour primaries kept all three major candidates in the race: Nystrom led with 38.2%, Robinson was next with 32.1%, and McDonough was a close third at 28.5% (see Table 13.5). Contrary to com-

mon public misperceptions, labour had not spoken with a single authoritative voice. Different unions had backed each of the three major candidates.
The CAW had endorsed Robinson; nationally the Steelworkers had supported McDonough (with some locals disagreeing); and the United Food and
Commercial Workers and the International Woodworkers of America had
backed Nystrom. Even at the leadership level opinions varied, with some CLC
officials remaining neutral and some supporting different candidates. And
within the labour caucus as a whole, one of the largest and strongest in the
party, internal differences emerged among the various unions.

When the results of the six primaries were combined, Svend Robinson
emerged as the winner of the most primaries, but the vote totals gave Lorne
Nystrom the lead at 44.7% (see Table 13.6)—tantalizingly close to 50%. A
result of over 50% would have presented the convention delegates with a very
real dilemma. Could they have ignored a majority vote? In any case, the differences between the primary process and the convention format meant that
it was perhaps unwise to read too much into the results of the primaries,[34] particularly in light of their low turnout rates (see Table 13.7), ranging from a
high of 59% in the small Quebec section to 23% in the most populous
province, Ontario; the average rate was only 28.3%. In general, the turnout
rate declined over time. The low participation rates of party members in the
primaries likely lessened the legitimacy of the primary process (for a fore-
warning of this problem, see Hayward and Whitehorn, 1991: 17–18), giving
the convention delegates greater latitude in their selection of a new leader.

ROUND TWO: THE NATIONAL CONVENTION

On the eve of the leadership convention, an editorial in the Tory-leaning
Globe and Mail endorsed the candidacy of the radical Svend Robinson. To
some observers, this seemed either a misguided or a mischievous attempt

Table 13.6
Combined Total Primary Vote by Region and Labour, 1995

| Primary | Candidate | | | | |
	Robinson	Nystrom	McDonough	Hardin	Total[b] (%)
Regional[a]	32.0	46.9	15.1	6.0	75
Labour[a]	32.1	38.2	28.5	1.2	25
Total	32.1	44.7	18.5	4.8	100

[a] Regional and labour totals derived from tables 13.4 and 13.5.
[b] Totals to be based on weighted ratio of regional primaries to union primaries mandated at 3:1 (i.e., 75% vs 25%).
SOURCE: NDP.

Table 13.7
Voter Turnout at Regional Primaries, 1995

Region[a]	%
Quebec	58.6
Atlantic	31.7
Ontario	23.2
BC/North	28.6
Prairies	27.8
Total[b]	28.3

[a] Regional turnout rates; excludes late ballots.
[b] Total includes all ballots (see Tables 13.1 and 13.3); 22,312 votes were cast out of a possible 78,815.
SOURCE: Calculated from data provided by the NDP.

by the neo-conservative newspaper to encourage the NDP to marginalize itself even further by moving to the left. For Robinson himself, to be endorsed by such a staunchly right-wing, pro-capitalist paper must have been galling, and it may have been the kiss of death in the eyes of some social-democrat delegates.

The federal convention was to a considerable degree overshadowed by a scandal surrounding the Harcourt NDP government in British Columbia. Beginning with a dramatic RCMP raid on the provincial NDP headquarters on the eve of the federal convention, the NCHS[35] scandal ('Bingogate') would eventually cause Harcourt to resign as premier. The crisis was a major distraction for all the BC delegates[36] and the key factor in the absence of some of the most senior BC NDP officials, including Premier Harcourt, from the convention (see provincial and federal council data in Table 13.8).

At the convention itself, the largest number of delegates came from riding associations (see Table 13.8); Ontario led the way, followed by Saskatchewan and British Columbia. Official labour delegates accounted for just over one-quarter of the delegates (26.1%). As usual, very few delegates registered through the official youth wing.

Once again, labour bodies sent far fewer delegates than they were entitled to (64% for central labour and 56% for affiliated locals; see also Chapter 4). The two regions with the lowest rates were Saskatchewan and British Columbia. Perhaps the energies and finances of the Saskatchewan section had been strained by the provincial election held earlier the same year; in any case, it seems likely that the low turnout from Saskatchewan delegates made a significant difference to the Nystrom vote (see Mitchell, 1996, who also notes that a significant number of Saskatchewan delegates had Ontario addresses).

Employing both a direct ballot and a convention to select the new NDP leader meant that two very different audiences were involved. The direct

Table 13.8
Convention Delegate Entitlements vs Attendance, 1995

	Entitlement	Attendance
Federal council and caucus	189	129
BC	243	226
Alberta	66	65
Saskatchewan	294	245
Manitoba	119	113
Ontario	396	386
Quebec	75	72
New Brunswick	18	14
Nova Scotia	42	40
PEI	9	9
Newfoundland and Labrador	10	9
NWT and Yukon	6	6
Youth	34	31
Central labour bodies	178	114
Affiliated union locals	647	360
Total	2,326	1,819

ballot engaged rank-and-file members, not all of whom were necessarily experienced activists; indeed, some were newcomers to the party, recruited by the various leadership candidates.[37] By contrast, convention delegates are usually highly experienced—in many cases, elected riding association and party officials (see Chapter 2). It was possible that these two distinct groups would vote quite differently, and the NDP faced serious embarrassment if one candidate were to win the primary ballot and another the convention. In this case, it would be hard to imagine a more divisive outcome for the new leader—a risk that the struggling party could ill afford.

One area of overlap between the primaries and the convention was the necessity for the convention to accept the procedures for the primaries, as well as their results. Accordingly, at the outset of the convention the delegates were asked to ratify the leadership selection rules and accept the criteria established for candidates to appear on the convention ballot. The delegates approved both, and Hardin did not continue in the leadership race.

As we noted in Chapters 11 and 12, delegates attending leadership contests can be asked not only their first choice for leader but also their second choice. A candidate who is not the first choice of most delegates may still be a compromise choice when other candidates are perceived as too far to one side or the other of the party's political spectrum.[38] By most accounts, British Columbia's Svend Robinson was seen as the candidate furthest to the left,[39] while Saskatchewan-based Lorne Nystrom was identified as the more traditional, right-leaning figure. In the eyes of observers and strategists alike, Alexa McDonough, as the only other candidate at the convention, occupied the middle of the NDP political spectrum and seemed ideally placed to pick up the largest number of second-choice votes if one of the preferred candidates had to drop off the ballot in subsequent rounds. She outperformed Nystrom, particularly in the speeches, and had a very strong organizational team.

On the eve of the convention vote, uncertainty was extremely high for two reasons. First, no one knew what impact, if any, the primaries would have on the convention delegates. Would their choices differ from those of the primary votes? Or would they feel compelled to support the leading candidate from the primary vote?

The second uncertainty was how close the results of the upcoming vote would be. While there was relatively little disagreement about who was likely to carry the first convention ballot, the size of his lead was impossible to predict, as was the identity of the runner-up. Robinson's chances of victory differed dramatically, depending on these factors. For example, if he came very close to the 50% required for victory, he might have sufficient momentum to win. However, most people believed his growth potential was limited. If his second-place rival was the right-leaning Nystrom, McDonough's centrist supporters would split, with many going over to the left-leaning Robinson. However, if McDonough was in second place, her centrist positioning would make her the ideal candidate to receive the majority of votes from the former Nystrom supporters. The left–right gulf between the Robinson and Nystrom supporters would be too great to bridge for the majority of delegates in the two camps. In short, Robinson's left-wing stance meant that his best chance to win second-round support was if McDonough, the more centrist candidate, dropped off. If it was Nystrom, the more right-leaning candidate, who was eliminated, Robinson was unlikely to gain significant new support on the second ballot.

The last scenario proved to be correct. The first ballot saw a very close three-way split, with each candidate getting about one-third of the vote:

Table 13.9
Convention Vote (one ballot only)[a]

Candidate	Votes	%
Robinson	655	37.7
McDonough	566	32.6
Nystrom	514	29.6
Spoiled	3	
Total	1738	100

[a] After the first ballot, Nystrom was automatically dropped off the ballot in preparation for the second round, but Robinson, the front-runner, withdrew from the second round; thus McDonough won the leadership by acclamation.

Robinson had 37.7%, McDonough 32.6%, and Nystrom 29.6% (see Table
13.9). McDonough had improved her standing significantly over the primary vote (by 14.1), moving from third to second place, while Nystrom's
vote had slipped dramatically (−15.1%), plummeting from first to third.
Significantly, only 52 votes separated second and third place: if only 26
McDonough voters had switched to Nystrom,[40] not only would the sec-
ond- and third-place finishers have been reversed, but Robinson would
likely have won the leadership. The balloting had been close, but what followed in the next few minutes was high drama.

Robinson, one of the brightest MPs in the House of Commons, knew
instantly what the first-ballot results meant. Instead of waiting for a second
ballot, and even though he was the front-runner, he calculated he had little chance to increase his delegate support, and thus chose to withdraw
from the contest immediately.[41] Characteristically, he moved swiftly and
consulted relatively few of his supporters. He approached McDonough and
congratulated her. Although at first she, like many others, did not understand what he meant by his gesture, he indicated that he was withdrawing
from any further round of balloting and was moving to have the convention make her selection unanimous. What made this case so unusual, not
simply a formality, was that McDonough had not been the leader in the
first round of balloting. For the front-runner to concede was a rare, if not
unique, event at a leadership convention.

Unfortunately, most of the delegates supporting Robinson, young and
old alike, were not so dispassionate, and many felt that, having given their
time and money to his campaign, they should have been allowed to play
out the final round.[42] The common view was that their champion should
not have conceded quite so swiftly.

Several young delegates threw away their convention badges; others
stormed out in disgust, hurling insults. Most of Robinson's supporters were
in shock. A considerable number were in tears, and not just the young.
While the new leader, Alexa McDonough, took part in a frantic scrum in
the convention hall, Robinson, one floor below in a packed hallway, had to
deal with his supporters' intense reactions. Emotions were raw. Even Mel
Watkins (1996), a veteran of the polarized 1971 Laxer–Lewis contest, was
bewildered and upset by Robinson's actions.

CONCLUSIONS

The number of candidates in the 1995 leadership contest was smaller than
in 1989; in addition, no visible minority candidate ran. Especially since the
new process was supposed to be more democratic, this was disappointing,

and suggests at least one possible flaw in the new system. Certainly the direct ballot contest was more complex, organizationally, and more costly for candidates than the old system[43] (see Table 13.2): instead of having to lobby a few thousand delegates, the new process meant that the candidates had to try to reach as many as 100,000 individual party members and potentially an even larger number of affiliated members. The challenge of reaching such a large number of potential voters was daunting, and probably a major reason why so few candidates declared. Of course, the grim electoral prospects facing the federal NDP were also a contributing factor.

Another troubling feature of the 1995 contest was the low participation rate among party members (see Table 13.7). The same problem has been observed in other cases where Canadian parties have held primaries. As anticipated, incorporating the affiliated unions was problematic, and the format of the labour vote was the least satisfying. Of the tens of thousands of ordinary unionists, a mere 430 'union primary' delegates—fewer than in any of the regional primaries except for the tiny Quebec section—determined 25% of the outcome of the total primary vote. The labour unions participating included those directly affiliated to the NDP and others that had contributed financially to the party.[44] The various experiences with the direct ballot by the NDP at the federal level and by other parties at the provincial level (see Latouche and Woolstencroft in Carty et al., 1992) indicate that this procedure does not uniformly increase participation rates, although in some instances it has done so (see Courtney, 1995; MacIvor, 1994, 1996; Preyra, 1996). The NDP, as a mass party, can ill afford a low turnout rate, particularly given its current weak electoral position.

Evidence to date suggests that leadership selection by direct ballot is not a panacea for an ailing party. A year after Alexa McDonough's election, she and her party remain at a low level in the polls. In addition, the 1995 contest left a serious division in the party, reminiscent in some ways of the one that resulted from the polarized 1971 leadership race (Hackett, 1979, 1980; Laxer, 1996; Richards, 1981; Watkins, 1973, 1992), although Robinson, as an MP, has been far more supportive of the party than Laxer was. Did the new format contribute to this division? Was McDonough's leadership hurt by a format that produced a split decision? Some speculate that Robinson hopes to build on his primary and convention support and some day become leader.

In 1995, the new format offered a way around the existing constitutional impediments to a revised system for leadership selection. In the event that the party considers using the same format again, it is important to ask whether such a complex process really does enhance democracy. If the primary process is not binding—if it's little more than a preliminary beauty

contest,[45] with the real decision-making happening at the convention—
does it simply mask the real locus of political power and present a mislead-
ing democratic façade? If, on the other hand, the primary process is binding (as Nystrom favours), what happens if a candidate receives 50% of the
vote in the primary round? Does the leadership convention become redun-
dant? Would it be cancelled? Clearly, combining two very different process-
es of leadership selection does not necessarily achieve the best of both
worlds. In 1995, many party strategists were jolted to realize that in fact the
primary vote could go one way and the convention itself another. Next
time the party may not be so lucky: the various factions may not be so
restrained in their responses, and the candidates may not be so gracious. In
deciding on the process for the next leadership convention, the federal NDP
needs to weigh carefully the pros and cons of each option.[46] To date, it does
not seem to have seriously considered this issue. Instead it has been preoccupied with organizational survival in the next federal election. If the election goes badly, however, the party should be prepared for the possibility of
a new leadership race beginning almost immediately.[47]

NOTES

Portions of this chapter are based on Whitehorn (1994, 1995a, 1995b).

1 See Canada's New Democrats (1994).

2 These are the official categories used by the NDP at its renewal conferences.

3 The last re-statement of the party's purpose, in 1983, was not particularly dated
   (see Whitehorn, 1992), but neither was it widely discussed.

4 It was hoped that the new format would generate publicity, and in fact it did
   help to raise an estimated $400,000 for the party. However, it was not without
   problems. For example, when Fraser Green, the federal secretary, mailed out the
   ballots for the regional primaries, he included a fund-raising letter. Not surprisingly, this dual mailing gave rise to considerable confusion among party members and triggered criticism about disrupting the integrity of the balloting
   process with a commercial appeal for funds.

5 A year later, the new format did not seem to have significantly increased the
   party's profile, support, or membership.

6 Another possible, though unstated, reason for not holding a convention to
   change the leadership selection procedures was the constitutional requirement to
   hold a vote on the leader at each convention. If such a vote elected a new leader
   (and it seemed unlikely that McLaughlin's leadership would have gone unchallenged), then any new leader would have been chosen by the old rules and the
   prospect of developing a new format delayed. Thus the mechanism for changing
   the leadership selection procedure called for some creativity.

7   The NDP officially called the process a 'nominating ballot'.

8   In fact, the CLC eventually decided to allow some non-affiliated unions that had previously contributed substantial sums to the party to participate in the labour primaries (interviews with Pat Kerwin and Nancy Riche, Jan. 1997).

9   Interestingly, the first CCF leaders were also selected through a two-step process. It involved gaining support within the parliamentary caucus, followed by election at the party's national convention (Lewis, 1981: 499; Whitehorn, 1992: 139). However, the first step in the 1995 competition was quite different in style and level of participation, with the membership primary being far more inclusive.

10 Some activists believed that Alexa McDonough's support in Ontario meant she was in some ways a surrogate Ontario candidate. She certainly was the only candidate from east of Manitoba, and this may have contributed to some Western activists' view of her as part of the Eastern establishment.

11 Earlier indications of the decline in the Ontario wing of the party were evident in the 1993 federal and 1995 provincial election results.

12 This point was highlighted by the fact that the Quebec referendum was to be held just two weeks after the NDP convention.

13 An example was Robinson's and the party's call for reliance on an economic boycott of Iraq instead of support for the allied Gulf War to liberate Kuwait. More than six years after the war, an extended economic boycott had not significantly altered Saddam Hussein's behaviour. A boycott was highly unlikely to have induced this military dictator to leave Kuwait.

14 For a similar conclusion, see Barrett (1996).

15 Certainly Robinson's stance on gun control was at variance with that of more traditional Saskatchewan NDP supporters. It was, however, completely in keeping with the attitudes of many federal NDP activists from key metropolitan areas.

16 Some of Robinson's closest supporters and advisers continue to believe this was the most important factor in his defeat (interviews with Whitehorn, Vancouver, May–June, 1996). One possible reply to this claim is to note that of all the major Canadian parties, the NDP has been the most sympathetic to gay rights. For data on NDP delegates' views and gay/lesbian caucus activity, see Tables 7.5, 7.7, 10.3, 10.4; for earlier delegates' responses, see Whitehorn, 1992: 130–5, particularly Table 5.16.

17 Perhaps most notable was Robinson's televised press conference announcing his '1-800-95-Svend' campaign phone number.

18 Most BC MLAs did not support Robinson's candidacy, and several of those who did were from the Burnaby area where his federal riding was located. This suggests that even among the few MLAs who supported him, electoral self-interest may have been a factor.

19 Robinson was one of Audrey McLaughlin's strongest supporters early in her leadership. However, when he commenced his campaign for the leadership, he seemed to distance himself from his former ally. Some suggested this was evi-

dence of Robinson's lack of personal loyalty to colleagues. In fairness to Robinson, it is hard to imagine that any leadership candidate in 1995 would have wanted to be closely linked to the leader in the 1993 election campaign.

20 Some observers have called the Saskatchewan CCF–NDP the governing party of Saskatchewan. It has won most of the provincial elections since 1944. Coming from Saskatchewan, Nystrom was a strong provincial-rights advocate and embraced the decentralized vision of Canada proposed in the failed Charlottetown Accord. It was a vision with which some New Democrats, such as former BC MP (now BC MLA) Ian Waddell, disagreed.

21 In 1975, two leadership contests earlier, Nystrom had been a candidate and had placed a close third to Rosemary Brown (Whitehorn, 1992: 115). Nystrom had chosen not to run in the 1989 leadership race, a decision that was probably fortunate, given the shoplifting charge. Although he was eventually aquitted, the incident seemed a handicap in his 1995 candidacy. A more serious factor, however, was the death of his mother just prior to the convention. This personal loss may help to explain his weaker performance at the 1995 convention.

22 This difference in gender support was reconfirmed in the 1996 BC provincial election (interview by Whitehorn with members of the BC Election Planning Committee, June 1996, Vancouver) and recent Canadian public opinion data (e.g., Environics, November 1996).

23 The 1996 election of the NDP's first-ever MLA in Prince Edward Island and the fact that as of December 1996 all four Atlantic Canada provincial NDP leaders are sitting members in their respective legislatures attests to the growth in NDP support in the region. However, this is still only a modest start.

24 The scheduling of the primaries did not correspond precisely to the size of party membership. For example, the Ontario primary preceded that in BC, although the Ontario section was slightly larger. In addition, although the union primaries were held last, collectively they counted for less than the Prairie regional primary.

25 Not surprisingly, Robinson favoured this sequence.

26 Herschel Hardin was also bilingual.

27 As Nystrom himself suggested, it might have been even higher if the Prairie primary had been held a week or two earlier, permitting more time for counting late ballots from that region (interview, Jan. 1977). In fact, the Prairie turnout rate was lower than might have been expected, but not dramatically different from that of other regions.

28 This conclusion is not surprising, since Saskatchewan accounts for the largest party membership by far on the Prairies (see Tables 5.1, 5.2, and especially 13.1).

29 Some believed that McDonough and Nystrom tapped a common anti-Robinson sentiment that would carry over into the convention.

30 For similar conclusions, see case studies by Latouche (1992) and Woolstencroft (1992). According to the latter, 'Direct election will mean that party members will approach political questions from the parochial perspectives of local areas

and constituency associations and without the broadening effect that comes from meeting members from other parts of the system' (in Carty et al., 1992: 224).

31 Because labour delegates generally have a lower turnout rate than constituency delegates, the proportion of labour delegates actually attending is usually in the range of 20–25% (see Chapter 4).

32 The labour unions participating included those directly affiliated to the NDP and others that had contributed financially to the party. Labour officials opted to hold three primaries: one for CAW unions, conducted at the union's national council meeting; one for Eastern unions (including Manitoba), conducted in Toronto; and one for Western unions, conducted in Vancouver. In each case the unions adopted a representative format for balloting, limiting participation to delegated union activists. In relying on delegates (as at a convention), this procedure super-imposed the principle of representative democracy on the direct democracy principle of the primary format adopted by the party. Both are legitimate meth-ods and styles of democracy. In choosing the representative method, the union leadership (which historically has been more supportive of the NDP than rank-and-file union members) significantly increased the probability that all those vot-ing would in fact be supporters of the NDP (rather than some other party). This strategy appears to have been effective: since the CAW vote was held at a nation-al council meeting, those present were all key union representatives, while large proportions of those voting in the Eastern and Western primaries also appeared to be experienced union activists.

33 The regional variation within the union movement was also evident in the fact that almost all the union members from Atlantic Canada—particularly Nova Scotia—supported McDonough, regardless of what their national union execu-tive bodies had decided.

34 Most political reporters apparently did read too much into these results and were consequently surprised by the convention outcome.

35 The NCHS (Nanaimo Commonwealth Holding Society) was a Nanaimo-based charity that had financial ties primarily to the local NDP riding association, but also some links to the provincial party (see BC NDP, 1996).

36 Provincial NDP president Patrice Pratt convened meetings of the BC NDP caucus during the convention and informed the BC delegates of the unfolding crisis. How much this affected the organizational efforts of the BC delegates, and thus Robinson's candidacy, is hard to tell, but it clearly had an impact.

37 This was particularly noticeable in the Robinson camp, which to some observers came to resemble a youth crusade (see Laxer, 1996, Chapter 7).

38 Joe Clark proved this in the Tory leadership contest of 1976.

39 Since Herschel Hardin was not on the convention ballot, he is not included in the following analysis.

40 This makes the low turnout of Saskatchewan delegates even more significant. Clearly, if the convention had been held in Saskatchewan—as was originally planned—it would have made a significant difference in that province's turnout

and probably in the result as well (see also Mitchell, 1996). It should also be noted that a surprising number of registered delegates (81) did not vote on the first and only ballot (see Tables 13.8 and 13.9).

41 Technically, Robinson's analysis was sound: it was quite unlikely that many of Nystrom's supporters would have redirected their second ballot to the left-leaning Robinson, and McDonough would most likely have won. Psychologically, however, his action was probably a serious mistake with respect to his supporters.

42 One commentator compared Robinson's action to walking out of a Shakespearean play at the end of the first act. Even if one senses in advance the final outcome of the tragedy, it is nevertheless useful to see the following acts for their cathartic effect. Robinson's dramatic gesture denied his supporters the chance for one last hope in the final round of balloting.

43 Unfortunately, more than a year after the convention final financial statements were not available for all candidates. Robinson's final report, the first received, indicated income and expenditures over $200,000. By contrast, the highest expenditure in 1989 was $128,575, by McLaughlin; see Archer (1991a: 42).

44 The latter fact was not widely known at the time, but the more flexible format of union 'semi-affiliation' is being explored for the upcoming federal NDP convention (interview with Nancy Riche and Pat Kerwin, Jan. 1997).

45 It is true that the primaries were effective in attracting badly needed funds and publicity for the NDP.

46 While an initial study was done in 1991, an updated report on the actual experience in 1995 is now possible.

47 As of December 1996, polls showed the party in a virtual tie with the Reform, BQ, and PC parties, well behind the Liberals.

Part V

Conclusion

CHAPTER
14

Conclusion

According to Johnston et al. (1992: 82), most Canadian voters tend to 'identify with' or 'feel closer to' one political party or another. Nevertheless, as the 1993 election showed, party identifications in Canada can be unstable, and they are clearly subject to change as new political issues or leaders arise (Clarke et al., 1996; Johnston et al., 1992). For most Canadians, in fact, the psychological tie to a particular party is relatively weak, and very few (less than 5% of eligible voters) formally become members of any party. Those who do so have a disproportionate impact on the political process. For party activists, the party convention provides a key forum for their activity in the extra-parliamentary wing of the party.

Linking the parliamentary and extra-parliamentary wings of the party, the biennial conventions of the New Democratic Party play an important role in party governance. In theory, the convention is the supreme authority in the NDP, and bears ultimate responsibility for amending the party constitution, setting its policy, choosing its leader, and electing its key officials. In the day-to-day management of the party, however, the convention is not and cannot be the locus of power.

For example, although convention delegates spend considerable time and effort debating and ultimately adopting policy resolutions that the party is pledged to follow in the event of forming a government, in practice there is no guarantee that these resolutions will be implemented. Since the federal NDP has never come to power at the national level, it is not possible to know with certainty the degree to which it would follow official policy. However, as the Rae government in Ontario showed, provincial NDP governments can take considerable latitude with respect to party resolutions. The fact that resolutions books do not prioritize the policies to which the government is committed means that members of the legislative caucus—or more likely the cabinet and premier—are able to set their own agenda. Their priorities may well differ from those of convention delegates, and even the ways in which policy is enacted can differ substantially from delegates' intentions.

Parties in government face pressures and representational demands that are far more complex than those of parties in opposition. A party out of power, particularly when it is meeting in convention in its extra-parliamentary forum, is responsible above all for articulating the interests of its members and supporters. Even though the party may define its 'core' supporters in quite broad terms, this group will never make up more than a part of the electorate. A party in government is confronted by much wider representational demands (Whitehorn, 1993). During its term of office, the governing party is responsible for representing the interests of all members of the society, not just its own members or voters. In attempting to fulfil this more complex representational function, the cabinet and premier may at times feel compelled to make decisions that actually run counter to party policy. An example can be seen in the 'social contract' legislation of the Rae government.[1]

Another factor limiting the efficacy of conventions in determining a party's path is the manner in which modern election campaigns are conducted. In the first decade of the NDP, party strategists developed a labour-intensive method of campaigning that centred on using to the fullest the party's mass membership to conduct door-to-door canvassing.[2] In recent decades, however, election campaigning has changed significantly even for the NDP (Courtney, 1995; Frizzell et al., 1989, 1994). The dynamics of campaigning have shifted from a personal dialogue between canvasser and voter to a one-way barrage of television ads. Whereas in the past a party was able to outline its program through a carefully planned series of pamphlets reflecting the decisions made at convention, the current emphasis on television coverage means that a party must be prepared to respond immediately to each day's political events. As a result, the NDP's campaign process has had to become less inclusive. As an election approaches, there is a *de facto* shift in the locus of decision-making, away from the mass membership represented at conventions and towards the party's Strategy and Election Planning Committee (SEPC) (Whitehorn, 1994). This small group of professionals, which includes the pollster, advertising consultant, and treasurer, plays the decisive role in defining both the message and the image of the party and its leader.

It is probably inevitable that such a group will tend to become isolated even from regular party activists, let alone rank-and-file members. It is probably equally inevitable that such a shift in decision-making power during election campaigns will create tensions within a mass party such as the NDP, which has a strong participatory ethos and a body of activists who expect their voices to be heard. A striking example of these tensions can be found in the 1988 election.

The party's US-based pollster, Vic Fingerhut, found that the dominant issue of the campaign, the Canada–US Free Trade Agreement, was perceived by the public as a 'managing the economy' issue—a type of issue on which the NDP has traditionally been perceived as weak (Whitehorn, 1989: 48). Accordingly, the strategists decided to 'soft-pedal' the free-trade issue, instead stressing the party's commitment to health care and the environment, and capitalizing on the positive public images of leader Ed Broadbent. However, free trade soon became the overriding issue, and the NDP's strategists scrambled, without success, to find a different plank with which to salvage their campaign.

The 1988 campaign clearly illustrates the isolation of campaign strategists from the rest of the party. In Chapter 3 we observed that NDP delegates almost unanimously rejected greater Canadian–American economic integration (i.e., continentalism), and when asked specifically about freer trade with the US, most strongly opposed such a policy. Yet the strategists were not deterred from their course even when union leaders urged them to incorporate a stronger anti-free trade message in the party's campaign (Whitehorn, 1989: 48). In a post-election letter, Bob White, then president of the CAW, expressed the frustration of the labour movement: 'This party doesn't belong to a handful of people who ultimately think they have all the answers. . . .' (quoted in Whitehorn, 1989: 52). After the 1988 election a number of reforms were introduced to make the SEPC more inclusive and representative of the party's constituent groups. But the problem is endemic to mass parties today: elections fought on nightly television news broadcasts require that a party respond quickly and have a single authoritative spokesperson. The tension between the needs of the centralized medium of television and the democratic ethos of a mass party is one that is unlikely to be resolved.

Despite changes in the locus of power in political parties and a heightened profile for party leaders, conventions continue to play an important role in the NDP. The convention is an important mechanism of representation within the party. The socio-demographic characteristics of delegates attending a convention say a great deal about a party's base of support. In examining the delegates at party conventions we can observe important differences between the NDP and other parties in Canada, as well as important changes occurring within the NDP over time.

In some respects the composition of the NDP's convention is simpler than that of the two older parties, the Liberals and Progressive Conservatives. Whereas the latter have had up to 18 different categories of delegates, the NDP has only six. However, this initial simplicity is complicated by two factors that add a significant collectivist element to the structure of delegate representation. The first is the party's federated membership structures. With the notable exception of Quebec,[3] an individual becomes a member of the federal NDP by joining the provincial wing of the party. This rule ensures that one cannot simultaneously be a member of the federal NDP and a different provincial party. Thus even those who join the party as individual members are obliged to be members of a collective entity—a provincial section—as well. This has practical implications in reinforcing provincial identifications and strengthening provincial caucuses at federal NDP conventions.

The importance of provincial sections is formalized in the organizational structure of the NDP, and the provincial caucuses are a further extension of regional influence. Unlike the Liberal and Conservative parties, which award equal numbers of delegates to each constituency throughout the country, the NDP awards delegates according to the size of the party's membership in each riding. Thus the provinces east of Ontario, with relatively few members, are represented by relatively few constituency delegates, and the largest groups typically come from Ontario, British Columbia and Saskatchewan. The fact that the bulk of union delegates also come from Ontario and, to a lesser extent, British Columbia, exacerbates the provincial imbalance in representation. Although bloc voting among constituency delegates does not formally occur, the existence of provincial caucuses ensures that the provinces with the most delegates are able to exert a powerful influence on the decisions of the convention and hence the party's course.

The second, and more significant, collectivist element at NDP conventions consists in the representation of trade unions. The Co-operative Commonwealth Federation began accepting the affiliation of trade unions as early as 1938 (Lewis, 1981: 153). When a union local affiliated with the party, all its members automatically became 'affiliated members' of the party. When the CCF and the CLC jointly created the NDP in 1961, similar procedures for union affiliation were adopted. While the rates of affiliation have been disappointing (see Chapter 4; see also Archer, 1985, 1990), affiliate membership remains a cornerstone of the party's organizational structure.

Union delegates have an important, albeit minority, voice at NDP conventions, usually accounting for about one-quarter of those attending. Although the NDP does not have bloc union voting, the labour caucus at convention can help to strengthen union delegates' group ties, and when union delegates vote in a consistent way, they can carry considerable weight. Nevertheless, as we have seen, the two most recent federal leadership conventions indicate that union delegates can differ significantly, at least in their leadership preferences.

Because of their special role in its founding, unions possess an important status within the NDP, and the party is still the 'political arm of labour'

(Horowitz, 1968). Increasingly, though, other groups seeking more effective political representation have called on the party to widen the decision-making circle. Foremost among these, perhaps, are women. After decades of under-representation in the upper reaches of the party hierarchy, women seeking greater gender parity on party councils and in senior administrative posts have met with considerable success. Not only have the two most recent federal NDP leaders been women, but so have four of the last five party presidents. Today the principle of gender parity among the party's executive officers is well established. Where gender parity has been more difficult to achieve is at conventions, a fact that is attributable largely to the overwhelmingly male membership of affiliated unions (although, even here, significant strides have been made). No doubt a large part of this success can be attributed to the efforts of the women's caucus (POW committee), which has helped to compensate for women's numerical weakness by giving them a strong united voice. By any measure, it is now one of the pre-eminent caucuses at NDP conventions.

In addition to the provincial, trade-union, and women's caucuses, delegates may attend various other caucuses: youth, environment, left, gay and lesbian. Although attendance is entirely voluntary, and although the secret ballot precludes formal bloc voting by any caucus, our data have indicated that caucuses do have an important effect in mobilizing like-minded individuals both in policy development and in leadership selection. There is always a risk that a caucus may become so powerful and well-organized as to constitute, in effect, a party within the party, as occurred with the Waffle in the early 1970s. However, caucuses appear to be a natural outgrowth of both society's and the NDP's collectivist structure, and they can serve as an important link between the party and organized interest groups.

In any case, the emergence of the newer caucuses does not appear to have weakened NDP activists' commitment to the welfare state and socialist and social-democratic principles. They still view the state in a positive light for the most part, with an interventionist role; they are still committed to expansion of and universality in social programs; and they still support sustained government spending on health, education, and welfare. Similarly, in the area of defence and foreign policy, delegates in general continue to reflect the party's historic emphasis on non-violent and internationalist solutions to conflict, (e.g., peacekeeping, fostering international human rights, increasing foreign aid, and promoting sustainable development); however, their stance on Canadian–American relations remains staunchly nationalist. At the same time, the newer caucuses are focusing attention on a number of concerns associated with the 'new politics', including women's issues, environmentalism, and quality of life, that could create divisions between the new postmaterialist groups and the more materially oriented labour caucus. However, the evidence so far suggests that, even on these issues, agreement within the NDP generally remains high, especially in comparison with activists in the Liberal and Conservative parties.

Leadership selection methods have evolved over the years. The change from an internal parliamentary caucus decision to leadership conventions was one historic step in the democratization of parties (Duverger, 1963). And in a recent book on leadership conventions, John Courtney (1995) argued that leadership selection through national party conventions may soon be replaced. In general, there has been a growing tendency for parties at the provincial level to replace selection by a delegated convention with some form of universal balloting by all party members. Arguments for such reform, typically based on the premise that universal balloting is more democratic, have also won adherents at the federal level. For example, at a national meeting of the Progressive Conservatives in April 1995, the Conservatives adopted a Universal Membership Vote that, according to Courtney (1995: 256), 'amounts to an all-member, direct vote with equal weight to all ridings. . . . With the selection of Jean Charest's successor, whenever that might be, leadership conventions in the Conservative party will have become a thing of the past.' In 1992, the federal Liberal Party adopted a hybrid voting mechanism, similar to the one used by the Ontario Liberals earlier that year, for its next leadership convention; it combines elements of proportional representation with a delegate convention. Constituency members would receive two ballots at the delegate selection meeting; the first would be used to allocate constituency votes for the leadership candidates on a proportional basis, and the second would be used to select delegates for the convention from a slate of activists, each of whom would be a declared supporter of a particular leadership candidate. At the federal convention, delegates would be given a ballot on the first round with only the name of their preferred leadership candidate. Their options would be either to support their declared candidate or not to vote at all. If no candidate won a majority of votes on the first ballot, delegates would be free to vote for whomever they liked on subsequent ballots (see Courtney, 1995: 259–73).

As we discussed in detail in Chapter 13, the NDP has not been immune to pressures to democratize the party still further by providing a stronger voice to the rank-and-file in the selection of party leader. But the changes introduced in 1995 had serious disadvantages. The use of a hybrid mechanism consisting of, first, a series of primaries in the regions and among the affiliated unions and, later, a convention of elected delegates, actually produced two significantly different results. Lorne Nystrom, who came first in the regional and union primaries, finished third on the first (and only) ballot at the convention. Conversely, the eventual winner, Alexa McDonough, had finished only third in the primaries. With the contradictory hybrid format, the NDP initially appeared to give a stronger voice to the rank-and-file party members, but in the end the outcome was still determined by the delegates and the various caucuses at the convention.

It is too early to know for certain whether the NDP's new leadership selection process will endure or will prove only an interim measure on the road to even further reforms. Recent experiences at the provincial level suggest that as one party introduces a direct ballot for its rank-and-file, the other parties feel pressure to follow suit. For example, the Ontario Conservatives first used a form of universal balloting to select their party leader in 1990 (Woolstencroft, 1992), and the Ontario Liberals followed with their own version in 1992 (Courtney, 1995). The Alberta Conservatives used a universal membership voting method in electing Ralph Klein in 1992, and the Alberta Liberals in turn used a universal membership tele-vote mechanism in November 1994 (Archer and Stewart, 1995; Stewart, 1997; Stewart and Archer, 1996). In neither of these provinces, however, did the provincial NDP feel compelled to follow the examples set by its rivals. The Ontario New Democrats used a leadership convention to elect Howard Hampton as their leader in June 1996 (Whitehorn, 1996b). Similarly, the Alberta New Democrats stayed with conventions to elect Ross Harvey in February 1994 and Pam Barrett in September 1996. Most notably, the two current NDP premiers, Glen Clark of British Columbia and Roy Romanow of Saskatchewan, were selected by conventions. Thus it does not appear by any means inevitable that the federal party will adopt a direct-ballot system of leadership selection.

The mixed success of the federal NDP's changes in its method of leadership selection, coupled with the reluctance of the party's provincial wings to experiment with new methods of leadership selection, may appear paradoxical in view of the NDP's commitment to openness and more participatory, democratic methods of decision-making. Part of the key to this paradox lies in the distinction between individualist and collectivist orientations. If a party's basic unit is the individual member, as is the case with the Liberal, Conservative and Reform parties, initiatives that enhance the role or importance of individual party members may be appealing and relatively easy to implement. However, membership in the NDP has an important collectivist component not only for affiliated union members but for 'individual' members from the provincial sections as well. And, as we have seen, the emphasis on the group is reinforced by the caucuses within which much of the activity at conventions takes place. Although universal membership voting can be adjusted to weight the votes of various groups (such as labour unions in the NDP), the principle of universal membership voting does not seem to resonate with the same intensity in the collectivist-orientated NDP as it does in some other parties. As the federal Liberals, Conservatives, and Reformers begin to provide a larger role for ordinary party members in leadership selection, the NDP may appear to be insufficiently democratic—and overly beholden to labour—if it adheres to the convention format. However, the pressure to accommodate the party's rank and file will be counter-balanced by the need to recognize the importance of key groups within the party. Although the introduction of primary balloting in 1995 recognized the collectivities of regions and unions, the other groups—women, environmentalists, the party's left wing, youth, gays and lesbians—that find strength in convention caucuses would stand to lose some of their status and power should a universal membership voting mechanism be adopted. Certainly the party's collectivist orientation points to a continuing role for conventions in leadership selection.

In the time span covered in this book there have been three federal NDP leaders. Commencing with Ed Broadbent, who won the leadership in 1975, the party has seen a new generation of leaders emerge. As the first leader without a direct connection to the CCF, Broadbent represented a significant break with the party's past, and in one important respect he personified the image that the NDP sought to cultivate. Coming from Oshawa, where the United Auto Workers (now Canadian Auto Workers) union was a key pillar of support for the NDP, and rising from his working-class roots to become a university professor, he represented a blend of left-wing intellectualism (present from the party's inception as the CCF), and modern industrial unionism (an important component in the founding of the NDP) (Levitt, 1996).

Over his fourteen years as leader, Broadbent led the party in four election campaigns. He was widely respected and one of the most popular party leaders of this era (Clarke et al., 1991: 90). In fact, by 1988 he was the only party leader to receive above-average assessments in public opinion polls on both 'competency' and 'character' rating scales (Johnston et al., 1992: 178). And even though the last election in which he served as leader was a bitter disappointment, it gave the NDP its best popular vote ever (more than 20%) and a peak of 43 seats in Parliament (Frizzell et al., 1989: 133). Nevertheless, faced with increased criticism about the way the party's election strategy was developed and implemented, Broadbent resigned.

Audrey McLaughlin's election, in December 1989, as the first woman to lead a major national party in Canada signalled the growing strength of the women's movement in general and the NDP's women's caucus (POW) in particular. Her leadership victory was a narrow one, reflecting in part her relative inexperience in national politics and Parliament, and in part a somewhat lacklustre campaign. But most New Democrats expected that she would polish her performance prior to the next election. Although she initially did well as party leader, particularly on 'honesty and ethics', the longer she stayed on, the lower her public ratings became. By 1993 she was rated behind Jean Chrétien in Canada at large, Lucien Bouchard in Quebec, and Preston Manning outside Quebec on an overall 'feeling thermometer'. She was ahead of only one other leader: Kim Campbell.[4] Both led their parties into electoral disaster (Clarke et al., 1996: 77–80), and McLaughlin, like her Conservative counterpart, resigned as leader after only one election.

Alexa McDonough won the federal leadership in 1995 having previously served as provincial leader of the Nova Scotia NDP, but by the spring of 1997 she still did not have a seat in Parliament. That the gender issue did not seriously handicap her in the 1995 leadership contest is a measure of the changes that have taken place in attitudes towards women both in the NDP and in Canadian politics more generally. Indeed, it may have been an important asset, as her candidacy was warmly supported by women, Ontario, and some key unions (e.g., the Steelworkers). Lorne Nystrom received the support of the Saskatchewan caucus and other unions (e.g., the United Farm and Commercial Workers), while Svend Robinson was championed by the youth and the gay and lesbian caucuses, a significant number of women, and still other unionists (CAW). (See also Chapter 13.)

The New Democratic Party confronts many challenges at the close of the twentieth century. It was one of the big losers in the fractionalization of the party system in 1993, when its poor electoral performance cost the party its 'official' status in the Commons;[5] it has continued to fare poorly in public opinion polls; its new leader has no experience in the federal Parliament; and she remains relatively unknown to large numbers of voters. The ability of the NDP governments in Saskatchewan and British Columbia to win re-election in 1995 and 1996, respectively, suggests that a moderate social-democratic message can still be relevant to large numbers of Canadians. But the federal party will have to continue trying to broaden its appeal, perhaps reaching out to offer a political home to an even wider range of political interests.[6] Fortunately, it has learned over the years to accommodate new groups and greater complexity (e.g., through the formation of caucuses representing emerging groups and interests). Such groups will have to compete and co-operate with others already within the party in the ongoing effort to select leaders and formulate policy that will attract electoral support while upholding the ideological principles that set the NDP apart. In the NDP, the main forum for these activities remains the party convention.

NOTES

1 In an effort to stem the ballooning public deficit, the Rae government passed Bill 48, the Social Contract Act, in June 1993. The most contentious provision of this bill was a rollback in wages for public-sector employees (Archer, 1995; Beaud and Prévost, 1995). This legislation was particularly controversial because it ran counter to the party's policies that governments should not interfere in the collective bargaining process and that wages negotiated in a fair and open manner should not be rolled back arbitrarily or unilaterally (Jenson and Mahon, 1995; Tanguay, 1995). In singling out unionized public-sector workers, the social contract ran the risk of alienating one of the party's traditional support bases.

   Despite its status as the party's 'supreme governing authority', in practice the convention could do little to reverse this unpopular policy. The Ontario Federation of Labour, meeting in convention in November 1993, passed a resolution stating that it would not support the NDP in the next provincial election unless Bill 48 was repealed. A group of unionists opposed to this resolution, comprising approximately 40% of OFL delegates, marched out of the convention in protest, and the leadership of this 'Pink Group' issued a statement declaring that the proposed policy did not speak for them and that they would work to re-elect the NDP government (Archer, 1995: 38). But many other union members, including some who were members of unions that had traditionally supported the NDP, such as the Canadian Auto Workers, did withdraw their support, and the government was not re-elected. It would be overly simplistic, and largely inaccurate, to conclude that the Rae government was defeated solely on account of the social contract; however, this legislation was certainly a contributing factor. This episode illustrates the impossibility, even for a social-democratic party, of ensuring that the parliamentary wing of the party will always remain faithful to the policies adopted by the extra-parliamentary wing at convention.

2 The strategy was to visit each dwelling as many as three times during the campaign to drop literature and to try to identify the party's supporters. Known as the Riverdale technique (Morton, 1974: 53–5), after the Toronto constituency in which it was fully developed, this strategy allows the party to focus on basic principles, and is a relatively inclusive process, relying on scores of party activists.

3 In Quebec, the federal and provincial wings of the party are formally separate entities, and it is possible to join the federal NDP directly (Royal Commission on Electoral Reform and Party Financing, 1991; 234–5).

4 In the 1993 federal election, the BQ ran candidates only in Quebec and the Reform Party ran candidates in the nine other provinces. The National Election Study survey therefore posed leader evaluation questions on these two leaders only in those regions/provinces where their parties were running candidates.

5 As a result, the party has less money to support its parliamentary caucus, fewer staff members, and a diminished profile in the House of Commons, particularly during Question Period and in debates on matters such as the Throne Speech and budget.

6 To complicate matters, not only has the party system in Canada become frac-
   tionalized, but the numbers and diversity of interest groups have increased significantly. While interest groups and political parties may complement one
   another, such groups can also compete directly with parties for activists' commitment and financial support. Further, interest groups are not obliged to make
   the compromises that are so often a necessary feature of a party's existence. As
   the NDP attempts to rebuild for the twenty-first century, it must do so within a
   social environment that is far more complex than the one that existed when the
   party was created, more than three decades ago.

BIBLIOGRAPHY

Abcarian, G., and S. Stanage
1973 'The Ideology of the Radical Right'. In J. Gould and W. Truitt, eds, *Political Ideologies*. New York: Macmillan.

Alford, R.
1963 *Party and Society*. Westport, CT: Greenwood Press.

Almond, G., and G. Powell
1992 *Comparative Politics Today: A World View*. New York: Harper Collins.

Amyot, G.
1986 'The New Politics'. *Queen's Quarterly* 93: 952-55.

Anderson, D.
1991 *The Unfinished Revolution: The Status of Women in Twelve Countries*. Toronto: Doubleday.

Archer, K.
1985 'The Failure of the New Democratic Party: Unions, Unionists and Politics in Canada'. *Canadian Journal of Political Science* 18, 2.
1987 'Canadian Unions, the New Democratic Party, and the Problem of Collective Action'. *Labour/Le Travail* 20.
1987a 'A Simultaneous Equation Model of Canadian Voting Behaviour'. *Canadian Journal of Political Science* 21.
1990 *Political Choices and Electoral Consequences: A Study of Organized Labour and the New Democratic Party*. Montreal and Kingston: McGill–Queen's University Press.
1991a 'Leadership Selection in the New Democratic Party'. In Bakvis (1991).
1991b 'The New Democrats, Organized Labour and the Prospects of Electoral Reform'. In Bakvis (1991).
1995 'Unions and the NDP: An Uneasy Relationship'. *Policy Options* 16, 8.

Archer, K., and F. Ellis
1994 'Opinion Structure of Reform Party Activists' *Canadian Journal of Political Science* 27, 2.
1996 'Activists in the Reform Party of Canada'. In Thorburn (1996).

Archer, K., and Gibbins, R.
1997 'What Do Albertans Think? The Klein Agenda on the Public Opinion Landscape'. In C. Bruce, R. Kneebone, and K. McKenzie, eds, *A Government Reinvented*. Toronto: Oxford University Press.

Archer, K., R. Gibbins, R. Knopff, and L. Pal
1995 *Parameters of Power: Canada's Political Institutions*. Scarborough, Ont.: Nelson.

Archer, K., and M. Johnson
1988 'Inflation, Unemployment and Canadian Federal Voting Behaviour'. *Canadian Journal of Political Science* 21, 3.

Archer, K., and D. Stewart

1995   'Democracy, Representation and the Selection of Party Leaders in Alberta'. Paper presented at the annual meeting of the Atlantic Provinces Political Studies Association, University of New Brunswick, Fredericton, NB, 13–15 Oct. 1995.

Archer, K., and A. Whitehorn

1990   'Opinion Structure Among New Democratic Party Activists: A Comparison with Liberals and Conservatives'. *Canadian Journal of Political Science* 23, 1. Reprinted with revisions as 'Opinion Structure Among Party Activists: A Comparison of New Democrats, Liberals and Conservatives' in Thorburn (1991, 1996).

1993   *Canadian Trade Unions and the New Democratic Party.* Queen's University: Industrial Relations Centre Press.

Armstrong, P., and H. Armstrong

1978   *The Double Ghetto: Canadian Women and Their Segregated Work.* Toronto: McClelland and Stewart.

Arrow, K.

1961   *Social Choice and Individual Values.* New Haven: Yale University Press.

Badgley, R., and S. Wolfe

1967   *Doctors' Strike: Medical Care and Conflict in Saskatchewan.* Toronto: Macmillan.

Bakvis, H., ed.

1991   *Canadian Political Parties: Leaders, Candidates and Organization.* Vol. 13 of the research studies of the Royal Commission on Electoral Reform and Party Financing. Toronto: Dundurn.

Barrett, D.

1995   *Barrett: A Passionate Political Life.* Vancouver: Douglas and MacIntyre.

1996   'Losing Innocence: Taking Responsibility'. *Simon Fraser Alumni Journal* (Summer).

Bashevkin, S.

1985a   'Women's Participation in the Ontario Political Parties'. In Bashevkin, ed., *Canadian Political Behaviour: Introductory Readings.* Toronto: Methuen.

1985b   *Toeing the Lines: Women and Party Politics in English Canada.* Toronto: University of Toronto Press.

1989   'Political Parties and the Representation of Women'. In Gagnon and Tanguay (1989).

1991   'Women's Participation in Political Parties'. In Megyery (1991).

1993   *Toeing the Lines: Women and Party Politics in English Canada.* 2nd ed. Toronto: Oxford University Press.

Bashevkin, S., and M. Holder

1985   'The Politics of Female Participation'. In D. MacDonald, ed., *The Government and Politics of Ontario.* Toronto: Nelson.

Baum, G.

1980   *Catholics and Canadian Socialism: Political Thought in the Thirties and Forties.* Toronto: Lorimer.

BC New Democratic Party
1996   *Report of the Renewal Commission for Party Reform*. [Blakeney Report].
        February 1996.

Beaud, J.-P., and J.-G. Prévost, eds
1995   *Late Twentieth Century Social Democracy*. Sainte-Foy: Presses de l'Université
        de Québec.

Beeby, D.
1982   'Women in the Ontario CCF, 1940–1950'. *Ontario History* 74, 4.

Bell, D.
1962   *The End of Ideology: On the Exhaustion of Political Ideas in the Fifties*.
        New York: Free Press.

Bibby, R., and D. Posterski
1985   *The Emerging Generation: An Inside Look at Canada's Teenagers*. Toronto:
        Irwin.
1992   *Teen Trends: A Nation in Motion*. Toronto: Stoddart.

Blais, A., and E. Gidengil
1991   *Making Representative Democracy Work: The Views of Canadians*. Vol. 17 of the
        research studies of the Royal Commission on Electoral Reform and Party
        Financing. Toronto: Dundurn

Blake, D.
1988   'Division and Cohesion: The Major Parties'. In Perlin (1988).

Blake, D., and K. Carty
1994   'Televoting for the Leader of the British Columbia Liberal Party'. Paper
        presented to the annual meeting of the Canadian Political Association,
        Calgary.

Blake, D., K. Carty, and L. Erickson
1991   *Grassroots Politicians: Party Activists in British Columbia*. Vancouver: University
        of British Columbia Press.

Blishen, B.
1978   'Perceptions of National Identity'. *Canadian Review of Sociology and
        Anthropology* 15, 2.

Bookchin, M.
1990   *Remaking Society: Pathways to a Green Future*. Boston: South End Press.

Brackman H., S. Erie, and M. Rain
1988   'Wedded to the Welfare State'. In J. Jenson, E. Hagen, and C. Reddy, eds,
        Feminization of the Labour Force. New York: Oxford.

Bradford, N.
1989   'Ideas, Intellectuals, and Social Democracy in Canada'. In Gagnon and
        Tanguay (1989).

Brams, S.
1985   *Rational Politics: Decisions, Games and Strategy*. Boston: Academic Press.

Brennan, J., ed.
1984   *Building the Co-operative Commonwealth*. Regina: Canadian Plains Research
        Center.

Brodie, J.

1985a 'From Waffles to Grits: A Decade in the Life of the New Democratic Party'. In Thorburn (1985).

1985b *Women and Politics in Canada.* Toronto: McGraw-Hill.

1988 'The Gender Factor and National Leadership Conventions in Canada'. In Perlin (1988).

1990 *The Political Economy of Canadian Regionalism.* Toronto: Harcourt Brace Jovanovich.

1991 'Women and the Electoral Process in Canada'. In Megyery (1991).

Brodie, J., and J. Jenson

1980 *Crisis, Challenge and Change: Party and Class in Canada.* Toronto: Methuen.

1988 *Crisis, Challenge and Change: Party and Class in Canada Revisited.* Toronto: Methuen.

1989 'Piercing the Smokescreen: Brokerage Parties and Class Politics'. In Gagnon and Tanguay (1989).

Brodie, J., and J. Vickers

1981 'The More Things Change . . . Women in the 1979 Federal Campaign'. In H. Penniman, ed., *Canada At the Polls: 1979 and 1980: A Study of the General Elections.* Washington: American Enterprise Institute.

Brown, R.

1989 *Being Brown: A Very Public Life.* Toronto: Random House.

Brym, R.

1985 *The Structure of the Canadian Capitalist Class.* Toronto: Garamond.

1989 *From Culture to Power: The Sociology of English Canada.* Toronto: Oxford University Press.

Butler, D., and D. Stokes

1974 *Political Change in Britain: The Evolution of Electoral Choice.* 2nd ed. New York: St Martins.

Cairns, A.

1968 'The Electoral System and the Party System in Canada, 1921–1965'. *Canadian Journal of Political Science* 1, 1.

1986 'The Embedded State: State-Society Relations in Canada'. In K. Banting, ed., *State and Society: Canada in Comparative Perspective.* Toronto: University of Toronto Press.

Campbell, A., P. Converse, W. Miller, and D. Stokes

1960 *The American Voter.* New York: Wiley.

Canada Chief Electoral Officer

1993 *Official Voting Results* (Ottawa: Elections Canada).

Canada's New Democrats

1994 *Ottawa Renewal Conference,* 27–8 August.

Caplan, G.

1973 *The Dilemma of Canadian Socialism: The CCF in Ontario.* Toronto: McClelland and Stewart.

Carbert, L.
1997   'Governing on "the Correct, the Compassionate, the Saskatchewan Side of the Border"'. In J. Arscott and L. Trimble, eds, *In the Presence of Women: Representation in Canadian Governments.* Toronto: Harcourt Brace.

Carr, E.
1964   *The Twenty Year Crisis, 1919–1939.* New York: Harper and Row.

Carty, K.
1988   'Campaigning in the Trenches: The Transformation of Constituency Politics'. In Perlin (1988).
1991   *Canadian Political Parties in the Constituencies.* Vol. 23 of the research studies of the Royal Commission on Electoral Reform and Party Financing. Toronto: Dundurn.

Carty, K., L. Erickson and D. Blake, eds
1992   *Leaders and Parties in Canadian Politics: Experiences of the Provinces.* Toronto: Harcourt Brace Jovanovich.

Casgrain, T.
1972   *A Woman in a Man's World.* Toronto: McClelland and Stewart.

CBC Research
1985   *CBC Election '84: 1984 Election Survey.* Toronto: CBC.

Christian, W., and C. Campbell
1990   *Political Parties and Ideologies in Canada.* Toronto: McGraw-Hill Ryerson.
1996   *Parties, Leaders, and Ideologies in Canada.* Toronto: McGraw-Hill Ryerson.

Clarke, H., J. Jenson, L. LeDuc, and J. Pammett
1979   *Political Choice in Canada.* Toronto: McGraw-Hill Ryerson.
1980   *Political Choice in Canada.* Abridged ed. Toronto: McGraw-Hill Ryerson.
1984   *Absent Mandate: The Politics of Discontent in Canada.* Toronto: Gage.
1991   *Absent Mandate: Interpreting Change in Canadian Elections.* 2nd ed. Toronto: Gage.
1996   *Absent Mandate: Canadian Electoral Politics in an Era of Restructuring.* 3rd ed. Toronto: Gage.

Clarke, H., and A. Kornberg
1992   'Support for the Canadian Progressive Conservative Party since 1988: The Impact of Economic Evaluations and Economic Issues'. *Canadian Journal of Political Science* 25, 1.

Cole, G.D.H.
1918   *Self-Government in Industry.* London: Jonathan Cape.

Connelly, P.
1978   *Last Hired, First Fired: Women and the Canadian Work Force.* Toronto: Women's Press.

Converse, P.
1964   'The Nature of Belief Systems in Mass Publics'. In D. Apter, ed., *Ideology and Discontent.* New York: Free Press.

Coulon, J.
1991   *En première ligne.* N.p.: Le jour.

Courtney, J.
1973   *The Selection of National Party Leaders in Canada.* Toronto: Macmillan.
1986   'Leadership Conventions and the Development of the National Political Community in Canada'. In R. Carty and W. Ward, eds, *National Politics and Community in Canada.* Vancouver: University of British Columbia Press.
1995   *Do Conventions Matter? Choosing National Party Leaders in Canada.* Montreal and Kingston: McGill–Queen's University Press.

Cross, M., ed.
1974   *The Decline and Fall of a Good Idea: CCF–NDP Manifestoes, 1932 to 1969.* Toronto: New Hogtown.

Crowley, T.
1990   *Agnes Macphail and the Politics of Equality.* Toronto: Lorimer.

Dalton, R.
1988   *Citizen Politics in Western Democracies.* Chatham: Chatham House.

Dean, D.
1961   'Alienation: Its Meaning and Measurement'. *American Sociological Review* 26, 5: 753–8.

Djwa, S., and R. Macdonald, eds
1983   *On F.R. Scott: Essays on His Contribution to Law, Literature and Politics.* Kingston: McGill–Queen's University Press.

Dobson, A., ed.
1991   *The Green Reader.* London: André Deutsch.

Downs, A.
1957   *An Economic Theory of Democracy.* New York: Harper and Row.

Duverger, M.
1963   *Political Parties.* New York: John Wiley.

Dyck, R.
1986   *Provincial Politics in Canada.* Scarborough, Ont.: Prentice-Hall.
1991   *Provincial Politics in Canada.* 2nd ed. Scarborough, Ont.: Prentice-Hall.
1993   *Canadian Politics: Critical Approaches .* Scarborough: Nelson.
1996   'Relations Between Federal and Provincial Parties'. In Tanguay and Gagnon (1996).

Eagles, M., J.P. Bickerton, A.-G. Gagnon, and P.J. Smith
1991   *The Almanac of Canadian Politics.* Peterborough, Ont.: Broadview.
1995   *The Almanac of Canadian Politics.* 2nd ed. Toronto: Oxford University Press.

Ehring, G., and W. Roberts
1993   *Giving Away a Miracle: Lost Dreams, Broken Promises and the Ontario NDP.* Oakville: Mosaic.

Elections Canada
1991   *Registered Parties' Fiscal Period Returns, 1990.* Ottawa: Elections Canada.

Elkins, D.
1974   'The Perceived Structure of the Canadian Party System'. *Canadian Journal of Political Science* 7.

Elkins, D., and R. Simeon
1980   *Small Worlds.* Toronto: Methuen.

Ellis, F., and K. Archer
1994   'Reform: Electoral Breakthrough'. In Frizzell et al. (1994).

Engelmann, F.
1954   'The Co-operative Commonwealth Federation of Canada: A Study of Membership Participation in Party Policy-Making'. Ph.D. dissertation, Yale University.

Everitt, J.
1994   'The Gender Gap on Social Welfare Issues: 1966–1990'. Paper presented to the Canadian Political Science Association, Calgary.

Farrell, A.
1994   *Grace MacInnis.* Toronto: Fitzhenry and Whiteside.

Flanagan, S.
1987   'Values in Industrial Societies'. *American Political Science Review* 81.

Flanagan, T.
1995   *Waiting for the Wave: The Reform Party and Preston Manning.* Don Mills, Ont.: Stoddart.

Fletcher, F., and R. Drummond
1979   *Canadian Attitude Trends 1960–1978.* Montreal: Institute for Research on Public Policy.

Forsey, E.
1982   *Trade Unions in Canada 1812–1902.* Toronto: University of Toronto Press.

Fortmann, M. and E. Cloutier
1991   'The Domestic Context of Canadian Defence Policy: The Contours of an Emerging Debate'. *Canadian Defence Quarterly* 21, 1.

Frizzell, A., J. Pammett, and A. Westell, eds
1989   *The Canadian General Election of 1988.* Ottawa: Carleton University Press.
1994   *The Canadian General Election of 1993.* Ottawa: Carleton University Press.

Gagnon, A.-G., and B. Tanguay, eds
1989   *Canadian Parties in Transition: Discourse, Organization and Representation.* Scarborough: Nelson.

Garson, D.
1977   *Worker Self-Management in Industry: The West European Experience.* New York: Praeger.

Gawthrop, Daniel
1996   *Highwire Act: Power, Pragmatism, and the Harcourt Legacy.* Vancouver: New Star.

Gelb, J.
1989   *Feminism and Politics: A Comparative Perspective.* Berkeley: University of California Press.

Geyer, R.F., and D. Schweitzer, eds
1976   *Theories of Alienation: Critical Perspectives in Philosophy and the Social Sciences.* Leiden: Martinus Nijhoff.
1981   *Alienation: Problems of Meaning, Theory and Method.* London: Routledge and Kegan Paul.

Gibbins, R.
1980   *Prairie Politics and Society.* Toronto: Butterworths.
1982   *Regionalism: Territorial Politics in Canada and the United States.* Toronto: Butterworths.

Gibbins, R., and S. Arrison
1995   *Western Visions: Perspectives on the West in Canada.* Peterborough, Ont.: Broadview.

Gibbins, R., and N. Nevitte
1985   'Canadian Political Ideology: A Comparative Analysis'. *Canadian Journal of Political Science* 18: 592–7.

Gindin, S.
1995   *The Canadian Auto Workers.* Toronto: Lorimer.

Godfrey, D., and M. Watkins
1970   *Gordon to Watkins to You: Documentary: The Battle for Control of our Economy.* Toronto: New Press.

Goldfarb, M., and T. Axworthy
1988   *Marching to a Different Drummer: An Essay on Liberals and Conservatives in Convention.* Toronto: Stoddart.

Goldstein, A.
1996   *The Ugly Duckling's Waffle: The Story of the* CCF–NDP *Youth.* N.p.: Ontario New Democratic Youth.

Gorz, A.
1980   *Ecology as Politics.* Montreal: Black Rose Press.

Gotell, L., and J. Brodie.
1991   'Women and Parties: More than an Issue of Numbers'. In Thorburn (1991).

Granatstein, J.
1996   *Yankee Go Home? Canadians and Anti-Americanism.* Toronto: Harper Collins.

Groome, Agnes
1967   'M.J. Coldwell and C.C.F. Foreign Policy, 1932–1950'. M.A. thesis, University of Saskatchewan.

Gruending, D.
1990   *Promises to Keep: A Political Biography of Allan Blakeney.* Saskatoon: Western Producer Prairie Books.

Hackett, R.
1979   'The Waffle Conflict in the NDP'. In Thorburn (1979).
1980   'Pie in the Sky: A History of the Ontario Waffle'. *Canadian Dimension.* Oct.–Nov. 1980 [special edition].

Happy, J.
1986   'Voter Sensitivity to Economic Conditions: A Canadian–American Comparison'. *Comparative Politics 19, 54.*

Harcourt, M.
1996   *Mike Harcourt: A Measure of Defiance.* Vancouver: Douglas and McIntyre.

Hardin, Herschel
1974   *A Nation Unaware: The Canadian Economic Culture.* Vancouver: Douglas.
1990   *The Privatization Putsch.* Halifax: Institute for Research on Public Policy.
1991   *The New Bureaucracy: Waste and Folly in the Private Sector.* Toronto: McClelland and Stewart.

Hayward, S., and A. Whitehorn.
1991   'Leadership Selection: Which Method?'. Paper presented to the Douglas–Coldwell Foundation.

Horn, M.
1980   *The League For Social Reconstruction: Intellectual Origins of the Democratic Left in Canada 1930–1942.* Toronto: University of Toronto Press.

Horowitz, G.
1968   *Canadian Labour in Politics.* Toronto: University of Toronto Press.

Howard, I.
1992   *The Struggle for Social Justice in British Columbia: Helena Gutteridge, the Unknown Reformer.* Vancouver: University of British Columbia Press.

Hulsberg, W.
1988   *The German Greens: A Social and Political Profile.* London, New York: Verso.

Hunnius, G., ed.
1970   *Industrial Democracy and Canadian Labour.* Montreal: Black Rose.
1971   *Participatory Democracy for Canadians.* Montreal: Black Rose.

Hunnius, G., G.D. Garson, and J. Case, eds
1973   *Workers' Control: A Reader on Labour and Social Change.* New York: Vintage.

Hurtig, M.
1992a *A New and Better Canada: Principles and Policies of a New Canadian Political Party.* Toronto: Stoddart.
1992b *The Betrayal of Canada.* Toronto: Stoddart.
1996   *At Twilight in the Country: Memoirs of a Canadian Nationalist.* Don Mills, Ont.: Stoddart.

Inglehart, R.
1977   *The Silent Revolution: Changing Values and Political Styles Among Western Publics.* Princeton: Princeton University Press.
1990   *Culture Shifts in Advanced Industrial Society.* Princeton: Princeton University Press.

Jennings, K.
1990   'Women in Party Politics'. In C. Tilly and P. Gurin, eds, *Women, Politics and Change.* New York: Russell Sage.

Jennings, K., and B. Farah
1981   'Social Roles and Political Resources: An Over-Time Study of Men and Women in Party Elites'. *American Journal of Political Science* 25, 3.

Jenson, J., and P.R. Mahon
1995   'From "Premier Bob" to "Rae Days": The Impasse of the Ontario New Democrats'. In Beaud and Prévost (1995).

Johnston, R.
1986   *Public Opinion and Public Policy in Canada.* Toronto: University of Toronto Press.
1987   'The Politics of Class and Religion in Canada'. Paper presented to the Canadian Political Science Association.
1988   'The Ideological Structure of Opinion on Policy'. In Perlin (1988).

Johnston, R., A. Blais, H. Brady, and J. Crête
1992   *Letting the People Decide: Dynamics of a Canadian Election.* Montreal: McGill-Queen's.

Kavic, L., and G. Nixon
1979   *The 1200 Days.* Coquitlam: Kaen.

Kay, B.J., R.D. Lambert, S.D. Brown, and J.E. Curtis
1987   'Gender and Political Activity in Canada, 1965–1984'. *Canadian Journal of Political Science* 20.

Kealy, L., and J. Sangster
1989   *Beyond the Vote: Canadian Women and Politics.* Toronto: University of Toronto Press.

Kemp, P., and D. Wall
1990   *A Green Manifesto for the 1990's.* London: Penguin Books.

Kenniston, K.
1971   *Youth and Dissent.* New York: Harcourt Brace Jovanovich.

Kerans, M.
1996   *Muriel Duckworth: A Very Active Pacifist.* Halifax: Fernwood.

Kerr, D., ed.
1981   *Western Canadian Politics: The Radical Tradition.* Edmonton: NeWest.

King, W.L.M.
1918/   *Industry and Humanity.* Toronto: Allen. Reprinted 1973. Toronto: University
1973   of Toronto Press.

Kirkpatrick, J.
1976   *The New Presidential Elite: Men, Women and National Politics.* New York: Russell Sage.

Kitschelt, H.
1989   *The Logics of Party Formation.* Ithaca: Cornell University Press.
1994   *The Transformation of European Social Democracy.* Cambridge: Cambridge University Press.

Kome, P., ed.
1985   *Women of Influence: Canadian Women and Politics.* Toronto: Doubleday.

Kornberg, A., W. Mishler, and H. Clarke
1982   *Representative Democracy in the Canadian Provinces.* Scarborough, Ont.: Prentice-Hall.

Kornberg, A., and H. Clarke
1992   *Citizens and Community: Political Support in a Representative Democracy.* Cambridge: Cambridge University Press.

Kornberg, A., W. Mishler, and J. Smith
1975   'Political Elite and Mass Perceptions of Party Locations in Issue Space: Some Tests of Two Positions'. *British Journal of Political Science* 5.

Kornberg, A., J. Smith, and H. Clarke
1979   *Citizen Politicians—Canada*. Durham, NC: Carolina Academic Press.

Krause, R., and L. LeDuc
1979   'Voting Behavior and Electoral Strategies in the Progressive Conservative Leadership Convention of 1976'. *Canadian Journal of Political Science* 12, 1.

Lambert, R., J. Curtis, S. Brown, and B. Kay
1986   'In Search of Left/Right Beliefs in the Canadian Electorate'. *Canadian Journal of Political Science* 19.

Laponce, J.
1981   *Left and Right: The Topography of Political Perceptions*. Toronto: University of Toronto Press.

Latouche, D.
1992   'Universal Democracy and Effective Leadership: Lessons from the Parti Québécois Experience'. In Carty et al. (1992).

Laxer, J.
1970   *The Energy Poker Game: The Politics of the Continental Resources Deal*. Toronto: New Press.
1996   *In Search of a New Left: Canadian Politics After the Neo-Conservative Assault*. Toronto: Viking.

Laxer, R., ed.
1973   *(Canada) Ltd.: The Political Economy of Dependency*. Toronto: McClelland and Stewart.

Laycock, D.
1990   *Populist and Democratic Thought in the Canadian Prairies 1910 to 1945*. Toronto: University of Toronto Press.

Lazarus, M.
1983   *Six Women Who Dared*. Toronto: Carswell.

LeDuc, L.
1971   'Party Decision-making: Some Empirical Observations on the Leadership Selection Process'. *Canadian Journal of Political Science* 4, 1.

LeDuc, L., H. Clarke, J. Jenson, and J. Pammett
1984   'Partisan Instability in Canada: Evidence from a New Panel Study'. *American Political Science Review* 78, 2.

Lele, J., G. Perlin, and H. Thorburn
1979   'The National Party Convention'. In Thorburn (1979).

Levesque, T.
1983   'On the Outcome of the 1983 Conservative Leadership Convention: How They Shot Themselves in the Other Foot'. *Canadian Journal of Political Science* 16, 4.

Levitt, J.
1996   *Fighting Back for Jobs: Ed Broadbent in Parliament*. Ottawa: LLA Publishing.

Levitt, K.
1970   *Silent Surrender: The Multinational Corporation in Canada.* Toronto: Macmillan.

Lewis, D.
1981   *The Good Fight: Political Memoirs 1919–1958.* Toronto: Macmillan.

Lewis, S.
1993   *Grace: The Life of Grace MacInnis.* Madeira Park, BC: Harbour.

Lipset, S.
1960   *Political Man: The Social Bases of Politics.* Garden City, NJ: Doubleday.
1968   *Revolution and Counterrevolution.* New York: Basic Books.

Lipset, S.M., and S. Rokkan
1967   *Party Systems and Voter Alignments: Crossnational Perspectives.* New York: Free Press.

Lipson, L.
1960   *The Great Issues of Politics: An Introduction to Political Science.* 2nd ed. Englewood Cliffs, NJ: Prentice-Hall.

Lipton, C.
1966   *The Trade Union Movement of Canada, 1827–1959.* Montreal: Canadian Social Publications.

Logan, H.
1948   *Trade Unions in Canada.* Toronto: Macmillan.

Lovenduski, J., and J. Hills, eds
1981   *The Politics of the Second Electorate: Women and Public Participation.* London: Routledge and Kegan Paul.

McAllister, J.
1984   *The Government of Edward Schreyer.* Montreal and Kingston: McGill–Queen's University Press.

McBride, S.
1996   'The Continuing Crisis of Social Democracy: Ontario's Social Contract in Perspective' *Studies in Political Economy: A Socialist Review* 50 (Summer).

McCormick, R.
1977   *Reformers, Rebels and Revolutionaries: The Western Canadian Radical Movement 1899–1919.* Toronto: University of Toronto Press.

McCready, D., and C. Winn
1976   'Geographic Cleavage: Core vs. Periphery'. In C. Winn and J. McMenemy, eds, *Political Parties in Canada.* Toronto: McGraw-Hill.

McDaniel, S.
1986   *Canada's Aging Population.* Toronto: Butterworths.

McDonald, L.
1987   *The Party That Changed Canada: The New Democratic Party Then and Now.* Toronto: Macmillan.

McHenry, D.
1950   *The Third Force in Canada.* Berkeley: University of California Press.

MacIvor, H.
1994   'The Leadership Convention: An Institution Under Stress'. In Mancuso et al. (1994).
1996   'Do Canadian Political Parties Form a Cartel?' *Canadian Journal of Political Science* 29.

McLaughlin, A.
1992   *A Woman's Place: My Life and Politics.* Toronto: Macfarlane, Walter and Ross.

McLeod, I.
1994   *Under Siege: The Federal NDP in the Nineties.* Toronto: Lorimer.

McNaught, K.
1959   *A Prophet in Politics: A Biography of J.S. Woodsworth.* Toronto: University of Toronto Press.

MacPherson, I.
1979   *The Co-operative Movement on the Prairies, 1900–1955.* Ottawa: Canadian Historical Association.

Mancuso, M., R. Price, and R. Wagenberg
1994   *Leaders and Leadership in Canada.* Toronto: Oxford University Press.

Manley, J.
1980   'Women and the Left in the 1930s: The Case of the Toronto CCF Women's Joint Committee'. *Atlantis* 5, 2.

Martin, P., A. Gregg, and G. Perlin
1983   *Contenders: The Tory Quest for Power.* Scarborough, Ont.: Prentice-Hall.

Maslow, A.
1954   *Motivation and Personality.* New York: Harper and Row.

Mathews, R.
1988   *The Canadian Identity.* Ottawa: Steel Rail.

Mathews, R., and J. Steele, eds
1969   *The Struggle for Canadian Universities: A Dossier.* Toronto: New Press.

Megyery, K., ed.
1991   *Women in Canadian Politics: Toward Equity in Representation.* Vol. 6 of the research studies of the Royal Commission on Electoral Reform and Party Financing. Toronto: Dundurn.

Meisel, J.
1975   *Working Papers on Canadian Politics.* Montreal: McGill–Queen's University Press.

Melnyk, O.
1989   *No Bankers in Heaven: Remembering the CCF.* Toronto: McGraw-Hill Ryerson.

Michels, R.
1962   *Political Parties: A Sociological Study of the Oligarchic Tendencies of Modern Democracy.* New York: Free Press.

Milbrath, L.
1965   *Political Participation: How and Why Do People Get Involved in Politics.* Chicago: Rand McNally.

1984   *Environmentalists: Vanguard for a New Society*. Albany: State University of New York Press.

Miller, A.
1974   'Political Issues and Trust in Government: 1964–1970'. *American Political Science Review* 81.

Mitchell, D.
1996   'NDP Federal Delegate Credentials'. *Briarpatch* 25, 1.

Monahan, P.
1995   *Storming the Pink Palace: The NDP in Power: A Cautionary Tale*. Toronto: Lester.

Monroe, K., and L. Erickson
1986   'The Economy and Political Support'. *Journal of Politics* 48.

Mooney, G.
1938   *Co-operatives: Today and Tomorrow*. Montreal: Survey Committee.

Morley, J.T.
1984   *Secular Socialists: The CCF–NDP in Ontario: A Biography*. Montreal and Kingston: McGill–Queen's University Press.

Morris, M.
1979   *Measuring the Condition of the World's Poor: The Physical Quality of Life Index*. London: Frank Cass.

Morton, D.
1974   *NDP: The Dream of Power*. Toronto: Hakkert.
1977   *NDP: Social Democracy in Canada*. Toronto: Hakkert.
1980   *Working People: An Illustrated History of the Canadian Labour Movement*. Ottawa: Deneau and Greenberg.
1986   *The New Democrats 1961–1986: The Politics of Change*. Toronto: Copp Clark Pitman.

Nevitte, N., H. Bakvis, and R. Gibbins
1989   'The Ideological Contours of "New Politics" in Canada: Policy, Mobilization and Partisan Support'. *Canadian Journal of Political Science* 22, 3.

Nevitte, N., and R. Gibbins
1990   *New Elites in Old States: Ideologies in Anglo-American Democracies*. Toronto: Oxford University Press.

New Democratic Party
1975   *Leadership Rules 1975*.
1981   'Peace, Security and Justice.' Report of the International Affairs Committee.
1989   Memorandum to 'Official Agents for Federal NDP Leadership Campaign', from Dick Proctor (then federal secretary), Re: Tax Receipting, 2 Oct.
1991   *Constitution*. As Amended by the Federal Convention.
1995   *Leadership Rules 1995*.

Ogmundson, R.
1975   'On the Measurement of Party Class Positions: The Case of Canadian Federal Political Parties'. *Canadian Review of Sociology and Anthropology* 12.

Oldenquist, A., and M. Rosner, eds
1991 *Alienation, Community, and Work.* New York: Greenwood Press.

Oliver, M., ed.
1961 *Social Purpose For Canada.* Toronto: University of Toronto Press.

O'Toole, R.
1977 *The Precipitous Path.* Toronto: Peter Martin.

Pal, L.
1993 *Interests of State.* Montreal and Kingston: McGill–Queen's University Press.

Paltiel, K.
1989 'Political Marketing, Party Finance and the Decline of Canadian Parties'. In Gagnon and Tanguay (1989).

Pammett, J.
1987 'Class Voting and Class Consciousness in Canada'. *Canadian Review of Sociology and Anthropology* 24.
1989 'The 1988 Vote'. In Frizzell et al. (1989).
1994 'Tracking the Votes'. In Frizzell et al. (1994).

Panitch L., and D. Swartz
1993 *The Assault on Trade Union Freedoms: From Wage Controls to Social Contract* Toronto: Garamond.

Pennington, D.
1990 *Agnes Macphail: Reformer, Canada's First Female M.P.* Toronto: Simon and Pierre.

Perlin, G.
1980 *The Tory Syndrome.* Montreal: McGill–Queen's University Press.
1983 'Did the Best Candidate Win? A Comment on Levesque's Analysis' *Canadian Journal of Political Science* 16.
1991 'Attitudes of Liberal Convention Delegates Toward Proposals for Reform of the Process of Leadership Selection'. In Bakvis (1991).

Perlin, G., ed.
1988 *Party Democracy in Canada: The Politics of National Party Conventions.* Scarborough, Ont.: Prentice-Hall.

Perlin, G., A. Sutherland, and M. Desjardins
1988 'The Impact of Age Cleavage on Convention Politics'. In Perlin (1988).

Phillips, P.
1982 *Regional Disparities.* Toronto: Lorimer.

Phillips, S.
1996 'Competing, Connecting and Complementing: Parties, Interest Groups and New Social Movements'. In Tanguay and Gagnon (1996).

Pitkin, H.
1967 *The Concept of Representation.* Berkeley: University of California Press.

Porrit, J.
1984 *Seeing Green: The Politics of Ecology Explained.* Oxford: Basil Blackwell.

Porter, J.
1965 *The Vertical Mosaic.* Toronto: University of Toronto Press.

Power, C.
1966   *A Party Politician*. Toronto: Macmillan.

Prentice, A., et al.
1988   *Canadian Women: A History*. Toronto: Harcourt Brace Jovanovich.

Presthus, R.
1978   *A Comparative Study of Political Elites*. Englewood Cliffs, NJ: Prentice-Hall.

Preyra, L.
1996   'Plebiscitarian Democracy and Party Leadership Selection in Canada'. In Thorburn (1996).

Pross, P.
1986   *Group Politics and Public Policy*. Toronto: Oxford University Press.

Rae, B.
1996   *From Protest to Power: Personal Reflections on a Life in Politics*. Toronto: Viking.

Reid, E.
1996   'The Rise of National Parties in Canada'. In Thorburn (1996).

Richards, J.
1979   *Prairie Capitalism: Power and Influence in the New West*. Toronto: McClelland and Stewart.
1981   'The Left of the NDP'. In Kerr (1981).
1983   'Social Democracy and the Unions: What's Left?'. Paper presented to the annual meeting of the Quebec Political Science Society.
1988   'Populism'. In J. Marsh, ed. *The Canadian Encyclopedia*. Edmonton: Hurtig.

Richards, J., R.D. Cairns, and L. Pratt, eds
1991   *Social Democracy Without Illusions*. Toronto: McClelland and Stewart.

Roome, P.
1989   'Amelia Turner and Calgary Labour Women, 1919–1935'. In Kealey and Sangster (1989).

Rosenblum, S., and P. Findlay, eds
1991   *Debating Canada's Future: Views From the Left*. Toronto: Lorimer.

Roy, L.
1992   *Brown Girl in the Ring: Rosemary Brown: A Biography for Young People*. Toronto: Black Women and Women of Colour Press.

Royal Commission on Electoral Reform and Party Financing
1991   *Reforming Electoral Democracy: Volume 1*. Ottawa: Supply and Services.

Sangster, J.
1989   *Dreams of Equality: Women On The Canadian Left, 1920–1950*. Toronto: McClelland and Stewart.

Sartori, G.
1976   *Parties and Party Systems: A Framework for Analysis*. Cambridge: Cambridge University Press.

Sauvé, R.
1990   *Canadian People Patterns*. Saskatoon: Western Producer Prairie Books.
1994   *Border Lines*. Toronto: McGraw-Hill Ryerson.

Schwartz, M.
1974   *Politics and Territory.* Montreal: McGill–Queen's University Press.
1994   'North American Social Democracy in the 1990s: The NDP in Ontario'.
        Canadian–American Public Policy 17 (April).

Scott, F.
1977   *Essays on the Constitution.* Toronto: University of Toronto Press.
1986   *A New Endeavour: Selected Political Essays, Letters and Addresses.* Ed. M.
        Horn. Toronto: University of Toronto Press.

Scotton, A., ed.
1977   *New Democratic Policies 1961–1976.* Ottawa: Mutual Press.

Seeman, M.
1959   'On the Meaning of Alienation'. *American Sociological Review.* 24, 6: 783–91.

Seidel, F.
1989   'The Canadian Electoral System and Proposals for its Reform'. In
        Gagnon and Tanguay (1989).

Sharp, P.
1948   *The Agrarian Revolt in Western Canada: A Survey Showing American Parallels.*
        Minneapolis: University of Minnesota Press.

Sharpe, S.
1994   *The Gilded Ghetto.* Toronto: Harper Collins.

Siegal, A.
1996   *Politics and the Media in Canada.* 2nd ed. Toronto: McGraw-Hill Ryerson.

Simmel, G.
1955   *Conflict and the Web of Group-Affiliations.* New York: Free Press.

Sims, R.
1977   'Conceptions of War: The Co-operative Commonwealth Federation of
        Canada: 1932–1940'. M.A. thesis, Carleton University.

Smith, A.
1983   *Theories of Nationalism.* London: Duckworth.

Sokolsky, J.
1989   *Defending Canada: US–Canadian Defence Policies.* New York: Priority Press.

Stanbury, W.
1989   'Financing Federal Political Parties in Canada, 1974–1986'. In Gagnon
        and Tanguay (1989).
1991   *Money in Politics: Financing Federal Parties and Candidates in Canada.* Vol. 1
        of the research studies of the Royal Commission on Electoral Reform
        and Party Financing. Toronto: Dundurn.
1996   'Regulating the Financing of Federal Parties and Candidates'. In Tanguay
        and Gagnon (1996).

Stewart, D.
1997   'The Changing Leadership Electorate? An Examination of Participants in
        the 1992 Alberta Conservative Leadership Election'. *Canadian Journal of
        Political Science* (forthcoming).

Stewart, D., and K. Archer
1996   'Electronic Fiasco: An Examination of the 1994 Liberal Leadership Selection in Alberta'. Paper presented to the annual meeting of the Canadian Political Science Association, Brock University, St Catharines, Ont., 2–4 June 1996.

Stewart, M., and D. French
1959   *Ask No Quarter: A Biography of Agnes Macphail.* Toronto: Longmans, Green.

Sufrin, E.
1983   *The Eaton Drive: The Campaign to Organize Canada's Largest Department Store, 1948 to 1952.* Toronto: Fitzhenry and Whiteside.

Surrey-Newton NDP
1994   *Then and Now: A Celebration of CCF/NDP Women.* Surrey, BC.

Tanguay, A.B.
1995   'Social Democracy on Trial: The Parti Québécois, the Ontario NDP, and the Search for a New Social Contract'. In Beaud and Prévost (1995).

Tanguay, A.B., and A.-G. Gagnon, eds
1996   *Canadian Parties in Transition.* 2nd ed. Scarborough, Ont.: Nelson.

Teeple, G.
1972   '"Liberals in a Hurry": Socialism and the CCF–NDP'. In Teeple, ed., *Capitalism and the National Question in Canada.* Toronto: University of Toronto Press.

Thomas, T.
1995   'New Forms of Political Representation: European Ecological Politics and the Montreal Citizens' Movement', *Canadian Journal of Political Science* 28, 3.

Thomlinson, N.
1993   'Intra-Party Caucuses and NDP Leadership Selection in 1989'. Paper presented to the annual meeting of the Canadian Political Science Association, Carleton University, Ottawa.

Thorburn, H.
1986   'The New Democratic Party and National Defence'. In N. Orvik, ed., *Semi-Alignment and Western Security.* London: Croom Helm.

Thorburn, H., ed.
1979   *Party Politics in Canada.* 4th ed. Scarborough, Ont.: Prentice-Hall.
1985   *Party Politics in Canada.* 5th ed. Scarborough, Ont.: Prentice-Hall.
1991   *Party Politics in Canada.* 6th ed. Scarborough, Ont.: Prentice-Hall.
1996   *Party Politics in Canada.* 7th ed. Scarborough, Ont.: Prentice-Hall.

Tollefson, E.
1963   *Bitter Medicine: The Saskatchewan Medicare Feud.* Saskatoon: Modern Press.

Trofimenkoff, S.
1989   'Thérèse Casgrain and the CCF in Quebec'. In Kealey and Sangster (1989).

Tyre, R.
1962   *Douglas in Saskatchewan.* Vancouver: Mitchell.

Underhill, F.
1960   *In Search of Canadian Liberalism.* Toronto: University of Toronto Press.
1974   *Canadian Political Parties.* Ottawa: Canadian Historical Association.

Vickers, J.
1989   'Feminist Approaches to Women in Politics'. In Kealey and Sangster (1989).

Vickers, J., and J. Brodie
1981   'Canada'. In J. Lovenduski and J. Hills, eds, *The Politics of the Second Electorate: Women and Public Participation*. London: Routledge and Kegan Paul.

Waffle
1969   'Toward an Independent Socialist Canada'(Waffle Manifesto). In Cross (1974).

Walkom, T.
1994   *Rae Days: The Rise and Follies of the NDP.* Toronto: Key Porter.

Watkins, M.
1973   'Contradictions and Alternatives in Canada's Future'. In R. Laxer (1973).
1992   *Madness and Ruin: Politics and the Economy in the Neoconservative Age.* Toronto: Between the Lines.
1996   'May the Party Flounder On'. *This Magazine* (January).

Wearing, J.
1988   *Strained Relations: Canadian Parties and Voters.* Toronto: McClelland and Stewart.

Wearing, P., and J. Wearing
1991   'Does Gender Make A Difference in Voting Behaviour?'. In J. Wearing, ed., *The Ballot and Its Message: Voting in Canada.* Toronto: Copp Clark Pitman.

Webster, D.
n.d.   *Growth of the NDP in BC.* Vancouver: BC NDP.

White, J.
1980   *Women and Unions.* Ottawa: Government of Canada.
1993   *Sisters and Solidarity: Women and Unions in Canada.* Toronto: Thompson Educational Publishing.

Whitehorn, A.
1974   'Alienation and Workers' Self-Management'. *Canadian Slavonic Papers* 14, 2.
1978   'Yugoslav Workers' Self-Management: A Blueprint for Industrial Democracy?'. *Canadian Slavonic Papers,* September.
1979a   'Alienation and Industrial Society: A Case Study of Workers' Self-Management'. *Canadian Review of Sociology and Anthropology,* May.
1979b   'Yugoslavia: A Case Study of Self-Managing Socialism?'. In A. Liebich, ed., *The Future of Socialism in Europe.* Montreal: InterUniversity Centre for European Studies.
1985   'The CCF–NDP: Fifty Years After'. In Thorburn (1985).
1988   'The New Democratic Party in Convention'. In Perlin (1988).
1989   'The New Democratic Party Election Campaign: Dashed Hopes'. In Frizzell et. al. (1989).
1991   'The CCF–NDP and the End of the Broadbent Era'. In Thorburn (1991).
1992   *Canadian Socialism: Essays on the CCF–NDP.* Toronto: Oxford University Press.

1993   'Some Preliminary Thoughts on the Labour Movement and the New Democratic Party'. Paper presented to the Canadian Labour Congress.
1994   'The NDP's Quest for Survival'. In Frizzell et al. (1994).
1995a   'How the NDP Chooses'. *Canadian Forum* (September).
1995b   'An NDP Historian's Handicap of the Race'. *Vancouver Sun*, 13 Oct.
1996a   'Audrey McLaughlin and the Decline of the Federal NDP'. In Thorburn (1996).
1996b   'Leadership Selection in the CCF–NDP'. *The New Ontario Democrat* (June).

Whitehorn, A., and K. Archer
1994   'Party Activists and Political Leadership: A Case Study of the NDP'. In Mancuso et al. (1994).
1995   'The Gender Gap Amongst Party Activists: A Case Study of Women and the New Democratic Party'. In F.-P. Gingras, ed. *Gender and Politics in Contemporary Canada*. Toronto: Oxford University Press.

Whiteley, P.
1983   *The Labour Party in Crisis*. London: Methuen.

Wilson, D., ed.
1985   *Democratic Socialism: The Challenge of the Eighties and Beyond*. Vancouver: New Star.

Wilson, J.
1974   'The Canadian Political Cultures: Towards a Redefinition of the Nature of the Canadian Political System'. *Canadian Journal of Political Science* 7, 3.

Wiseman, N.
1983   *Social Democracy in Manitoba: A History of the CCF–NDP*. Winnipeg: University of Manitoba Press.

Woolstencroft, P.
1983   'Social Choice Theory and the Reconstruction of Elections: A Comment on Levesque's Analysis'. *Canadian Journal of Political Science* 16, 4.
1992   '"Tories Kick Machine to Bits": Leadership Selection and the Ontario Progressive Conservative Party'. In Carty et al. (1992).

Wright, J.
1965   *The Louise Lucas Story: This Time Tomorrow*. Montreal: Harvest House.

Young, L.
1991   'Legislative Turnover in the Election of Women to the House of Commons'. In Megyery (1991).

Young, W.
1969   *The Anatomy of a Party: The National CCF, 1932–61*. Toronto: University of Toronto Press.

Zakuta, L.
1964   *A Protest Movement Becalmed: A Study of Change in the CCF*. Toronto: University of Toronto Press.

INDEX

Aboriginal people, 6, 7

abortion, 31, 95, 97

affirmative action: delegates' views, 22; *see also* gender parity

age: and attitudes to monarchy, 145; and cultural attitudes, 123, 124; and defence/foreign policy, 169–73; and delegate experience, 118–19; and demographic profiles, 115–17; and education, 117; and ideology, 119–20; and issue indexes, 125–6; and leadership voting, 221, 222; and left-right positioning, 119; and policy attitudes, 121–4; and postmaterialist issues, 182, 186; *see also* young delegates

alienation, 71, 142–4; and region, 74, 75, 80; Western, 82

All-Canadian Congress of Labour (ACCL), 48

American Federation of Labour (AFL), 48

Argue, Hazen, 197, 198, 240, 242

Atlantic Canada: convention attendance, 17–18, 67; delegates' attitudes, 75, 80, 81, 169; in primaries (1995), 245, 246; union affiliation, 51

attitude constraint (activists/mass public), 178–9

Axworthy, Chris, 242

Barrett, Dave, 116, 119, 211, 212, 239–40; campaign spending, 205; determinants of support, 221–2, 225, 227–9; preference rankings, 217–20, 229–30; support by age, 221; support by caucus attendance, 190–1; voting results, 212–16; *see also* leadership contest (1995)

bilingualism index, 39; and age, 126; and gender, 100; inter-party differences, 28–30, 31, 34, 36, 37; and region, 80,

81; and union/non-union status, 56–7; *see also* Quebec issues

Blake, Donald (1988), 27–38

Blakeney, Allan, 145, 239

Bloc Québécois, 2, 176; and regionalism, 65, 83

Borda count, 219–20

Bouchard, Lucien, 147, 268

British Columbia: convention attendance, 17, 67, 68; at convention (1995), 249; delegates' age, 116; delegates' attitudes, 75, 80, 82; Harcourt government, 249; in primaries (1995), 246; *see also* Western Canada

Broadbent, Ed, 22, 87, 197, 198, 211, 233, 240, 241, 262; and Meech Lake Accord, 69

Brodie, Janine, and Jane Jenson (1988), 3

Brown, Rosemary, 91, 198, 241

business, 55, 82; *see also* corporate power

Business Council on National Issues, 2

Campbell, Kim, 204, 230, 268

Canadian Auto Workers (CAW): and election (1988), 46, 247, 248; and Ontario 'social contract', 60, 62

Canadian Catholic Confederation of Labour (CCCL), 47

Canadian Labour Congress (CLC), 5, 48, 50, 62, 225; in election campaigns, 61; post-mortem of 1993 election, 62, 234

candidate nominations: 'clustering', 92

capital punishment, 31

Carr, Shirley, 225

Casgrain, Thérèse, 91, 102n.1, 143

caucuses, 3, 264; attendance, 187–91; and leadership voting, 189–91; *see also* individual caucuses (environment, gay/lesbian, labour, provincial, women's, youth)

Green Party, 177
Gulf War, 157, 173

Hardin, Herschel, 244, 251; campaign
  spending, 206; in primaries, 245, 246
Harris, Mike, 54
hawkishness index, 38; and age, 125;
  and gender, 100–1; inter-party
  differences, 28–30, 31, 34, 36; and
  region, 80, 81; and union/non-union
  status, 56; see also defence; foreign
  policy
Heap, Dan, 241
Hebb, Tessa, 91
Hurtig, Mel, 167

ideology, 7; and age, 119; and attitude
  consistency (constraint), 27, 31,
  40n.3, 75; delegates' self-images,
  19–20, 53–4, 120; 'end of ideology',
  30; index of difference, 28; issue
  areas, 28; and mass parties, 8; party
  comparisons, 28–38; research on,
  26–7; and voting behaviour, 26,
  43n.27; see also class self-image; left-
  right positioning
immigration, 31, 168, 169, 173, 180–1;
  and age, 186
industrialization, 4, 5
inequality, see class issues
interest groups: relations with political
  parties, 11n.12, 270n.6
International Woodworkers of America,
  248
issue indexes, 32–6, 38–40; and age,
  125–6; and delegate type, 55–8; and
  gender, 100–1; scoring, 32; 'standard
  difference in means'/'adjusted standard deviation', 35; see also bilingualism; civil liberties; continentalism;
  corporate power; hawkishness; moral
  conservatism; privatization; social
  security

job creation, 140, 182
Johnston, Richard (1988), 27, 220
justice, criminal, 154

Knowles, Stanley, 49

labour, organized, 46–62; affiliation
  with CCF–NDP, 3, 5, 263; central
  bodies, 50; as conservative force, 46,
  47, 61–2, 178, 193; delegates' attitudes,
  58–61, 62; influence within NDP, 22;
  and Ontario 'social contract', 47, 234;
  and primary direct ballot (1995),
  247–8, 253, 257n.31; as progressive
  force, 47, 58; relationship with
  CCF–NDP, 47–50; and young delegates, 122–3, 124; see also labour
  caucus; union delegates
labour caucus, 22, 187–8, 263; and
  leadership voting, 190
labour clubs, 4
labour market: changes in, 2; job
  security, 2
Labour Party (Britain), 49, 202
labour relations: delegates' attitudes, 31,
  58, 122–3, 135
Lagassé, Roger, 119, 211, 212, 213, 214
Langdon, Stephen, 119, 211–12; campaign spending, 205; determinants of
  support, 222–7, 229; preference rankings, 217–20, 229–30; voting results,
  212–16
Laxer, James, 50, 110, 198, 211, 241
leadership: attitudes towards, 7; delegates' views on, 22–3: and ideology,
  27; nomination, 196; by region, 198;
  review, 196; see also leadership contests; leadership voting
leadership contest (1971), 22, 50, 227
leadership contest (1989), 128, 210–31;
  campaign financing, 205; candidates,
  201, 211–12; and left-right positioning, 225–7, 229; results, 212–17; see
  also leadership voting
leadership contest (1995), 249–52,
  265–6; campaign financing, 206;
  candidates, 239–44, 252–3; reasons
  for new method, 234, 235–6, 237–8;
  results, 251–2; scheduling, 11n.15,
  235, 238; see also leadership voting;
  primaries
leadership contests: campaign contributions, 206; campaign spending,
  204–5; convention vs direct ballot,
  235–7, 250 (see also direct ballot);
  financial statements, 205; financing,
  203–7; minority candidates, 198;

privatization index, 39–40; and age, 125, 126; and gender, 100–1; inter-party differences, 28–30, 31, 34, 35, 36, 37; and region, 80, 81, 82; and union/non-union status, 56; *see also* ownership, public/private

Progressive Conservative Party, 2, 233; as 'brokerage' party, 27, 37; convention surveys, 28; delegate allocation, 17; delegate selection, 199, 200–1, 202; delegates' family incomes, 18; 'Flora syndrome', 230; and ideology, 27; 'instant' members, 113, 199; and interest groups, 11n.12; internal agreement, 34–5, 265; leadership selection, 227, 265, 266, 267; membership, 13, 266; organizational structure, 3; party spending, 203; policy differences with NDP and Liberals, 28–30, 35–6, 37; regional representation, 83; spending by leadership candidates, 204; 'Tory syndrome', 208; youth wing, 17, 111–12

provincial caucuses, 6, 18, 127, 187, 263; *see also* regions

provincial parties, 233; delegates' attitudes towards, 14, 23

quality of life, 176, 180; and age, 186; *see also* postmaterialism

Quebec, 200; age of delegates, 116; convention attendance, 17–18, 67–8; as convention location, 17; delegates' attitudes, 74, 75, 81, 83, 169; in primaries (1995), 244, 248; provincial NDP, 75; Quiet Revolution, 5; referendum (1995), 9, 147; trade unions, 5, 47, 48; union affiliation, 51; *see also* Quebec issues

Quebec issues, 82; attitudes by region, 68–9, 75; intra-party differences, 74; and Reform Party, 42n.20; *see also* bilingualism

Rae, Bob, 138, 243, 211, 239; *see also* Ontario

Reform Party, 2; and bilingualism, 42n.20; and cultural conservatism, 123; delegate entitlement, 63n.4; membership, 13, 266; and older voters, 123, 129; organizational structure, 3; and regionalism, 65, 83, 176, 233

Regina Manifesto (1933), 158

regional entities: delegates' attitudes, 68–73

regionalism, 65; and attitude differences, 83, 84; and Reform Party, 233; and self-interest, 83; *see also* regions

regions, 2, 65; and Canada–US relations, 37; and leadership voting, 221, 222, 225, 228; and party leaders, 240; and primary voting (1995), 246–7; and union/non-union differences, 67; *see also* caucuses, provincial; issue indexes; regional entities; regionalism

renewal conferences (post-1993), 235

Richards, John, 138

Riche, Nancy, 62, 91

Riis, Nelson, 211

Robinson, Svend, 111, 198, 211, 240–2, 253; campaign spending, 206; at convention (1995), 250, 251–2; *Globe* endorsement, 248–9; and interest groups, 241; in labour primary, 247–8; and new leadership selection method, 238, 241; in regional primaries, 244–6; support 268; and young delegates, 128–9

Rodriguez, John, 241

Romanow, Roy, 138, 211

Royal Commission on Electoral Reform and Party Financing, 105n.18

Russia, *see* USSR

Saskatchewan, 138, 200, 242; age of delegates, 116; at convention (1995), 249; in primaries (1995), 244, 245; youth wing, 108; *see also* Western Canada

Schreyer, Ed, 239

Scott, Frank, 143, 144

Second World War, 158

Senate, 143

social democrats, 132, 155, 264; *see also* ideology

social programs, access to, 31, 152–3

social security index, 38–9; and age, 125; and gender, 100–1; inter-party differences, 28–30, 31, 34, 36; and region, 80, 81, 82; and union/non-

97–100, 102, 168; convention atten-dance, 7; demographic profiles, 94–5; leadership voting, 190–1; and post-materialist issues, 183–6 ; and union delegates, 7

women's caucus: attendance, 22, 127–8, 187, 188–9; and leadership voting, 190–1

Woodsworth, J.S., 157, 158, 164, 197, 240

Young, Rod, 108

young delegates: and caucus attendance, 70–2; definitions, 113, 114; demo-graphic profiles, 115–17; education, 117; union/non-union, 117–18; voting behaviour, 217; *see also* age; youth caucus; youth wing

youth caucus, 127; and leadership voting, 128

youth wing, 7; convention attendance, 14, 17; delegate selection, 199; history, 107–10

Yukon, 200